Our Monthly Newspapers from Year 3

October – December 2013
January – December 2014

ISBN: 978-0-6923-9779-4

Published by Gabriel Communications, Inc.
916 Harpeth Valley Place
Nashville, TN 37221

To order more copies:
www.cfrvideos.com
www.larrycountrydiner.com
800-820-5405

CONTENTS

Church signs, humorous & thought provoking

Signs reading: "SON SCREEN PREVENTS SIN BURN"; "KEEP USING MY NAME IN VAIN I'LL MAKE RUSH HOUR LONGER -GOD"; "'TRY JESUS' IF YOU DON'T LIKE HIM. THE DEVIL WILL TAKE YOU BACK"; "ETERNITY: SMOKING OR NONSMOKING"; "CHURCH PARKING ONLY! VIOLATERS WILL BE BAPTIZED"

Every church has one. Sometimes the writing on them is merely informative, but sometimes it uses scripture or even humor to get the reader's attention.

There are now entire websites devoted to funny church signs, so it should be no surprise that Nadine, the church lady from Larry's Country Diner now has a book of church signs entitled "Nadine's 101 Favorite Church Signs."

Nadine's book is small enough to fit in your pocket or purse and is filled with church signs, a scripture reflecting on the sign and Nadine's comments, as well. You'll laugh as you reflect on these sometimes humorous signs. Some of the signs are very serious and thought provoking and will make you ponder them as you move on from one to the next.

Nadine's book is for sale on her website, www.nadinenadine.com, for $12.95 plus $6.95 shipping and handling. See her ad on page 2.

Does your church use humor on its sign? Or have you passed funny sign on your travels? If so, please send it to us at the CFR News, P.O. Box 201709, Nashville, TN 37221 or send it by email to paula@ gabrielcommunications.com and we'll try to use it in the newspaper.

The Little Brown Church in the Vale

On a busy day over a dozen couples will tie the knot in this little brown church.

Deep in the corn country of Iowa a little church not only has a spiritual history in song but a romantic story that began in 1857, when William Pitts wrote Church in the Wildwood also known as The Little Brown Church in the Vale that ranks along with classic songs of faith like The Old Rugged Cross and Rock of Ages.

The story begins with a young music teacher named William Pitts traveling by stagecoach to visit his future wife. While the stagecoach paused for the passengers to stretch their legs and the horses to be changed, he walked down Cedar Street a street of the then bustling Bradford, dreaming of his future. Being a romantic young man he sited a picturesque

setting among a grove of pines and the thought came to him of what a charming setting the spot would make for a church. Returning home from his travels he reflected about the setting and wrote a poem and set it to music. He put it away in a drawer and forgot it.

The story could have ended but a return trip through Bradford came as a shocking surprise as he saw a little brown church nestled in the very trees where he had stood some years before. Farmers who'd never heard the hymn tucked away in a drawer, built the church during the Civil War. They painted it brown because that was the cheapest paint they could find. He went home and found the song and the hymn and the church became one.

History was hard on the Little Brown Church built in 1864 and in the early 1900's a Society for the Preservation of The Little Brown Church was started and by 1914, services were again held, as they are now.

People today regard the Little Brown Church as on of Cupid's favorite chapels. Some 250 weddings take place each year in this little brown wooden church with the big bell tower. People marrying in the church say it holds a special meaning, one that stays with them forever. It's a quiet spot in a noisy world but most of all it is a loving spot.

The Little Brown Church in Nashua, Iowa has been the setting for over 73,000 weddings

The current preacher, James Mann, also known as Pastor Jim, encourages couples to recognize that God gives us the gift of love so we may understand the depth of love He has for us.

***NOTE: Jim Ed Brown sings "The Little Brown Church in the Vale" on Country's Family Reunion Gospel series and also on the series "Lookin Back".

There's something about a church cookbook & potluck dinner

No matter what the denomination, it seems that all churches have potluck dinners and publish cookbooks. We recently recevied a cookbook from one of our Larry's Country Diner viewers from the St. Jude Catholic Church in Richland, Missouri.

St. Jude's Catholic Church was formally organized in the spring of 1972. Services were held in the United Methodist Church, the American Legion Hall, and the Richland Housing Community Center before the present church was built on Highway 7. This building was formally dedicated on April 6, 1975 and has now served parishioners for almost 40 years.

Here are a couple of the recipes from the book.

Crockpot Potatoes
- Karen Glawson

8 to 10 potatoes, sliced
1 can cream of mushroom soup
2 to 3 med. onions, sliced
1can cheddar cheese soup
salt and pepper to taste

Place half of sliced potatoes and onions in crockpot or baking dish. Pour half of the soups over them. Add remaining potatoes and onions, then remainder of soups. Salt and pepper to taste. Cook in crockpot 8 to 10 hours on low or 4 hours on high or bake in dish at 450 degrees for about 1 hour.

Spinach Salad
- Terri Kiling

Spinach
Fresh Mushrooms
Hard boiled eggs
Red onion

Dressing
1 cup oil
1/4 cup vinegar
2 tsp. salt
3/4 tsp. sugar
1 tsp. Worchestershire sauce
1/3 cup catsup

1 medium onion, chopped
Blend dressing ingredients together. Serve over spinach mixture.

Pork Chops
- Juaniata R. Haller

4 (1-inch) pork chops

Brine:
5 cups water
1/4 cup kosher salt
1/4 cup sugar

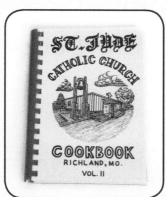

Marinade
1 tsp. dried thyme leaves, crumbled
1 tsp. dried rosemary, crushed
2 garlic cloves, pressed
2 T. balsamic vinegar
2 T. olive oil

Cover pork chops in brine overnight. Rinse chops in cold water and let stand in water 1 minutes. Pat dry. Marinate for 1 hour. Saute in 2 T. hot oil. Sear chops on each side. Roast at 375 degrees until done. Can also be grilled.

Pumpkin Bundt Cake

1 pkg. yellow cake mix
1 (3.4 oz) pkg. instant butterscotch pudding mix
4 eggs
1/4 cup. water
1/4 cup vegetable oil
1 cup pumpkin
2 tsp. pumpkin pie spice
Whipped topping

Combine all ingredients. Beat on low for 30 seconds. Beat on medium for 4 minutes. Pour into a greased and floured 10 inch fluted tube pan. Bake at 350 degrees for 50-55 minutes. Cool in pan 15 minutes. Cool on Rack. Serve with whipped topping.

Nadine's Cooking Corner

Cupcakes are great for church potluck dinners 'cause they come in single serving sizes! And you can make them a Halloween treat by adding frosting!

Brown Bottom Cupcakes

8 to 10 potatoes, sliced
1 ½ cups flour
½ tsp. salt
1 cup sugar
1 cup water
¼ cup unsweetened chocolate, melted
1/3 cup cooking oil
1 tsp. vinegar
1 tsp. soda
1 tsp. vanilla

Mix all ingredients in a large mixing bowl. Beat well. Fill lined muffin tins 1/3 full.

Filling:

1 (8 oz.) package cream cheese
1/8 tsp. salt
1 egg
1/3 cup sugar
1 cup chocolate chips

Combine cream cheese, egg, salt, and sugar. Beat well. Stir in chocolate chips. Place a heaping teaspoon of filling mixture on batter in each muffin cup. Bake 350 degrees for 30 minutes.

The CFR News
is published monthly by Gabriel Communications, Inc.
P.O. Box 210796, Nashville, TN 37221
615-673-2846
Larry Black, Publisher
Renae Johnson, General Manager
Paula Underwood Winters, Editor
Subscriptions: $29.95 yearly

George Strait's Final *The Cowboy Rides Away* Tour

In the fall of 2012, country music icon George Strait announced his final tour. While he's not retiring from music altogether, the King of Country did lay out his plans for the two-year The Cowboy Rides Away Tour, which will be his last full-scale outing.

The 2013 leg included 21 dates in winter and spring, giving fans an opportunity to see the 60-year-old's fantastic live show one last time. While the first run wrapped up in San Antonio, the second leg will start back in 2014. Below is his schedule.

1/30/14 San Jose, CA	1/31/14 San Diego, CA
2/1/14 Las Vegas, NV	2/7/14 Phoenix, AZ
2/8/14 Los Angeles, CA	2/14/14 Auburn Hills, MI
2/15/14 Columbus, OH	2/28/14 Philadelphia, PA
3/1/14 Newark, NJ	3/7/14 Louisville, KY
3/8/14 Chicago, IL	3/21/14 Nashville, TN
3/22/14 Atlanta, GA	4/4/14 Wichita, KS
4/5/14 Denver, CO	4/11/14 Portland, OR
4/12/14 Tacoma, WA	4/18/14 Des Moines, IA
4/19/14 Tulsa, OK	5/23/14 Baton Rouge, LA
5/31/14 Foxboro, MA	TBA Arlington, TX

Man starts fire, tries to burn down Ryman

A man was charged with arson after police said he attempted to set the Ryman Auditorium on fire.

According to an affidavit, surveillance showed 52-year-old Jeffrey Parsley piled newspapers outside the back doors of "Mother Church" and set them on fire on August 18.

The flames rose several feet high against the doorway, but firefighters were able to extinguish the blaze before it spread.

His bond was set at $20,000.

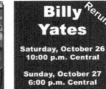

Don't miss a single episode of Larry's Country Diner

NEW...If you are a Larry's Country Diner fan who's used to watching the show from your rocking chair, be prepared....Larry's Country Diner shows can be seen anytime on your laptop or PC or even your phone or tablet. You don't have to have cable, direct or dish..just connect directly to our new website at www.larryscountrydiner.com and click on DINER TV. The site is excellent and the video quality is absolutely stunning. The website is simple to navigate and the TV shows are easy to find. We have three full length Larry's Country Diner episodes for you to watch before you decide which membership is good for you. TRY IT NOW FREE!!

We have three membership options to fit your budget...monthly, yearly, or lifetime. Once you become a member you will have access to all of our seasons through season 7. No commercials to fast forward through, and you can watch full-screen viewing. We will continue to add current seasons that you can watch anytime, anywhere. All you need is an internet/WiFi connection.

And that's not all....on our NEW website you can find out which show your favorite artists were on and the original air date! So don't wait, check it out now!

We're back in Branson at the Starlite Theatre

For tickets call the Starlite at 417-337-9333.

September 24-26: Gene Watson

October 1-3: Dailey and Vincent

October 4-6: Wilson Fairchild

October 15-17: The Grascals

Enjoy comedy and music in the beautiful Starlite Theatre conveniently located one block East of Titanic on world-famous 76 Country Music Boulevard.

Fans of the popular RFD-TV series "Larry's Country Diner" will be thrilled to see the return of Larry's Country Diner LIVE to the Starlite Theatre stage! Join Larry and the entire cast of the hit series including Renae, The Sheriff, Keith Bilbrey and everyone's favorite gossipy busybody, the church-lady Nadine.

Big time in Branson with Rhonda Vincent...

Larry's Country Diner and the cast was back in Branson in September and will also be there in October for some mid-week shows at the Starlite Theatre. The featured artists at the Diner have been Jimmy Fortune, Rhonda Vincent and Gene Watson. If you ever want to see the Diner cast live and on stage with your favorite singer, this is the show for you. The stage looks like the Diner itself, including the diner counter and tables and chairs. Renae the waitress brings folks on stage to eat pie while they lsiten to the "day in history, the Promise" and see Nadine drop by. You feel like you are right there watching the TV show, except the artists actually performs most of the evening. It's like seeing two shows in one. AND....Nadine has been known to dance a little on stage. But don't tell her pastor.

Just like on the TV show you never know who's gonna drop by and eat some pie with us. Mel Tillis, Teea Goans, The Gatlin Brothers, and Miles (formerly of The Cleverly's) all stopped by in September. AND....5 of Larry's grandchilden showed up in chicken hats on stage to promote Spring Mountain farm chicken.

Larry's Country Diner cast will only be in Branson for a few more shows in 2013. October shows include Daily and Vincent, Wilson Fairchild and The Grascals.

Renae the Waitress welcomes first granddaughter, Rio!

THE NEWS

On Christmas Day Phil and I learned we were going to be grandparents. It was a day filled with tears and unbelief and a Christmas I will never forget. We had shed so many tears at Christmas since our son, Justin had gotten killed that I thought it would never hold the same kind of joy. But the tears seemed to heal my heartbreak with the news and hope of our little new one. Our daughter, Chi and husband, Elliott whom many of you have heard me talk about, had recently moved back to Nashville from California. We were so happy about their decision that the news of the next 9 months was over the top !! From the first doctors visit to hear the heart beat, to the doctor's visit to find out she was a girl, to the sonogram that allowed us to see her tiny features, we loved her.

9 MONTHS

Chi, who is a professional dancer and choreographer had an amazing pregnancy.

Watching her thin fit dancer body change with the miracle of life growing inside her was amazing. She actually continued to work in the "dance" world until 2 weeks before her delivery proving you can enjoy the experience to the fullest. I do have to admit her last job 2 weeks before delivery made me a little nervous. She had accepted a choreography job in St Louis for Dollar General. And although she wasn't actually doing the dancing she was going over 200 hundred miles away from home with the thought she could actually deliver early. But she was convinced she would be fine and she was. And ... she was able to work with Star Trek star William Shatner.

THE DELIVERY

However ... two weeks later when she actually did start labor she delivered in 2 ½ hours. Phil and I barely had time to get to the hospital before she was ready to deliver. And it was amazing. Rio was born at 5:08 PM on August 16th. She was 7 lb 5 oz and 20 inches long. I have to admit I was mesmerized watching our daughter, husband and child bond. The miracle of life ... our beautiful little granddaughter was perfect. But then she cried and the mix of confusion as to what to do next broke the trance. She was here ... beautiful, perfect and ready to be heard.

Rio has enchanted us all. She has these adorable dimples that appear with the slightest animation. Her long fingers and toes respond with the slightest encouragement as she constantly arches her back and stretches her arms upward. We are convinced she will be twirling on her toes before she walks !! But never fear ... there will be tons of photos.

THE GRANDPARENTS CLUB

We are so proud to be apart of the Grandparent club!! It's a club that has no boundaries ... no rules ... and no strangers. Where ever we go we meet other grandparents that are willing to share stories and photos. It's like a wink or nod and you just know who's a member. AND ... we have our own special day "National Grandparents Day" . Wow ... who could ask for a better club ... lol

Special Drawing from Guy Gilchrist

When Rio was 2 days old I posted her photo on Facebook. The next day I received an email with a sketch he was working on. Cartoonist Guy Gilchrist who is the writer and artist for the classic newspaper cartoon Nancy, the Muppets, Looney Toons and others, saw Rio's photo and began drawing her with his cartoon characters. I was speachless…..what a treasure. Guy had visited our tapings of Larry's Country Diner a couple of times and drew some special sketches for Larry and Nadine but this was for my Grandbaby Rio is a very lucky little girl. Thank you, Guy!

Grandma's Heart

When I heard you were on the way,
I smiled and wiped my tears away.
I cried a tear because I knew
My heart had held a place for you.

As each day your Mommy grew,
I thought and thought and thought of you.
I wondered what games we would play,
And how we would spend a day.

Would we talk or read or bake?
Oh, what special friends we'd make!
Would we dance or skip or sing?
What would be your favorite thing?
Would we cuddle, kiss and hug?
What would give my heart a tug?

When you were born, I held you close,
It's what I'd dreamed of most.
I touched your tiny fingers and toes,
I kissed your head, your cheeks and nose.

Hello little granddaughter, it is me,
My heart as happy as can be.
I wish for you the sun and moon,
I wish for you a happy tune.

Know that Grandma's always near,
I'd do anything, anything for you my dear.
I cried a tear because I knew,
My heart would always belong to you.

Bonus DVD gives viewers chance to see stage show

If you liked the FIRST Marty Robbins Spotlight Collection, you're gonna LOVE Volume Two—

Back in the 1980's Marty Robbins did a television series featuring some of the best artists in country music. All shot in Nashville in an unscripted setting—The country stars share stories and songs with the AMAZING Marty Robbins...

Volume Two includes some of the biggest names in Country music... Legends like Bobby Bare, Mickey Gilley, Roy Acuff, Johnny Rodriguez, Jimmy Dean, Barbara Fairchild, Jack Greene, Boots Randolph, The Kendalls, Porter Wagoner, Ernest Tubb, Charlie Daniels, Jim Ed Brown and Helen Cornelius, Hank Snow, Bob Luman, Sammi Smith, Freddy Fender, Don Gibson...

Perhaps the best thing about this offer is the FREE bonus DVD called A Man and His Music.

Marty Robbins recorded A Man and His Music live at the Opry in 1980. Funnin around was what Marty called it and that's precisley what this DVD is about. Packed with live recordings including Among My Souvenirs, Big Boss Man, Big Iron, Devil Woman, Don't Worry, Earl's Breakdown, El Paso, Foggy Mountain Breakdown, Jenny, Love Me, My Woman My Woman My Wife, Ribbon Of Darkness, Singing The Blues, That's Alright Mama, Touch Me With Magic, and White Sport Coat.

You also have the opportunity to see and hear Don Winters, Marty's long time friend and singer/yodeler perform Jambalaya and Chime Bells. Don joined Marty Robbins in 1962 and stayed with him until Marty's death. He was a regular part of Marty's shows as well as part of the Marty Robbins Trio.

A Man and his Music is a 55 minute concert featuring the great hits performed by the one-of-a-kind, Marty Robbins.

Country Questions
By Dick Boise, CMH

Send questions to:
Dick Boise, , c/o CFR News,
P.O. Box 201796, Nashville,
TN 37221.

Q. I've been trying to locate the name of the man that had an old recording of the song called Ice Cold Love. Can you help me with this? Thanks,

John Riley Shamokin, PA

A. The man that you are wondering about would be the late Benny Martin. He was a great song writer, singer, and best of all an excellent fiddle player. He wrote that song and recorded it on the Mercury label, back in the 78 RPM era. Many folks do not know that he is also known for playing an eight string fiddle.
I first saw him when he was playing fiddle with the Johnny and Jack and Kitty Wells show. A true entertainer!

Q. Two questions. Is Bobby Lord deceased? If so, when, how many children and is his wife living? Also, I read Bill Anderson is single, widowed or divorced?

Thanks from Libery, KY

A. Thanks for the four questions and I'll do my best, espeicaly for Liberty! Bobby Lord passed away February 16, 2008. He was a fine singer and one of the original members of Red Foley's Ozark Jubilee TV show from Springfield in the late 1950s.

He joined the Grand Ole Opry in 1960. Bobby left three children, several grand children, and his wife, Mozell. (See Precious Memories on page 12 for more) And yes, Whisperin' Bill Anderson is divorced.

Q. Who was the singer of the song Funny Face and wher ewas she born? Enjoy CFR News very much. Thanks for the nice paper.

Lou Thompson

A. Donna Fargo was no tonly the singer of that hit song, but the writer as well. She was born Yvonne Vaughn, in Mt. Airy, NC on November 10 1945. Her first big hit, Happiest Girl in the Whole USA in 1969 was also written by this talented lady.

Thanks for asking and your nice comments about the CFR News.

Q. I'm trying to remember the steel guitar player that Eddy Arnold had on his many early records. What was his name and are there any records of his playing?

Mark Jones

A. There was a very nice story about "Little" Roy Wiggins in the September issue of the CFR News.
He was born in Nashville and played on many early recordings. I have found infomation that states he had 4 albums and several cassettes of his steel guitar artistry. Another name that helped make country music.

David Frizzell shares a country family legacy

His life and his career are tightly woven into the fabric of country music history and lore. He is both legacy and legend with an unmistakable voice and a captivating style.

David Frizzell is one of the greatest voices in country music with a haunting resemblance to his older brother, the ultimate stylist, Lefty Frizzell. Both share that raw, forlorn quality that is essential to the interpretation of traditional country themes, but David's voice is even more resonant and nuanced; a perfect instrument for conveying the deepest emotion of every lyric.

While still just a teenager, David Frizzell left home to perform and tour with his legendary brother, working the concert circuit with many of the mightiest names in country music. By his 18th birthday, Frizzell was recording country and rockabilly albums for Columbia Records. A four-year hitch in the military slowed his burgeoning musical career, but upon his discharge, Frizzell was immediately re-signed to Columbia.

David emerged from the significant shadow of his brother to create his own artistic identity. He recorded and charted the first country version of "L.A. International Airport" (months before it became a hit by Susan Raye) and followed that song with a Top 40 rendition of "I Just Can't Help Believing." Frizzell parlayed his recording success into headlining country shows in Las Vegas, a bold move that paved the way for other country acts in Las Vegas.

In the early 1980s, Frizzell founded the musical duo of Frizzell & West with the gorgeous and gifted Shelly West, daughter of country superstar Dottie West. Their recording of "You're The Reason God Made Oklahoma" made its way to Clint Eastwood, who insisted on adding the tune to the soundtrack of his forthcoming film, Any Which Way You Can … despite the fact that every major label had previously passed on the song and the duo. This vote of confidence earned Frizzell & West a contract with Viva/Warner Bros. and the wheels began to turn quickly. A small radio station in Tulare, California began to play the album track. Other stations followed, prompting Warner Bros. to release the song as a single. Soon, the song that nobody wanted became a smash hit.

Frizzell & West remains one of the most-awarded acts in entertainment; one that sold out arenas worldwide and produced five albums. The duo twice won the Country Music Association's Vocal Duo of the Year award, twice won the Academy of Country Music award for Vocal Duet of the Year and were awarded the ACM Song of the Year award. They also received the Music City News Award for Duet of the Year twice and Song of the Year as well.

During his duet years with West, Frizzell continued a vibrant solo career. He scored a huge chart-topping hit with "I'm Gonna Hire A Wino To Decorate Our Home." The record is a country music standard, and has been featured on CMT's 40 Greatest Drinking Songs in Country Music, making #17 in the countdown. Also, making #6 in CMT's countdown of the 100 Greatest Duets is "You're The Reason God Made Oklahoma."

Along with his CMA awards, Frizzell has won numerous performing and recording trophies from the Academy of Country Music, Billboard and Music City News. He has been nominated for three Grammys, both as part of Frizzell & West and as a solo artist.

As producer and Host of the popular Frizzell & Friends series of projects, TV, CD's and DVD's David brings together some of the top performers in the business for both live and recorded projects. On his own Nashville America Records label, Frizzell & Friends guest performances have included Merle Haggard, Crystal Gayle, Johnny Lee, Gene Watson, Joe Stampley, Jeannie Seely, T. Graham Brown, Lacy J. Dalton, Bobby Bare, Helen Cornelius, Jimmy Fortune (Statler Brothers), John Cowan (New Grass Revival), Johnny Rodriguez, Amy Clawson, brother Allen Frizzell and niece Tess Frizzell.

In 2011, David released his long awaited book, a tribute to the life and career of Lefty Frizzell. "I Love You A Thousand Ways: The Lefty Frizzell Story" features a forward by Merle Haggard and chronicles the turbulent life and career of one of America's most influential voices. The book was named by CMT as one of the Best Music Books of the year. An audio book is now available and David is working on a screenplay of the story.

In addition to the Lefty project honoring the brother who loved, taught and inspired him, David has plans to give back in other ways. He has teamed up with M.A.D.D. (Mothers Against Drunk Drivers) to raise awareness of the dangers of driving impaired, and of the tremendous service provided by the organization. The Frizzell family itself was touched by loss in the wake of an accident with a drunk driver and this project is one way for David to both thank MADD, and strive to help and inspire others. With the moving song, *"Say Hello To Heaven,"* David paints a story of loss with the palpable emotion that only his inimitable voice can deliver. The song and a segment focused on

MADD will be part of a Frizzell & Friends television show on the RFD network.

Writing, producing, touring and performing … David Frizzell is not one to rest on his many accolades. This timeless entertainer continues to share his gifts to the delight of fans old and new across the US and throughout the world.

Dottie West's ex-husband, Bill West dies

Bill West, ex-husband of Dottie West and father of Shelly West, died Wednesday night, September 18. Visitation was held on Sunday, September 22 at Springhill Funeral Home in Nashville. A graveside service was held at Forest Lawn Cemetery.

Bill and Dottie West in Cleveland, Ohio

Duck Dynasty family stands ground on God.

"You can't judge a book by its cover" is very true with the Duck Dynasty guys. You'd never know by looking at them they daddy Phil Robertson has a Masters Degree in Education and that all of them live very Christian based lives. So much so that because they pray at the end of each show, some viewers asked A & E network to make them stop. To which the Robertsons responded with a resounding "NO".

Anyone who has ever raised boys knows how rowdy they can be, and these boys are no exception. Except that they are millionaires and have their own television show. And while each episode shows the boys being silly and getting into mischief, they are very serious about their business and their devotion to God and family.

Phil Robertson was born and raised in Vivian, Louisiana, a small town near Shreveport. With seven children in his family, money was scarce and very early on, hunting became an important part of his life.

Praying for the victims of the Oklahoma tornados. Each of the shows is ended with a prayer.

As a high-school athlete, Phil was All-State in football, baseball, and track which afforded him the opportunity to attend Louisiana Tech University on a football scholarship. There he played first string quarterback ahead of Terry Bradshaw. Phil's been quoted as saying "Terry went for the bucks, and I chased after the ducks." After receiving his Bachelor's Degree in Physical Education and a Master's in Education, he spent several years teaching. While his students claim he was an excellent teacher, spending time in a classroom brought Phil to the conclusion that his time and talents would be better spent in the woods.

Phil and his family, which by this time included wife Kay, and four boys, Alan, Jase, Willie, and Jeptha began a quest to turn his passion for hunting and fishing into a livelihood.

Never satisfied with the duck calls that were on the market, Phil began to experiment with making a call that would produce the exact sound of a duck. A duck call for duck killers, not "world champion-style duck callers." Claiming, "No duck would even place in a duck calling contest." And so, in 1972, the first Duck Commander call was born. Phil received a patent for this call and the Duck Commander Company was incorporated in 1973.

His home became his "factory" from where the calls were assembled, packaged, and shipped. Phil traveled store to store in the early days, with most ending in rejections. A certain large store in Stuttgart, AR laughed him out of the building (that store is now one of Duck Commander's largest accounts.) Phil's wife and four sons assisted in the packaging and shipments of the calls along with helping to run the nets, and take the fish to the market. This family side business of commercial fishing kept food on the table while Duck Commander Company was getting off the ground.

In the mid-70's, Phil turned his life over to the Lord and made some dramatic changes in the way he was living. Phil Robertson is not only known as the Duck Commander but is now building a reputation all over the country for his faith and belief in the Almighty. He is invited to speak to hundreds of different churches and organizations every year, telling them what the Lord has done for him and can do for them.

Duck Commander is still a family business with all four sons and their wives working for the company at one time or another. Duck calls are still being built, blown, packaged and shipped in the Robertson's home on the Ouachita River, although now their home is surrounded by several offices and warehouses to help the company smoothly, and the nets are still being run, only now the fish that they catch feed all the Duck Commander employees. Yes it's a rough life, but as Phil says "somebody's gotta do it."

It isn't often a person can live a dream, but Phil Robertson, aka The Duck Commander, has proven it is possible with vision, hard work, helping hands, and an unshakable faith in the Almighty. If you ever wind up at the end of Mouth of Cypress Road, sitting face to face with Phil Robertson, you will see that his enthusiasm and passion for duck hunting and the Lord is no act- it is truly who he is.

Si Robertson, the youngest brother of Phil Robertson, can be seen on almost every Duckmen DVD as well as the Duck Commander TV show. Si has worked and hunted for Duck Commander since retiring from the United States Army in 1993. Si spends his time making all of the reeds for the Duck Commander calls, working out at the land with Phil preparing for the next duck season, and, of course, when season rolls around, you'll find him in the blind.

Si lives in West Monroe, La with his wife Christine.

Phil's son, Willie, has been in and around hunting all his life. Growing up with the family business, he has handled most tasks at Duck Commander from sanding and packaging calls as a youngster, to now serving as president of the company. Despite a busy travel schedule, Willie is a regular in the Robertson family blind where his comic relief helps when the season gets long and the birds are not flying.

In 2006, Willie began a new pursuit when he started Buck Commander. Willie and the Buckmen travel all over the country chasing white-tail deer, having a good time at hunting camp, and creating the Buckmen series of DVD's and the popular television show Buck Commander Protected by Under Armour on Outdoor Channel.

Willie is executive producer of both TV shows and has a passion for inspiring future hunters by showing the outdoor lifestyle and hunting experience in the most fun and entertaining way. His unique perspective helps makes Duck and Buck Commander TV shows, DVD's and products stand out in the crowd.

He loves being outdoors with his family and friends and is happiest at home in West Monroe, La with his wife Korie and children, John Luke, Sadie, Will and Bella. When he is not working you will catch him on his tractor bush-hogging a field, earphones blaring, thinking of the next idea that will keep his companies at the top of the heap.

Growing up with his father as the Duck Commander, Jase Robertson soon realized that if he wanted to spend time with him, he'd have to meet him in the blind. But it soon became evident that Jase had the same passion for duck hunting as his dad. From the age of 8 years old, Jase spent as much time in the woods as he possibly could, even missing the maximum number of days from school each year that the law would allow.

Even today he shows that same passion and drive to meet his dad in the blind each and every day of duck season for one common goal ... limiting out. Hunting, along with helping the family business to succeed, consumes most of Jase's time. Aside from his current role as a duckman in the Duck Commander DVD series and TV Show, Benelli Presents Duck Commander, he runs the manufacturing part of Duck Commander, making sure that every call is hand-tuned, in large part by himself. This part of the business is very important to him as he knows consumers want the best call possible. It is his ambition to give them what they want.

Jase lives in West Monroe, Louisiana, with his wife Missy and their three children, Reed, Cole and Mia.

The youngest son of Phil and Kay Robertson, Jules Jeptha "Jep" Robertson, grew up in the duck blind. Utilizing these years of experience for his role as the cameraman and editor for the family business, Jep is able to think like a hunter behind the camera and therefore, capture excellent footage for the Duckmen DVD series and the television show, Benelli Presents Duck Commander.

Jep continues with the goal his father began years ago, to bring the "Duckmen style" of hunting out of the swamps, into the editing room, and into the homes of duck hunting enthusiasts around the world. Jep's

passion for capturing the hunt on camera was stoked when he made his filming debut in "Duckmen X", and it remains his favorite Duckmen DVD to date.

Jep resides in Louisiana with his wife Jessica and four children, Lily, Merritt, Priscilla, and River.

Alan is the oldest son of the Duck Commander. He grew up hunting and fishing and helping build the foundation of the family business in the 1970's & '80's. Back in the day, he and Phil would travel around Louisiana and Arkansas selling duck calls to stores right out of the truck! The sales pitch back then was the same as today: "These calls are the best 'cause they sound just like a duck!"

He left the duck call business when he received the call for full time ministry in 1988 and now serves as a senior pastor in West Monroe, LA. Alan is still a part of the family's commitment to spreading the gospel of Christ through their love of hunting and the great outdoors. He calls himself a Jacob in a family of Esaus...

The Wives of Duck Dynasty.

Dean Acres/Green Acres, not even a comparison!

It may rhyme with Green Acres, but Dean Acres is nothing like the fictional home of Oliver and Lisa Douglas from the old TV show.

Green Acres set

Dean Acres is the home of Grammy Winning Country Music Star Billy Dean. On your tour of Nashville, in addition to visiting the Grand Ole Opry, and the Country music Hall of fame, come on out and check it out. Located 1 hour East of Nashville TN, (4134 Dale Ridge Rd, Liberty, TN, 37095)Dean Acres offers music enthusiasts live music concerts to remember. Live Country Music concerts by Grammy Award winning artists, and Country Music Hall of Fame Singer/Songwriters, and even American Idol Contestants make Dean Acres the place to be!

What's better than a barn wedding in Tennessee? Having it in the barn of a Country Music Star! Dean Acres offers indoor/outdoor weddings with country elegance. Their 1800's barn has been almost completely rebuilt re-purposing the old material to give it a rustic charm.

You can even book your own private concert at Dean Acres! Do you have clients you would like to entertain? This is the ULTIMATE Country Music Concert! Let Dean Acres be your personal venue. They will work with you to customize the concert and find Country Stars that are tailored to your liking.

Or relax and unplug in an idyllic country setting when you stay in an adorable little cabin they call The Sugar Shack.

The Sugar Shack is made from logs that date back to the 1800's (incidentally, Billy purchased the logs from Kathy Mattea). Billy decided to add a few modern additions for comfort, like a deck off the back. You will feel like you have been transported back to a simpler time!

The Sugar Shack is perfect get away for two adults, or a single wishing to go country, rough it a bit and get away from the "real world". Perfect for songwriters to dream up hit songs, writers to write, or just to sit on the deck and clear your head! Billy and Stephanie often sit on the deck and spend an afternoon just unwinding.

So whether you're looking for a day trip or an overnight, check out Dean Acres! And see Billy perform on Larry's Country Diner at www.larryscountrydiner.com.

Precious Memories; Remembering Bobby Lord

Performing with Patsy Cline.

Robert L. (Bobby) Lord was born Jan. 6, 1934, in Sanford, Lord later lived in Tampa.

Lord's music career began as a teenager in Tampa, where he had his own television show shortly after graduating from high school, "The Bobby Lord Homefolks Show." He was invited to appear on "Paul Whiteman's Teen Club," with Dick Clark as its announcer, an ABC television program that showcased promising young singers.

In 1953, legendary songwriter Boudleaux Bryant played a demo recording of Lord's for Don Law at Columbia Records, which immediately signed him to a recording contract. At age 19, he was Columbia's youngest recording star. He recorded several "rockabilly" and country hits for Columbia.

He was signed to become a featured performer on "The Ozark Jubilee," an ABC television network show hosted by Red Foley and based in Springfield, Mo., where he remained from 1955 to 1960.

In 1969, at age 35, Lord wanted to spend more time with his family and announced his partial retirement from the country music business. He developed Nettles Island for Outdoor Resorts of America, and was involved in the development of Ancient Oaks Resort in Okeechobee, Bryn Mar Resort in Vero Beach, and Indian River Plantation in Stuart.

"He fell in love with Stuart, and moved us here," said Rob Lord.

"He also founded Stuart Insurance with his son, Cabot," Rob Lord said.

In addition, Lord helped launch the Lyric Theatre, centerpiece for the reborn downtown Stuart.

He settled his family in North River Shores, a part of Stuart. Later he would move to Palm City and then Jensen Beach.

"Back in 1992 or 1993, when they were opening the Lyric, he was asked to help get an act to open the theater. He asked Bobby Bare to come, and he did perform for free. My dad was on stage with him. They played together," Rob Lord said.

Helping open the theater was just one of many things Lord did in the community, his son said.

"He was in the Kiwanis Club. He was a Mason. He would help raise funds when someone needed help. He worked with the Martin County Fair Association, helping them book acts, sometimes performing himself, and he was master of ceremonies for the Little Miss Martin County contests."

Survivors include by his wife of more than 53 years, Mozelle of Jensen Beach; three children, Rob Lord of Jensen Beach; Sarah Williams of Dothan, Ala.; and Cabot Lord of Stuart; brothers, John Lord and Steve Lord, both of Stuart; 10 grandchildren, and one great-grandchild..

Bobby performed on the Country's Family Reunion Celebration & Gospel, and Generations. all filmed in 1999, His performances are also on the Precious Memories series.

Jackson Misses Country Music on the Radio

Alan Jackson brought tears to his eyes, as well as everyone who watched him sing "He Stopped Lovin' Her Today" during George Jones' memorial service. So, a country singer, who clearly loves to hear and sing country music wonders where the traditional country sound has gone.

In a recent interview with the Baltimore Sun, Jackson said, "Right now, it seems like it's gone. It's not that I'm against all that's out there. There's some good music, good songwriting and good artists out there, but there's really no country stuff left."

The 54-year-old singer/songwriter who has won two Grammy Awards and has sold nearly 60 million albums worldwide doesn't hate the slick, pop sound that has become increasingly ingrained in country music. He just wishes the radio would balance things out with more traditional-sounding artists, too.

"What makes me sad today is that I think the real country, real roots-y traditional stuff, may be gone," commented Jackson, "I don't know if it'll ever be back on mainstream radio. You can't get it played anymore."

There's some truth to Jackson's statements, but can radio stations ignore the sound hitmaker Jackson loves most when his albums contain just that type of songs.

In June 2012, he proved his songwriting ability was still as good as ever with the release of his 17th studio album, "Thirty Miles West." The album's closing track, "When I Saw You Leaving (For Nisey)," is about Jackson's wife, Denise, and her December 2010 cancer diagnosis. Jackson described the time as "a total shock for us like it would be for anybody." Denise is now cancer-free, and the song written in her honor now helps fans through their own experiences.

After "Thirty Miles West" was completed, Jackson turned his attention to a project he had eyed since the mid-'90s. With the help of his band member Scott Coney, Jackson recruited acclaimed bluegrass musicians to create "The Bluegrass Album," which was released in September.

For Jackson, performing bluegrass — the improvisational American roots music made with acoustic-stringed instruments — is a matter of respect.

"I wanted to pay my respects to it because I think it's a great genre and it's real close to country," Jackson told the Baltimore Sun "Bluegrass is one of the last American music [genres] that's stayed somewhat close to its roots."

Whether it's bluegrass or traditional country, Jackson remains devoted to the craft of songwriting. It's a puzzle that never bores him. "Making the new music has always been the most fun for me."

Thankful that traditional country music survives the battle

As we look back over the battle that seems to rage on for the heart of country music we have survived. The fight that surrounds country music and what direction it should take was inflamed by remarks made by Blake Shelton. He recently said, "Nobody wants to listen to their grandpa's music." This both angered and bewildered Country Music Fans. Especially our Country's Family Reunion fans since Blake was very happy to sit in our circle and be apart of our Country's Family Reunion series we filmed in 2000, honoring and recognizing the legends who helped pave the way for country music. The arrogance and shortsightedness of his comments made many fans struggle with his dedicated apologists and contrived explanations.

The devout traditional fans are the ones with the biggest hearts but struggle as they watch their culture be stolen from them, and then re-sold as a parody.

Pop music has its place in our society, and has its place in country music, and don't let anyone tell you any different. Pop was there at the very beginning of country, but there's always been balance with the traditional influences. Pop may have been in country since it's beginning, but we must make sure pop doesn't become country music's end.

Traditional country music fans are steadfast, reliable, strong, powerful, and trustworthy. They will go to battle for the music they love because it exists in the very fabric of their lives, and the way Blake Shelton's comments were received is a testament to that. Traditional country is played in their homes as a force of habit; it serenades them at their funerals. A pop country fan's love is fleeting, pliable, relying on the winds of trend to define its ever-transient nucleus.

This Thanksgiving give thanks to the Lord God Almighty as we survive the battles that will surely keep traditional country music strong.

Who set dates for Thanksgiving & Black Friday

Lincoln Sets Date

On October 3, 1863, Lincoln issued a Thanksgiving Proclamation that declared the last Thursday in November (based on Washington's date) to be a day of "thanksgiving and praise." For the first time, Thanksgiving became a national, annual holiday with a specific date

FDR Changes It

For 75 years after Lincoln issued his Thanksgiving Proclamation, succeeding presidents honored the tradition and annually issued their own Thanksgiving Proclamation, declaring the last Thursday in November as the day of Thanksgiving. However, in 1939, President Franklin D. Roosevelt

did not. In 1939, the last Thursday of November was going to be November 30. Retailers complained to FDR that this only left 24 shopping days to Christmas and begged him to push Thanksgiving just one week earlier. It was determined that most people do their Christmas shopping after Thanksgiving and retailers hoped that with an extra week of shopping, people would buy more.

So when FDR announced his Thanksgiving Proclamation in 1939, he declared the date of Thanksgiving to be Thursday, November 23, the second-to-last Thursday of the month.

Roasted Spicy Mayonnaise Chicken Breasts

1/2 cup mayonnaise
2 lemons, zest finely grated
2 teaspoons paprika
1 teaspoon celery seeds
1 teaspoon salt, plus additional for seasoning
1 teaspoon freshly ground black pepper,plus additional for seasoning
Pinch cayenne pepper
4 (8-ounce) boneless, skinless chicken breasts

Mix all ingredients in a large mixing bowl. Beat well. Fill lined muffin tins 1/3 full.

Directions:

Preheat the oven to 425 degrees F. Line a rimmed baking sheet with foil.

In a small bowl, whisk together the mayonnaise, lemon zest, paprika, celery seeds, salt, pepper, and cayenne. Season the chicken with additional salt and pepper, to taste. Arrange the chicken on the prepared baking sheet. Slather the mayonnaise mixture over the chicken. Bake until the juices run clear when the chicken is pricked with a fork, about 20 to 25 minutes. Transfer the chicken to a serving platter and serve hot.

Roasted Root Vegetables

Ingredients
1 pound carrots, peeled
1 pound parsnips, peeled
1 large sweet potato, peeled
1 small butternut squash, peeled and seeded (about 2 pounds)

3 tablespoons good olive oil
1 1/2 teaspoons kosher salt
1/2 teaspoon freshly ground black pepper
2 tablespoons chopped parsley

Directions:

Preheat the oven to 425 degrees F.

Cut the carrots, parsnips, sweet potato, and butternut squash in 1 to 1 1/4-inch cubes. All the vegetables will shrink while baking, so don't cut them too small.

Place all the cut vegetables in a single layer on 2 baking sheets. Drizzle them with olive oil, salt, and pepper. Toss well. Bake for 25 to 35 minutes, until all the vegetables are tender, turning once with a metal spatula.

Sprinkle with parsley, season to taste, and serve hot.

FAMILY-REUNION NEWS Larry's Country Diner

The CFR News
is published monthly by Gabriel Communications, Inc.
P.O. Box 210796, Nashville, TN 37221
615-673-2846
Larry Black, Publisher
Renae Johnson, General Manager
Paula Underwood Winters, Editor
Subscriptions: $29.95 yearly

Practicing my singing

With my brother Bobby

Prom Night

Annie Get Your Gun

At the White House

Fan presents Larry with Riffleman gun

Larry was recently surprised at the taping of Larry's Country Diner when Jimmy Porter, one of the show's fans, sent him a vintage rifle from TV show "The Rifleman."

"The Rifleman" aired on ABC from September 30, 1958 to April 8, 1963 as a production of Four Star Television. The series centers on Lucas McCain, a widowed Union Civil War veteran (a lieutenant in the 8th Indiana Infantry Regiment) and a homesteader. McCain and his son Mark live on his ranch outside the fictitious town of North Fork, New Mexico Territory. They had moved from Enid, Oklahoma after Lucas' wife had died when Mark was 6 years old. It was one of the first prime time series to have a widowed parent raise a child. The series was set during the 1880s; a wooden plaque next to the McCain home states that the home was rebuilt by Lucas McCain and his son Mark in August 1881.

Jimmy and Larry Black

Westerns were popular when The Rifleman premiered, and producers tried to find gimmicks to distinguish one show from another. The Rifleman's gimmick was a modified Winchester Model 1892 rifle, with a large ring lever drilled and tapped for a setscrew allowing for rapid fire by setting the screw to depress the trigger instead of a finger. It also enabled McCain to spin-cock the rifle. Despite the anachronism of a John Browning-designed rifle appearing in a show set 12 years before it was designed, Connors demonstrated its rapid-fire action during the opening credits on North Fork's main street.

The 1892 Winchester caliber .44-40 carbine with a standard 20-inch barrel used on the set of The Rifleman appeared with two different types of levers. The backwards, round-D-style loop was used in the early episodes. Sometimes the rifle McCain uses has a saddle ring.

The style later changed to a flatter lever (instead of the large loop) with no saddle ring. The 8-32 set screw tapped through the trigger guard for the rapid-fire action also came in different styles. Some were silver; others were black with a silver nut under the head of the screw. Sometimes Connors had the screw head turned inside close to the trigger, but he mostly had it on the outside of the trigger guard. In some episodes, the screw was taken out completely when rapid-fire action was not required.

The rapid-fire mechanism was originally designed to keep Connors' finger from getting punctured by the trigger as he quickly fired and cocked the rifle. The rifle and ammunition were provided by the now-defunct Stembridge Gunsmiths. Ammunition was quarter-load 5-in-1 blank cartridges containing smokeless powder, which did not produce the thick clouds of smoke the genuine black powder cartridges of the 1880s did. The 1892 Winchester rifle holds 12 shots, although a 13th shot was dubbed in to the show's opening scene. It is actually an echo from the 12th shot; his hand moves the lever only 12 times.

Although the rifle may have appeared in every episode, it was not always fired; some plots did not require violent solutions. McCain attempts to solve as many problems as possible without having to resort to shooting, yet still manages to kill approximately 113 villains over the show's five-year run.

A common thread in the series is that people deserve a second chance.

Behind the scenes SPOTLIGHT

We have so many talented folks that work behind the scenes of our television shows and tapings that we thought you should meet them. Their talents and experience surely humble us. This first spotlight features one of our favorite people:

Cheorkee Hart

Cherokee is a professional makeup artist with extensive experience in commercial, print, film, video and television for over seventeen years. She is the make-up-artist for "Larry's Country Diner" and "Country Family Reunion". Cherokee also works with networks such as A&E, MSNBC, CNN, CBS, NBC, FOX CBS, HGTV, RFDTV, CMT and Inside Edition

Other television shows she has worked with include: Nancy Grace, Hannity & Colmes, O' Rielly Factor, HGTV-Design Star, 700 Club, Ralph Emery, Jimmy Sturr, and Food Network to name a few.

The celebrities she has worked who have not been on our shows include: Dolly Parton, Bo Derek, Lou Rawls, Rebecca St James, Merle Haggard, Jack LeLanne, Brad Paisley, John Rich, Mel Tillis, Ray Price, Marty Stuart, Pam Tillis, Lorrie Morgan and Clint Black for starters.

Cherokee also travels with us on our Country's Family Reunion and Larry's Country Diner Cruises.

Larry's Country Diner RFD Show Schedule

B.J. Thomas
Saturday, Nov. 2
10:00 p.m. Central

Sunday, Nov. 3
6:00 p.m. Central

The Roys
Saturday, Nov. 9
10:00 p.m. Central

Sunday, Nov. 10
6:00 p.m. Cetnral

Jim Glaser
Saturday, Nov. 16
10:00 p.m. Central

Sunday, Nov. 17
6:00 p.m. Central

Tracy Lawrence
Saturday, Nov. 23
10:00 p.m. Central

Sunday, Nov. 24
6:00 p.m. Central

Jimmy Fortune and Dailey & Vincent
Saturday, Nov. 30
10:00 p.m. Central

Sunday, Dec. 1
6:00 p.m. Central

The above shows have been previously aired.

Happy Thanksgiving

Women music executives honored by SOURCE

Photo by Alan Mayor

SOURCE, along with Nashville's music community, celebrated the careers of seven special women at the 2013 SOURCE Awards, which took place at Musician's Hall of Fame and Museum in Nashville on Tuesday, September 24, 2013.

SOURCE is a nonprofit invitation-only organization unifying women executives who work in all facets of the Nashville Music Industry. Monthly programs are presented to SOURCE members addressing topical music and non-music industry related issues with invitations extended to industry leaders who share their knowledge and insights with the SOURCE membership.

The annual SOURCE Awards were established in 2003 to pay respect to and honor the women who helped develop and build upon the foundation of the music industry in Nashville. SOURCE also pays tribute to women who presently make major contributions with their work in the industry.

For this year's awards ceremony, SOURCE has selected the following honorees, left to right:

Bonnie Garner: Rothbaum Garner, Columbia Records, Dick Cavett Show

Paula Szeigis: Charlie Daniels Band, Inc.

Debi Fleischer-Robin: Fleischer-Robin Enterprises, Columbia/Sony Records, Crystal Gayle

Sarah Trahern: Great American Country, TNN, C-Span

Gerrie McDowell: Gerrieco, Curb, Capitol and Mercury Records

Bebe Evans: Charlie Daniels Band, Inc.

Donna Hilley: (d. 2012) Sony/ATV Publishing

Veterans Day National Ceremony at Arlington

The Veterans Day National Ceremony is held each year on November 11th at Arlington National Cemetery . The ceremony commences precisely at 11:00 a.m. with a wreath laying at the Tomb of the Unknowns and continues inside the Memorial Amphitheater with a parade of colors by veterans' organizations and remarks from dignitaries. The ceremony is intended to honor and thank all who served in the United States Armed Force.

Military veterans often receive special treatment in their respective countries due to the sacrifices they made during wars. Different countries handle this differently: some openly support veterans through government programs, while others ignore them. Veterans are also subject to illnesses directly related to their military service such as PTSD. War veterans are generally treated with great respect and honour for their contribution to the world and country by their own nationals. Conversely there are often negative feelings towards the veterans of foreign nations held long after the war is over;

for example towards the German Nazi soldiers, yet they are no less veterans of war than those of the winning side. There are exceptions. Veterans of unpopular conflicts, such as the Vietnam War, have been discriminated against. Others, such as veterans of conflicts like the Korean War, are often forgotten (even though the casualty rate in Korea was higher than that experienced in the Vietnam War) when compared with those who fought in the World Wars. In some countries with strong anti-military traditions (e.g., Germany after 1945), veterans are neither honoured in any special way by the general public, nor have their dedicated Veterans Day, although events are sometimes orchestrated by Neo-Nazis and other minority right-wing groups.

Many countries have longstanding traditions, ceremonies, and holidays to honour their veterans. In the UK "Remembrance Day" is held on November the 11th and is focused mostly on the veterans who died in service to the monarch and country. A red or white poppy is worn on the lapel (for remembrance or for peace, respectively) in the weeks up to the date, and wreaths and flowers laid at memorials to the dead.

In Russia, a tradition was established after the Second World War, where newly married couples would on their wedding day visit a military cemetery. In France, for instance, those wounded in war are given the first claim on any seat on public transit.

Country Bumpkin's Cal Smith dies at 81

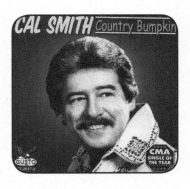

Cal Smith, who enjoyed a rich country career with some of the biggest hits of the 1960s and 1970s, passed away Thursday, October 10, 2013 at his home near Branson, Missouri. He was 81.

Smith was born Calvin Grant Shofner on April 7, 1932 in Gans, Oklahoma. However, as many did in the Great Depression, Smith's family headed west – settling in Oakland, California. He began his music career by performing at San Francisco's Remember Me Cafe in 1947. Unable to make a steady income as a musician, he also turned to other jobs, such as truck driving and the rodeo.

Smith enlisted in the military in the mid 1950s. Upon his discharge, he returned to the Bay area where he began playing in a local band. Country superstar Ernest Tubb heard the band play one night, and offered Smith a job playing guitar for his Texas Troubadours band. Not only a road band for Tubb, the group also backed him on his Decca recordings, so Smith was working plenty of Tubb's sessions as well.

Smith's vocals were brought to the attention of Kapp Records, who signed him in 1966. His debut single for the label, "I'll Just Go Home," failed to chart, but his second release, "The Only Thing I Want," hit the Billboard Country Singles chart in January 1967 – peaking at No. 58.

Subsequent releases would fare better for Smith, who left the Tubb show in 1969 – the same year he hit the top-40 for the first time with "Drinking Champagne" (later covered by George Strait). He moved to Decca in 1971, and hit the top ten for the first time with a cover of the Free Movement's "I've Found Someone Of My Own," a No. 4 release from the spring of 1972. By years' end, he would release "The Lord Knows I'm Drinking," a song written by Bill Anderson. It would become his first number one record in March 1973.

As big as that record was, it was nothing compared to his next major hit. "Country Bumpkin," a story song in the classic country tradition, was released in early 1974 – hitting the top in May. It netted him a CMA Award for Single Record of the Year, and also won the Song of the Year trophy for writer Don Wayne, as well.

The song was a favorite of many -- including a young Garth Brooks. During a mid 1990s appearance on TNN's "Music City Tonight," the singer said that "Country Bumpkin" was his favorite country song –

prompting Smith to give Brooks the CMA trophy he won for the song.

Another fan of Smith's was Loretta Lynn. In her 2002 autobiography "Still Woman Enough," the singer admitted to having a crush on Smith during her stint as duet partner with Ernest Tubb – claiming that husband Mooney would sometimes get jealous of the singer.

Cal Smith topped the charts for a third and final time with 1975's "It's Time To Pay The Fiddler," yet remained on the charts throughout the 1970s. One of his last major hits was his original version of "I Just Came Home To Count The Memories," a No. 15 hit from 1977 that helped put John Anderson on the map five years later. His last appearance on the charts was 1986's "King Lear," which peaked at No. 75 on the Step One label.

Smith is survived by wife Darlene, five children, and fifteen grandchildren.

World loses what could have been another generation as a country musician

He wasn't a professional musician, at least not yet, but he was the fourth generation in a line of professional country musicians. His name was Ryan Winters and he is the son of country and Southern rock musician Donnie Winters. He is the grandson of Don Winters, who sang with Marty Robbins for over 20 years. He is the great grandson of George Winters, who performed in the 30s and 40s as Pop Winters and the Southern Strollers in the South Georgia and Florida areas.

Ryan passed away on September 29. The cause is not yet known. He was 28 years old. Ryan played banjo, guitar, bass and drums.

Ryan is also the son of Paula Underwood Winters who works for Gabriel and the CFR News.

Ryan Winters playing his banjo on the streets of downtown Nashville.

Les Kerr, Donnie Winters and Ryan Winters perform at a fundraiser.

2nd Generation kids get back together & entertain

Thursday, October 10 was a magical night at Mickey Roo's Texas Style BBQ in Franklin, TN. The 2nd Generations kids (who got together for the taping of CFR's Generations and 2nd Generations DVDs), and some of their friends, got together to entertain a full house. Jo-el Ulmer & LeAnne Smith Ulmer and, their 2Country4Nashville Band backed up the artists which are pictured.

Also in the audience was Patsy Clines son, Randy Dick. Special guests who showed up to perform were: George Hamilton IV, Dave Rowland (Dave & Sugar) and, Baillie & The Boys and Donnie Winters (son of Don Winters who sang with Marty Robbins for over 20 years) received the only standing ovation of the night when he sang and yodeled his song, Rosita.

Jett Williams

Robyn Young

Melissa Luman Philips

Seidina Reed

Donnie Winters

Hawkshaw Hawkins Jr.

Dave Rowland

Baillie and the Boys

George Hamilton IV and George Hamilton V

Dean Smith

2Country4Nashville did a terrific job of backing up all the artists and did a great job during their set as well.

"Kids" Entertain at Starlite Theatre in Branson

Wilson Fairchild and Larry's Country Diner performed on stage at the Starlite Theater in Branson, Mo.

If you are not familiar with Wilson Fairchild then you are in for a treat. These two fine entertainers are the sons of Harold and Don Reid of the Statler Brothers and you will not have any trouble knowing who's who.

Langdon Reid is the son of Don Reid and Will is the son of Harold Reid formed a duo in the 1990's.

Much like their fathers in look and sound they make you feel right at home. Like most kids from famous entertainers Wilson Fairchild have tired to make their own mark in the country music. But with traditional country music fans if's like family. If you have embraced the fathers....you more than likely will embrace the sons. It's kind of a family thing. And these guys are well deserved. They have not only entertained on the Diner TV show but also on the Country's Family Reunion "Second Generation" and "Kinfolk" series available on DVD.

For several years they opened for the legend GEORGE JONES.

There were many fine moments in their show on stage at the Starlite Theater with the Diner cast. But the most memorable was their new "Cowboy" song they had written. It involved audience participation with everyone joining in with a "howl" when the word "Coyote" was sung. The crowd loved it and the Diner cast was really getting into it when all of

a sudden NADINE slid off her stool and decided to do a little "cowboy" dancing with Will. Well....it was Sunday night and her preacher wasn't there..... so she flat cut a rug, UNTIL her hat came flying off and flew across the stage. Langdon laughed so hard he was playing his guitar lying on the floor. Will who had been dancing sudden stopped......and didn't know what to do. The crowd was on their feet as Nadine composed herself and made her way back over to her stool.

If you ever come see our stage shows in Branson you will agree, "The cameras are always rollin' and we don't care"

The Statler Brothers were and American country music, gospel, and backing vocal group for Johnny Cash. The quartet was founded in 1955 and retired in 2002. Only two members of the group (Don and Harold Reid) are actual brothers and none have the surname Statller. The band, in fact, named themselves after a brand of facial tissue they had noticed in a hotel room. They have joked that they could have turned out to be the Kleenex Brothers. Don Reid sang lead, Harold Reid sang bass, Phil Balsley sang Baritone and Lew DeWitt sang tenor before being replaced by Jimmy Fortune in 1983 due to DeWitt's ill health. DeWitt died on August 15, 1990, of heart and kidney disease, stemming from complications of Crohn's disease.

"We took gospel harmonies" said Harold Reid, "and put them over in country music." Two of their best -known songs were"Flowers on the Wall" and "Bed of Roses". Between 1991-1998, they hosted their own show, "The Statler Brothers Show, a weekly variety show on TNN. Throughout their career, much of their appeal was related to their incorporation of comedy and parody into their musical act, thanks in large part to the humorous talent of Harold Reid.

The Statlers continue to be the most awarded act in the history of country music.

Farm Aid celebrates 28 years of entertaining & helping

Each year, Farm Aid board members Willie Nelson, Neil Young, John Mellencamp and Dave Matthews headline a Farm Aid concert to bring together a wide variety of musicians, farmers and fans for one mission: keeping family farmers on their land. Farm Aid is the longest running benefit concert series in America, raising more than $43 million to help family farmers thrive all over the country while inspiring millions of people to learn about the Good Food movement.

The Beginning, September 22, 1985 Champaign, Illinois

Farm Aid started as an idea at the Live Aid Concert when Bob Dylan said on stage, "Wouldn't it be great if we did something for our own farmers right here in America?" Willie Nelson, Neil Young and John Mellencamp agreed that family farmers were in dire need of assistance and decided to plan a concert for America. The show was put together in six weeks and was held on September 22, 1985 in Champaign, Illinois before a crowd of 80,000 people. It raised over $9 million for America's family farmers. Performers included Bob Dylan, Billy Joel, B.B. King, Loretta Lynn, Roy Orbison, Tom Petty, The Winters Brothers Band and many more.

Lorretta Lynn signing autographs at the first Farm Aid in 1985.

28 Years Later, September 21, 2013 Saratoga Springs, NY

On September 21, 2013, more than 25,000 people gathered at Farm Aid 2013 in Saratoga Springs, New York. The annual Farm Aid concert calls attention to the crucial importance of family farmers and the good food they grow for us and our families.

Merle Haggard being interviewed at 1985's Farm Aid

The music on the stage featured Farm Aid board members Willie Nelson, John Mellencamp, Neil Young and Dave Matthews, as well as Jack Johnson, Kacey Musgraves, Jamey Johnson, Amos Lee, and many more. A surprise appearance by 94-year-old Pete Seeger who led a sing-a-long of "This Land is Your Land" that brought the entire audience together as one voice.

Johnny Cash & June Carter Cash - 1985's Farm Aid

Willie Nelson, Dave Matthews, John Mellencamp and Neil Young

Country Questions
By Dick Boise, CMH

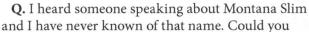

Send questions to:
Dick Boise, , c/o CFR News,
P.O. Box 201796, Nashville,
TN 37221.

Q. I heard someone speaking about Montana Slim and I have never known of that name. Could you help me with some information about this person?

Betty Dupree, Florence, AL

A. Betty, there was such a person as Montana Slim and his real name was Wilf Carter. He was born in Nova Scotia, December 18, 1904. He recorded under the name Montana Slim for the Canadian Bluebird label and when he came to the U.S., he joined the RCA Victor label. He passed away December 5, 1996.

Q. I seem to remember a song called "Blackland Farmer." Could you tell me who might have recorded it and how long ago. Thanks.

Norma Wardrep, Lansing, WV

A. Frankie Miller, a singer from Texas, had a record of that song in 1959. He had several good records on the Starday label and appeared on many radio shows.

Q. I have always wondered if Dale Evans was her real name? I have also been told that she and Roy Rogers had both been married before they were wed. Thanks for your column and its interesting tidbits.

Jill Wickham, Clinton, NY

A. Your question, Jill, caused me to remember the Saturday morning movies at Smalley's Theater. Dale Evans real name was Frances Octavia Smith, and she was born in Uvalde, TX, October 31, 1912. Roy's real name was Leonard Franklin Slye, and he was born November 5, 1911 in Cincinnati, Ohio. Both had been married before, and their marriage was the third for Roy and the fourth for Dale.

Q. Could you find the name of the guitar player who used to play with Roger Miller? His style was different than any I had seen before.

Dan Hale, Deer Lake, WI

A. That guitarist would be "Thumbs" Carlisle. He did have an unusual style of playing with his thumb and fingers pressing down on the top of the strings. He was talented and had four LPs to his credit, one titled, "Roger Miller presents Thumbs Carlisle." He passed away July of 1987.

Q. In a discussion about country music this past week, someone mentioned the name Ray Pennington. I would like some information about him.

Clark Musson, Mt. Carmel, PA

A. Ray Pennington is from Kentucky and is most known for his record company work. He is also a fine song writer and has songs like "Happy Tracks," "Three Hearts in a Tangle," and "Walkin' on New Grass." He is the head man of Stop Records and has recorded some great vocals with Buddy Emmons playing the steel guitar on the sessions. Thanks for asking.

Great way to chronicle your life and give lasting gift

When Larry and Luann Black wanted to give copies of their book, *A Montana Christmas to Remember,* to their grandchildren for Christmas a few years ago, they went to *Published by Westview,*

Inc., a small self-publishing company not far from the Gabriel Communications offices in Nashville. They could have gone anywhere, but they knew Westview could give them the kind of individualized attention their book called for.

Founded as a neighborhood newspaper by Doug Underwood in 1978, Westview began publishing books in 2003. Since then it has published 410 books for a total of 235 authors, with four more books currently in the works – numbers that clearly demonstrate how pleased authors are with Westview's services, because they keep coming back.

Many Westview books were written to chronicle a life – either that of the author or another family member. These contain everything from collections of letters written during wartime to collections of family memories, blogs, and newspaper columns. In addition to these life stories, Westview's books include poetry, novels, genealogies, history, fiction, humor, and children's books.

Other books were published so that the authors could give a lasting gift to their loved ones. One of these, My Elusive Memories, was designed with a "fill-in-the-blank" format, so that family members and loved ones could either chronicle the life of a loved one whose memories are slipping away, or could use it to create an heirloom for their own children and grandchildren. Westview also has available a classic game in an heirloom box, created just for the younger members of your family: Classic Snakes and Ladders.

Whether you've still got the letters and photos your great-grandparents sent each other in a box in

the attic, your unpublished novel or collection of poetry you'd like to preserve for the ages, or you've got a grandchild who would be thrilled to get their own words or artwork published as a Christmas gift, Westview can help you turn your ideas into books.

You can find out more about Westview at www.publishedbywestview.com,

Precious Memories;
Remembering Janette Carter

Janette Carter, the last surviving child of country music's founding Carter Family, who in recent years preserved her parents' oldtime style with weekly performances died January 22, 2006. She was 82.

A.P., Janette, Bill Rinehart, Sara and Maybelle in back, Helen, Anita and June in front, at XERA Radio Station in 1939. The Carter Family spent four seasons from 1938-1943 performing

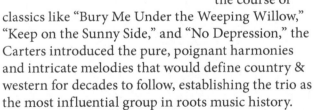

Janette Carter was the last surviving member of country's immortal Carter Family, championing the cause of traditional American roots music into the 21st century. Born July 2, 1923, in Maces Springs, VA, she was the youngest daughter of A.P. and Sara Carter, who with A.P.'s sister-in-law Maybelle comprised the original Carter Family that in 1927 signed with RCA Victor producer/talent scout Ralph Peer. Over the course of classics like "Bury Me Under the Weeping Willow," "Keep on the Sunny Side," and "No Depression," the Carters introduced the pure, poignant harmonies and intricate melodies that would define country & western for decades to follow, establishing the trio as the most influential group in roots music history.

Despite their commercial success A.P. and Sara Carter divorced in 1932. Seven years later, Sara married A.P.'s cousin Coy Bayes and relocated to California, taking her children with her.

The Carter Family concluded its recording career in 1941, but in 1952 both A.P. and Sara agreed to a comeback, enlisting Janette and her brother Joe before signing to the Acme label to record some 100 songs over the next four years.

Following her father's 1960 death, Janette – at the time an elementary school cook – dedicated her life to preserving their music and legacy, hosting informal music programs at A.P.'s Poor Valley, VA, retail store. Although she never earned the commercial or critical acclaim awarded her cousin, June Carter Cash, Janette also mounted a solo career, in 1972 releasing her debut LP, Storms Are on the Ocean, on the tiny Birch label. Howdayadoo followed on Traditional Records a year later. In 1976 she established the Hiltons, VA-based Carter Family Fold, a nonprofit amphitheater and museum site built from old railroad ties and school bus seats dedicated to the old-time music of rural Appalachia. Despite the Fold's strict adherence to traditional acoustic music, Janette eventually eased her restrictions in order to allow her cousin's husband, Johnny Cash, to play an electric set.

Carter continued hosting weekly concerts at the Fold into her eighties, and in 2004 the Bear Family label assembled Deliverance Will Come, compiling the entirety of her slim solo output. She died in Kingsport, TN, on January 20, 2006, following a long battle with Parkinson's disease and other illnesses.

The Grascals new song 'American Pickers' includes friends Mike Wolfe & Dierks Bentley

The Grascals, a three-time Grammy nominated band, has recently released the companion video for one song on their new album set for release on November 19. "American Pickers" was written by Jamie Johnson, Susanne Mumpower Johnson and Jeffrey East after members of The Grascals met and became friends with Mike Wolfe of the hit History Channel television show, American Pickers. Country superstar and Grascals' pal, Dierks Bentley, also played and sang on the album cut and appears in the music video, along with Wolfe.

"We just really love the American Pickers TV show, so it was a thrill to meet and get to know Mike," Jamie says. "I told him we'd like to write a song for him and he thought that was a pretty cool idea. The song and video have been such fun for all of us, including Dierks and Mike, and now we're happy to share it with fans."

The music video was shot on location during The Grascals' Rivestage appearance at the 2013 CMA Music Festival in Nashville and at the Cash Cabin Studio in Hendersonville, TN.

The Grascals are among the most beloved and acclaimed bands on the bluegrass scene. The Grascals have been repeatedly honored for their work. The reigning SPBGMA Instrumental Group of the Year (for the 3rd year in a row), the group was named SPBGMA's Bluegrass Band of the Year 2010. The Grascals have also received the IBMA (International Bluegrass Music Association) Emerging Artist of the Year award (2005) and Entertainer of the Year award (2006, 2007). Kristin Scott Benson is a four-time winner of the Banjo Player of the Year Award and Danny Roberts has been honored as Mandolin Player of the Year. The Grascals are three-time Grammy Award nominees. They have made more than 130 appearances on the legendary stage of the Grand Ole Opry.

The Grascals also recently added fiddler Adam Haynes to the band. Adam has an impressive pedigree having played with some of the finest: Melvin Goins & Windy Mountain, The James King Band, David Parmley & Continental Divide, Dailey & Vincent, Larry Stephenson Band, and most recently Grasstowne. Adam is originally from Norwalk, OH but spent quite some time in Eastern Kentucky where his family has roots as deep as bluegrass. Adam currently makes his home in Portland, TN with his wife, Janette, and two daughters, Bella (8) and Ellie (3).

Nadine's Cooking Corner

Christmas Sugar Cookies

INGREDIENTS:

Cookies:
2 cups all-purpose flour, plus more for dusting
2 teaspoons baking powder
1/2 teaspoon salt
1/2 cup (1 stick) butter
1 cup granulated sugar
1 large egg
1/2 teaspoon vanilla extract

Icing:
One 12-ounce box confectioners' sugar
3 tablespoons meringue powder
1/3 cup warm (80 to 90 degrees F) water
Food coloring, optional
Assorted sprinkles, colored sugar and small candy pieces

DIRECTIONS:

For the cookies: Sift together the flour, baking powder and salt. In a stand mixer, cream the butter and granulated sugar until light and fluffy. Add the egg and mix until combined. Gradually add the sifted dry ingredients, one spoonful at a time, until thoroughly combined. Add the vanilla. Chill the cookie dough in the refrigerator for at least 1 hour.

Preheat the oven to 400 degrees F.

Roll out half of the dough at a time, keeping the remainder of the dough in the refrigerator. On a lightly floured surface, roll out the dough to a 1/4-inch thickness and cut into desired shapes with a cookie cutter.

Place the cutout cookies 2 inches apart on an ungreased cookie sheet and put the cookie sheet in the refrigerator for a few minutes before baking. This will help the cookies to retain their shape. (You can roll out the scraps to make a few more cookies.) Bake until just before the edges of the cookies start to brown, 8 to 10 minutes. Cool the cookies for 1 to 2 minutes on the cookie sheet before removing to wire racks to cool completely.

Who says you can't make a Nativity scene out of food!?

Nadine
The Church Lady

For the icing: In a medium bowl, combine the confectioners' sugar, meringue powder and warm water with a wire whisk. Stir until the icing is smooth. Adjust the consistency of the icing by adding more confectioners' sugar or more water, as needed. Add food coloring, if desired, to the icing. Spread the icing on the cooled cookies and then top with assorted sprinkles and candies.

Notes

Cook's Note: Meringue powder is available in a can. (I use Wilton.) It is used in place of egg whites in many icing recipes.

The CFR News
is published monthly by Gabriel Communications, Inc.
P.O. Box 210796, Nashville, TN 37221
615-673-2846
Larry Black, Publisher
Renae Johnson, General Manager
Paula Underwood Winters, Editor
Subscriptions: $29.95 yearly

American Pickers show brings collectibles to Antique Archeaology

Mike Wolfe from the History Channel TV show *American Pickers* says he's been looking for treasures in the trash forever. "When I was five, I had my first big score when I found a pile of old bicycles in my neighborhood on trash day. And I was always bringing home old bottles and other random stuff. I never thought of it as junk: to me, it was beautiful."

He says he always loved bikes and even raced competitively while in his twenties which led him to open a bicycle store and repair shop in his hometown of Bettendorf, Iowa.

"Because of the store, people were always telling me about cool vintage bikes for sale, which I'd buy and flip for extra cash. When I added Italian scooters and motorcycles to the mix, picking became more than just a hobby," says Mike, "So I closed the shop, bought a van and hit the road. Antique Archeaology was born."

Now through the TV show American Pickers, he can share the experience with millions of people.

He has two Antique Archeaology stores. One Antique Archeaology is tucked away in the historic Mississippi River town of LeClaire, Iowa. It's the birthplace of Buffalo Bill. The two-story former fabrication shop now houses our best picks, a new merchandise store, and serves as the home base for the American Pickers Show.

Antique Archaeology Nashville is Mike's second location. Located just a few blocks away from downtown Nashville, you can find them in the old Marathon Automobile car factory dated from the early 1900s right along I-40. Here they'll have your favorite Antique Archaeology gear, including the latest Nashville-exclusive designs, plus new picks that you may have seen on the show. And you never know who's gonna "pop" in. Tune up your guitar and stay a while. Nashville's always been pickin'...

Cutlines: Mike Wolfe from American Pickers TV show, Renae the waitress from Larry's Country Diner and Jamie Johnson from The Grascals at Antique Archeaology in Nashville.

Dolly Parton stars in new Lifetime Christmas movie

Grammy® Award winner Dolly Parton (Nine to Five, Steel Magnolias), to star along with Megyn Price (Rules of Engagement), Brian McKnight (American Dreams), newcomer Desiree Ross (Crossing the River) in the Lifetime Original Movie A Country Christmas Story, which premiered Saturday, November 9.

A Country Christmas Story follows a young bi-racial Appalachian Mountain girl (Ross) as she defies her mother (Price) and goes against stereotype when she takes up guitar in pursuit of her dream of becoming a country star. Her journey to the stage at Dollywood and a singing competition hosted by Dolly Parton reunites her itinerant musician father (McKnight) with her family, as well as uncovering

the musical legacy of African Americans in the world of country music. Mary Kay Place (Big Love, Being John Malkovich) will portray her grandmother.

Dolly Parton's career has spanned nearly five decades and is showing no signs of slowing down. An internationally-renowned superstar, the iconic and irrepressible Parton has contributed countless treasures to the worlds of music, film and television. Some of her hit films have included Nine to Five, Steel Magnolias, The Best Little Whorehouse in Texas and Rhinestone. Parton received two Oscar® nominations – one for writing the title tune to Nine to Five and the other for Travelin' Thru from the film Transamerica. Throughout her career, she has penned such classic songs as Jolene, Coat of Many Colors, her mega-hit I Will Always Love You and Here You Come Again and garnered seven Grammy Awards. In 1986, Parton opened up her own them park called Dollywood, in Pigeon Forge, Tennessee, at the base of the Great Smoky Mountains.

EJ's Treasures help celebrate Larry Black's Birthday

The Larry's Country Diner cast were all on hand for the 13th year Celebration of EJ Treasures. The place was packed with shoppers and they got a real treat when Jimmy Fortune showed up to help celebrate a SURPRISE birthday for Larry Black. "Larry, who loves surprises, had no idea what we were up to" says Renae (the waitress). All of the customers were treated to a slice of birthday cake while shopping. FUN...seems to follow this cast around !!!

FIND THE 9 DIFFERENCES IN THESE 2 PICS

CMA Awards give nod and awards to some 'real' country music artists

There were definitely some interesting moments at the CMA Awards show in Nashville as Kanye West came on stage, but there was also a feeling that some of the world still knows and appreciates traditional country music. The night ended with George Strait winning his third entertainer of the year trophy on Wednesday, November 6.

Strait won the CMA's top honor for the first time since 1990 in something of a victory lap as he launches the final leg of his The Cowboy Rides Away tour -- his goodbye to touring.

"This blows me away," the 61-year-old legend, whose competition included Taylor Swift and Blake Shelton, told the audience after a standing ovation. "I just cannot believe it. You guys that are nominated are such powerful entertainers. I'm just thrilled to even be nominated again."

He later joked backstage, "The cowboy might be riding in again."

Swift, who performed a somber, acoustic version of her hit "Red" with Vince Gill, Alison Krauss and Sam Bush, was given the CMA's Pinnacle Award. The award goes to artists who take country music to a worldwide audience. Garth Brooks is the only previous winner in 2005.

George Strait and Alan Jackson joined together to salute the late George Jones with a rendition of "She Stopped Loving Him Today."

And in one of the night's most anticipated moments, Kenny Rogers received the CMA's Willie Nelson lifetime achievement award and was saluted

by Jennifer Nettles, Rucker and Rascal Flatts. Rogers sat on stage and mouthed along until he and Nettles finished the tribute by singing "Islands in the Stream."

"It's been a hell of a month," Rogers said. "The (Country Music) Hall of Fame last week, this this week. I can't wait to see what's coming next week."

And fans of traditional country are waiting as well.

Cutlines: (L-R) Joe Don Rooney, Jay DeMarcus, Willie Nelson Lifetime Achievement Award winner Kenny Rogers, Jennifer Nettles, Darius Rucker and Gary LeVox onstge during the 47th annual CMA awards at the Bridgestone Arena on November 6, 2013 in Nashville, United States.

Behind the scenes SPOTLIGHT

We have so many talented folks that work behind the scenes of our television shows and tapings that we thought you should meet them. Their talents and experience surely humble us. This first spotlight features one of our favorite people:

Lynn Edwards

Lynn helps 'edit' LCD & CFR on RFDTV and has directed a few episodes of Larry's Country Diner. He helps produce the 'Behind The Scenes' volume for the CFR products and is usually the one who interviews the artists.

Lynn is seen introducing Buddy Jewell on Larry's Country Diner.

"Most of the time I sit in a dark room and mash computer buttons," Lynn tells people who ask.

He has been working for Gabriel for the past 4.5 years. Before that he worked at CMT and once directed Taylor Swift, "but prefer it here!" he says emphatically.

His VERY FIRST REAL JOB was when he was 15 working for Bill Anderson's restaurant 'Po Folks'

Lynn's favorite artists include country music greats such as Uncle Dave Macon, The Skillet Lickers, Louvin Brothers, Tex Ritter, Roger MIller, Grandpa Jones and Dwight Yoakam.

Lynn Edwards was born & raised in Nashville, Tennessee. He and his wife, Honor, and son, Oliver, live in Bellevue (a suburb of Nashville), not far from the Gabriel corporate office.

When and how do I renew my subscription?

Every subscriber should get a notice at least one month prior to the expiration of the CFR NEWS, however, because computers don't always get it right, if you think it might be time for your subscription to run out, just call us at either our customer serivce number (800-820-5405) or the corporate office (615-673-2846) and we can check to see exactly when your subscription is due.

When you receive your renewal notice, you will need to send it back to us in time for us to receive it by the 15th of the month in order for us to get it processed prior to the paper going to print and being mailed on the 18-20 of the month. Otherwise, your name won't be on our mailing list and you won't get that month's issue.

In other words, if your paper is due to expire in January, you should receive a renewal notice by the first of December. You will need to return it to us by December 15 to get your January issue. If you think

you are expiring and haven't received a renewal notice, call and we can renew you by credit or debit card over the phone or you can send us a check.

If you do miss and issue or two, we are continuing to put together the annual book with the articles and photos from that year's paper. Year Two should be out shortly after the first of the year.

If you have any doubts, just call. We are more than happy to pull up your account and see what the status is and get you back on track.

Charlie Daniels' singer, Carolyn Corlew crowned Ms. Senior America in Atlantic City

Longtime Charlie Daniels Band background vocalist Carolyn Corlew was crowned Ms. Senior America today at the National pageant at Resorts Casino Hotel's Superstar Theater in Atlantic City, NJ. The competition featured 34 women age 60 and older from around the country. Corlew won the title of Ms. Senior Tennessee April 27th. While representing Wilson County at the Tennessee State convention, Corlew encouraged ladies that have reached the "Age of Elegance" to consider participating in the pageant.

"I am thrilled, honored and so excited about wearing this crown for the next year," said Corlew. "These women were over the top - there were professional dancers, opera singers from Broadway... I sang a bluesy Etta James song and we had a 93 year old that rocked the competition. I'm blown away. From this point it's spirit, mind and then body - it's gotta come from within. I've got a 20 pound dress on and a crown and I'm proud to represent all the senior women of America!"

Carolyn started working as a back up singer with Charlie Daniels in 1979 and moved to Nashville. She and her husband, long time Charlie Daniels employee, David Corlew, have two daughters.

Ms. Senior America, established by Dr. Al Mott in 1972, is the world's first and foremost pageant to emphasize and give honor to women who have reached the "Age of Elegance." It is a search for the gracious lady who best exemplifies the dignity, maturity and inner beauty of all senior Americans. By giving women 60 years of age and older an opportunity to display their "inner beauty," talents, and elegance, the Pageant seeks to draw attention to the achievements of senior women. The Pageant motivates and encourages women to utilize their full potential and share a positive outlook on life with others. Participants represent a cross section of America.

"Certainly youth is beauty that excites, but age is charm and character that inspires," Mott said. "One of the reasons this pageant is thriving is because it's a celebration of women who've reached -- perhaps "achieved" is the more apt term, the "age of elegance.""

The Pageant's philosophy is based upon the belief that seniors are the foundation of America, and our most valuable treasure. It is upon their knowledge, experience and resources that the younger generation has the opportunity to build a better society.

"These remarkable women have had successful careers, raised families, survived cancer, strokes, heart attacks; struggled, lived and thrived, yet they remain steadfastly elegant and inspiring," said Dr. Mott.

For more information on the Ms. Senior America Pageant, visit www.senioramerica.org

Well known video director, Sherman Halsey, dead at 56

Sherman filming the Merle Haggard & Kris Kristofferson Tour.

Sherman Halsey, 56, was found deceased on a couch in the living room of a home in Nashville where he was staying on Tuesday, October 29, by a local acquaintance who went to check on Halsey at the request of his family in Oklahoma. The family had not heard from him in several days. Halsey was an music video and television director, producer, and artist manager. Sherman Halsey has produced and directed hundreds of television shows and music videos for artists such as Tim McGraw, Brooks and Dunn, Alan Jackson, BB King, Michael Bolton, Dwight Yoakam, and many more.

He began his career in the country music business at the age of 13, putting up posters and show bills for his father Jim Halsey's Management and Concert promotion company in the family's home town of Independence, Kansas. This would be the start of a father and son collaboration that continues in business today as an important part of the country music industry. While studying film at the University of Kansas, Halsey promoted concerts with artists from the Jim Halsey Company's roster such as The Oak Ridge Boys, Freddy Fender, Hank Thompson, Don Williams and many others. While at the university, Halsey worked for Dick Clark Productions in Beverly Hills one summer on the NBC Special "The Wild, Sensational, and Shocking 70's". As a result of this experience with Dick Clark, he built relationships with several veteran, network directors who taught him the art of directing and producing.

After college, Halsey split his time between the Agency, Management and Record Company division headquartered in Tulsa, and their Beverly Hills office where he and Dick Howard developed the television production arm of the Jim Halsey Company. As vice chairman of the Jim Halsey Company, the largest agency in country music in the world at that time, he was involved in all aspects of the artists' careers. The Jim Halsey Company represented 47 of country music's top stars, Roy Clark, The Oak Ridge Boys, The Judds, Waylon Jennings, Reba McEntire, Merle Haggard, Roy Orbison and many others. Halsey was vice chairman of the Jim Halsey Company from 1980–1990 when the Halseys sold the Agency division to William Morris. The Halseys maintained ownership of the Management and Production divisions of the Company.

Halsey discovered and managed Dwight Yoakam. Drawing upon his directing talent, Halsey combined his management and marketing skills to design and implement a plan which would develop Yoakam's career through the newly emerging video market. As Yoakam's Manager, he produced and directed numerous music videos for Yoakam including one of the first big budget music videos, "Honky Tonk Man". This was the first country music video to be played on MTV and Yoakam's career exploded into instant stardom.[citation needed] Halsey also worked as manager of the group The Clark Family Experience. He discovered them after seeing a videotape of one of their performances, but with no contact information on the tape, it took him six months to find them. He asked them if they wanted to open for Tim McGraw, and got them signed to Curb Records, within a few weeks of meeting them.

Halsey became a prolific music video director, especially for Tim McGraw. Regarding their work together, McGraw said in an interview, ""Sherman has documented pretty much everything and almost all the videos I've done." McGraw delayed plans for a television network special, eventually titled, Tim McGraw: Sing Me Home, until he could be assured that Halsey would direct the special.

He also directed music videos for The Oak Ridge Boys, Dwight Yoakam, Los Lobos, Travis Tritt, The Mavericks, Lorrie Morgan, Collin Raye, Brooks & Dunn, Patty Loveless, John Anderson, Hal Ketchum, Mark Chesnutt, Alan Jackson and more.

The 19th Annual ICM Faith, Family & Country™ Awards

The 19th Annual ICM Faith, Family & Country™ Awards were held in October at The Fellowship at Two Rivers in Nashville to honor artists, songwriters, radio personalities and others in the genres of Christian and Inspirational Country Music. Winners included Rascal Flatts for "Mainstream Inspirational Country Song" and "Video," Martina McBride for "Mainstream Country Female Artist" and Scotty McCreery for "Mainstream Country Male Artist," along with the top Inspirational Country Music artists: Kali Rose, Tommy Brandt, Mary James, The Roys and many more.

Highlights of the evening included Gene Higgins being presented with the "Living Legend Award," as well as performances by Guy Penrod and special guest Sarah Darling, Dennis Agajanian , Aaron & Amanda Crabb, and Canton Junction. ICM favorite Andy Griggs took over hosting duties from Inside Edition's Megan Alexander for a portion of the show, with Miss Tennessee USA 2014 and Miss Tennessee Teen USA 2014 presenting the winners with their trophies. The star power did not end with performers. Presenters included American Idol's Melinda Doolittle, The Voice's Holly Tucker, Jim Ed Brown, Former NBA Player Mike Glenn and The Roys. The 19th Annual ICM Faith, Family & Country™ Awards were presented by Samaritan's Purse and Operation Christmas Child and Operation Troop Aid was this year's charity of choice. Airing on The TCT Network, GEB America, National Religious Broadcasters (NRB), The Worship Network and Total Living Network (TLN), this year's show reached a potential audience of 1.6 billion, it's largest to date.

2013 ICM Winners:

ENTERTAINER: Kali Rose

MALE VOCALIST: Tommy Brandt

FEMALE VOCALIST: Mary James

VOCAL DUO / VOCAL DUO PERFORMANCE: Steve Richard & Laura Dodd

VOCAL GROUP OR BAND: Sunday Drive

MAINSTREAM INSPIRATIONAL COUNTRY SONG: "Changed" Rascal Flatts

MAINSTREAM COUNTRY MALE ARTIST: Scotty McCreery

MAINSTREAM COUNTRY FEMALE ARTIST: Martina McBride

MAINSTREAM COUNTRY DUO OR GROUP: Joey+Rory

INSPIRATIONAL COUNTRY SONG: "They Don't Stay Little Long Enough" Chuck Hancock

SONGWRITER: Chuck Hancock

VIDEO: "Changed" - Rascal Flatts

MUSICIAN: Dennis Agajanian

COMEDIAN: Chonda Pierce

RADIO STATION/NETWORK: Inspirational Country Radio Network

NEW ARTIST: Charee White

YOUTH IN MUSIC AWARD: The McDougal Kids

FAITH, FAMILY, & COUNTRY MOVIE: Spirit of Love, the Mike Glenn Story – Film It Productions Produced by Darla Rae

RADIO PERSONALITY: Marty Smith

INSPIRATIONAL BLUEGRASS ARTIST: The Roys

MUSIC EVANGELIST: Russ Murphy

TELEVISION NETWORK: RFD TV

2013 LIVING LEGEND: Gene Higgins

The Roys make their Opry Debut Nov. 1

Bluegrass brother/sister duo The Roys made their Grand Ole Opry debut on November 1, when they joined Little Big Town, Josh Turner, The Marshall Tucker Band, Chris Janson, Sara Haze, Jeannie Seely, Jesse McReynolds, Jim Lauderdale and others for the Opry At The Ryman show.

For Lee and Elaine, the night was a dream come true. "It has been a lifelong dream to perform on the Grand Ole Opry and I'm still in excited shock that we will be living it tomorrow night," exclaims Lee. For his sister Elaine, "holding it together" best describes her reaction to the invitation. "My whole being went numb. This is just an incredible opportunity and an honor," she adds. "And I thank God for answering my prayers in His own way and in His own time."

The Roys' current Rural Rhythm Records CD, GYPSY RUNAWAY TRAIN, continues to top SiriusXM's Most-Played Albums list for October. The disc is #15 on Bluegrass Unlimited's Top 15 Bluegrass Albums chart and their single, "Gypsy Runaway Train," is #19 on the Bluegrass Unlimited National Bluegrass Top 30 Singles chart (November). The duo is still "reeling" from winning last week's Inspirational Country Music Award for Bluegrass Artist of the Year for the third consecutive year.

Previously honored with the five additional ICM awards (2012 No. 1 Inspirational Country Single, 2012 & 2011 Bluegrass Artist of the Year and the 2010 & 2009 Duo of the Year), THE ROYS continue to bring the best of Bluegrass to audiences near and far. They have toured across the U.S. and performed in Europe and in Australia and shared the stage with Lady Antebellum, Jason Aldean, Chris Young, Blake Shelton, Doyle Lawson, Janie Fricke, Collin Raye, Alan Jackson, Ricky Skaggs, Sara Evans, Rhonda Vincent and others. Lee and Elaine have enjoyed high-profile TV gigs, including performances on Fox & Friends, Daytime, The Daily Buzz, ABC's What's The Buzz, GAC's Headline Country, RFD's Campfire Café and Larry's Country Diner and more. THE ROYS were featured in the PBS television special Pa's Fiddle: Charles Ingalls, American Fiddler.

Comedian Steve Martin is avid banjo picker

Stephen Glenn "Steve" Martin was born August 14, 1945 in Waco, Texas but was raised in California. He is an American actor, comedian, musician, author, playwright and producer.

Martin came to public notice as a writer for the Smothers Brothers Comedy Hour, and later became a frequent guest on The Tonight Show. In the 1970s, Martin performed his offbeat, absurdist comedy routines before packed houses on national tours. In 2004, Comedy Central ranked Martin at sixth place in a list of the 100 greatest stand-up comics.

Since the 1980s, having branched away from stand-up comedy, Martin has become a successful actor, as well as an author, playwright, pianist and banjo player, eventually earning Emmy, Grammy and American Comedy awards, among other honors.

On his comedy albums, Martin's stand-up is self-referential and sometimes self-mocking. It mixes philosophical riffs with sudden spurts of "happy feet", he plays banjo and he is a master juggler.

Martin first picked up the banjo when he was around 17 years of age. Martin has claimed in several interviews and in his autobiography, "Born Standing Up", that he used to take 33 rpm bluegrass records and slow them down to 16 rpm and tune his banjo down, so the notes would sound the same. Martin was able to pick out each note, and perfect his playing.

Martin learned how to play the banjo with help from John McEuen, who later joined the Nitty Gritty Dirt Band. McEuen's brother later managed Martin as well as the Nitty Gritty Dirt Band. Martin did his stand-up routine opening for the band in the early 1970s. He had the band play on his hit song, "King Tut", being credited as "The Toot Uncommons" (as in Tutankhamun).

The banjo was a staple of Martin's 1970s stand-up career, and he periodically poked fun at his love for the instrument. On the Comedy Is Not Pretty! album he included an all-instrumental jam, titled "Drop Thumb Medley", and played the track on his 1979 concert tour. His final comedy album, The Steve Martin Brothers (1981), featured one side of Martin's typical stand-up material, with the other side featuring live performances of Steve playing banjo with a bluegrass band.

In 2001, he played banjo on Earl Scruggs's remake of "Foggy Mountain Breakdown". The recording was the winner of the Best Country Instrumental Performance category at the Grammy Awards of 2002. In 2008, Martin appeared with the band, In the Minds of the Living, during a show in Myrtle Beach, South Carolina.

In 2009, Martin released his first all-music album, The Crow: New Songs for the 5-String Banjo with appearances from stars such as Dolly Parton. The album won the Grammy Award for Best Bluegrass Album in 2010. Nitty Gritty Dirt Band member John McEuen produced the album.

Martin made his first appearance on The Grand Ole Opry on May 30, 2009. Martin has appeared at the New Orleans Jazzfest, Merlefest Bluegrass Festival in Wilkesboro, North Carolina, at Bonnaroo Music Festival, at the ROMP Bluegrass festival in Owensboro, Kentucky, at the Red Butte Garden Concert series and on the BBC's Later... with Jools Holland. In 2011, Martin also narrated and appeared in the PBS documentary "Give me the Banjo" chronicling the history of the Banjo in America.

Love Has Come For You, a collaboration with Edie Brickell, was released in April 2013. The two made musical guest appearances on talk shows, such as The View and Late Show with David Letterman, to promote the album.

Recently he has been touring with the Steep Canyon Rangers and Edie Brickell throughout the United States.

In 2010, Martin created the Steve Martin Prize for Excellence in Banjo and Bluegrass, an award established to reward artistry and bring greater visibility to bluegrass performers. The prize includes a $50,000 cash award, a bronze sculpture created by the artist Eric Fischl, and a chance to perform with Martin on the Late Show With David Letterman. Recipients include Noam Pikelny of the Punch Brothers band (2010), Sammy Shelor of Lonesome River Band (2011), Mark Johnson (2012) and Jens Kruger (2013).

On July 28, 2007, after three years together, Martin married Anne Stringfield, a writer and former staffer for The New Yorker magazine and at age 67, Martin became a first-time dad when Stringfield gave birth in December 2012.

Larry's Country Diner RFD Show Schedule
These shows have been previously aired.

Larry Mahan
Saturday, Dec. 7
10:00 p.m. Central

Sunday, Dec. 8 show preempted by RFD -TV

Rebecca Lynn Howard
Saturday, Dec. 14
10:00 p.m. Central

Sunday, Dec. 15 show preempted by RFD -TV

Exile
Saturday, Dec. 21
10:00 p.m. Central

Sunday, Dec. 22
6:00 p.m. Central

Billy Dean
Saturday, Dec. 28
10:00 p.m. Central

Sunday, Dec. 29
6:00 p.m. Central

Ricky Skaggs
Saturday, Jan. 4
10:00 p.m. Central

Sunday, Jan. 5
6:00 p.m. Central

NOTICE:
RFD-TV will be preempting Country's Family Reunion on Friday nights and Larry's Country Diner on Sunday nights from December 5-15.
Please check your RFD listings for possible change in air days & times during this period.

Country Questions
By Dick Boise, CMH

Send questions to:
Dick Boise, , c/o CFR News,
P.O. Box 201796, Nashville,
TN 37221.

Q. Where was the late Tennessee Ernie Ford born? I sure miss his humor an dhis fine voice. Thanks.

Ron Coleman, WY

A. Ernest Jennings Ford was born in Fordtown, TN, February 13, 1919. The "Ole Pea Picker" as he like to be called, died October 17, 1991. Yes, we all do miss him as well.

Q. I would like to find out which country music show was first, The Grand Ole Opry or the Wheeling Jamboree? Enjoy the paper each month, and appreciate any answer you may provide.

Emma Grover Oneida, TN

A. Well now, Emma, there were many radio shows featuring live country music back in the days gone by. The Grand Ole Opry started as the WSM Barn Dance on October 5, 1925, and the name changed to the Opry on December 8, 1928. The Wheeling Jamboree began with its first live audience show on April 1, 1933. Many shows around the states from Louisiana, Virginia, Texas and more, were heard on the radio and the first was from WLS in Chicago beginning its long run on April 9, 1924. What a wonderful time those early years were for country music.

Q. Could you tell me who was the Duke of Paducah that my grandfather mentioned a lot?

Kathy Getty Dover, DE

A. Benjamin Francis Ford, also called "Whitey" Ford, was a comic on several medicine shows in the early days. He became a famous member of the Grand Ole Opry and was noted for his famous line, "I'm going back to the wagon boys, these shoes are killing me!" Truly, a funny, funny man.

Q. What was the lady's name who sang the song "One Day At A Time"? I would like to know more about her.

Dorothy McArthur, AR

A. Christy Lane, from Peoria, IL, was the singer of that hit record. Her life story is a very interesting read. I'm sure that you could find a copy of her biography in your local library. It also has the title, "One Day At A Time", by Lee Stroller, her husband.

How many "BLUE" songs do you know

There are lots of songs with the word 'blue' in the title. Here are only 9 of them. How many can you list?

Send them to us at CFR News Contest, P.O. Box 210796, Nashville, TN 37221 and we'll enter you in our drawing for a Larry's Country Diner apron. We're giving away 5 of them, so don't delay. Send them in today. Deadline is December 18th!

Jimmy Capps one of Musician Hall of Fame Inductees

Twelve new inductees to the Musicians Hall of Fame were announced in Nashville on Monday, November 4. The 2014 Induction Ceremony will be held at the 10,000 seat arena of Nashville's Historic Municipal Auditorium on Tuesday, January 28, 2014. After a 3 year absence, this will be the first award show held at the Historic Nashville Municipal Auditorium, the new home of the Musicians Hall of Fame and Museum.

2014 Inductees are:

Jimmy Capps

As one of Country Music's finest guitar players, Jimmy Capps is a 'master of smoothness'. He is known in the studio for his ability to move flawlessly from 'electric to acoustic' with a polished and refined touch that he brings to every recording or performance he is part of. Some of the classics' that Jimmy has played on are "Stand By Your Man," "He Stopped Loving Her Today," and "The Gambler." Jimmy can also be seen performing on the Opry stage as a staff musician, which he has done since the 1960's. Jimmy also plays "The Sheriff" on Larry's Country Diner.

Barbara Mandrell

The first artist to win the CMA Entertainer Of The Year for two consecutive years and has won multiple awards from the CMA, ACM, American Music Awards, Grammys, People's Choice Awards and a Dove Award. Her variety show, "Barbara Mandrell and the Mandrell Sisters," on NBC drew millions of viewers weekly.

Along with being a member of the Steel Guitar Hall of Fame, her repertoire of instruments include: saxophone, banjo, guitar, dobro, mandolin, and bass, in addition to the accordion and the pedal steel guitar

Peter Frampton

Grammy Award winner Peter Frampton remains one of the most celebrated artists and guitarists in rock history. At 16, he was lead singer and guitarist for British band The Herd. At 18, he cofounded one of the first super groups, seminal rock act Humble Pie. His fifth solo album, the electrifying Frampton Comes Alive! is one of the top selling live records of all time.

Ben Keith (posthumously)

Known primarily for his work as a pedal steel guitarist with Neil Young, Keith was a fixture of the Nashville country music community in the 1950s and 1960s. He later worked with numerous successful rock, country and pop artists as both a producer and a multi instrumentalist sideman for over four decades. The very first song Ben recorded as a Nashville session player was Patsy Cline's timeless standard "I Fall To Pieces."

Velma Smith

A self taught musician, Smith learned to sing and play guitar at an early age. Velma was the first female to perform a solo on the NBC Network portion of the Grand Ole Opry. Velma was also the first female rhythm guitar player to play on records recorded in Nashville. Some of the artists Velma recorded with during her musical career were Eddy Arnold, Hank Locklin, Jim Reeves, Skeeter Davis, Roy Orbison, Waylon Jennings, Chet Atkins, Jerry Reed, Willie Nelson, Charlie Rich and Don Gibson.

Randy Bachman

A legendary figure in the rock and roll world through his talents as a guitarist with The Guess Who and Bachman Turner Overdrive, Randy is equally known for being a songwriter, session musician and producer. He has earned over 110 gold and platinum awards around the world for performing and producing. His songs have been recorded by numerous other artists and placed in dozens of television, movie and commercial soundtracks. His melodic guitar riffs have provided a veritable soundtrack of the last forty plus years of popular music.

Corki Casey O'Dell

In Phoenix, Arizona, in the mid Fifties, a small group of musicians were making groundbreaking recordings that would help to define the sound of Rock and Roll. Corki Casey O'Dell was the lone woman musician in this group.In 1956, she played rhythm guitar on Sanford Clark's The Fool, a Top Ten hit record. In 1957 and '58, she played rhythm guitar on Duane Eddy's Moovin' 'n Groovin' and Ramrod. She played on most of Eddy's recordings in Phoenix, including Peter Gunn,Forty Miles of Bad Road, and his signature tune, Rebel Rouser, which would be featured years later in the film Forrest Gump. Corki's rhythm guitar playing on so many pioneering hit records earned her the title of The First Rock and Roll Sidechick.

Will Lee

Best known for his work as the bass guitarist on the CBS television program Late Show with David Letterman as part of the CBS Orchestra. As a studio musician, Lee has played on more than 1700 albums, working with artists as diverse as Carly Simon, Barry Manilow, Mariah Carey, and Dave Matthews. Will is also a founding member of the world famous Beatles tribute band, The Fab Faux.

Stevie Ray Vaughan (posthumously) & Double Trouble

With Stevie on guitar, Chris Layton on drums, Tommy Shannon on bass guitar and Reese Wynans on keyboards, Stevie Ray Vaughan & Double Trouble are credited with igniting the Blues Revival in the 80's with sold out concerts and gold records. They played together from 1978 until Stevie's death in a helicopter crash after a concert August 27, 1990. Since then, Chris,

Tommy, and Reese have continued playing in other bands as well as session musicians for other artists.

Buddy Guy

Guy is a pioneer of the Chicago blues sound and has served as an influence to some of the most notable musicians of his generation, including Eric Clapton, Jimmy Page, Jimi Hendrix and Stevie Ray Vaughan. Rolling Stone magazine ranked Guy 30th on their list

of 100 Greatest Guitarists of All Time. Known for his showmanship on stage, he would play his guitar with drumsticks or stroll into the audience while playing solos. His song "Stone Crazy" was ranked 78th in Rolling Stone's list of the 100 Greatest Guitar Songs of All Time.

2014 Iconic Riff Award

Roy Orbison (posthumously) "Pretty Woman" Grammy winner Roy Orbison's induction as a member of the Songwriters Hall of Fame and Rock and Roll Hall of Fame are well documented, but not as well known, is that as a guitarist, Roy created one of the most covered and iconic guitar riffs of all time, "Pretty Woman".

Roy is the first recipient of this award.

Non Performing Award

Mike Curb

Mike Curb started out writing music for TV and film before creating his first record label in 1963. Later, he merged his company with MGM and became president of MGM Records and Verve Records. In the 70s, Curb wrote for and produced Roy Orbison, the Osmond Family, Lou Rawls, and Sammy Davis, Jr. In 1994, the former Lieutenant Governor of California moved to Nashville and formed Curb Records with country recording artists including Wynonna Judd, LeAnn Rimes, Hank Williams, Jr. Rodney Atkins, and Tim McGraw. Along with running Curb Records, Mike is also a civic leader and benefactor for many organizations including higher learning institutions that have helped ensure the entertainment industry will survive in perpetuity.

Precious Memories: Remembering John Hartford

John Hartford won Grammy awards in three different decades, recorded a catalog of more than 30 albums, and wrote one of the most popular songs of all time, Gentle On My Mind. He was a regular guest and contributor on the Glen Campbell Good Time Hour and the Smothers Brothers Show. He added music and narration to Ken Burns' landmark Civil War series, and was an integral part of the hugely popular "O Brother, Where Art Thou?" soundtrack and Down From The Mountain concert tour. But that hardly explains John Hartford.

John Hartford was an American original. He was a musician, songwriter, steamboat pilot, author, artist, disc jockey, calligrapher, dancer, folklorist, father, and historian.

Born John Cowan Harford in New York on December 30, 1937, John grew up in St. Louis. He was a descendent of Patrick Henry and cousin of Tennessee Williams. His grandfather was a founder of the Missouri Bar Association and his father was a prominent doctor.

At an early age, John fell in love with two things: music and the Mississippi River.

They were passions that would last his lifetime, and their pursuit would be his life's passage.

In 1965 he moved to Nashville. The following year he was signed to RCA Records by the legendary Chet Atkins. It was Atkins who convinced John to add a "t" to his last name, becoming John Hartford. In 1967 his second RCA release "Earthwords & Music" featured the single "Gentle on My Mind", a song Hartford wrote after seeing the movie Dr. Zhivago. That year, the song earned four Grammy awards. Hartford would take home two awards, one as the writer and one for his own recording of the song. The other two went to Glen Campbell who had heard Hartford's version on the radio and decided to record it. Campbell's rendition became an instant classic, and the song became one of the most recorded and performed songs of all time, covered by everyone from Elvis Presley to Aretha Franklin.

Hartford often said that Gentle On My Mind bought his freedom.

He used that freedom to explore his various creative curiosities, and was usually happy to take his friends along on the trip.

In 1968 John Hartford left Nashville for Los Angeles, where he played on the Byrds' classic album, Sweethearts of the Rodeo. He became a regular guest and contributor on CBS's Smothers Brothers Comedy Hour and later on The Glen Campbell Goodtime Hour. He would also earn his riverboat pilot's license by the end of the decade.

John Hartford became mentor and mystic for a generation of pickers, singers, and songwriters. His landmark record, Aereo-plain (1971) documented his work with Vassar Clements, Norman Blake, and Tut Taylor. Rooted firmly in tradition but sprouting at the top with hippie hair, the group's instrumental mastery and free-wheeling style bridged a musical gap between traditional bluegrass and a progressive new audience, making every song a cult favorite and every live performance the thing of legend. According to Sam Bush, "Without Aereo-plain, there would be no 'newgrass' music."

In 1976, John won another Grammy award for his contemporary folk masterpiece, Mark Twang. The album featured a set of quirky river-centric original songs, presented in stripped down arrangements, typically featuring only Hartford accompanying himself on banjo, fiddle, or guitar while tapping his feet on an amplified sheet of plywood. The combination was magical, and would become his trademark sound for many years as a solo act.

Summer days might find him piloting the Julia Belle Swain on her afternoon run, before entertaining the passengers at night. During festival season, his amazing instinct for single-handedly captivating an audience would often have him leaving the stage and leading a processional of joyful dancers through the grounds, like a fiddle-playing pied piper.

Later in his career, he would revisit different ensemble configurations, recording and touring with his son, Jamie, and with various incarnations of the John Hartford String Band.

At his house overlooking the Cumberland River, John continued to write, record, and fill his hours with music. Already a published author ("Steamboat in a Cornfield" and "Word Movies"), Hartford also developed an extensive manuscript on the life and music of fiddler, Ed Haley.

In 2001, he was awarded a Grammy award for his contribution to the soundtrack of "O Brother Where Art Thou". His bittersweet appearance on the subsequent "Down From The Mountain" tour was immortalized in the concert film. He died on June 4, 2001, after a long battle with non-hodgkin's lymphoma.

"John Hartford was one of the rarest of musical birds. He had one foot deeply rooted in the past and the other always at least a few steps into the future-and both were dancing."

Larry Groce, Mountain Stage

Every summer, fans and musicians will again gather as festivals draw tens of thousands of music lovers. For many, it is like a family reunion….where the uninitiated, cousins, friends, and in-laws are always welcome. And while John Hartford no longer performs, his music and memory continue to permeate both stage and campground.

His influence is everywhere. From Merlefest to Telluride to Bonnaroo

Just ask Bela Fleck or Sam Bush, or Yonder Mountain, or Tim O'Brien….or the guy at the next campfire.

_____

Biography from JohnHartford.com

Country's Family Reunion celebrates God & America

God Bless America Again is devoted to songs that make us proud to be Americans and songs that allow us to enjoy our spiritual roots. We're talking about the songs you sang in church when you were growing up and songs that recall a time in America when we were free to openly express our faith without fear of ridicule— A time that seems, on reflection, to have been filled with family, friends and faith.

Bill Anderson hosts this reunion that we're calling God Bless America Again . This series features our Country Family Reunion artists singing and sharing stories, songs and memories of a lifetime.

Artists on the series are Bill Anderson, Lee Greenwood, Bobby Bare, Jimmy Fortune, Aaron Tippin, Ed Bruce, Daryle Singletary, Jan Howard, Larry Gatlin and The Gatlin Brothers, Linda Davis, Jim Ed Brown, David Ball, John Conlee, Joey + Rory, Gene Watson, Ray Stevens, Teea Goans, Con Hunley, Marty Raybon, Jeannie Seely, Rhonda Vincent, Dailey & Vincent, Mark Wills, and Jean Shepard.

The series was filmed in November 2013 and will be sent out to our pre-order customers soon. It is sold along with our Simply Bluegrass series to be featured in next month's issue.

To order this series along with Simply Bluegrass see ad on page 7.

Check your CFR News expiration date below

Due to a glitch in our computer system, some subscribers did not get their renewal notices for the CFR NEWS. Please take a look at the address label (left) and see what your expiration date is. If you were due to expire in November, December or January and you did not get a renewal notice and would like to continue receiving the newspaper, please go ahead and send your check or money order for $29.95 to CFR NEWS, P.O. Box 210796, Nashville, TN 37221.

If you would like to renew with a credit card, please call customer service at 800-820-5405.

We apologize for any inconvenienceand how now fixed the problem.

Chicken Pot Pie

Ingredients

4 cups chicken broth
1 bouillon cube
1/2 cup (1 stick) butter
1 onion, finely chopped
1 rib celery, sliced
2 cloves garlic, chopped fine
Salt and freshly ground black pepper
1/2 cup all-purpose flour
1/4 cup heavy cream
1 store-bought 2-pound rotisserie chicken, shredded
1 (7-ounce) bag frozen pearl onions
1 (9-ounce) box frozen peas & carrots
2 (9-ounce) packages store-bought rolled out pie dough
1 egg beaten with 1 tablespoon water

Directions

Preheat your oven to 375 degrees F.

In a large saucepan heat chicken broth and bouillon cube over medium heat until hot.

In a Dutch oven, melt butter over medium heat. Add onions and garlic, and saute until tender. Season with salt and pepper. Add the flour and stir together until it becomes pasty and lump-free, about 2 minutes. Stir in the hot broth, heavy cream, sherry, chicken and frozen onions and peas. Bring to a boil then reduce to a simmer.

With a ladle, fill 6 ovenproof ramekins or bowls with the filling. Place on baking sheet.

Sprinkle flour on countertop. Roll out dough an extra inch. Using a biscuit round or mold, cut out dough to cover the tops of your oven-proof bowls, with about 1/2-inch hangover, depending on their size. Crimp the dough over the edge of the ramekin. Brush with the egg wash and make 4 small slits on the top. Sprinkle with kosher salt and place on a baking sheet. Bake for 35 minutes. Remove from the oven and serve.

Tootsie's Alley gets neon sign restored and rehung

The original sign from the Tootsie's alley is once again in its rightful place linking the famous purple building's back side to the redbricked Ryman Auditorium.

"Many artists came here to relax before or after the Grand Ole Opry including my dad Hank Williams" says Jett Williams.

The old neon sign that marked the alley entrance where Hank Williams, Patsy Cline and hundreds of others have walked through has been in storage rusting for many years, but it has now been restored and is back to light up the path for a new generation of country music lovers.

"When the Grand Ole Opry left, Tootsie stayed and then we kept it going." says Tootsie's owner Steve Smith.

Neon sign-making hasn't changed in 100 years, and Joslyn and Son Signs in Nashville, did an excellent job in bringing a little history back to the Nashville historical landmark.

"We took about 40 pounds of rust out of it, cleaned it up real good, repainted it and we've restored it back to its original glory. Hopefully it looks better today than it did 60 years ago," Bobby Joslyn said.

"When we started remodeling we decided to get the sign revamed they did a great job with it. It let's people know where the world famous entrance is as well" says Smith.

Not only is the sign back lighting the way, the alley itself was also named in honor of the legendary bar.

COUNTRY'S FAMILY REUNION SCRAPBOOK: SHEB WOOLEY

Sheb as Ben Miller in "High Noon"

Sheb and Beverly entertain the cast of Rawhide with Clint Eastwood and his first wife. Maggie

Good friend Johnny Cash at baby shower for Chrystie's birth.

Sheb's wife, Beverly

Beverly holding winner in "Purple People Eater" contest

Sheb holding daughter, Chrystie in pool at home in Ojai, CA.

Sheb and Chrystie singing.

Chrystie and son, Austin Ehrhart, 25. They reside in Franklin, TN

Chrystie's daughter, Dylan is a graduate from Art Institute of San Francisco, CA clothing designer Nd. Shebs Great Grandson Eli was born September 27th 2013 . They reside in Rio De Janiero Brazil .

Kenny Rogers & Dolly Parton nominated for the third time together for Grammy Awards

Is the third time a charm for Kenny Rogers & Dolly Parton? Kenny & Dolly received their third joint Grammy nomination on Friday night, December 6th for "You Can't Make Old Friends" for Best CountryDuo/Group Performance. The song is featured on Rogers' latest Warner Bros. album of the same name.

The nomination is the third for Kenny & Dolly as a duo. They were previously nominated for Best Pop Vocal Performance by a Duo or Group in 1984 for "Islands In The Stream," and then again in 1986 for Best Country Vocal Performance by a Duo or Group for "Real Love."

Kenny Rogers, the newest member of the Country Music Hall of Fame, and recent recipient of the Willie Nelson Lifetime Achievement Award at this year's CMA Awards had this to say about the nomination: "I'm excited and very flattered about this opportunity and am convinced I should work with Dolly more often if we're getting these kinds of results," remarked Rogers.

Country Music Hall of Fame member Dolly Parton added, "I was so excited and proud to hear that the Grammys have nominated Kenny and I for Best Country Duo/Group Performance on 'You Can't Make Old Friends.' I am also very proud

to hear that 'Jolene' made the Grammy's Hall of Fame. Thank you everyone!"

"You Can't Make Old Friends" and the 30-year friendship between the two Grammy Award winners is showcased in Kenny & Dolly: An Intimate Conversation, premiered on ET on December 9 on Great American Country. In a relaxed setting, the two stars chat about memories they've shared over the years and the chemistry they share that has led to one of the most enduring partnerships in popular music.

RFD Show Schedule

Ricky Skaggs

Saturday, Jan. 4
10:00 p.m. Central

Sunday, Jan. 5
6:00 p.m. Central

The Isaacs

Saturday, Jan. 11
10:00 p.m. Central

Sunday, Jan. 12
6:00 p.m. Central

The ABOVE shows are RERUNS.
The shows listed BELOW are NEW!

Suzy Bogguss

Saturday, Jan. 25
10:00 p.m. Central

Sunday, Jan. 26
6:00 p.m. Central

Bill & McKenna Medley

Saturday, Jan. 18
10:00 p.m. Central

Sunday, Jan. 19
6:00 p.m. Central

Happy New Year! Find the nine differences!

Answers to last month's puzzle

Circled in yellow, no snowflake on roof, window white, no cord on window, door window different color, yellow upper window, window awning different color, bell different color, nose differnet color.

Have A Cute Baby Pic?

Renae's grandbaby, Rio, came to the set of Larry's Country Diner recently and proud granddad, Phil, grabbed this shot. Do you have a cute grandbaby or great grandbaby? Send us your photo and we'll print it in the paper for you to brag about to all your friends. Send it to CFR NEWS, P.O. Box 210709, Nashville, TN 37221 or send it by email to us at paula@gabrielcommunications.com.

Nadine's guide to couponing

Get Some Coupons

The Sunday newspaper is a great place to clip coupons. Buy the newspaper in your area with the largest circulation in order to get the best coupons.

Ask your friends and family for coupons. If they get a newspaper but usually throw out the coupons then they'll probably be happy to give them to you.

If you have a computer, check the Internet. There are many great online printable coupons to be found!

Use a clipping service. If there is a great coupon that you would like to have multiples of, then you might consider ordering the coupons from a clipping service like The Coupon Clippers.

Check the store. Stores usually have lots of coupons. Some are even right by the items!

Organize Your Coupons

Envelopes. You can start by clipping and putting them all in an envelope or check file. Once you've been couponing for a few weeks you will need something bigger.

File by insert. With this method you just file your inserts by date in a box or use an online coupon database to find the coupon you need. This method doesn't require much work but you might miss out on unadvertised deals by not having all of your coupons with you at the store.

Coupon Binder. With this method you would clip all of your coupons and file them in baseball card holders in a three-ring binder. With this method you can carry your binder to the store and have all your coupons with you while you shop.

Know Your Store's Coupon Policy

Loyalty Cards. If your store offers a loyalty card then make sure to get one. Some stores only give the sale prices to card-holders. Loyalty cards are free!

Double/Triple coupons. Doubling or tripling coupons is when the store will take your 50¢ coupon and double it to make it worth $1. This is done automatically at the register; you do not have to do anything to take part in this promotion. First, find out if your store doubles or triples coupons. If they do, find out the maximum double/triple value and how many they will double/triple.

Stacking coupons. Some stores will allow you to use one store coupon (the discount is provided by the store) and one manufacturer coupon (the discount is provided by the manufacturer) per item.

Printable coupons. Find out if your store accepts printable coupons.

Competitor coupons. Some stores will accept competitors coupons.

Expired coupons. Some stores will accept expired coupons, though it is rare.

Make a Plan

Weekly Ads. Read the weekly store ads to see what is on sale and which stores have the best prices on the items you need. If you don't get the weekly ads delivered you can usually view them on the store's website.

Coupon Matchups. See if you can match coupons to the sale items to get an even better deal! Some websites do this for you.

Price Match. Some stores, like Walmart, will price match. This means that if grapes are on sale for 99¢/lb at Kroger, you can take the ad to Walmart and at checkout tell the cashier that you would like to price match the grapes. Show them the ad and they will sell you the grapes for 99¢/lb versus their higher price.

Make a List. Don't go to the store without a list. Lists remind you what you came for and keep you from buying items you don't need.

Rainchecks. If your store is out of the sale item, get a raincheck! Go to customer service and ask for a raincheck for the item you wanted. They will fill out a piece of paper with the item details and price. Then you can come back another day (usually no more than 30 days) and buy that item at the sale price by giving the cashier the raincheck. This also gives you more time to gather coupons for the item! You can still use a coupon if you are using a raincheck.

Don't Be Fooled

10/$10 promotions. You do not have to buy 10 items to get the $1 price! The only exception to this rule is if the ad states that you must! Those times are rare and are usually for items that are buy x get y free, final price 2/$5, etc.

Rock-bottom prices. Don't go out and use your coupon immediately! If you use that 25¢ off toilet paper right away when it's not on sale you aren't reaching your saving potential! Wait until toilet paper goes on sale for $1 then use the coupon. If your store triples coupons then your toilet paper coupon could be worth three times as much! Matching sales with coupons is getting a great price. Combining sales plus coupons plus another promotion (rebates, double coupons, store coupons) is getting the best price!

"One per Purchase." I've heard this so many times! Most coupons say "one coupon per purchase" somewhere in the fine print. Cashiers will try to tell you that that means you can only use one coupon per transaction/day. This is NOT true! One per purchase means that you can only use one coupon per item purchased! So if you are buying 10 items and have 10 coupons then you can use them all!

Make a Pricebook. Start paying attention to prices and keep a list of items you regularly buy with the best and regular prices for those items. This will help you when you see that canned veggies are on "sale" for 10/$10 but the regular price is actually 99¢!

Limits. Stores will sometimes put limits on the item to make you think it's a great price! If cereal is on sale for 2/$4 you might not even notice it. But if it's on sale "2/$4 — limit 2!" then you will likely think it's a great price since they had to put a limit on it!

Shop early. If you have couponers in your area then it's best to get to the store as early in the sale as you can!

"Bigger is better." The cost per unit of the bigger box of cereal may be less than the smaller one, but when combining coupons with sales, the smaller box is likely the better deal.

Watch the cashier. When checking out pay close attention to the price screen to make sure everything rings up at the correct price. Also, make sure that the cashier scans all of your coupons. Coupons sometimes stick together or get dropped or the cashier will scan the coupon but not realize that it didn't go through. Kindly point out that they missed one and they will correct it.

Ray Price sends final farewell to all his fans

Country Music Hall of Fame member and country music legend Ray Price, 87, left the East Texas Medical Center in Tyler on Thursday, December 12 to go to his home in Mount Pleasant where he was provided with hospice care. He slipped into a coma and passed away on Monday, December 16.

Rumors flew on Sunday, December 15 that he had passed away, however, his wife confirmed that he was in a coma, but still alive at that time.

Price, who is best known for his country classics, including Release Me, Crazy Arms and For the Good Times, has been battling pancreatic cancer since 2011. Since then, the disease has spread to his liver, intestines and lungs, even with aggressive treatment. Price and his wife, Janie, who have been married for 45 years, made the decision not to pursue further aggressive treatment for the cancer.

Janie stated, "With God's blessing he has not had extreme pain. But it's with great sadness that I announce to you today that my beloved husband has entered the final stages of his cancer that he has battled for 25 months. Anyone who knows Ray is aware that he has strong convictions and great faith in God. It's his decision to leave the hospital and return home to spend his final days on his beloved ranch surrounded by the comfort of his home, family and friends."

In a final message to his fans, Price said, "I love my fans and have devoted my life to reaching out to them. I appreciate their support all these years and I hope I haven't let them down. I am at peace. I love Jesus. I'm going to be just fine. Don't worry about me. I'll see you again one day."

Janie thanked Price's fans and said that fans may leave her a note on her Facebook page or by sending a card to:

Janie Price, P.O. Box 1986, Mt. Pleasant, TX 75456.

Price has earned numerous accolades throughout his career, including 62 albums that earned Academy of Country Music, Country Music Association and Grammy Awards. In 1996, he was inducted into the Country Music Hall of Fame.

Final 'No Show' George Jones Tribute was star studded success and testament to his fame

Lorrie Ann Crook, Larry Black and Charlie Chase.

By Renae the Waitress

Well, I can tell you it was a night to remember. Me and Nadine stayed well past Nadine's bedtime for this star studded event. Nearly 100 singers and musicians lined up to perform on stage and pay tribute to George Jones and send their love to Nancy who sat in the front row. Not only did we get to see many of the stars from Larry's Country Diner and Country's Family Reunion, but Larry Black and Keith Bilbrey were among the night's hosts. Larry told the crowd that when it was time for Larry's Country Diner to come on George would say, "Come on Nancy, it's time for the FAT BOY to come on TV." We understand he loved the show and rumor has it that Nancy will join us for our Alaska Cruise.

Keith & Emy Jo with George's empty chair.

Nancy Jones and Keith Bilbrey.

Join us for one of our great 7 day cruises

It's going to be a great time as Country's Family Reunion and Larry's Country Diner takes two seven day cruises in 2014. One to the Bahamas February 18 - 26, 2014 and one to Alaska July 19 - 26, 2014.

There are only a few cabins available for the Bahamas cruise with Bill Anderson, Gene Watson, Rhonda Vincent, Jim Ed Brown, Helen Cornelius, Billy Dean, David Frizzell, Bo Pitney and The Church Sisters. This cruise leaves out of Port Canaveral, Florida for seven sun filled days!

Our Alaska cruise with Bill Anderson, Jeannie Seely, Gene Watson, Rhonda Vincent, Joey and Rory, Jim Ed Brown, Sweethearts of the Rodeo, Dailey and Vincent and Moe Bandy leaves from Seattle,

Washington and travels up to see the majestic scenery.

As a participant of this special group your package on either cruise includes:

- 5 live Country Music shows!

- Exclusive chance to meet the stars!

- Autograph and photo signings!

- Nadine's comedy show!

- You'll join Larry, Renae the waitress, the Sheriff, Keith, and NADINE for an uproarious Larry's Country Diner stage show!

Country Questions
By Dick Boise, CMH

Send questions to:
Dick Boise, , c/o CFR News,
P.O. Box 201796, Nashville,
TN 37221.

Q. Could you tell me who the singer is that has the song, "Holds In The Floor of Heaven"? I hear it now and then, but never hear the singer's name. Thanks.

Betty Ann Palmer, NY

A. Steve Wariner is the vocalist on that nice song. He is a great singer and plays a very good guitar as well. Born in Noblesville, IN, Christmas day, 1954, he was named Steven Noel Wariner. He got his first break in show business playing bass for the great Dotty West.

Q. My grandfather tells me about old time music that he used to listen to and has mentioned the name Pie Plane Pete. I can't seem to find anything about him, can you help? Appreciate anything you can tell me.

Willie Wellman, AR

A. The man you have mentioned was more of an old time radio entertainer and later did some children's TV shows in the late 1950s. His real name was Claud Moye, born July 9, 1906 and died in 1988. Over the years he entertained with greats like Bradley Kincaid, and Bashful Harmonica Joe Troyan. He did a little recording for the American Recording Co. around 1935-36. Not much of his records are available.

Q. How old was Brenda Lee when she first began singing? I'm told she was not a teenager when she began to be heard nationally.

Alice Livingston, NM

A. Brenda Mae Trapley, or Brenda Lee as we know her, first sang on the radio in Atlanta, GA at the age of 7. Then some TV in Atlanta got her discovered by Red Foley's manager and she was on the Ozark Jubilee at around the age of 11. It was the first major country music TV show and her talent was soon on national shows like Ed Sullivan, Red Skelton, and the Steve Allen Show. The rest is history for the talented lady.

Q. We saw a pretty young lady singing "I Want To Be A Cowboy's Sweetheart" on the TV and did not hear her name. Could you possibly find out who she was for me? I'm older and do remember Patsy Montana singing that song. Thanks for your help.

Amelia Bunk, VA

A. Not knowing what the TV show was, it's hard to say for sure. If I had to use my old country music guess, I would say it was probably Suzy Bogguss. She had a fine recording of that song in 1988. Now, Patsy Montana, whose real name was Ruby Blevins, had a hit record with that song in 1935. I believe it was mentioned in some articles as being the first female record to sell a million copies. Thanks for your memories of the real, old country music.

Chicken Surprise at Larry's Country Diner!

Gus Arrandale was sure surpised during the December taping of Larry's Country Diner when a large chicken came and stood at his table holding a Spring Mountain Farm sign. Gus wasn't sure whether to be happy or make a run for it! Be sure to watch Larry's Country Diner to see everyone else's reaction....especially Jean Shepard!

An Opry first, DeFord Bailey, makes history

Growing up in Smith County

DeFord Bailey was born on December 14, 1899, the grandson of slaves, Bailey was born near the Bellwood community in Smith County, Tennessee, about forty miles east of downtown Nashville. DeFord's mother, Mary Reedy, named him after two of her former schoolteachers, Mr. DeBerry and Mrs. Ford. When he was a little over a year old, his mother died of an unknown illness. DeFord's father, John Henry, had a younger sister named Barbara Lou who helped care for DeFord. Gradually, she took over complete care of DeFord and became his foster mother. Barbara Lou gave DeFord his first harmonica (or mouth harp).

"My folks didn't give me no rattler, they gave me a harp, and I ain't been without one since."

At the age of three, DeFord contracted infantile paralysis (polio). At the time, the disease was almost always fatal. He was confined to bed for a year and was only able to move his head and his arms. It was at this time that he started to develop his playing style. He would lie in bed and listen to the sounds of dogs howling, of wild geese flying overhead, of the wind blowing through cracks in the wall, and most importantly, of trains rumbling in the distance. Eventually he recovered, although the disease severely stunted his growth and left him with a slight hunchback.

Music continued to be a large part of DeFord's upbringing in Smith County. Most members of his family played instruments and his grandfather, Lewis Bailey, was a champion fiddler. The tunes they played were part of a rich tradition of string band music, a style DeFord called black hillbilly music.

[My family] "could all sing and dance. Everyone could play at least one instrument."

Moving to Nashville

In 1918, DeFord's biological father died and DeFord left rural middle Tennessee and joined Barbara Lou and his foster father, Clark Odum, in Nashville. His foster parents were working for Mr. and Mrs. J.C. Bradford, one of Nashville's prominent families, and Clark arranged for DeFord to become a houseboy. At first, DeFord's work included running errands, helping set the table, and cleaning and polishing silver, but when Mrs. Bradford learned of DeFord's musical talent, his role changed.

"One day I was in the yard and she heard me playing. She said, 'I didn't know you could play like that. How long have you been playing?' I told her, 'all my life,' From then on she had me stand in the corner of the room and play my harp for her company. I'd wear a white coat, black leather tie, and white hat. I'd have a good shoeshine. That all suits me. That's my make-up. I never did no more good work. My work was playing the harp."

In 1923, DeFord's foster mother, Barbara Lou, died. The entire family was devastated, especially DeFord. With her death, the family began to drift apart. DeFord's foster father moved to Detroit, where thousands of other southerners, black and white, were going to make their way in the new Henry Ford automobile industry, while DeFord stayed in Nashville and worked a number of odd jobs for several years.

During one of DeFord's jobs as an elevator operator in the Hitchcock building in downtown Nashville, a secretary from the National Life and Accident Insurance Company heard him play the harmonica. She hired him to entertain at a formal dinner at the company's new building. He thought little of it at the time, but later when he looked back, he realized that it was an odd foreshadowing of things to come.

Getting on the Opry

On October 5, 1925, a new broadcast station, WSM, went on the air. The station, which was created by the National Life and Accident Insurance Company, was interested in presenting a first-class image so it hired George D. Hay, one of America's most popular announcers. Hay (who was nicknamed Judge Hay) had a fondness for folk music and had started a variety program known as "The National Barn Dance" while working at WLS in Chicago. Shortly after he arrived in Nashville, Hay aired a similar program with a local champion fiddler named Uncle Jimmy Thompson. The show received a huge response. On December 27, 1925, WSM and Judge Hay sent out a press release announcing that WSM would begin a regular broadcast of an hour or two of old familiar tunes — a show that became known as "The Barn Dance," and later the "Grand Ole Opry."

Nashville was home to another radio station that started in the fall of 1925. WDAD went on the air a few months earlier than WSM and was operated by a local radio supply store called Dad's. Pop Exum, the manager of the store and one of DeFord's biggest fans, made DeFord a regular on WDAD. Pop had met DeFord at an auto accessory store that he had managed prior to Dad's and where DeFord would come to buy auto parts for his bicycle. Another one of Dad's regulars was Dr. Humphrey Bate, a country doctor who also played the harmonica. Dr. Bate's band, later called the Possum Hunters, played on both WDAD and WSM. When Dr. Bates heard DeFord play, he insisted that DeFord join him on WSM's new Saturday night "Barn Dance" program. One night, DeFord agreed to come and played on that evening's show without an audition. The show's announcer, Judge Hay, liked DeFord so much he asked him to perform regularly from that point forward.

Bailey was fired by WSM in 1941 because of a licensing conflict with BMI-ASCAP, which prevented him from playing his best known tunes on the radio. This effectively ended his performance career, and he spent the rest of his life shining shoes and renting out rooms in his home to make a living. Though he continued to play the harp, he almost never performed publicly.

The Shoeshine Business

Once he left the Opry, DeFord took up shining shoes full time. The experience was traumatic but it was also a watershed in his life.

"I could make it on my own. I walked out of WSM with a smile. I told myself, 'God gave every man five senses and I'm going to use them. I ain't gonna work for another man as long as I live.' I'd work for myself."

His first shop was in the back room of his house on 13th Avenue South, just a few blocks from the Ryman stage, where the Opry continued to play every Saturday night for years to come. Because of his radio fame, white customers would seek him out, no matter where his shop was located. He welcomed them on an equal basis with his black customers, all sitting side by side and waiting their turns.

DeFord said a white barber once asked him how he could mix races up in his shoeshine shop. He said,

"They all know me and all

want to hear the same tune."

Soon DeFord had more business than he could handle. He moved his shop several times and had an elaborate setup, including nine chairs and as many employees on 12th Avenue South. The only sign he had outside his shop simply displayed the price of a shoeshine, but his customers could always find him.

Later Life amd Death

One of his rare appearances occurred in 1974, when he agreed to make one more appearance on the Opry. This became the occasion for the Opry's first annual Old Timers' Show. He died on July 2, 1982 in Nashville. and is buried in Greenwood Cemetery there.

In 2005, Nashville Public Television produced the documentary DeFord Bailey: A Legend Lost. The documentary was broadcast nationally through PBS. Later that year, Bailey was inducted into the Country Music Hall of Fame on November 15, 2005. Joining him in the 2005 class were country-pop superstar Glen Campbell and the band Alabama. On June 27, 2007, the DeFord Bailey Tribute Garden was dedicated at the George Washington Carver Food Park in Nashville. The Encyclopedia of Country Music called him "the most significant black country star before World War II."

Music City Roots, Live at the Loveless Cafe with Keith Bilbrey & Jim Lauderdale

Not only does Keith Bilbrey do an excellent job as the announcer on Larry's Country Diner, but he is also the announcer each week at Music City Roots, Live From The Loveless Café in Nashville, Tennessee. Jim Lauderdale, who has appeared on the Diner is the show's host each week. Music City Roots is a weekly, two-hour radio show that revives the historic legacy of live musical radio production. Broadcast on Wednesday nights from 7 p.m. to 9 p.m., CST, It can be heard on the internet on www.hippieradio945. com. Music City Roots, Live From The Loveless Cafe showcases Nashville's astonishing music scene, from country and Americana to more progressive interpreters of tradition. It is a format that brings together fans of different tastes and generations. The show is presented live from the stage of the Loveless Barn.

Music fans worldwide know Nashville as the home of country music, and Music City Roots embraces and builds on that foundation. MCR is broadcast to a global audience. There has never been a time of greater variety, abundance and quality in Nashville's creative community, and Music City Roots looks to put that talent on a worldwide stage.

Each broadcast will feature 4-5 artists in 20 minute segments and short interviews, and also encourages collaboration with a nightly Loveless Jam where all musical guests embrace the spirit of Music City.

Music City Roots offers a most affordable and enjoyable experience whether you come by yourself or as a group. Doors open at 6:00 p.m., show starts at 7:00 p.m. and goes until around 9:30 p.m.

Ticket prices are $10 per person, general admission. For groups of 25- 49 prices drop to $9 per ticket, groups of 50 or more are $8.50 per person. Group tickets must be purchased as a block and do not include tax or handling fee. Seating is general admission; groups of 20 or more, we can reserve seats – seats will be held until 15 minutes prior to showtime.

Food vouchers may be purchased for $7 per person and include one menu item such as fried chicken

and biscuits, pork barbecue with side item, veggie quesadillas, and sweet treats.

For more information on Music City Roots, Live At The Loveless Cafe, go to www.musiccityroots.com

Precious Memories; Remembering Sheb Wooley

Shelby F. "Sheb" Wooley was born April 10, 1921 in Erick, OK. He is best known for his huge novelty hit "Purple People Eater," which sold over three million copies in the late 1950's and early 60s. However, among fans of country and western music, Sheb is considered the real article: a genuine cowboy singer. Sheb started riding horses as a boy in rodeos, and was making a living on the rodeo circuit as a teenager. He was competing in local rodeos before he was ten years old. By his teenage years, Sheb was one of the top young riders on the rodeo circuit. Music was also one of his interests, and he got his first guitar when his father traded a shotgun for a steel string.

While working the oil fields of Oklahoma as a welder, Sheb led his own country band in high school. Like many Oklahomans seeking opportunity, he headed to California and worked at a packing plant, moving crates of oranges. It was during this period that Sheb married Melba Miller, the older sister of future country music star Roger Miller. They were from the same home town of Erick.

At the outset World War II, Sheb found himself labeled 4-F (ineligible for military service) because of injuries he'd sustained as a rodeo rider. He assisted the war effort by working in defense plants.

By 1945 he was divorced and made it to Nashville, Music City USA, where he made his first records for the Bullet label, and began appearing as a singer/guitarist on WLAC. The gig wasn't a paying one, but allowed Sheb to promote himself and his music. His Bullet sides were cut at WSM, home of the Grand Ole Opry, but sadly they saw almost no play or exposure of any kind.

Frustrated with the opportunities in Nashville, a year later he moved to Fort Worth, TX, and got a regular spot on radio there, sponsored by Calumet Baking Powder. In 1949, at the suggestion of a friend at WSM, Sheb left Texas for California in hope of breaking into the film industry. Around this same time, he was signed as a songwriter to Hill & Range, the publishing company and signed with MGM Records in 1950, home of the sensation Hank Williams.

Sheb made an investment in acting lessons to help win some work on the silver screen, and succeeded brilliantly, appearing in small parts in 40 feature films, beginning with Rocky Mountain, Errol Flynn's final Western, in 1949. His most notable screen came two years later in the classic High Noon (1952), in which he played Ben Miller, the leader of the outlaw gang gunning for town marshal Gary Cooper. He also played an important supporting role in the historical drama Little Big Horn (1951), starring Lloyd Bridges and John Ireland, and was seen in The Man Without a Star (1955), Giant (1956), and Rio Bravo (1959), starring John Wayne.

In 1954 Sheb met his future wife, Beverly, while she was on a date with the owner of the Palomino Club in LA, a famous country bar. They fell in love and married. At that time, Sheb was still a struggling actor and singer. Beverly had the job and the house. They remained married for 23 years and Beverly is the mother of Sheb's only child, Chrystie.

Sheb continued recording and writing songs during his busy acting schedule. It wasn't until 1958, however, that he had a hit, and it was a most unexpected song. He had written several songs that were hits for other singers, most notably "Are You Satisfied," which got to number 11 on the country charts as recorded by Rusty Draper in 1955. Sheb had always displayed a gift for parody, and the song he finally scaled the pop charts with was "Purple People Eater," a parody of various pop culture crazes including monster movies (some people at the time suggested — incorrectly — that the scifi/ horror classic The Blob, starring Steve McQueen, which was released at around the same time as Sheb's song, was virtually a film of the song). He had to fight to get the song released, and it ultimately became one of the biggest hit singles in the history of MGM Records.

In 1958, Sheb was cast in the role of Pete Nolan in the television Western Rawhide, starring Eric Fleming and Clint Eastwood, which premiered in January of 1959. He later wrote some scripts for the series as well, and in 1959, in order to fulfill public demand for a recording of the series' title song, he recorded his own version of the Rawhide theme song and an entire album of Western songs, which failed to chart. He later recorded an album of folk-style material that was released in the wake of the MGM wide-screen epic blockbuster movie How the West Was Won, but this also failed to catch on with the public.

His film work continued during this time, and it was because of movie and television commitments that he was unable to record the song "Don't Go Near the Indians." Instead, former movie cowboy/singer Rex Allen recorded it and had a hit with it. In response to his bad luck, he cut a joke parody follow-up to the song, entitled "Don't Go Near the Eskimos," and his alter-ego, Ben Colder was born.

Around this time, Sheb and Beverly moved their family to Ojai from LA because of Johnny Cash. They were both country boys and they wanted to be away from Los Angeles. They even built a shopping Center together there called Purple Wagon Mall. Vivian, Johnny's first wife and Beverly owned a beauty shop together there.

Following his success with "The Purple People Eater," Sheb enjoyed a string of country hits, his most successful being "That's My Pa," which reached No. 1 of Billboard magazine's Hot C&W Sides chart in March 1962.

He is considered by many to be the most likely voice actor for the Wilhelm scream, having appeared on a memo as a voice extra for Distant Drums. This particular recording of a scream has been used by sound effects teams in over 149 films.

Sheb continued occasional television and film appearances through the 1990s, including a notable appearance as Cletus Summers, the principal of Hickory High School in the 1986 film Hoosiers.

In 1998, Sheb was diagnosed with leukemia and spent the next few years in and out of hospitals battling the condition. On September 16, 2003 Sheb Wooley passed away at the age of 82. The previous year he had been honored by Tennessee Senator Fred Thompson, who referred to the singer/songwriter/actor as an "American treasure."

Great country duets past and present

Over the years there have been some truly remarkable duets by country artists. Even though some of the artists have passed away, we can always go back and listen to these great songs and there are even some newer artists coming along with memorable duets as well. Some of the CFR News favorite country duets are listed here.

"JACKSON"
Johnny Cash & June Carter

"Jackson" was written in 1963 by Billy Edd Wheeler and Jerry Leiber and first recorded by Wheeler. It was a country hit single by Johnny Cash and June Carter, which has become more appreciated by non-country audiences in recent years.

Johnny Cash and June Carter released their version in February 1967, reaching #2 on the US Country charts and winning a Grammy Award in 1968 for Best Country & Western Performance Duet, Trio or Group. This version was reprised by Joaquin Phoenix and Reese Witherspoon, performing as Johnny Cash and June Carter, in the 2005 film, Walk the Line, and also appears on the soundtrack of 2011 film The Help.

"JUST SOMEONE I USED TO KNOW"
Porter Wagoner & Dolly Parton

"Just Someone I Used To Know" was written in 1969 by Cowboy Jack Clement and recorded by Porter Wagoner and Dolly Parton.

In 1967, Porter Wagoner introduced then-obscure singer Dolly Parton on his long-running television show, and they were a well-known vocal duo throughout the late 1960s and early 1970s.

From 1967 to 1974 they were singing partners, though Porter claimed they had been more, Dolly disagreed. When the partnership ended, Dolly wrote 'I Will Always Love You' for him. But there wasn't much love in 1979, when Porter filed a $3 million breach of contract suit against her.

The two made up and in 1988, they performed together on Dolly's TV variety show. And she was at Porter's bedside when he died in 2007.

"AFTER THE FIRE IS GONE"
Loretta Lynn & Conway Twitty

"After the Fire Is Gone" was written by L.E. White, and recorded by American country music artists Loretta Lynn and Conway Twitty as a duet. It was released in January 1971 as the only single from the LP We Only Make Believe. After the Fire Is Gone was the first number one on the U.S. country chart for Lynn and Twitty as a duo. It spent two weeks at number one and a total of 14 weeks on the chart. On the Billboard Hot 100, the single peaked at number 56.

From 1971 to 1976, Twitty & Lynn received a string of Country Music Association awards for their duets.

"GOLDEN RING"
George Jones & Tammy Wynette

Golden Ring, written by Bobby Braddock, is a song off the same titled album by American country music artists George Jones and Tammy Wynette, released in 1976 on the Epic Records label. It reached #1 on the Billboard Country Album chart. The singles Near You and Golden Ring both reached #1 on the Country Singles chart. Their next album together would not come until five years later called Together Again in 1981.

Tammy Wynette was married to George Jones from 1969–75. Even after their 1975 divorce their professional collaboration continued with regularity through 1980; years later in 1995, they made a reunion album entitled One. It was well received, although it didn't achieve their earlier chart success.

"I DON'T WANNA HAVE TO MARRY YOU"
Jim Ed Brown & Helen Cornelius

I Don't Want to Have to Marry You is a 1976 single by the duo of Jim Ed Brown and Helen Cornelius. It would be the most successful single for both Jim Ed Brown and Helen Cornelius as both a duo and as solo artists. The single was the only number one of their careers and stayed at number one for two weeks and spent a total of ten weeks on the country chart.

Their next duet, Saying Hello, Saying I Love You, Saying Goodbye. was another smash, and the pair began playing on the TV show Nashville on the Road. She continued to record with Brown, releasing the hits I'll Never Be Free, If the World Ran Out of Love Tonight, Don't Bother to Knock, Lying in Love with You, and finally notching a solo hit with Whatcha Doin' After Midnight Baby. In 1981, after topping the U.S. country charts one last time with Morning Comes too Early, the duet separated.

They do get together occasionally to sing a duet or two and have been featured on several of the Country's Family Reunion and Larry's Country Diner shows.

"ISLANDS IN THE STREAM"
Dolly Parton & Kenny Rogers

Islands in the Stream is a song written by the Bee Gees whose title is named after the Ernest Hemingway novel and sung by American country music artists Kenny Rogers and Dolly Parton. It was released in August 1983 as the first single from Rogers' album Eyes That See in the Dark and the second pop number-one for both Rogers and Parton (after Rogers' Lady in 1980 and Parton's 9 to 5 in 1981).

It also spent two weeks as the number one country song and in the year's final countdown was the number one song of the year of 1983. In December of that year it was certified Platinum by the Recording Industry Association of America for shipping two million physical copies in the US.[1] It has also sold 569,000 digital copies in the US as of November 2013. In Australia, the song was number one for one week in December 1983 and becoming one of the highest selling singles of 1984. In 2005, the song topped CMT's poll of the best country duets of all time; Parton and Rogers reunited to perform the song on the CMT special.

In April 2008, South Bend, Indiana radio station WZOW played the song continuously for several days on end. This was a stunt used to draw attention to the station's format change from alternative rock to adult contemporary.

Rogers and Parton went on to record a Christmas album together, and had an additional hit with their 1985 duet Real Love. The Gibbs originally wrote the song for Marvin Gaye in an R&B style, only later to change it for the Kenny Rogers album.

Nadine's Cooking Corner

Crockpot Chicken Recipes

These recipes are great winter recipes that can be thrown in the crockpot and forgotten until dinner time.

Chicken Tortilla Soup

INGREDIENTS:
1 1/2 cups shredded cooked chicken
1/2 cup chopped onion
2 (14oz) cans diced tomatoes with their juices
1 can (10oz) Rotel
1 can (15oz) Ranch Style Beans
1 cup chopped fresh veggies (celery, carrots)
4 cloves garlic chopped or crushed
1 teaspoon cumin
3 or 4 cups chicken broth (gauge how thick it looks, if it looks too thick, add the 4th cup)
1 (15oz) can white hominy (or add roasted corn, frozen or canned)

DIRECTIONS:

Using a 4 quart slow cooker, add all your ingredients. Cover and cook on low for 8 hours or high for 4 hours.

Adorn the top with sour cream, cubed avocado, olives and crushed tortilla chips.

The Rotel makes it spicy, so if you have little ones in the house, you may want to add regular tomatoes instead, then use spices like cayenne pepper, cumin, chili powder accordingly to taste. I've even been knows to throw just a packet of taco seasoning in and a little ranch dressing spice packet.

Chicken Dinner in a Pot

INGREDIENTS:
4 halves boneless chicken breast
2 pounds small white potatoes, peeled and cut in 1-inch cubes

2 medium carrots, cut in chunks
1 medium onion, cut in thin wedges
1 teaspoon dried parsley flakes
1 teaspoon salt
1/4 teaspoon pepper
4 tablespoons melted butter, divided
2 tablespoons Spanish smoked paprika
1 tablespoon lemon juice
1 teaspoon Worcestershire sauce
1 tablespoon honey
Dash salt
Dash cumin

DIRECTIONS:

Wash chicken and pat dry. Combine potatoes, carrots, and onion wedges in a 4- to 6-quart slow cooker with parsley, 1 teaspoon salt, 1/4 teaspoon pepper, and 2 tablespoons of the melted butter; toss.

Combine the remaining 2 tablespoons of butter with the smoked paprika, lemon juice, Worcestershire sauce, honey, and dash of salt and dash of cumin. Rub chicken breasts with the paprika mixture; arrange on vegetables.

Cooking Waylon's Way, a tribute to Waylon from Jessi

According to Waylon's wife, Jessi Colter, this book is a very personal food chronicle that begins with the early days of traveling on the road, and shows a history of how the food was served and presented at Southern Comfort, the Brentwood Tennessee home of Waylon and Jessi. It is an intimate view into the lives and celebrations of family and friends. Experience the christening of Shooter, the sobriety party for Johnny Cash, as well as wonderful family dinners.

Waylon was very proud of the food that was served at Southern Comfort and he much preferred to eat and entertain there. He pushed for this project to happen, because he believed the best food he could get was at home.

The book shows the many family happenings, and the wide variety of foods, for all occasions, and reflects the changes that for a healthier life style. This book is not just recipes, it also has wonderful stories, beautiful pictures, and memories of Waylon and Jessi's life together.

The project started many years ago, and was put on the shelf because of illness and the untimely passing of Waylon.

"Waylon was born in West Texas, I was born in Arizona" Jessi says, "and Maureen Raffety, our "chief of staff," hails from Kentucky. Between the three of us, we have come up with meals that incorporate the taste of the West and the flair of the South. Our menus were created by Maureen, while Waylon and I helped guide the delicate balance of unforgettable flavors. This is how the three of us spent much of our time. Waylon had a voracious appetite and enjoyed a bountiful table three times a day. This inspired Maureen, whose culinary skills have thrilled guests that have joined us from all over the world. We invite you into Southern Comfort, our Nashville, Tennessee home, where we have loved and laughed our way through life's ups and downs. We want to share these times with you. Our hope is that you will enjoy the humor along with the recipes that we have developed while working our way from rich, creamy butter to light, virgin olive oil."

In it's initial publication, this book is exclusively available to fans via www.officialjessicolter.com, but is currently out of print.

COUNTRY'S FAMILY REUNION SCRAPBOOK:
WAYLON JENNINGS

Waylon & mom, Lorene

Waylon, Tommy & mom, Lorene & dad, Albert

Waylon and Faron Young

Waylon & J.D.

The Highwaymen

Waylon & Jessi

Willie Nelson, Waylon, Kris Kristofferson, Johnny Cash

Waylon & son Terry

Waylon & fans

Waylon, Jessi & son Shooter

Mark Lowry: comedian, songwriter, singer

Mark Alan Lowry was born June 24, 1958 in Houston, Texas to Charles, an attorney, and Beverly Lowry. He started making music at age 11. He often uses anecdotes of his young life in his comedy, as well as speaking of his experience with Hyperactivity and Attention Deficit Disorder in his performances. Lowry is a self-described "Poster Boy for Hyperactivity".

While attending Liberty Baptist College (now known as Liberty University), Lowry joined a college evangelistic team made of Charles Hughes and David Musselman and began singing. Lowry's comedy career inadvertently began from here. There would be an long pause in his singing performance while he waited for the soundtrack to be changed. Lowry began to fill this pause with a monologue. Lowry soon realized that the audiences at his performances were laughing not at him but at his monologues.

In 1978, Lowry was badly injured in an car accident near Carlisle, PA, while touring with a college evangelistic team. He sustained eleven broken bones, and spent a good deal of time in physical therapy recovering from the accident.

In 1984, Lowry wrote the lyrics to the song "Mary, Did You Know?" He was asked to write a script for a church Christmas play. Lowry wrote a series of questions that he would like to ask Mary, the mother of Jesus. These questions were used in between the scenes of the play. Over the next decade, Lowry tried to find the music that would complete the song. Twelve years after writing the lyrics, musician and songwriter Buddy Greene wrote the music to the song. The Christmas play script became the song.

The song has become a popular Christmas song performed by more than thirty artists including Cee Lo Green, Clay Aiken, Kenny Rogers, Wynonna Judd, Michael English, Daniel Childs, Natalie Cole, Pippa Wilson, Kathy Mattea and Michael Crawford.

In 1988, Lowry was approached by Bill Gaither and asked to join the Gaither Vocal Band as the baritone. Lowry's career with the Gaither Vocal Band spanned thirteen years during his first stint with the group. During this time Lowry's on-stage antics became popular with audiences. As a result, Lowry became the co-host of the many concerts and shows performed by Gaither and the Vocal Band with Gaither playing the straight man to Lowry's antics.

In June 2001, Lowry resigned from the Gaither Vocal Band after performing longer with the group than any previous member except Bill Gaither himself. After that, Lowry released several solo albums, including I Love to Tell the Story, A Hymns Collection. On January 14, 2009, it was announced that Lowry would be returning to the Gaither Vocal Band.

Lowry continues to tour the United States performing his music and comedy concerts as well as recording music and comedy CD albums and videos. In addition, Lowry records and publishes several iPod podcasts; in particular, Saturdays with Mark and Tony, a weekly podcast with Tony Campolo. Lowry is also co-hosting "Bill Gaither's Homecoming Radio" with Bill Gaither and Phil Brower.

Lowry is single and has no children. He has two siblings – an older brother Mike of Lynchburg, Virginia and a younger sister, Melissa "Missy" L. Carter also of Lynchburg. He also has three nieces and three nephews, on both his brother's and sister's sides of the family.

Country music's working couples & how they do it

Brad Paisley & Kimberly Williams-Paisley

Brad Paisley's wife Kimberly Williams-Paisley played someone's mistress on the hit show 'Nashville,' but in real life, she and her superstar husband are totally committed to one another, despite rumors.

In reality, Williams-Paisley describes her family as down-to-earth, explaining, "We have family Sundays together." She and her country star husband, who have been married for 10 years, have two kids, Huck and Jasper, whom they love spending those special days with. "We spend as much time as we can," she reveals. "We come from good families, and we appreciate family."

Along with a commitment to their marriage and each other, there's something else that holds the couple together. Paisley's wife elaborates, "His sense of humor. [He makes me laugh] not all the time, but when it's important!"

The rumor mills can take a breather, because the Williams-Paisley household is tight as can be — and they plan on keeping it that way.

Keith Urban & Nicole Kidman

Nicole Kidman doesn't let her husband wallow when he's feeling down in the dumps.

In an issue of GQ Australia, Keith Urban explains why his wife doesn't put up with his moping. "Negativity and doubt are always creeping into my life and having to be kept at bay. Thankfully, Nic is great at calling me on it, and our marriage is at the stage where she doesn't have to say anything," Urban says. "I hear myself prattling on with negative crap and her loaded silence shuts me up."

Nicole Kidman says her marriage to Tom Cruise was "intoxicating," but calls her current husband Keith Urban her "great love."

"I was so young," Nicole Kidman told December's Vanity Fair magazine about her first marriage to Cruise when she was 23 years old. "And you know, with no disrespect to what I had with Tom, I've met my great love now."

"And I really did not know if that was going to happen. I wanted it, but I didn't want it for a while, because I didn't want to jump from one relationship to another. I had a lot of time alone, which was really, really good, because I was a child, really, when I got married. And I needed to grow up," Kidman said.

Kidman's life with country singer and "American Idol" judge Urban is much more low key. The couple live in Nashville with their two daughters. Kidman said she doesn't miss Hollywood either.

"For me" says Urban, " so long as I keep family prioritized, my marriage my priority, then everything works. I always put my marriage first. I just do, and everything falls into line after that."

Marty Stuart & Connie Smith

Twenty-six years after they met on one Indian reservation in Mississippi, country singers Marty Stuart and Connie Smith married one another in South Dakota "She's an angel," says Marty. "She is a spiritual person who gives my heart great hope and my life guidance."

They had been friends for years--but Marty remembered clearly the day he first laid eyes on Connie. He was a pre-teen mandolin player growing up in Philadelphia, Mississippi. Connie was a young star with hits such as "Once A Day," "Ain't Had No Lovin' " and "The Hurtin's All Over."

"I met Connie when I was 12 years old," he recalls. "She came to the Indian reservation in my hometown to work at a fair. She hasn't changed a bit. She looked great then and she looks great now." At first, Marty jokes about his reasons for choosing to get married on the Pine Ridge Indian Reservation in southwestern South Dakota. "I didn't have to do a blood test there," he says, laughing. "I pass out whenever I give blood."

But there are more serious reasons behind the easy laughter. The reservation is one of Marty's favorite places. "It's where Wounded Knee happened," says

Marty, who is part Choctaw Indian. "It's a strong spiritual center. You know, it gets kind of crazy being in the country music business and, every now and then, you need to go back and plant your feet on the ground."

These days the two are busy with the hit RFD-TV's The Marty Stuart Show where each week's show treats viewers to Country Music Hall of Fame member (and Stuart's "Mrs.") Connie Smith, reverentially known in country music circles for her influence on generations of singers and as the "Rolls Royce of female country vocalists" and a multitude of wonderful guest artists.

Garth Brooks & Trisha Yearwood

Connie Smith & Marty Stuart

"Being married, it's got to be right," Garth said in an interview last year of his marriage to his first wife Sandy. "This is who you went to college with, and you were married in front of God and your family and everything. So you keep hacking, and you work and you work and you work. And then comes that time where you're looking at the rest of your life going, 'How do you want to live it?'"

He and Sandy went onto to have three daughters before divorcing in 2000. Yearwood who had two failed marriages behind her was also single and the pair began dating before marrying in December 2005.

"This was somebody I always enjoyed being around. And we had a lot more in common than I ever dreamed we did. And so we started seeing each other after the divorce," he recalled. "We'd known each other music-wise (since the 1980s), but we got to see each other as people. And I've got to tell you, if you like her and don't know her, you'll love her. If you love her and don't know her, you'll worship her. She's the real deal."

And it seems that Brooks is just as besotted with his missus as the first time he ever met her.

. "I never knew that everyday you could wake up and feel like this. And I have God and I have Ms. Yearwood to thank for this."

He also bragged about her many side ventures like a Food Network cooking show and three cookbooks.

"I'm part of the working wives club," he joked. "I lay out at the pool with the other husbands." That will change in 2014 with Garth's recently announced world tour.

"She's the bomb, man. She does it all," he said proudly. But the one thing that Yearwood does the best? (according to her hubby) "Make no mistake -- Ms. Yearwood was born to sing. That's just what she does...I'll put her in the top five female voices of all time. She's that good," Brooks declared.

Clint Black & Lisa Hartman Black

It was 22 years ago (Oct. 20, 1991), that Clint Black wed his wife, Lisa Hartman Black.

The couple met in 1990 when the actress and her mother attended the country singer's New Year's Eve concert in their shared hometown of Houston, Texas, and sparks immediately flew between the two. But while they knew they wanted to be together, they both admit they hesitated to walk down the aisle.

"I always felt you go through life and you have relationships and you learn and you grow and you change, and that's what life is," Hartman Black told People magazine. "The thought of spending my whole life with just one person didn't make sense to me."

"I always liked the idea of a relationship, but with my schedule it never worked out," Black added.

Clearly, it worked out just fine for the happy couple. The two wed on the singer's 180-acre farm outside of Houston, and settled into happily married life. "The feeling that I get from taking care of him is very potent," she says. "I'd never felt that before."

Fans got a glimpse into their love story when they sang together on the duet, 'When I Said I Do,' from Black's 'D'lectrified' album. The song won the pair an ACM Award for Vocal Event of the Year.

The difference between Bluegrass & Country

What is the difference between 'country' and 'bluegrass' music? Bluegrass music is more about the musicians and less about the song than 'country'. It's also a faster tempo. If you listen to a bluegrass band play a song, each member of the band will usually take an instrumental solo. When you listen to a country song, the singer makes the song more about the story and usually the band is simply backing up the singer.

Back in the 1940's Bill Munroe, Ralph Stanley, and some others, decided it would be fun to "kick the music up a notch" by swinging the rhythm, adding in instrumental solos, harmonizing the vocals, and balancing out the back-up instrumentation and thus was the beginning of bluegrass (named for Bill Monroe's Blue Grass Boys) as we know it.

Country descended from old time Appalachian music, too (earlier than Bluegrass). It's the extension of the folk music and storytelling . As the players started writing new songs to sing, they did it in the style they were used to singing and with the instrumentation they were accustomed to using. Country music is about telling the story of the "country folk".

Ricky Skagg's Highway 40 Blues is in the style of bluegrass (notice the emphasis on each musician taking a turn at the break) whereas Loretta Lynn's Coal Miner's Daughter is strictly country (all about the story and not about the musicians).

Western (for a long time the genre was Country and Western) descended from the same music and musicians as Country but did so in a different place (West Texas, Oklahoma, etc...) so had a different story to tell. The style and instrumentation though is very similar.

If you listen to some bluegrass you'll notice an inclination to observe things like "wow, that banjo player can pick" while when listening to country it's more about "what an interesting story".

LARRY'S Country DINER

RFD Show Schedule

Mark Lowry

Saturday, Feb. 1
10:00 p.m. Central

Sunday, Feb. 2
6:00 p.m. Central

Jett Williams

Saturday, Feb. 8
10:00 p.m. Central

Sunday, Feb. 9
6:00 p.m. Central

Mandy Barnette

Saturday, Feb. 15
10:00 p.m. Central

Sunday, Feb. 16
6:00 p.m. Central

Bill Anderson

Saturday, Feb. 22
10:00 p.m. Central

Sunday, Feb. 23
6:00 p.m. Central

The Fruit Jar Drinkers on WSM's Barndance

Bands that regularly played on the Barn Dance show (later Grand Ole Opry) during its early days included Bill Monroe, the Possum Hunters (with Dr. Humphrey Bate), the Fruit Jar Drinkers, the Crook Brothers, the Binkley Brothers' Dixie Clodhoppers, Uncle Dave Macon, Sid Harkreader, Deford Bailey, Fiddlin' Arthur Smith, and the Gully Jumpers.

In 1926, Uncle Dave Macon, a Tennessee banjo player who had recorded several songs and toured the vaudeville circuit, became its first real star formed The Fruit Jar Drinkers in 1926. It was composed of Macon, Sam McGee, Kirk McGee and Mazy Todd. The Fruit Jar Drinkers recorded for the first time on May 7, 1927. Although the group's repertoire was mainly traditional songs and fiddle numbers, they occasionally recorded religious songs, for which Macon would alter the group's name to the Dixie Sacred Singers. Later the band members included; "Grandpappy" George Wilkerson (lead), Claude Lampley, Tommy Leffew, Mazy Todd and Howard Ragsdale.

Judge Hay liked the Fruit Jar Drinkers and asked them to appear last on each show because he wanted to always close each segment with "red hot fiddle playing." They were the second band accepted on Barn Dance, with the Crook Brothers being the first. When the Opry began having square dancers on the show, the Fruit Jar Drinkers always played for them.

Some places credit George Wilkerson as forming the Fruit Jar Drinkers and others reference Dave Macon as actually being the one who formed the group.

UNCLE DAVE MACON
AND HIS FRUIT-JAR DRINKERS

Sail with us & see the magnificent views of Alaska

Sailing to Alaska in July is just the right month to get out and see the beauty that Alaska offers. Average temperatures in the coastal areas of Alaska during the month of July have the highs around 65 and lows around 50. Perfect weather for walking through the historic cities.

Sailing out of Seattle, then traveling up to Alaska and British Columbia, Canada, you will see magnificent scenery, so be sure to take a camera. Here are the ports of call for the Alaska Cruise:

Seattle, Washington

In Seattle you simply can't skip the Central Public Library – a modern architectural marvel of glass grids, unusual shapes, and a "book spiral" that climbs four stories. Stroll over to Pike's Place Market to visit the original Starbucks and play catch with a fishmonger. In the heart of the city lies Chihuly Garden and Glass, which will dazzle you with its colorful and delicate works. Glide to the top of the Space Needle for panoramic views of the surrounding mountain ranges and Puget Sound.

Ketchikan, Alaska

Ketchikan is a city in Ketchikan Gateway Borough, Alaska, United States, the southeasternmost sizable city in the state. It is named after Ketchikan Creek, which flows through the town. Ketchikan comes from the Tlingit name for the creek, Kitschk-hin, the meaning of which is unclear. It may mean "the river belonging to Kitschk"; other accounts claim it means "Thundering Wings of an Eagle."

Ketchikan also has the world's largest collection of standing totem poles, located at three major locations: Saxman Village, Totem Bight, and the Totem Heritage Center. nd fresh cut chives.

Jeneau, Alaska

Before Juneau was Juneau, it was Rockwell. Before that, it was Harrisburg. And even before that, it was a settlement for several tribes of native Indians.

It wasn't until a man named Joseph Juneau and his buddy, Richard Harris, teamed up with a Tlingit native that this plot of land got its big break: gold. The first rush of 40 miners brought a mix of trading posts, saloons, and missionaries to the area. Soon, Juneau became a bonafide town, the first to be settled after Alaska's purchase from Russia.

Today, Juneau is a thriving city offering a great blend of city amenities and small-town hospitality, all in the heart of Alaska's majestic mountains, rivers, glaciers, and forests. Nearly 31,000 people call Juneau home - many of them working in government, tourism, mining, and fishing, and all of them instilled with a deep love for this place. Such a mix of personalities makes Juneau unique

Skagway, Alaska

A place exists in Alaska where the past lives on, where the cries of "gold in the Yukon" still echo from steep canyon walls, where the sounds of barroom pianos and boomtown crowds ring out in the night. A place where the romance and excitement of yesteryear linger around every street corner, every bend in the trail. That place is Skagway!

Corrington's Alaskan Ivory and Museum is an outstanding private collection that spans the long and surprising history of Alaska (pre-historic times, Russian Period, U.S. Civil War, Gold Rush, through statehood in 1959) that charges no admission fee. It is located at Fifth and Broadway at the far end of the "Old Town" tourist area.

Victoria, British Columbia, Canada

Victoria is the capital of the province of British Columbia, Canada. It is located near the southern tip of Vancouver Island. It is a medium sized and beautiful city. Nicknamed the Garden City for Butchart Gardens and much green space

To get to downtown Victoria from Ogden Point, cruise ship visitors have many options: take a pleasant 30-minutes walk through the James Bay residential area (Dallas St. along the Strait of Juan de Fuca, then north on Menzies St.), hop on ($2.50) the public bus #30 or #31 that runs along Dallas St., use the Cruise Victoria shuttle at the terminal, or hail a taxi/limo lined up at the pier.

See ad on the next page to book your cruise!

Rhonda Vincent & The Rage nominated for six SPBGMA Awards

"When Rhonda Vincent opens her mouth, it's great…whether she's singing country or bluegrass, God gave Rhonda an unbelievable voice and I am so thankful that we get to enjoy it. I love her like a sister and enjoy her music as her biggest fan," – Dolly Parton

Rhonda Vincent & The Rage, the most awarded band in bluegrass, could be adding more awards to their prestigious list of honors as they have been nominated for 6 SPBGMA (Society for the Preservation of Bluegrass Music of America) awards. These nominations come as Vincent readies the release of her forthcoming album Only Me, which was released on January 28th.

Only Me is a specialty album for Vincent, containing two-discs with six songs each, where half of the music is country and the other half features Vincent's signature bluegrass sound! Only Me features song collaborations with Willie Nelson and Daryle Singletary.

"The bluegrass pickers on this song are some of the best that I have ever heard. When I think of bluegrass, this is the sound that I hear. Your voice is beautiful," says Willie Nelson.

Rhonda Vincent & The Rage are nominated for the following categories:

• Entertainer of the Year: Rhonda Vincent

• Entertaining Group of the Year: Rhonda Vincent & The Rage

• Instrumental Group of the Year: Rhonda Vincent & The Rage

• Guitar Performer of the Year: Josh Williams

• Fiddle Player of the Year: Hunter Berry

• Bass Performer of the Year: Mickey Harris

The Martha White Bluegrass Express will be making stops all across America in 2014, as Vincent remains the spokeswoman for the historic flour company Martha White.

Texting with Nadine!

ATD :	At the Doctor
BFF:	Best Friends Funeral
BTW:	Bring the Wheelchair

BYOT:	Bring Your Own Teeth
CBM:	Covered by Medicare
CUATSC:	See You at the Senior Center
DWI:	Driving While Incontinent
FWTW:	Forgot Where I Was
GGPBL:	Gotta Go, Pacemaker Battery Low
GHA:	Got Heartburn Again
HGBM:	Had Good Bowel Movement
LMDO:	Laughing My Dentures Out
LOL:	Living on Lipitor
OMSG:	Oh My! Sorry, Gas
TOT:	Texting on Toliet
WAITT:	Who Am I Talking To?

Country Questions
By Dick Boise, CMH

Send questions to:
Dick Boise, , c/o CFR News,
P.O. Box 201796, Nashville,
TN 37221.

Q. My cousin and I just heard a song with the words "murder on 16th Avenue." Beautiful and true song. Who recorded it? Thanks,

Georgia Jones, Fresno, CA

A. Georgia, the actual title is "Murder On Music Row" which is 16th Avenue in Nashvlle. The song was written by Larry Cordle and Larry Shell. There have been several recordings of the song, however, the most popular one was by George Strait and Alan Jackson. Thanks for reading the CFR News out there on the left coast.

Q. Back in the mid 1950s, I remember hearing a song that said something like you better not do something. Could you find out more information regarding this song for me? Thanks.

Bill Collins, Vestal, NY

A. That was a cute little novelty number written and recorded by Tommy Collins. The song title was "You Better Not Do That." I believe it was a Capitol Record around 1954 and was possibly about number 2 on the record charts. Tommy Collins, whose real name was Leonard Sipes, was a great song writer and Merle Haggard wrote a tribute song about him titled "Leonard."

Q. Could you find out for me how long ago the "Teddy Bear" song by Red Sovine was popular? I have always thought it was one of the best trucker songs ever.

Elsie Morrison, VA

A. It was around 1975 that Red had a hit with the "Teddy Bear" song. He had a hit in 1966 or so with "Giddy-up Go" and about a year later had another great record with "Phantom 309." Truely he had a way with truck driving songs and recitations.

Q. I have always been a Roger Miller fan and could you tell me when he was born? Miss him very much.

Sandra Hobbs, WI

A. Sandra, there are may of us that miss that talented man. His birthday was mentioned by many on the internet last month. He was born January 2, 1936 in Fort Worth, Texas. In fact, I found an old interview of Roger on the "net" and he made that comment, that as a youngster he alwayswanted to be a comedian, but everybody kept laughing at him! True Roger Miller humor.

Simply BLUEGRASS is simply bluegrass at its best!

B̲ack in 1999, we asked Mac Wiseman to pull together a Who's Who of Bluegrass. He did, and we were able to honor and pay tribute to many of the pioneers of Bluegrass.

Well if you've been listening, Bluegrass is still growing and adding many new performers to the ranks. We asked Ricky Skaggs to pull together some of the best of the past, present and future of Bluegrass performers for Simply Bluegrass filmed in 2013.

Hosted by Ricky Skaggs and Bill Anderson, this is a reunion that all Bluegrass and Country fans will enjoy. Some of the attendees were Bobby Osborne, Jesse McReynolds, Doyle Lawson, Dierks Bentley, Dailey and Vincent, Larry Cordle, Carl Jackson, Ronnie Reno, The Grascals, The Roys, Kyle Cantrell, Ramona Jones, Sam Bush, Mac Wiseman, The Whites, Rhonda Vincent, and many more.

This series will be available soon for $79.80 plus $6.95 shipping and handling. Call 800-820-5405 or go to www.cfrvideos to order.

Ricky Skaggs

Bill Anderson

Rhonda Vincent

Mac Wiseman

The Whites

Bobby Osborne

Dailey & Vincent

Doyle Lawson

Dierks Bentley

The Roys

10 Tips for Happy Marriages

Good marriages are a lot of work. Just ask anyone who has been married any length of time. Many couple have their heads in the clouds when they marry, but marriage needs to have two people who really want the marriage to succeed in order to remain happily married. Here are our 10 Tips for Happy Marriages:

1) Be Honest with Each Other

Some people think that making the other person happy is the best plan in a marriage. But eventually, if you are always giving in to the other person's wishes, while shoving your own wants and needs under the rug, resentment will build up inside you. Whether it is major decisions such as whether or not your spouse should take a new job and move the two of you out of state, to smaller things, like what restaurant do you want to eat in, be honest with your spouse. Of course, there may be times you truly don't care, and at those times it's fine to let your partner decide. But being honest with your spouse is one of the best ways to have a healthy relationship. As a precaution here, being too honest so that you hurt someone's feelings is not a good plan either. And wording can also be important. It is definitely better to say something like "It's not the best color for you" than it is to say "You look so pale it looks like you're a corpse!"

2) Communication is Important in a Healthy Marriage

What does communication between a married couple actually mean? Just because you talk everyday doesn't necessarily mean you are "communicating." You should be able to discuss your wants and needs. It should definitely include some discussions about money, because money issues are often the caul most often linked to marital discord. Some people get aggravated by their spouse for years and never bring it up. Then when they announce they want a divorce and the spouse asks why, they give them an entire laundry list of things they have done wrong over the years. Husbands and wives should love each other enough to be able to talk about these issues as they arise and not let them fester and build up over the years.

3) Variety is the Spice of Life

And no, I'm not talking about just in the bedroom, although variet there is important, too. It's healty for married couples to experience new things together. Doing the same types of things every week, or every year can be very boring. Find new activities to try, try new vacation places, try a new restaurant. If money is an issue, try new experiences together, play a new board game, take up a new sport, find a new trail to walk or learn to dance.

4) Find interesting Ways to Show That You Care

There are lots of ways to show a husband or wife that they are important to you or that you are thinking about them. Send them a card, text them something nice. Leave a love note on the bathroom mirror or in the car. Another great surprise would be to bring home a cup of their favorite coffee on a Saturday morning or make a meal or dessert you know they would love. It will bring back that spark that was there in the beginning of a relationship.

5) Don't Try to Change Your Husband or Wife

It has been said that many women marry a man with the thought that they will change them after they get married. A wise woman will know it's better to accept the man she loves as he is. If he drops his dirty socks on the floor constantly, that won't change if the wife nags him daily to pick them up. And men usually go into a marriage thinking their wives will accept them for who they are an dbe happy. A man would be wise to try to make some considerations to make his wife happy. If a husband knows it really bothers his wife that he drops his socks on the floor, he will probably make an effort to pick them up. It's all about trying to do something that makes the other person happy. A man may make changes to make his wife happy, but it's best if he does it on his own and a nagging wife will only cause resentment.

6) Show Love for Each Other Physically

If public displays of affection are okay with both husband and sife, then feel free to connect with each other that way both in and out of the home. Showing affection in physical ways is important to the health of a marriage. Hug and kiss often, or at least when you leave each other in the morning and at night before bedtime.

7) Agree on How to Raise Children

If you have children, agree in advance on how to raise them. That way the kids can't pit one of you against the other. Always talk about discipline issues togheter before you present decisions to your children. YOu want to present a united front to your children. Setting an example that your spouse is the most important person in your life will help your children feel secure in their family.

8) Say, "I Love You" Every Day

Life can be full of surprises and you never know what day may be your last. Always tell your spouse that you love them, every day, so you will have no regrests if something does happen. If it's hard to actually verbalize these words, and for some people it is, a hand written note, a card, or text works well, too.

9) Don't Ever Go to Bed Mad

Always talk things out before bed so that you can both get a a good night's sleep. There's a saying about never letting the sun go down on your anger. This is especially true for married couples. When you end one day in resentment and anger, you'll probably start the next day in the same mood. Not only is it not good for a person's mood, but not good for his/her health either.

10) Allow Your Spouse to Change and Grow

When you get married, you plan on spending the rest of your lives together. Assuming that a spouse will be the exact same person for all time is unrealistic. Hopefully, they will evolve into a more interesting, more loving, and more kind person. If they go on to school, they will probably even be more intelligent. Allowing a spouse to become the best person they can be and to use all their gifts will allow for a happier and better marriage. Remember to nurture your spouse and allow them to change and you will change, too.

Precious Memories; Remembering Goldie Hill

Born Jan. 11, 1933, in Coy City, Texas, Argolda Voncile (Goldie) Hill began singing with her brothers, Tommy and Ken Hill, while she was in her teens.

Argolda Voncile (Goldie) Hill was born January 11, 1933 in Coy City, Texas, a small town southeast of San Antonio. Goldie played a big role in the Hill family. During her early years, she picked cotton in the fields by her house with her family. Soon Goldie's older brothers, Ken and Tommy, left cotton-picking to become country singers. Within a few years the two were backing up such country singers as Johnny Horton, Webb Pierce, and Hank Williams. Goldie was determined to also make it as a country singer.

In 1952, she and Tommy joined Webb Pierce's band and began performing with him on the Louisiana Hayride on radio station KWKH in Shreveport.

When Pierce journeyed to Nashville to record in 1952, Hill went along with him. While there, she auditioned for Pierce's label, Decca Records, and was signed immediately. She was soon dubbed "The Golden Hillbilly." Hill's first single was "Why Talk to My Heart," an "answer song" to the Ray Price hit, "Talk to Your Heart." It failed to chart.

In 1953, however, Hill went No. 1 for three weeks with "I Let the Stars Get in My Eyes," an answer to Slim Willet's wildly popular "Don't Let the Stars Get in Your Eyes." The answer song was written by her brother Tommy, who also wrote Pierce's big 1954 hit, "Slowly." She was one of the first women in country music, and became one of the first women to reach the top of the country music charts with her No. 1 1953 hit, "I Let the Stars Get In My Eyes". Along with Kitty Wells, she helped set the standard for later women in country music.

On September 19, 1957, Hill married Carl Smith and retired from show business to their horse farm south of Nashville, where she raised their children. She resumed recording in 1968 for Epic Records. Although she cut two albums for Epic Goldie Sings Again and Country Gentleman's Lady, only one single made the charts. "Lovable Fool," released under the name Goldie Hill Smith, reached the No. 73 spot, but she never charted after that.

Goldie died February 24, 2005, in Nashville's Baptist Hospital of complications from cancer. She was 72.

She and Carl had three children, Carl Jr., Larry Dean and Lori Lynn. Smith and his first wife, the late June Carter Cash, are the parents of singer-songwriter Carlene Carter.

MARCH
★

Dan Miller's Cowboy Music Revue in Cody

Irma Hotel

Long before Dan was hosting television shows like PBR Bull Riding, American Magazine and Due West, he was playing the showrooms of Nevada with The Dan Miller Band. While working on a dairy farm in Indiana he dreamed of movies, music and the entertainment industry.

After attending college on a football scholarship he headed to Los Angeles to pursue his dreams. In L.A. Dan studied acting, worked in radio and television and performed in clubs. Those jobs led to the stages of Reno, Tahoe and Las Vegas and a touring schedule that took him from Alaska to Florida.

When he moved to Nashville to pursue a recording career, Dan found more opportunities existed for him there in television, commercials and voice over work including You Can Be A Star with Jim Ed Brown, the Cable ACE award winning Top Card, and conventions for national corporations including Toyota and Subaru.

After Dan and his family moved to Cody, Wyoming, Dan continued to host television shows including "Xtreme Bulls" on GAC and "The Best of the West" on the Outdoor Channel.

Many of Dan's fellow musicians in Nashville have accepted his invitation to perform in Cody— performers such as Mel Tillis, The Bellamy Brothers, Kathy Mattea, Billy Dean, Suzy Bogguss and Ed Bruce have entertained audiences in Cody as part of Dan's "Cody Wild West Shows."

For the past nine years, Dan and his "Empty Saddles Band" have entertained over 85,000 people from 50+ countries with his show.

Dan and his Band have been featured in USA Today, on television networks such as The Travel Channel, ESPN and GAC, and have been invited to perform at many conferences, events and churches throughout Wyoming and Montana. Their musical style ranges from Americana and western to bluegrass and gospel. Dan's younger daughter, Hannah, has been onstage with her dad since the age of 6. She plays fiddle and mandolin and sings in the show. Wendy Corr plays the bass guitar and sings harmony and lead vocals. Her musical background includes starring in local theatre productions and participating in community chorales and events. Ed Cook is featured on the lead guitar. His vast musical experience includes many years as a studio musician and now as a member of the music department at Northwest College in Powell, Wyoming.

The theater is open May through September and is located at 1171 Sheridan Ave, Cody, WY. The box office opens at 7:30 pm for the show and the cost is $14.00 per person.

For more information on Dan Miller's Cowboy Music Revue, visit www.cowboymusicrevue.com/.

And when you go to Cody to see Dan Miller and his Cowboy Music Review, you can stay in Yellowstone National Park or in the hotels of Cody. The hotels include: Beartooth Inn of Cody, Cody Legacy Inn, Chamberlin Inn, Best Western Sunset Motor Inn, Big Bear Motel, Buffalo Bill's Antlers Inn, Buffalo Bill's Irma Hotel, Cody Super 8, Comfort Inn at Buffalo Bill Village Resort, Econo Lodge Moose Creek, Holiday Inn Cody Convention Center and Sunrise Motor Inn.

You can step back in time... into the old west of today, at the Irma Hotel, – a place that Buffalo Bill Cody called "a gem" just across from Dan Miller's Cowboy Revue. Stay in historic rooms that housed some of the most famous personalities the world have ever known such as Frederic Remington, Annie Oakley & Calamity Jane. You can even stay in Buffalo Bill's private suite, or in a host of other historic or non-historic rooms, all with up-to-date amenities and air conditioning.

Rhonda Vincent releases new CD

Rhonda Vincent – the fiery vocalist, multi-instrumentalist and songwriter dubbed "the new queen of bluegrass" by the Wall Street Journal released her new two-disc album Only Me on January 28, 2014. In addition to receiving an unprecedented seven consecutive "Female Vocalist of the Year" awards from the International Bluegrass Music Association (IBMA), being named IBMA's 2001 "Entertainer of the Year," and being the co-author of the 2004 IBMA "Song of the Year," Vincent was nominated for a 2006 Grammy® award for "Best Bluegrass Album" for Ragin' Live, as well as a double nomination in 2007 for "Best Bluegrass Album" for All American Bluegrass Girl, along with "Best Country Collaboration with Vocals" for Midnight Angel featuring Bobby Osborne.

Since her debut, Rhonda has met with increasing acclaim for her dynamic, infectious take on bluegrass. Her gift for balancing classic bluegrass sounds with subtle contemporary touches is featured throughout music. Gleaming with hope, resilience, and gratitude, Rhonda presents a set of songs that range from timelessly straight-ahead bluegrass to classic country. Joining her on the album is Willie Nelson on the title track, Daryle Singletary featured on "We Must Have Been Out of Our Minds", and members of Diamond Rio.

"When Rhonda Vincent opens her mouth, it's great... whether she's singing country or bluegrass. This collection of songs on "Only Me" is incredible. God gave Rhonda an unbelievable voice and I am so thankful that we get to enjoy it. I love her like a sister and enjoy her music as her biggest fan," says Dolly Parton.

As part of the promotional blitz for Only Me, Rhonda will be featured in a special two-part Today Show segment that was taped in Nashville and aired the first of February, as well as RFD's Cumberland Highlanders, GAC Top 20 Countdown, RFD's Rural Evening News, CMT.com, Country Weekly, Bluegrass Unlimited, Huffington Post, the Tennessean, Woodsongs, Billboard, The Boot, Bluegrass Today, AOL, and much more.

Track Listing:

Disc One/Bluegrass
1. Busy City
2. I'd Rather Hear I Don't Love You (Than Nothing At All)
3. Only Me (Featuring Willie Nelson)
4. I Need Somebody Bad Tonight
5. We Must Have Been Out of Our Minds (Featuring Daryle Singletary)
6. It's Never Too Late

Musician Credits:
Hunter Berry - fiddles
Brent Burke - resophonic guitar
Mickey Harris - upright bass
Aaron McDaris - banjo
Rhonda Vincent - mandolin
Josh Williams - acoustic guitar

Disc Two/Country
1. Teardrops Over You
2. Once A Day
3. Beneath Still Waters
4. Bright Lights & Country Music
5. When The Grass Grows Over Me
6. Drivin' Nails

Musician Credits:
Tim Crouch - fiddles
Kevin Grantt - upright bass
Carl Jackson - acoustic guitar
Mike Johnson - steel guitar
Catherine Marx - piano (all songs except Drivin' Nails)
James Mitchell - electric guitar
Michael Rojas - piano (Drivin' Nails)
Lonnie Wilson - drum

Learn more about Rhonda Vincent at www.rhondavincent.com

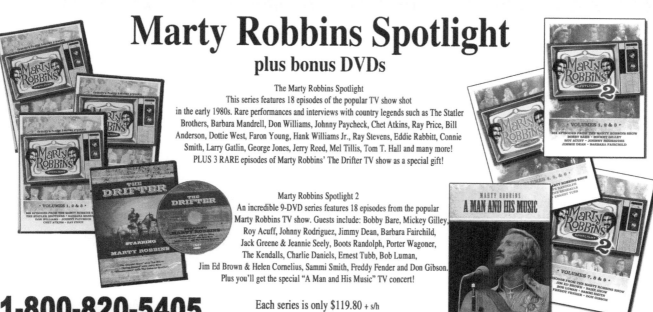

Nadine's Cooking Corner

Caribbean BBQ Salmon with Mango Salsa

Ingredients

Barbecue Sauce:
3 T vegetable oil
2 yellow onions, chopped
8 oz guava paste, cut into chunks
2 T tomato paste
2 T apple cider vinegar
1/4 cup light or dark brown sugar
2 whole star anise
1/2 t ground allspice
1/4 t curry powder
2 T lime juice
1 T dark rum

Salsa:
1/2 cup olive oil, plus extra for greasing the baking dish
3 cloves garlic finely minced
1/4 cup lime juice (from about 2 limes), plus 2 limes cut into wedges, for serving
1 t salt
1 t freshly ground black pepper
2 mangoes, peeled, fruit cut off seed and diced
1 red bell pepper, halved, seeded, and finely diced
1 green bell pepper, halved, seeded and finely diced
1 yellow bell pepper, halved, seeded and finely diced
1 large red onion, halved and finely chopped
1 serrano chile, finely chopped, optional
1/2 cup finely chopped fresh cilantro leaves
1 (15 oz) can black beans, drained and rinsed
1 whole side salmon (about 3 1/2 to 4 pounds)

Directions

For the barbecue sauce:

Heat the oil in a large skillet over medium-high heat for 1 minute. Reduce the heat to medium and add the onion, cooking until it's soft and a little brown around the edges, about 5 to 7 minutes, stirring often. Stir in the guava paste, tomato paste, vinegar, brown sugar, star anise, allspice, and curry powder.

Simmer until the guava paste has melted, about 15 minutes, stirring occasionally. Turn off the heat and let the sauce cool slightly. Discard the star anise; transfer the mixture to your blender and puree. With the motor running add the lime juice and rum. Transfer to a small bowl and set aside, or refrigerate for up to 2 weeks.

For the salsa:

Whisk the olive oil, garlic, lime juice, salt and pepper together in a large bowl. Add the mangoes, peppers, red onions, chile, and cilantro and toss to coat. Add the beans and gently toss everything together.

For the salmon:

Heat your broiler to high. Line a large baking dish or rimmed baking sheet with a double layer of aluminum foil and grease the foil with some olive oil or nonstick cooking spray.

Place the salmon in the prepared baking dish and tuck about 2-inches of the tail end under the fish, so you have a somewhat uniform shape. Pour the barbecue sauce over the salmon and cook it under the broiler until the sauce caramelizes and chars around the edges and the salmon is firm and flakes easily, 8 to 12 minutes for rare (the salmon will still be pink in the middle) or 12 to 15 minutes for well done (the salmon will be cooked throughout).

Spread the salsa on the serving platter and carefully lift the salmon out of the baking dish and arrange it on top of the salsa (use 2 large spatulas to transfer it).

Squeeze a few lime wedges over the fish and serve with additional lime wedges on the side.

COUNTRY'S FAMILY REUNION SCRAPBOOK: DAN MILLER

Dan's daughters

Hannah

Dan on stage with Hannah and Wendy Corr

Behind the Scenes SPOTLIGHT

Paula Underwood Winters

We have so many talented folks that work behind the scenes of our television shows and tapings that we thought you should meet them. Their talents and experience surely humble us.

Paula started working for Gabriel in May 2011 in the corporate office in Nashville.

Paula worked over 30 years in a family owned community newspaper in the Bellevue area of Nashville. When her father passed away in 1995, she and her mother ran the newspaper together, but in 2010 they decided her mom needed to retire and Paula wanted to do something different.

Paula's father, Doug Underwood, had been a news photographer and reporter in Nashville, working several years with WSM-TV. Paula grew up in the television studios watching shows like Bobby Lord, Porter Wagner, and Flatt and Scruggs as they were on the air and had a love of country music.

Later Paula married Donnie Winters, son of Don Winters, who sang with Marty Robbins for over 20 years, so she had another country music connection.

"I was looking for a job, but was worried how I would fit in at a corporate office when a friend of mine called and told me about a job that was about to be advertised," says Paula. "I called and told Renae that I was perfect for the job and that she didn't need to look any further. Thankfully, they hired me."

Paula does a lot of the office work that needs to be done on a day to day basis and answers the phones, but it wasn't long before the idea of a newspaper about traditional country music became a topic of conversation. That's when the CFR News became a reality. With Paula coming up with much of the content and doing the layout. They print at Franklin Web Printing in Franklin, TN where she printed her community newspaper. They also take care of mailing the newspaper out each month.

Besides the office work and the newspaper, Paula also schedules the audience for Larry's Country Diner. Over the last few years this has become quite a job. "We have a list of people, some of whom have been trying to get to the diner for over two years," she says. "We are working really hard to get everyone who wants to come, into the diner."

Larry's Country Diner tapes the first Monday and Tuesday of February, June, August and December and has only 25 seats for guests per show. "We tape seven shows per taping, so that's only 175 seats per month, times four months, for a total of 700 people." With a list of well over 200 people and each person bringing 2 to 4 people, it gets harder and harder to accommodate everyone. "But we try our best and are always trying to come up with a better way to get people scheduled to come."

Paula and her husband live on her family's farm, Mt. Airy, which she is working on turning into an event venue with her niece and nephew. "I only live 3 miles from work, so I love that." She and her husband have a son, Derek, 25 and recently lost their son, Ryan, 28. Others on the family farm include her mother, Evelyn, and her husband, Roy Miles Jr., her nephew, niece, sister, and their families. "I sometimes say it's like Southfork on the old TV show Dallas, except without the money or the fighting! We love being able to live on the farm together. Between my own family and my work family, I am truly blessed."

The music & compassion of Mark Wills

Mark Wills was born Daryl Mark Williams on August 8, 1973 to in Cleveland, Tennessee and later moved to Georgia. In his teenage years, Wills played in garage bands playing mostly rock. During his young adulthood, however, he began to take an interest in country music. He entered and won a local talent contest in Marietta, Georgia, at age 17, and after which he began to perform locally. Later he moved to Nashville as a demo singer.

Mark and Nadine on the set of Larry's

"I think I'm a good storyteller to make a song meaningful. Whether romantic or 'reality,' my focus is on the music delivery to make it my own for the people who listen—so that they can make it their own."

His list of accolades is his testament. Mark Wills is a multi-platinum selling country music star with eight top 10 hits to his name including "19 Something," "Wish You Were Here" and "Don't Laugh At Me;" all of which received nominations for Single, Song and Video of the Year by the Country Music Association. Wills won the Academy of Country Music 's award for Top New Male Vocalist in 1998. In 2002, his single "19 Something" spent six consecutive weeks at No. 1, was Billboard's top country hit of the year and was the second most-played song of the decade in 2009.

Since garnering his Top New Male Vocalist recognition in 1998, Mark has become a staple in country music. Mark is married and has two daughters.

"I think I'm at a point where I've seen all sides of me! I've become more aware of who I am not only as an artist, but as a father, a husband and a friend. And as a dad, I want to put out music my children can listen to; all in all, I take more ownership in it."

His ownership is made evident in his newest collection of recordings on the CD entitled LOOKING FOR AMERICA; an assortment of tunes Mark describes as different, yet the same.

LOOKING FOR AMERICA is a project with no 'sacrifices.' With titles like "Smoking Gun," "Where Did I Lose You," "A Whole World" and "Rocking The Country," the tracks are not just about a rhyme and a hook, they're a menagerie of people-stories--a musical exhibition of heart-heavy, romantic, comedic all-American existence with apple pie flavor. Describing the hue of the music, Wills colors his music "dark blue."

"I'm a man of many personalities with a lot that I want to say. There's a fun, down-home side of me, and then there's an emotional, serious side. I think LOOKING FOR AMERICA, topically, is a human interest story of love, tragedy and life's unexpected."

Anyone who has ever seen him in concert, or has met with him personally, knows that inside this humble, good ol' boy, country singer dwells a soul who just wants to speak to and for all with his music.

Mark has made more than seven trips to entertain our troops; he is familiar with the places they've been. His trips have taken him to Iraq , Afghanistan and Kuwait . He has also performed at several events for the Champions for Champions Organization, the USO and a variety of Fallen Soldier Charities here in the U.S. Having become personally acquainted with the faces of our brothers and sisters of the military, LOOKING FOR AMERICA is dedicated in part to these brave individuals.

" First of all, it's a privilege to provide a little joy and entertainment for these people. The first time I went, it was a life-changing experience. The freedom that we have is not something that I take for granted--they're literally giving their lives for us. By playing a show for them or releasing a song that shares their emotional story, it's my way, however minimal, to say 'Thank You.'"

Supporting our troops is just one of a number of philanthropic endeavors Mark Wills dedicates his time and effort to. He has aligned with USA Cares to launch a national awareness campaign surrounding the severity of Post Traumatic Stress Disorder (PTSD) and Traumatic Brain Injury (TBI). Since 2007, Mark has been the spokesperson for the Children's Miracle Network and its annual celebrations.

As an active representative, he accompanies miracle children to Walt Disney World and then to Washington each year as part of a national awareness campaign; the children enjoy lunch with Congress and a trip to the White House to meet with the President.

And Mark has had his own brush with death when he was caught by surprise by an unexpected, eye-opening crisis. In October 2010, Mark experienced what felt like a "poke" in his side that was followed by flu-like symptoms. A visit to the doctor took him straight to the emergency room. "The nurse said, 'we have to admit you immediately,' I said, 'I need to go home to let the girls know,' her response to me was, 'You don't have the time." Mark suffered from an intestinal infection that could have taken his life, but he pulled through with a nine-inch long scar to remind him of its value.

"It was a dire circumstance and it gave me a whole new perspective in all aspects of my life."

TIDBITS About Mark Wills

BEING A DAD HAS CHANGED ME...
For the absolute better. I love my little girls.

IF I COULD BE ANYONE FOR A DAY, I'D BE...
The President of the United States

IF I COULD BE AN ANIMAL, I'D BE..
A lion. I'm a Leo.

HATE TO...
Get up early.

FIRST CAR:
A tan VW Rabbit.

THE SONG I SING IN THE SHOWER MOST IS:
"I Thought It Was You" by Doug Stone

WORDS OF ADVICE:
Be true to yourself.

PHOBIA:
Snakes

FIRST KISS:
7th Grade

AFFILIATIONS:
National Rifle Assoc. / USA Cares / Children's Miracle Network / Sworn Sheriff in GA

WHICH TV SHOW ARE YOU EMBARRASSED TO SAY YOU WATCH?
"Hee Haw"

WHAT IS THE LAST MOVIE OR SONG THAT BROUGHT YOU TO TEARS?
Tangled got me! When the King and Queen lit the lanterns for their daughter, I lost it.

Nadine Overboard on CFR/LCD Cruise!

Nadine will once again be featured in her own comedy show on board the "Larry's Country Diner and Country's Family Reunion Cruise." This year's show is called "Nadine Overboard" and features her advise and wisdom to the ladies about aging. But never fear...she won't be letting the guys get off the hook. She will give equal time to those gents out there who don't seem to listen or pay attention. This high seas show is sure to be full of advise, church gossip and full of fun and surpises. Last's year's cruise had a surprise appearance by HOMER. The show last year, called "Nadine Out To Sea" is available for purchase from CFR Videos (see ad below). And don't miss next month's issue that will have photos from this year's show.

If you haven't gotten her new book "Nadine's 101 Favorite Church Signs" you need to order it now.

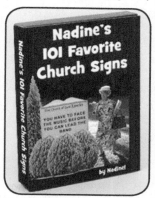

She has not only included some of the chruch signs sent in by FANS, but she also adds some special comments and scriptures. It's just like Nadine to add her 2 cents. It is available for $12.95 through her website at www.nadinenadine.com or by sending a check for 12.95 plus $6.95 s/h to Nadine, P.O. Box 680489, Franklin, TN 37068.

NASHVILLE

The character of Scarlett on the TV show Nashville, is trying to keep her traditional country sound even though the record executives are pushing her to be more commercial. Some of her songs are very haunting and beautiful sung. All the songs are actually recorded by the

With every episode of the hit television show, Nashville, viewers have essentially had an album of new, original music revealed to them one, two, three tracks at a time. The songs are making quite a commercial mark.

Nashville's first season was overseen by the show's executive music producer and co-composer, Oscar winner T Bone Burnett, whose TV and film credits include O Brother, Where Art Thou?, The Hunger Games and Crazy Heart, and who's married to the show's writer and creative executive producer, Callie Khouri (Thelma & Louise).

"Callie has an incredible ear," executive producer Steve Buchanan says. "Working to find songs that really fit for that script, that moment, and in giving those songs an emotional edge that matches what's going on with the character."

Inspired by the popularity of music on both reality and scripted television, it was Buchanan (who is also president of the Grand Ole Opry Group) who came up with the idea for Nashville with the intention of using it as a vehicle to sell new music. ABC later cut a deal with Big Machine Records (home to Tim McGraw and Taylor Swift) to release the show's songs.

"My sense about our show is that it's not something that we've ever seen before on TV," star Connie Britton told Rolling Stone in an interview. "Every song you see is something that you're hearing performed live, or you're watching a character write the song or hearing it on the radio.".

Although Miller, Burnett and Khouri have reached out to other friends in high places, such as Gillian Welch, Nashville duo the Civil Wars and Elvis Costello, for contributions, they're also taking an old-school A&R approach and scouting the city for pavement-pounding, working-class songwriters for material – songwriters not unlike the show's Gunnar Scott and Avery Barkley.

"Having [a song] in the show, it's just been incredible," says Trent Dabbs, who co-wrote "Undermine" with Kacey Musgraves. The show is reaching out to artists on edges of the industry, where the Americana movement is booming and to people who thought they didn't like country music, but are finding out they really do.

Billy Dean cruising and then on to Starlite Theater

William Harold "Billy" Dean, Jr. was born in Quincy, Florida, on April 2, 1962. His father, also known as Billy Dean, maintained a band called The Country Rock in his spare time, and by the time he was eight, Billy began playing in his father's band. Throughout high school, at Robert F. Munroe Day School, he continued to play music, both in his father's band and with other local musicians. He soon began touring in local clubs, and sang Frank Sinatra's "My Way" at his high school graduation.

He played basketball in high school and was offered a scholarship to college where he attended one year before dropping out to pursue his music. By the time he was 20, Billy made the finals on the Wrangler Country Star Search, followed by a Male Vocalist win on the television competition Star Search six years later. He also worked as a demo singer and took acting lessons, appearing in television commercials for McDonald's, Chevrolet and Valvoline. By the end of the decade, he had signed to a publishing contract with EMI Music, as well as a recording contract with SBK Records, a subsidiary of Liberty Records.

He has recorded 8 studio albums since 1990, of which 4 have been certified "Gold." He has generated more than 20 hit singles on the Billboard country charts including 11 Top Ten hits. His biggest hits include "Only Here For A Little While," "Somewhere In My Broken Heart," "You Don't Count The Cost," "Only The Wind," "Billy The Kid," "It's What I Do," "Buy Me A Rose," and "Let Them Be Little."

Billy has transcended genres with his unique repertoire earning numerous awards, including: The Academy of Country Music's Song of the Year "Somewhere In My Broken Heart," ACM New Male Vocalist of The Year, BMI Pop Awards, BMI Song Awards, BMI Million Air Plays Award, Country Music Television Rising Star Award, NSAI Song of The Year, and a Grammy for a Country Tribute "Amazing Grace."

In addition to recording and touring, Dean is branching into using music for corporate marketing. One of his ventures, Song Sessions, combines songwriting and corporate team building exercises.

Billy took over the lead role (formerly played by Kenny Rogers), playing Hank Longley, in "The Toy Shoppe" (a musical written by Kenny Rogers and Kelly Junkerman) at the Starlite Theater in Branson, Missouri which ran through the end of 2013.

Billy will be on the Country's Family Reunion and Larry's Country Diner cruise February 22 – March 2 then he is set to return to the Starlite Theatre later in March with an all-new show that showcases his big hits with laughs and variety added. Billy Dean will kick-off his show March 19th and continue through selected dates to November 19th.

Billy's Birthday Bash and Barbeque is a great time to join Country Singer Billy Dean celebrate his birthday with family and friends. Tickets will be sold for Friday, April 25 or Saturday, April 26. Each night from 5 – 10 p.m. will be different experiences but will have the same promise of a great time at the home of Billy Dean at Dean Acres in Liberty, TN. Tickets are on sale at www.billydean.com for $125 per person.

Larry's Country Diner & Friends at Starlite

Larry's Country Diner will be back in Branson at the Starlite Theatre May 6-11 and September 23-28 of this year.

The 880-seat Starlite Theatre is a Branson landmark conveniently located on historic Highway 76 within walking distance of popular attractions like Hollywood Wax Museum and the Titanic Museum. It is also a short walk to Howard Johnson's, Best Western Center Pointe and several other lodging options.

The Starlite Theatre features Branson's only five-story glass atrium with 19,560 feet of glass encasing a downtown street that includes the entire Starlite Diner and the Starlite Gift Shop. You can dine "outdoors" in climate-controlled comfort whatever the weather.

It is also one of Branson's most technologically-advanced and features state-of-the-art audio and video systems and stunning light displays. These features serve to enhance the best selection of shows on any Branson stage: the The Texas Tenors, Billy Dean, Larry's Country Diner, Paul Harris & The Cleverlys and Larry Gatlin & The Gatlin Brothers.

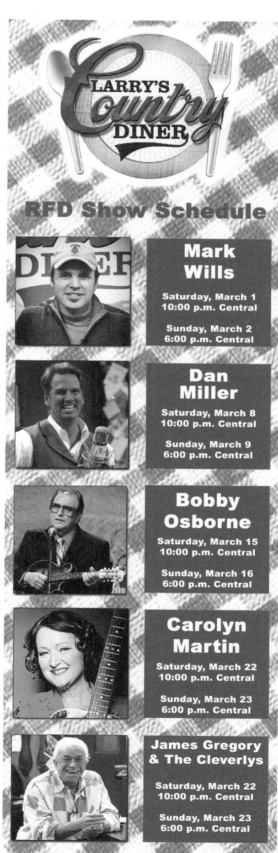

RFD Show Schedule

Mark Wills
Saturday, March 1
10:00 p.m. Central

Sunday, March 2
6:00 p.m. Central

Dan Miller
Saturday, March 8
10:00 p.m. Central

Sunday, March 9
6:00 p.m. Central

Bobby Osborne
Saturday, March 15
10:00 p.m. Central

Sunday, March 16
6:00 p.m. Central

Carolyn Martin
Saturday, March 22
10:00 p.m. Central

Sunday, March 23
6:00 p.m. Central

James Gregory & The Cleverlys
Saturday, March 22
10:00 p.m. Central

Sunday, March 23
6:00 p.m. Central

Jim Ed Brown cruisin' with Country's Family Reunion

Jim Ed Brown was scheduled to cruise with the Country's Family Reunion and Larry's Country Diner crew in 2013, but at the last minute he had some health issues that prevented him from sailing. But this year, he and his wife Becky are ready to go! Jim Ed will also be on the Alaska cruise in July.

James Edward (Jim Ed) Brown and his sisters, Maxine and Bonnie formed a singing group in the early 1950s after they moved to Pine Bluff, Arkansas. They also sang individually until 1954, when Jim Ed and Maxine signed a record contract as a duo. They earned national recognition and a guest spot on Ernest Tubb's radio show for their humorous song "Looking Back To See", which hit the top ten and stayed on the charts through the summer of 1954.

Jim Ed and Maxine were joined in 1955 by 18-year-old Bonnie, and The Browns began performing on Louisiana Hayride in Shreveport, Louisiana. By the end of 1955, the trio was appearing on KWTO-AM in Springfield, Missouri, and had another top ten hit with "Here Today and Gone Tomorrow", which got a boost by their national appearances on ABC-TV's Ozark Jubilee. They signed with RCA Victor in 1956, and soon had two major hits, "I Take the Chance" and "I Heard the Bluebirds Sing". When Jim Ed was drafted in 1957, the group continued to record while he was on leave, and sister Norma filled in for him on tours.

In 1959, The Browns scored their biggest hit when their folk-pop single "The Three Bells" reached No. 1 on the Billboard Hot 100 pop and country charts. The song also peaked at No. 10 on Billboard's Rhythm and Blues listing. Remakes of the pop hits "Scarlet Ribbons" and "The Old Lamplighter"

continued the hit streak, reaching the top 15 on Billboard's Pop and Country surveys. The trio had moderate successes on the country music charts for seven years thereafter. In 1963, they joined the Grand Ole Opry and in 1967 the group disbanded.

Jim Ed continued to record for RCA and had a number of country hits, starting in 1965 while still with his sisters. In 1967, he released his first solo top ten hit, "Pop a Top", which became his signature song. In 1970, he gained a crossover hit with "Morning" which went to No. 4 on the country charts and No. 47 on the pop charts. Other hits included "Angel's Sunday" (1971), "Southern Loving" (1973), "Sometime Sunshine" (1974) and "It's That Time Of Night" (1974).

Beginning in 1976, Brown released a string of major duet hits with Helen Cornelius starting with the No. 1 hit, "I Don't Want to Have to Marry You". Other hits for the duo included "Saying Hello, Saying I Love You, Saying Goodbye" (1977), "Born Believer" (1977), "I'll Never Be Free" (1978), "If the World Ran Out of Love Tonight" (1978), "You Don't Bring Me Flowers" (a cover of the then-recent Neil Diamond-Barbra Streisand hit) (1979), "Lying In Love With You" (1979), "Fools" (1979), "Morning Comes Too Early" (1980) and "Don't Bother to Knock" (1981).

Brown hosted the syndicated country radio show Jim Ed Brown's Country Place and the television show Nashville On The Road. He also hosted The Nashville Network programs, You Can Be A Star (a talent show), and Going Our Way, which featured Brown and his wife traveling the U.S. in an RV.

He remains an active and popular member of the Grand Ole Opry, where he has been a member since 1963. He still occasionally reunites onstage with Helen Cornelius.

Carolyn Martin is one of the best at Western Swing

exudes passion and experience – the soulful elegance that is the very essence of music. Besides her solo career, she was part of the impressive Nashville group Time Jumpers.

Carolyn's music draws inspiration not only from the classic western swing groups of the 1930s through the 1950s, but also from the big band swing era, broadway show tunes, and southern blues. Her CD "Cookin' With Carolyn" was named the 2011 Best Western Swing Album by the Western Music Association while her prior project, "Swing" was named as one of the top Swing CD's of the year in 2009. Carolyn was recently named the 2010 Western Swing Female Vocalist of the Year by the Academy of Western Artists, what nominated by the Western Music Association for 4 awards in 2010 (including, Album of the year and Female Vocalist of the Year) and was inducted into the Texas Western Swing Hall Of Fame in 2011.

S inger Carolyn Martin has been described as "… a winning throwback to the days where emotion was measured and artful rather than loud and histrionic." From European concert halls to intimate venues at home in Nashville, fans have come to know Carolyn as a vocalist with a unique sense of musical style, a charismatic stage presence and a voice that

Carolyn's latest CD, "Tennessee Local" continues to stretch the bounds of traditional western swing - in addition to her original songs, the album includes songs from composers like Irving Berlin and George Gershwin as well as western swing composers like Cindy Walker and Fred Rose.

Country Questions
By Dick Boise, CMH

Send questions to:
Dick Boise, , c/o CFR News,
P.O. Box 201796, Nashville,
TN 37221.

Q. I would like to ask if Roger Miller wrote the song he recorded called Little Green Apples? Like that song very much.

Betty Burdick, Albany, IN

A. That song was written by the late Bobby Russell and he also had several other hits like Honey and The Night The Lights Went Out In Georgia. He passed away in 1992 and was inducted into The Songwriters Hall of Fame in 1994. Both he and Roger are talents that are missed.

Q. Could you find out for me who the first million selling recording artist was? I've heard that Patsy Montana was the first lady to sell a million. Enjoy the CFR News each month at our house.

Sandra Harrington, VT

A. Thank you for your kind words about the News, Sandra. Vernon Dalhard its claimed to have had the first million selling record with the song, "Wreck of the Old 97." It was around 1924 and his real name was Marion Slaughter. He also recorded under several other names: Vernon Dale, Harry Harris, Bob White and many others. It is reported that he had a list of over 5,000 recordings to his claim in the 78 RPM era.

Q. I would like to find out the birthplace of George Hay who started the Grand Ole Opry.
Thanks for any information you can give me.

Ralph Wolfe, Roaring Springs, PA

A. George D. Hay, "The Solemn Old Judge" was born in Attica, Indiana November 9, 1895. He was a reporter for a Memphis newspaper and when the newspaper started a radio station he was made an announcer for the new venture. He was hired by Chicago's WLS and became an announcer for the National Barn Dance. Joining the WSM station in 1925, as the station manager, he gave the Grand Ole Opry its name in 1927. He passed away May of 1968. In Mammoth Springs there is a Foundation and Music Hall of Fame named in his honor.

Q. I have heard several good country songs by a girl named Michelle Wright. I can't find any information about her. Enjoy her voice very much. Thanks.

Elsie Thomas, TX

A. Michelle Wright is Canadian and was born July 1, 1961. She is a very talented young lady. She had won several awards in Canada including CCMA Female Vocalist of the Year and had Album of the years as well. She is a highly nominated artist in Canada circles and we here in the states do not get as much information on her as we would like. Fine talent and I'm sure she will be entertaining for a long time.

Jimmy Capps inducted in the Musicians Hall of Fame

Nashville Mayor Karl Dean recognized 2014's inductees to the Musician's Hall of Fame as "ingredients that make Nashville known as Music City." He continued by saying Joe Chambers, was "going to save this building, to make it into something that all Nashville can be proud of, here on out."

Nearly all of 2014's living inductees (with the exception of an absent Buddy Guy, and Frampton, who was busy rehearsing for the night's concert) gathered at the Museum to receive their medallions.

After a cocktail hour, the inductees and their friends, family and fans gathered upstairs at Municipal for a musical celebration of the songs they helped make famous.

Barbara Mandrell was the night's first honoree and was celebrated not just as a country star, but as an accomplished multi-instrumentalist.

Some of the inductees were no strangers to the spotlight. But for others, the moment was a little overwhelming.

"I'm not used to the hot seat," Capps told the crowd after performing "I'm the 'Man In Back'"and "Elvira"with the Oak Ridge Boys,

"You know, everybody has these big shows for the hood ornament," Neil Young said from the podium. "Everybody's cheering for the hood ornament. Don't forget what's under the hood. That's all you back there, keeping it going for everybody else. Without that, there's nothing happening but the chrome."

The 2014 Musicians Hall of Fame inductees were: Randy Bachman, Jimmy Capps, Peter Frampton, Buddy Guy, Ben Keith, Will Lee, Barbara Mandrell, Corki Casey O'Dell, Velma Smith, Stevie Ray Vaughan & Double Trouble

2014 Iconic Riff Award – Roy Orbison for "Oh, Pretty Woman"

2014 Industry Icon Award – Mike Curb

Jimmy Fortune and his wife with Stephen Kirby and Jimmy and Michele Capps.

At the Musicians Hall of Fame Induction after-party last night with seven favorite people - Hall of Fame inductee Jimmy Capps, Jeannie Seely, Jimmy Fortune and his wife with Stephen Kirby and Jimmy and Michele Capps. and Gene Ward.

Jimmy (left) performing with the Oak Ridge Boys

Larry's Country Diner In Tennessee magazine

Larry's Country Diner seems to be getting write ups in all sorts of places these days, including right here at home in the Tennessee Magazine which is published as a communication for Electric Cooperative Consumers.

Letting their customers know everything about the Diner, Larry Black and the cast of the diner, the magazine does a great job of giving an overview of what makes the show so special to both viewers and artists who come to perform. "It's such a thrill to give these artists another run at it," Larry told the magazine. "To give these great singers and songwriters another place to be heard when country radio has all but forgotten them, that's the reason I do this."

It also has information on the website and Diner TV as well as the cruises that Country's Family Reunion and Larry's Country Diner folks take each year.

To see the write up, go to www.tnmagazine.org

Kids Corner

This photo is from July Killigo who says, "These are our twins Chloe and Casey. They had just lost their first tooth and discovered a baby lizard at Grammie and Papa's house.

Do you have a cute or funny baby or kid pic? Send it to us at CFR NEWS, P.O. Box 210796, Nashville, TN 37221.

Precious Memories;
Remembering Bill Carlisle

Bill Carlisle was a singer, a comedian, a superb guitarist, a gifted songwriter, and a showman extraordinaire. Born William Toliver Carlisle in 1908, he was part of country music's first generation of professionals. By his early twenties he and his brother Cliff were working in their family's band on radio station WLAP in Lexington, Kentucky. Beginning in the mid-1930s Bill and Cliff became two of country music's most popular performers, working solo and in tandem on a number of southeastern radio stations, most notably WNOX in Knoxville.

While in Knoxville Bill perfected his comic alter ego, Hot Shot Elmer, whose outlandish costumes and onstage antics kept audiences in stitches on the Mid-Day Merry-Go-Round and the Tennessee Barn Dance. Donning boxing gloves, Hot Shot Elmer would pretend to fight with cast members such as the diminutive Little Robert Van Winkle. "Bill was hilarious," recalled Nashville studio guitarist Ray Edenton, who worked at WNOX in the late 1940s, "Little Robert would jump up, land on his hands, and then kick like a mule. Bill had his rough 'Hot Shot' voice, sort of like a frog, and he'd shout, 'I don't know which end he's gonna fight with!' Everybody loved it."

In 1933, as the Carlisle Brothers, Bill and Cliff made their first records as a duo for the American Record Corporation; many of their numbers featured Bill's hot lead-guitar licks. The team later recorded for Decca, although their #5 hit "Rainbow at Midnight" (1946) was released on King. Excellent yodelers, both brothers recorded solo as well, and Bill gained his first big hit with "Rattlesnake Daddy," recorded for Vocalion in 1933. He later recorded for RCA, and in 1948 he scored a #14 hit with "Tramp on the Street" on King.

By this time Cliff Carlisle was beginning to wind down his career. Bill organized his own group, which

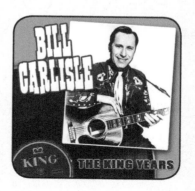

he eventually named the Carlisles. Signed to Mercury Records, the Carlisles recorded a string of what Bill called his "crazy songs," beginning with the #6 novelty hit "Too Old to Cut the Mustard" in 1951. This was followed in 1953 by the #1 smash "No Help Wanted," on which Bill heightened the rhythmic impact of his guitar by putting paper in the strings, thereby providing a solid foundation for Chet Atkins's jazzy electric guitar accompaniment.

Other Carlisles hits of 1953 included "Knothole" (#3), "Is Zat You, Myrtle" (#2), and "Tain't Nice (to Talk Like That)" (#5). These recordings took Bill and the group first to Shreveport, Louisiana's KWKH Louisiana Hayride, and then, in November 1953, to WSM's Grand Ole Opry.

Although Bill penned "Knothole," "No Help Wanted," and "Too Old to Cut the Mustard," his songwriting talents weren't limited to novelties. Inspired by the death of his grandfather, Bill's gospel number "Gone Home" became one of his own regularly performed songs and later became the signature song of the Hee Haw Gospel Quartet.

Bill Carlisle had a major impact on country music for seventy years. He wanted to be remembered as someone who inspired others. A compassionate family man, Bill endured the passing of Leona King Carlisle, his wife of sixty-two years, and his daughter, Sheila, and kept entertaining Opry fans almost until the end. "Jumpin' Bill Carlisle," as he was affectionately called, became a member of the Grand Ole Opry in 1953. He last appeared on the Opry March 7, 2003.

Bill can be seen on the Country's Family Reunion DVD series as well as the Precious Memories series which is for sale for $79.80 plus shipping and handling.

Son of God brings faith to the big screen

Getting great reviews from CFR News readers, the larger-than-life story of The New Testament gets a larger-than life treatment in the stand-alone feature SON OF GOD. Nadine said she thinks it's about time this story was told with the scope and scale of an action epic. The film features powerful performances, exotic locales, dazzling visual effects and a rich orchestral score from Oscar®-winner Hans Zimmer. Portuguese actor Diogo Morgado portrays Jesus as the film spans from his humble birth through his teachings, crucifixion and ultimate resurrection.

The Hollywood husband-and-wife team that made "The Bible" mini-series a smash hit is hoping to parlay that success onto the big screen with their new biblical movie, "Son of God."

Actress Roma Downey, best known for her leading role on the TV series "Touched by an Angel," and her husband, reality TV show producer Mark Burnett of "Survivor," "Shark Tank" and "The Voice" fame, are the creative team behind "Son of God," which opened nationwide on February 28.

"Jesus hasn't been on the big screen for 10 years since 'The Passion of the Christ,'" Downey said.

The couple is hoping "Son of God" will strike a chord with a new generation of moviegoers.

"We're aware that many people learn through visual storytelling," Downey said. "And for so many people, people who don't go to church, people who maybe have never read the Bible, this movie, 'Son of God,' will be the first time that they hear and see the story of Jesus come to life."

In the movie, Downey plays what is really the female lead — the Virgin Mary.

"It was profoundly moving to step into the role, because we know Mary was the mother of the son of God, but she was also the mother of a son," she said. "She knew that he was born to be extraordinary."

Last year, Burnett and Downey produced "The Bible" mini-series for the History Channel. The Sunday school epic was wildly successful, becoming the number one drama series of 2013 with more than 100 million viewers.

"Son of God" is the first of several old-fashioned Bible movies due out this year. There's also "Noah," starring Russell Crowe; "Exodus," with Christian Bale in the role of Moses; and "Mary, Mother of Christ." All have 2014 release dates.

Ever since Charlton Heston parted the Red Sea as Moses in the 1956 epic "The Ten Commandments," Hollywood has had a thirst for more. In today's dollars (adjusted for inflation) "The Ten Commandments" and "Ben Hur," Heston's other Bible epic, are counted among the most successful Hollywood movies ever made.

"I grew up in Ireland and I was raised on all those old Bible movies," Downey said. "We would sit there on rainy Sunday afternoons on the couch. ... I couldn't consider thinking about Moses and not, in some way, remember Charlton Heston."

"We had a massive responsibility in making this movie, and we enlisted the help of over 40 academics and church leaders across all faiths, including rabbis, Catholic leaders, Protestant leaders, to make sure that we were faithful to the text and considerate and respectful across faith," he said.

"If you didn't know Jesus and you came to this movie for the first time, I think you would get a beautiful understanding of what he came to do, of how he loved," Downey said. "We've tried to tell the movie as a thriller to create the tension and the drama to make it compelling, to keep you interested."

Nadine's Cooking Corner

Vanilla Cupcakes

INGREDIENTS:

1½ cups all-purpose flour
1 cup granulated sugar
1½ teaspoons baking powder
½ teaspoon table salt
8 tablespoons unsalted butter (1 stick), room temperature
½ cup sour cream
1 large egg , room temperature
2 large egg yolks , room temperature
1½ teaspoons vanilla extract

DIRECTIONS:

Adjust oven rack to middle position; heat oven to 350 degrees F. Line standard muffin/cupcake tin with paper or foil liners.

Whisk together flour, sugar, baking powder, and salt in bowl of standing mixer fitted with paddle attachment. Add butter, sour cream, egg and egg yolks, and vanilla; beat at medium speed until smooth and satiny, about 30 seconds. Scrape down sides of bowl with rubber spatula and mix by hand until smooth and no flour pockets remain.

Divide batter evenly among cups of prepared tin. Bake until cupcake tops are pale gold and toothpick or skewer inserted into center comes out clean, 20 to 24 minutes. Remove the cupcakes from tin and transfer to wire rack; cool cupcakes to room temperature before frosting.

Red Velvet Cupcakes

4 tablespoons unsalted butter, at room temperature
¾ cup granulated sugar
1 egg
2½ tablespoons unsweetened cocoa powder
3 tablespoons red food coloring
½ teaspoon vanilla extract
½ cup buttermilk
1 cup + 2 tablespoons all-purpose flour
½ teaspoon salt
½ teaspoon baking soda
1½ teaspoons distilled white vinegar

DIRECTIONS:

Preheat oven to 350 degrees F. Line a standard muffin/cupcake pan with liners.

On medium-high speed, cream the butter and sugar until light and fluffy, about 3 minutes. Turn the mixer to high and add the egg. Scrape down the bowl and beat until well incorporated.

In a separate small bowl, mix together the cocoa powder, vanilla extract and red food coloring to make a thick paste. Add to the batter and mix on medium speed until completely combined. You may need to stop the mixer to scrape the bottom of the bowl, making sure that all the batter gets color.

Reduce the mixer speed to low and slowly add half of the buttermilk. Add half of the flour and mix until combined. Scrape the bowl and repeat the process with the remaining milk and flour. Beat on high until smooth.

Again, reduce the mixer speed to low and add the salt, baking soda and vinegar. Turn to high and beat for another couple of minutes until completely combined and smooth.

Divide the batter evenly between the cupcake liners and bake for about 20 minutes, or until a thin knife or skewer inserted into the center of the largest cupcake comes out clean.

Cool for 10 minutes and then remove cupcakes from the pan and place them on a cooling rack to cool completely before frosting.

Country singer Penny DeHaven gone at 65

Country singer Penny DeHaven died Sunday, Feb. 23, at the age of 65.

Best known for a series of singles recorded for United Artists and Mercury Records in the 1970s, DeHaven had her biggest hit in 1970 as the duet partner of the late Del Reeves (1933-2007) on "Land Mark Tavern."

She was born Charlotte DeHaven in Winchester, VA in 1948. Following her high school graduation, she began appearing on WWVA's Wheeling Jamboree in West Virginia. She first made the country popularity charts as "Penny Starr" in 1967. DeHaven moved to Nashville two years later.

Her biggest solo hit was 1969's "Mama Lou." DeHaven's other singles included country remakes of such pop hits as The Beatles' "I Feel Fine" (1970), The Everly Brothers' "Crying in the Rain" (with Reeves, 1972), Marvin Gaye's "I'll Be Doggone" (1974) and Billy Joe Royal's "Down in the Boondocks" (1969).

Her albums included 1972's Penny DeHaven and 2011's gospel collection A Penny Saved. She also appeared on some of the final albums by Country Music Hall of Fame member Porter Wagoner (1927-2007), as well as on a 1982 CD by Boxcar Willie (Lecil Martin, 1931-1999).

Penny DeHaven was in the films Valley of Blood (1973), Traveling Light (1971) and Country Music Story (1972). In addition, she appeared on the 1982 soundtrack of Clint Eastwood's film Honkytonk Man, singing "Bayou Lullaby."

According to publicist Vernell Hackett, Penny DeHaven died of cancer. She had most recently been living in Atlanta.

Happy Easter

The CFR News
is published monthly by Gabriel Communications, Inc.
P.O. Box 210796, Nashville, TN 37221
615-673-2846
Larry Black, Publisher
Renae Johnson, General Manager
Paula Underwood Winters, Editor
Subscriptions: $29.95 yearly

Tommy Hill   Goldie, age 9

Kenny Hill

Carl and Goldie with son, Dean, Sept. '65

Carl Smith and Jimmy Dean

Dean and Carl

Carl, Jr. LoriLynn, Goldie, Dean, Carl

Carl, Jr. and wife Pam, LoriLynn, Dean and wife Tammy
Carl and Goldie

LoriLynn, Carl, Tammy Piggott, Dean,
Goldie, Carl, Jr. at Tammy and Dean's
1993 wedding

Behind the Scenes SPOTLIGHT

We have so many talented folks that work behind the scenes of our television shows and tapings that we thought you should meet them. Their talents and experience surely humble us.

DeAnn Moosman
Customer Service

If you have any questions about any of our DVDs, shows, cruises, advertisements, etc, DeAnn is the person you need to call. She handles customer service at our toll free number (800-820-5405). It's always nice to put a face with a voice and it is great to have DeAnn as part of the Gabriel family. She has worked with with the company since 2006 and like Larry says, "knows where all the bodies are buried."

"DeAnn, Paula and I talk on a daily basis and usually several times a day. It's like she is in the office next door, not hundreds of miles away," says Renae.

"I love my job. I get to talk to a lot of interesting people and hear their stories and how much they love our Country Family Reunion collections," DeAnn says.

If DeAnn is not taking orders she is usually helping book a cruise, checking on orders, processing mail orders, looking up folks accounts or answering questions. She has worked with the company so long that she even recognizes customer's voices. Last year Larry Black brought her on the Caribbean cruise just to meet some of the folks.

DeAnn was born and raised in Price, UT and grew up listening to country music. Her parents had a band and DeAnn loved listening to her father sing.

She and Lex, her husband of 25 years, have three daughters, Sharon, 22, Karen, 17, and Sierra, 12. They also have one grandson, Michael, who is 3.

When she isn't working she hangs out with her family who all live nearby.

LARRY'S Country DINER

RFD Show Schedule

Gary Chapman

Saturday, April 5
10:00 p.m. Central

Sunday, April 6
6:00 p.m. Central

Mickey Gilley

Saturday, April 12
10:00 p.m. Central

Sunday, April 13
6:00 p.m. Central

T.G. Sheppard

Saturday, April 19
10:00 p.m. Central

Sunday, April 20
6:00 p.m. Central

The ABOVE shows are NEW!
The show listed BELOW is a RERUN!

Suzy Bogguss

Saturday, April 26
10:00 p.m. Central

Sunday, April 27
6:00 p.m. Central

Gary Chapman follows his heart and the music with his 'Hymn A Week' project

Gary Chapman was born in Waurika, Oklahoma, the son of an Assemblies of God pastor, Terry Chapman. He grew up in De Leon, Texas.

He performed in bands throughout high school and college. After going to Bible college at what is now Southwestern Assemblies of God University, he moved to Nashville, Tennessee and was hired as guitar player.

He got a big break in 1979, when his song "Father's Eyes" was recorded as the title track to Amy Grant's Grammy-nominated second album My Father's Eyes. He also received a Dove Award as Songwriter of the Year from the Gospel Music Association in 1981. Chapman married Amy Grant on June 19, 1982. Also in 1982, his song "Finally" recorded by T. G. Sheppard

During the rest of the 1980s and the early 1990s, Chapman continued to write, record, and produce music, while touring as an opening act for various artists. He sang "Brave Hearts" in 1987 for the Touchstone Pictures film Ernest Goes to Camp.

He was nominated for a Grammy Award for Best Pop/Contemporary Gospel Album in 1994. The Light Inside also resulted in a Dove Award nomination for Male Vocalist of the Year. It also yielded a contemporary Christian music chart No. 1 song, "Sweet Glow of Mercy." He won a second Dove Award in 1994 for co-producing the album, Songs from the Loft, featuring various artists.

In April 1996, Chapman won Male Vocalist of the Year at the GMA Dove Awards. His 1996 album, Shelter, delivered another No. 1, "One of Two", with "Man After Your Own Heart" resulting in a Dove Award for Inspirational Recorded Song of the Year and featuring on the Dove award winning Special Event Album of the Year, My Utmost for His Highest. Shelter also received a 1997 Grammy nomination for Best Pop/Contemporary Gospel Album. At the 1998 Dove Awards, his album also featuring other artists, Hymns From The Ryman, won Country Album of the Year.

In the middle of 1996, The Nashville Network announced Chapman would replace Tom Wopat as host of their evening talk show, Prime Time Country. The show ended after 1999. Chapman went on to produce "Muzik Mafia" on CMT as well as appear numerous times on the network's "Gone Country" as a songwriting mentor. Chapman, along with John Rich and Big Kenny (the country duo, Big and Rich) traveled to Viet Nam to document the story of Niles Harris, a Viet Nam vet in the production of "The 8th of November: A True Story of Pain and Honor". Chapman produced, wrote, directed and scored the documentary.

Citing "irreconcilable differences", Grant filed for divorce from Chapman in March 1999 and the divorce was finalized in June 1999.

On December 22, 2008, Chapman married Cassie Piersol. The couple began a project called A Hymn a Week in 2010 to honor the musical heritage left to Chapman by his parents. Chapman has stated that both his parents, who were small town pastors for their entire lives, had a strong influence in his life and they "implanted the hymns into [his] heart". Chapman's mother, Mary, died on December 26, 2002. His father Terry died on April 12, 2009, after a lengthy battle with Parkinson's disease and a form of cancer called multiple myeloma. During his last years, he lived with Chapman and his wife. During that time, Chapman played and sang old hymns at his father's bedside. They then began filming the brief history and personal connection to a different hymn each week along with a guitar and vocal performance of the work and posting them on Facebook, on a page called A Hymn a Week.

Chapman and his wife are involved in many charities and organizations: Nashville Rescue Mission, Agape Animal Rescue, T.J. Martell Foundation, Make a Wish Foundation.

Great time at Country's Family Reunion & Larry's Country Diner Cruise 2014

Show 1 with Bill Anderson, Rhonda Vincent, David Fizzell, Helen Cornelius and Mo Pitney.

Show 2 with Jim Ed Brown, Gene Watson, Bill Anderson, The Church Sisters & Billy Dean.

Bill Anderson

Mo Pitney

Rhonda Vincent

David Frizzell

Helen Cornelius

Sarah & Savannah Church - The Church Sisters

Jim Ed Brown

Gene Watson

Billy Dean

Nadine's "Overboard" show was a big hit!

Larry's Country Diner show had Billy Dean and Rhonda Vincent....and Michele sang a solo.

The Diner show had all the regulars, The Sheriff, Keith, Renae, Larry and, of course, Nadine!

The fans got up close and personal as Billy Dean gave "Nurse Goodbody" a kiss.

The autograph sessions brought the crowds out for photos and talk.

Bill Anderson also had a moment with a fan, holding her hand and singing to her.

Country's Family Reunion show 3 was the finale and had all the artists, Rhonda Vincent, Jim Ed Brown, Helen Cornelius, Billy Dean, Bill Anderson, Mo Pitney, Savannah and Sarah Church, David Frizzell and Gene Watson!

Juneau is spectacular from the ground or in the air

In town for just a few hours or all day, there's plenty to enjoy during a quick stay.

Some local residents live their whole lives here and still don't experience everything to see and do in America's most beautiful capital city.

This place will definitely fill your day—and then some. Old-growth forest, snow-capped mountains, glaciers, ice caves, spawning salmon steams, prime bear habitat, and migratory whale routes all lie within city limits. A short boat or seaplane ride can bring spouting humpbacks, breeching orcas, and some of the best sport fishing on the planet. Hop in a kayak, jump on a bike, or lace up your (waterproof!) hiking boots for some human-powered exploration.

Of course, there's more to Juneau than natural beauty. Set against our stunning backdrop are original Gold Rush-era buildings, art galleries, museums, historic and Native heritage sites, restaurants, bars, cafes, shopping, and seafood that doesn't get any fresher.

Popular attractions and activities easily tackled in a day:
~ Historic Downtown
~ Mendenhall Glacier and Visitor Center
~ Juneau Icefield Flightseeing, Trekking or Dogsledding
~ Humpback Whale Watching - If it's whales you want, it's whales you're gonna get. The best time to whale watch is from April to November. Whale watching tours are offered in Juneau and near Glacier Bay. Daily boat tours to Tracy Arm rarely return without whale sightings - and you'll often spot many on a single trip.
~ Salmon or Halibut Sportfishing
~ Outdoor Activities - Aerial tours provide the best ways to see glaciers and the Juneau Icefield, and on a helicopter flightseeing tour you'll land right on a glacier itself.

Punography

~ I tried to catch some Fog. I mist.
~ When chemists die, they barium.
~ Jokes about German sausage are the wurst.
~ A soldier who survived mustard gas and pepper spray is now a seasoned veteran.
~ I know a guy who's addicted to brake fluid. He says he can stop anytime.
~ How does Moses make tea? Hebrews it.
~ I stayed up all night to see where the sun went. Then it dawned on me.
~ This girl said she recognized me from the vegetarian club, but I'd never met herbivore.
~ I'm reading a book about anti-gravity. I can't put it down.
~ I did a theatrical performance about puns. It was a play on words.
~ They told me I had type A blood, but it was a Type O.
~ A dyslexic man walks into a bra.
~ Why were the Indians here first? They had reservations.
~ Class trip to the Coca-Cola factory. I hope there's no pop quiz.
~ Energizer Bunny arrested: Charged with battery.
~ I didn't like my beard at first. Then it grew on me.
~ What do you call a dinosaur with an extensive vocabulary? A thesaurus.
~ When you get a bladder infection, urine trouble.
~ I wondered why the baseball was getting bigger. Then it hit me!
~ Broken pencils are pointless.

The one & only Ralph Emery, Live!

Walter Ralph Emery was born March 10, 1933 in McEwen, Tennessee. He gained national fame hosting the syndicated television music series, Pop! Goes the Country, from 1974 to 1980 and the nightly Nashville Network television program, Nashville Now, from 1983 to 1993. Emery can currently be seen in reruns, hosting the weekly program, Ralph Emery Live, on Family Net, a satellite and cable television channel.

Emery first earned fame as the late-night disc jockey on Nashville's WSM. Due to the clear-channel broadcasting range of the station at night, Emery's country music show could be heard over most of the Eastern and Central U.S.-- and by many overnight long-haul truck drivers, who were often fans of country music. The all-night show was a mecca for country music stars of all kinds, many of whom were personal friends of Emery. One in particular was singer and movie star, and Nashville resident, Tex Ritter. Ritter actually co-hosted the show with Emery for a while. Many well-known stars, most notably Marty Robbins, would often drop in unannounced.

Emery also gave national exposure to many up-and-coming and previously unknown country music singers, for which these singers often owed their careers. Emery later wrote several best-selling books chronicling his memories of the many Nashville singers and musicians that appeared on his various radio and TV shows. The second of Emery's three wives was Opry star Skeeter Davis.

Emery is credited for developing the gab of NASCAR driver (and Middle Tennessean) Darrell Waltrip, who was a frequent guest on his late-night radio show during his early days racing in Nashville. That eventually led to substitute gigs on WSM and Nashville Now.

Emery attained his greatest popularity on Nashville Now, with his rich voice and easy affability with guests making the show a national phenomenon. He would converse with a wide range of country music stars from all eras, and also used a Muppet-like 'co-host,' "Shotgun Red," during several seasons.

From the mid-1960s until the early 1990s (except for several years in the 1960s when hosted by country singer Bobby Lord and a two-year period between 1970 and 1972), Emery also hosted a weekday morning show on WSM television (now WSMV), which, until the early 1980s, was a sister property of WSM radio. The program, which featured an in-studio band of local session musicians and aspiring singers (among them a teenaged Lorrie Morgan, daughter of Emery's longtime friend, Grand Ole Opry star George Morgan) along with news and weather updates and in-studio live commercials, became the highest-rated local morning television program in the U.S. for some years in the 1970s and 1980s. His eye and ear for talent was inclusive in breaking color barriers and started the careers of younger African-American singers such as Joyce Cobb; she was included as a part of his studio band in the early 1970s. Emery also hosted a late-afternoon program on WSM-TV in the late 1960s, Sixteenth Avenue South (named for one of the streets on Nashville's famed Music Row of recording studios), with the same format. Because of the morning show's popularity and demands on his time, Emery ended his long run on the overnight shift on WSM radio in 1972; Hairl Hensley replaced him and went on to a thirty-year career with the station. Beginning in 1971, Emery hosted The Ralph Emery Show on radio. It was a weekly, syndicated show that aired daily on country stations in five parts Mondays through Fridays. Each week Emery would profile a guest star, while playing the hot country hits of the week. It was distributed by "Show Biz Inc." and lasted until sometime in the 1980s.

Legendary songwriter Mickey Newbury remembered Ralph Emery on his 1979 album, The Sailor, in the song The Night You Wrote That Song.

In 2001, Emery attempted a television comeback on Nashville Fox affiliate WZTV, but only spent seven days on the air before being sidelined first by continuing coverage of the September 11 attacks and then an illness. Substitute host Charlie Chase, a former WSM disc jockey in his own right, took over Tennessee Mornings permanently. In October 2005, Emery launched The Nashville Show, a free weekly webcast with Shotgun Red as co-host.

Emery was among the 2007 inductees to the Country Music Hall of Fame, and in 2010 he was ultimately inducted into the National Radio Hall of Fame.

Country Questions
By Dick Boise, CMH

Send questions to:
Dick Boise, , c/o CFR News,
P.O. Box 201796, Nashville,
TN 37221.

Q. I received my copy of the CFR "Golden Years" and was excited about an entertainer listed in the cast. It was a member of the Grand Ole Opry, Dr. Lew Childre. What can you tell me about him? Any musci available? Thanks,

Darwin K. Dickerson, Comanche, Texas

A. Lew Childre was born in Opp, Alabama, November 1, 1901. He was a very talented man and could sing, dance, and played several instruments. He was most noted for his comedy and playing a small Martin guitar with a steel bar, Hawaiian style. Dr. Lew's music "might" be found on an old Starday LP, titled "Old Time Get Together" with Cowboy Copas, and Josh Graves. You could try OLD HOMESTEAD, a company that has a vast collection of older country records. They are in Howell, MI 48843. Dr. Lew Childre passed away December 3, 1961.

Q. Dick, we received a call at the CFR NEWS office today and the lady wanted to know if Eddie Hill and Tommy Hill were brothers. She also wanted to know if they are related to Goldie Hill. Thanks,

Paula (CFR News)

A. "Smiling" Eddie Hill was a WSM announcer and had all the all night radio show in the mid-1950s. He was from Delano, TX, and was famous for his "W Yes Mam" instead of WSM on the radio. To the best of my information he is no relation to Tommy or Goldie Hill, who were brother and sister, however, and did have a brother who was named Kenny. Tommy produced records for Hill, whose real name was Angolda Hill, an early Decca artist who had the hit "I Let The Stars Get In My Eyes." She later married Carl Smith and both went into retirement from music appearances. Goldie did make an appearance on Country's Family Reunion show and sang the song I mentioned.

Q. I had a casette several years ago that had the song "Amber Waves of Grain" and "The Farmers Daughter" by Merle Haggard. I must have loaned it and could you help me find them? Thanks,

Robert Monoco, Rio Vista, CA

A. Those songs are available at the Ernest Tubb Record Shop and the title is "Kern River/Amber Waves of Grain." During my research I counted that Merle had a total of 90 CDs and box sets of his great music. Also found both songs on YouTube if you have a computer. I loved "The Farmers Daughter," as it hits home. I have two daughters and can understand the find thoughts of the writer.

Q. Hi Dick, did Sonny Osborne retire or did he pass away? I was surprised he wasn't on my latest CFR Bluegrass DVD with his brother Bobby. I love Larry Black's newspaper. Thanks,

Joyce Kidder, Wells, ME

A. Thanks for the nice comment on CFR News. Sonny Osborne retired in 2003 when rotater cuff surgery was needed. He still stays involved in music as a fine record producer. He started at age 14 playing banjo on several of Bill Monroe's recordings. Sonny was inducted into the Bluegrass Hall of Fame in 1954.

Larry's Country Diner goes to Starlite Theatre in Branson

The cast of Larry's Country Diner makes a road trip to the Starlite Theatre in Branson again in 2014 bringing special guests to entertain everyone in the finest of Diner fashion.

Jimmy Fortune will be the guest on May 6, followed by Gene Watson on May 7th. The great Dailey & Vincent will appear on stage for two days on May 8th and 9th and Mandy Barnett will be there on May 10th.

To make reservations or to find out more information about the Starlite Theatre, call 417-337-9333.

And they'll be back again in September, so be sure to call or check our websites at www.larryscountrydiner.com or www.starlitetheatre.com to find out who will be the special guests!

Come See Us!
May 6-11, 2014
Sept. 23-28, 2014
Oct. 21-26, 2014

For reservations or more information, call 417-337-9333

Nadine's look alike was on the cruise and took time out to get her photo taken with the original!

Kids Corner

Nettie Blair sent in this photo of her great granddaughter, Penelope Kate.

Do you have a cute or funny baby or kid pic? Send it to us at CFR NEWS, P.O. Box 210796, Nashville, TN 37221.

Kids LOVE drinking from their own Larry's Country Diner Cup!

Larry's Country Diner Kids Cup
Blue 14 oz durable plastic cup. It's easy to grip and fun to drink out of. Comes with 2 per order and makes a great gift for the grandkids.

2 for $12.95 + s/h

800-820-5405
www.larryscountrydiner.com

Congrats to Joey & Rory who welcomed daughter, Indiana Boon Feek on February 17. More to come in May's issue!

Dr. Humphrey Bate and his Possum Hunters

Dr. Humphrey Bate (May 25, 1875-June 12, 1936) was a country physician from Castillian Springs, Tennessee who founded the Possum Hunters. Oscar Stone and Bill Barret played the fiddles; Staley Walton and James Hart on guitars; Walter Leggett on banjo; and Oscar Albright on bowed bass. Alcyon Bate (Beasley), Bate's daughter, was also in the band playing uke, but did not record. They recorded 16 titles for Brunswick/ Vocalion in 1928. The band's recordings, while scant, are considered some of the most distinctive and complex string band compositions in the old-time genre.

In November 1925, WSM hired announcer George Hay, who had developed a popular program called National Barn Dance for Chicago radio station WLS. Hay kept the barn dance format for WSM, and sought rural musicians from the Nashville area to play on the program. WSM's Barn Dance first aired on November 28, 1925 with legendary fiddler Uncle Jimmy Thompson as its first performer.

Bate made his first appearance on the program three weeks later. The band was first introduced as "Dr. Humphrey Bate and His Augmented String Orchestra," but Hay eventually changed the name to the more rural-sounding "Dr. Humphrey Bate and His Possum Hunters."

Hay insisted the group change its name to the Possum Hunters in one of his typical attempts to establish "hick" personalities for his performers. The good Dr. Bate was told to dress in overalls when he played his harmonica, and his ukulele-strumming daughter Alcyone Bate Beasley was forced into the kind of rustic gingham dress that no one in Nashville would ever be caught wearing.

Dr. Bate and the Possum Hunters always opened the eight o'clock program with "There'll Be a Hot Time in the Old Town Tonight."

The Possum Hunters played a very early style of old-time music and continued to play well into the 1940's.

Dr. Bate learned many of his old instrumental tunes from an old slave when he was a boy shortly after the Civil War. You can hear some of the blues influence on the band's recordings like "Goin' Uptown," "Take Your Food Out of the Mud and Put It in the Sand," and "Old Joe." He had several bands going at the same time around World War I, including an Hawaiian Band. His daughter recalled playing at "socials" on steamboat excursions down the Cumberland River.

When Dr. Bate died in 1936, George Hay wrote a glowing tribute to him. "WSM lost the dean of its Grand Ole Opry," he said, "His sterling character was appreciated by all who knew him, and especially the boys and girls who were associated with him on the program."

Many credit George Hay as being the pioneer in bringing country music to the radio, however, it was Dr. Bate, who even before Hay came to Nashville, who saw the potential for using the radio as a medium for country music.

CUTLINE: In 1926, when the "barn dance" was just starting, Dr. Humphrey Bate and his Possum Hunters posed in business suits (above), but by 1928 (below) they reflected George Hay's decision to create a rustic image for the program. Bate was the first to play country music over the radio.

The Possum Hunters
(Circa 1925–1936)

Harmonica and Vocals		*Additional Vocals*
Dr. Humphrey Bate		Alcyone Bate (Beasley)
Buster Bate		

Fiddle	*Guitars*	*Banjo*
Oscar Stone	Stanley Walton	Walter Leggett
Bill Barret	James Hart	
Buster Bate		

Bowed String Bass	*Ukelele*	*Tipple*
Oscar Albright	Alcyon Bate (Beasley)	Buster Bate

Jew's Harp	*Piano*	
Buster Bate	Alcyone Bate (Beasley)	

Precious Memories: Remembering Charlie Walker

Charlie Levi Walker, Jr., was born in Copeville, Texas, on November 2, 1926. He grew up on a farm, spending his days picking cotton. By the age of seventeen, Charlie was making a living performing live, singing in honky tonks throughout Dallas and soon became a vocalist for Bill Boyd's band the "Cowboy Ramblers."

Charlie continued to perform with the "Cowboy Ramblers" until he joined the military. After serving two years for the United States Army, he moved to San Antonio, Texas, and began working for a radio station. Shortly after going to work there, he became one of the nation's top ten country music disc jockeys. In 1962, he received one of the highest honors by the state of Texas, and that was being named "Favorite Son of Texas."

After being a disc jockey for a while, Charlie decided to pursue a music career, which produced his first song "Tell Her Lies and Feed Her Candy." This was not the biggest hit of his career, but it did get him a lot of credit and put him on the national charts.

Shortly after this, Charlie recorded a tune that was written by Harlan Howard called "Pick Me Up On Your Way Down." It became a smash hit, eventually selling millions. This tune also helped garner him a spot as a member of the Grand Ole Opry. He was inducted on August 17, 1967. Other hits that shortly followed were "Don't Squeeze My Sharmon," "Close All The Honky Tonks," and "Little Ole Wine Drinker Me."

Charlie's love for country music showed on every stage that he performed. He toured every state in the United States as well as numerous other countries including Norway, England, Japan, Italy, and Sweden, just to name a few. Charlie also dipped his toe into acting by playing the role of Hawkshaw Hawkins in the movie "Sweet Dreams," which was about the plane crash that killed Patsy Cline, Hawkshaw Hawkins, and Cowboy Copas.

Charlie Walker passed away on September 12, 2008 in Henderson, TN. He was 81, and had recently been diagnosed with colon cancer.

Roger Miller on rhythm guitar Charlie Walker singing and Buddy Emmons on steel.

Jean Shepard's book finally available

The last line in Jean Shepard's book may be the most profound... "I wanted to sit down and have a personal conversation with every reader of this book." And that's exactly what you get with her book "Down Through The Years."

Growing up poor, but loved, in a family of twelve, Jean loved singing and her parents encouraged her. Stories about growing up, her high school days singing with her band, and later as a member of the Grand Ole Opry, make this book a must have for any country music fan.

I love Jean. I love touring with her. I love being out on the road with her and Benny. Because number one, you never know what to expect! And number two, you know you're going to laugh. Jean is such a wonderfully warm, funny, and caring person. I just can't think of anybody that I love any more.

—BILL ANDERSON, Grand Ole Opry Star

Her story about her Opry induction is just one of the insights into her life.

The date was November 21, 1955. Jim Denny was the manager of the Grand Ole Opry. We were at the Andrew Jackson Hotel on Sixth & Deaderick Street downtown in one of their conference rooms. (That historic hotel was demolished in '71 when the Tennessee Performing Arts Center was built.) Mr. Denny was making some announcements, and right at the end of one of them, I heard this:

"By the way, we would like to welcome the newest member of the Grand Ole Opry, Jean Shepard. Happy Birthday!"

I was twenty-two years old. What a way to spend my birthday! It was the most wonderful feeling in the world. I had listened to the Grand Ole Opry on that old battery radio all those years and never dreamed that one day I would be a part of it.

But there are many more stories about being on the road, her relationships with other entertainers, her late husband Hawkshaw Hawkins, the music industry and her 40-plus year marriage to her husband, Benny.

I think one of the greatest pleasures was working with Cousin Minnie Pearl. I never, ever worked with Minnie that I didn't learn some little something. For instance, how to take a bow, or how to acknowledge applause better – so many little things that Minnie was such a pro at.

It wasn't always fun, as readers will learn as they read about the hard times in Jean's life. Losing her husband while she was expecting their second child was one of the lowest.

It was about ten-thirty or eleven when the phone rang. A woman by the name of Eileen Tait, a representative of Hawk's fan club, was calling. She asked me what was I doing. I said, "Well I was trying to go to sleep."

She started to cry and kept crying. She said, "Then you haven't heard?" And she told me the plane was missing. She kept carrying on and I couldn't hardly get her off the phone, bless her heart....

...Harold Franklin Hawkins II was born on April 8, 1963, just one month after Hawk died. When Harold was born, I was both happy and sad. I knew that Hawk would never see his boys grow up.

But for every sad story there are more than enough humorous stories.

Grandpa Jones and Bill Carlisle was talking one night, and Bill found out that he had lost a beef steer. Bill told him, "Call me in the morning after church, and I will come over and help you look for that steer." As everyone knows, Grandpa was a real forgetful person. So Bill waited until two or three o'clock in the afternoon and Grandpa had not called him, so he called Grandpa.

Bill said, "You didn't call me to help you find that steer." Grandpa said, "I found him." Bill said, "You did, where?"

"In the freezer."

I have known Jean Shepard for a lot of years. She came here in 1955 and I came in 1956. We toured the Northwest together that following winter with her and Hawkshaw Hawkins. We went through a lot and had all kinds of experiences. We have been friends ever since. All through the years, she has had so many hits. *She is an Opry natural and a pioneer in country music. She is a wonderful lady. She is the real deal.*

—JIMMY C. NEWMAN, Grand Ole Opry Star

Jean's book is the "real deal." It can be purchased for $19.99 plus $6.95 shipping and handling at www.cfrvideos.com or by calling 800-820-5405.

Jean with her good friends Gus Arrendale and Larry Black at the printer watching the first of her books come off the press.

Music City Roots radio show trades Barn for The Factory

After spending its first five years at the Barn of the Loveless Cafe Barn, the weekly live music and radio show, Music City Roots, will trade the Loveless' biscuits and barn this summer for a new home in the Factory at Franklin.

The move, on July 9, will give the Americana music radio and webcast, producers and fans, access to the Factory's two larger performance spaces — the 800-seat, Jamison Hall and the 2,000-seat Liberty Hall — for the show's weekly performances. The Loveless Cafe Barn seats about 600.

"We've loved the Loveless Cafe Barn," said John Walker, Music City Roots executive producer. "We don't want to go to some huge facility where we lose the intimacy. At the same time, we need a little more space." Quickly pointing out that the change doesn't mean there were any issues between the Loveless Café and Music City Roots.

The show's final spring season at the Loveless Cafe Barn kicks off at 7 p.m. Wednesday and runs through June 18.

"Loveless Cafe is pleased to have been the original setting for Music City Roots," said Jessica Charlton, Loveless Cafe Brand Manager in a statement. "We celebrate the show's growth and look forward to continued partnership opportunities."

Built in 1929, the Factory is a renovated manufacturing space and is listed on the National Register of Historic Places. In 2012, billionaire Brad Kelley bought the Factory from its previous owner Calvin Lehew. The addition of Music City Roots adds another music-themed business to the Factory at Franklin, which now includes the Americana Music Association, Sugar Hill Records, and Dark Horse studios.

Despite the change in venue, the show's radio and online broadcasts won't change. Music City Roots will still be heard on Hippie Radio 94.5 FM and musiccityroots.com. The show's streaming service RootsRadio.com plans to build a broadcast booth in The Factory's main hall for other live programming and interviews, officials said.

And there is still the possibility of future Music City Roots shows at the Loveless Cafe Barn or other venues, says Walker.

Nadine's Cleaning Corner

Cleaning Tips for SENIORS

1. Before you even get started spring-cleaning….buy a Larry's Country Diner apron, stash your essential spring-cleaning supplies in the pockets and use it as you go from room to room. It will leave your hands free to scrub and polish and you won't have to lug a heavy cleaning bucket around. Or if you were Nadine you wouldn't have to lug a heavy bible around the house.

2. If you are using a cleaning powder that has holes in the top…only tear off ½ the seal. It will give you better control of the flow and won't come pouring out. Remember that your kitchen sink has more bacteria than your toilet seat so use a disinfectant.

3. When cleaning bottles that are hard to clean… just fill it up with water and drop a tablet or two of your denture cleaner and let it stand overnight. Then clean it easily with a brush and rinse.

4. Clean the wax out of your candles like a pro by placing them in freezer for a few hours. Once frozen, the wax will shrink and you can pop out left over wax.

5. Here is a bright idea for cleaning fabric lampshades. Use an adhesive lint roller.

6. Clean windows with rubber-edge squeegees instead of using your CFR News newspaper.

7. Change the direction of your ceiling fans about the same time you set your clocks. Counterclockwise direction during warm months and clockwise during cold weather.

8. As much as we like leftovers the refrigerator does need cleaning. Go ahead and throw away left over food and use a toothbrush to clean out crannies. Wiping down shelves with 2TBS baking soda per quart of warm water.

9. For floors that need vacuuming make sure you have a clean vacuum bag before you begin. Food particles and dog hair left in a bag can create an odor for future cleaning.

10. Replace the batteries in your smoke detectors and clocks when you also set your clocks. (You might want to check your hearing aid batteries at the same time)

11. Zap your cleaning sponge in your microwave on high for a minute. Make sure it is squeezed out… then replace it once it gets smelly.

Look what we get from our fans!

We have the BEST fans, and sometimes they send us things they have made. Some are funny, some are sweet, some are useful and some are just plain interesting, but we love them all. One day, many of them will have a special place in the 'real' diner!

Want to sit on stage at the Diner in Branson?

Are you going to Branson to see the Larry's Country Diner at the Starlite Theater? Don't miss this opportunity to sit on stage and be a part of the Diner show. You get to eat pie and meet Nadine! It's FREE, but there are limited seats on stage, so come by our merchandise table at the Starlite and get on the list early.

Show sets almost as important as the artists

Sometimes the sets are almost as important as the guest artists on a show. It might be a small item that you see in the background or the chairs the artists are sitting in, or it could be the old car behind the band that brings back nostalgic memories. Whatever it is, it's thanks to the hard work of the set designers, and for Gabriel, that means Scott Moore and Elaine Hensley.

Their keen eye for detail makes the sets a huge part of each series. But not only do they have to have a good eye, they have to know where to find the items for the sets.

"I have known about this 1928 Pontiac for several years and have had it in my back pocket to use someday. When Larry asked me to design a Bluegrass show, I knew it would be perfect!" said Scott, "We hadn't used any automobiles, so it was the perfect opportunity. It belongs to a "car wrangler" as we know it in the film business, a guy who wrangles automobiles, for film sets and I've used him on other shoots."

So the next time you watch any show, take a look at the set and think about the designers who came up with the idea, found just the right pieces, and put it all together. And see if you see anything that looks familiar.

Behind the Scenes SPOTLIGHT

We have so many talented folks that work behind the scenes of our television shows and tapings that we thought you should meet them. Their talents and experience surely humble us.

Scott Moore & Elaine Hensley

Production Set Designers

Scott Moore is a self-taught visual artist who has built a solid reputation with his production design in film, as well with his large scale modern paintings, that can be found in many public and private collections.

Elaine is an Emmy Award winning art director, and an energetic set dresser with an eye for creative shopping. Her talents are evident through her work in photography, video, editorial, and film.

Scott and Elaine are two creative people, whose paths crossed thru the cosmic intention of the universe, visual merchandising backgrounds, and a few friends in common.

"We have worked with Larry and Gabriel for many years, I personally started with Larry on all the sports tapings, and then Elaine joined the fun for CFR shows." Scott says, "We always look forward to Gabriel, because Larry has always let us soar with our creativity.

Working as film production designers, for 16 years doing TV Shows, National Commercials, Music Videos (with everyone from Allison Krauss to Taylor Swift), Interior Design Projects, and now partners in their own boutique shoppe, MOXIE FEARLESS FURNISHINGS, featuring a modern, ever-changing collection of re-imagined furniture, art, and objects from unexpected sources. MOXIE is located in the "Five Points" area of East Nashville, at The Shoppes on Fatherland. (1006 Fatherland, suite 303) Nashville, Tennessee 37206.

Strait retiring from tours, wins ACM Entertainer of Year

Twenty five years ago, George Strait won Entertainer of the Year at the Academy of Country Music Awards, and he did it again this year! It wasn't unexpected as the 61-year old won the same award at the Country Music Association Awards five months ago, but the difference is that the ACM Awards is fan-voted. This fact had many wondering if Strait's older fan base would have enough votes.

"I've always said I have the best fans in the world," Strait told the crowd. "I heard this was a fan-voted thing, so I rest my case."

He may be retiring from the road, but he still plans on recording, and that's a good thing for his fans.

Other highlights of the ACM show was when Miranda Lambert participated in a tribute to Merle Haggard. But perhaps the most moving performance was by the audience at the MGM Grand, which broke into "Happy Birthday" as Haggard walked to the stage on his 77th birthday to receive the academy's Crystal Milestone Award.

"Country music has been great to me all my life and it's great again tonight," Haggard said.

So, while the younger and more rock artists are winning a lot of the awards, it was nice to see some of the more traditional country artists can still give them a little competition.

Randy Travis makes appearance at charity event

During that time, Travis suffered a stroke and had to undergo emergency neurosurgery, but he soon was transferred to a physical therapy facility to focus on restoring functions such as walking and talking.

Nearly six months after the medical scare, Travis was in good spirits as he attended a charity concert on Friday, February 14 in Dallas, Texas.

Country singer and friend Neal McCoy posted a photo of himself with Travis on Facebook. Both are grinning ear to ear.

McCoy writes, "Randy Travis and I recently backstage before I went on, at a Smiles For Life concert in Dallas Texas. Pretty honored this was Randy's first time out and his first time to have Cowboy boots on since his illness. Gettin Better!!!"

Despite his remarkable progress Travis has made over the last 6 months, his friends are unsure if he will ever be able to perform again.

Singer Neal MCCoy told People magazine, "He looks great but is still struggling to use both of his hands. I don't know if he'll ever fully recover, but he's a tough guy with a work ethic."

His family insists his goal is still to get back to the stage and he is working toward that goal.

Country legend Randy Travis, 54, made his first public appearance since suffering a stroke on July 13, 2013, and he appears to be on the mend after his harrowing ordeal.

The singer was admitted to a hospital for idiopathic cardiomyopathy and was put on life support for 48 hours.

Larry's Country Diner RFD Show Schedule May, 2014
These shows have previously aired

Bill & McKenna Medley
Saturday, May 3
10:00 p.m. Central
Sunday, May 4
6:00 p.m. Central

Mark Lowry
Saturday, May 10
10:00 p.m. Central
Sunday, May 11
6:00 p.m. Central

Jett Williams
Saturday, May 17
10:00 p.m. Central
Sunday, May 18
6:00 p.m. Central

Mandy Barnette
Saturday, May 24
10:00 p.m. Central
Sunday, May 25
6:00 p.m. Central

Bill Anderson
Saturday, May 31
10:00 p.m. Central
Sunday, June 1
6:00 p.m. Central

Five more of our favorite duet partners

Just Between the Two of Us"
Merle Haggard & Bonnie Owens

In 1965 country legend Merle Haggard married fellow Bakersfield, Calif. singer Bonnie Owens (who used to be married to Buck Owens), they cut "Just Between The Two of Us." Their voices worked together beautifully, taking the Liz Anderson composition all the way to the Top 5. Their marriage ended in 1978, but the two remained friends. In fact, Owens sang backup in Haggard's band starting in the 1960s all the way until her death in 2006.

"Sweethearts in Heaven"
Buck Owens & Rose Maddox

Buck Owens and fellow California country legend Rose Maddox (of the family group the Maddox Brothers & Rose) cut a number of duets together in the 1960s, including the divorce duet "Mental Cruelty" (which hit No. 8 in 1961) and a great version of "Loose Talk." Written by Owens, "Sweethearts in Heaven" was the B-side to the duo's 1963 single "We're The Talk Of The Town." It's about a couple vowing that, should one "go first" and leave the other behind "to face life alone," that he'll be there "waiting" for her "just inside the pearly gates."

"You're the Reason God Made Oklahoma"
David Frizzell & Shelly West

In April 1979 "You're the Reason God Make Oklahoma" reached the top of the country charts. It was the highest ranking of 7 duets from David Frizzell and Shelly West.

The song was also chosen to be part of the Clint Eastwood movie, 'Any Which Way You Can', and was listed as #6 on CMT's 100 Greatest Duets of all time. This vote of confidence earned Frizzell & West a contract with Viva/Warner Bros. and the wheels began to turn quickly. A small radio station in Tulare, California began to play the album track. Other stations followed, prompting Warner Bros. to release the song as a single. Soon, the song that nobody wanted became a smash hit.

Frizzell & West remains one of the most-awarded acts in entertainment; one that sold out arenas worldwide and produced five albums. The duo twice won the Country Music Association's Vocal Duo of the Year award, twice won the Academy of Country Music award for Vocal Duet of the Year and were awarded the ACM Song of the Year award. They also received the Music City News Award for Duet of the Year twice and Song of the Year as well.

"If I Needed You"
Don Williams & Emmylou Harris

Emmylou Harris' pure, angelic voice has been in constant demand since she emerged in the early 1970s. Some always jump out. For this release, Harris teamed up with another of the richest country vocalists to emerge during the 1970s, the "Gentle Giant" Don Williams. The song is a classic by the late, great Townes Van Zandt, and it was released on Emmylou's 1981 album Cimarron. It's beautifully low-key version of Townes' gentle love song, so it's little wonder that it turned into a Top 3 single for the duo.

"Wish I Didn't Have to Miss You"
Jeannie Seely & Jack Greene

Jeannie Seely is among a select group of country artists who have scored No. 1 hits as a solo artist, as a duet partner, and as a songwriter.

A 1969 duet recorded with fellow Opry member Jack Greene titled "Wish I Didn't Have to Miss You" went to No. 1 on the charts and launched one of the most successful duos and road shows in country music history.

Nominated for numerous Country Music Association (CMA) and Grammy awards, Jack Greene and Jeannie Seely toured together for over ten years, performing everywhere from New York's Madison Square Garden to London's Wembley Arena.

The duo changed the format of "package shows" and were considered forerunners in opening doors and bringing country music to wider audiences around the world. Through a special invitation from the White House they were named Goodwill Ambassadors to the annual United Nations Concert.

Ken Curtis was so much more than 'Festus'

Most people know Curtis Wain Gates as Ken Curtis. What they don't know is that he was a singer and a serious actor before he became Festus on the television show Gunsmoke.

He was born July 2, 1916 in Lamar, Colorado, but was reared west of there in Las Animas, the seat of Bent County. His father, Dan Gates, was the Bent County sheriff. The family lived above the jail and his mother, Nellie Sneed Gates, cooked for the prisoners. The jail is now located for historical preservation purposes on the grounds of the Bent County courthouse in Las Animas.

Curtis played quarterback for his high school football team before serving as a member of the infantry during WWII.

He combined his talent of both singing and acting once he entered films, performing with the popular Sons of the Pioneers from 1949 to 1953 as well as singing with the Tommy Dorsey band. Curtis replaced Frank Sinatra as vocalist for the Dorsey band for a time in 1941.

Columbia Pictures signed Curtis to a contract in 1945. He starred in a series of musical westerns with The Hoosier Hot Shots, playing singing-cowboy romantic leads. For much of 1948, Curtis was a featured singer and host of the long-running country music radio program WWVA Jamboree.

Curtis was a son-in-law of director John Ford by his first wife and was featured in many of his films as well as others.

Curtis guest-starred twice on the TV Series Western Have Gun Will Travel. He also guest-starred as circus performer Tim Durant on an episode of Perry Mason, "The Case of the Clumsy Clown", which aired on November 5, 1960. He then co-starred with Larry Pennell in the 1961-1963 syndicated television series Ripcord, a half-hour drama about a skydiving service company. Curtis played the role of "Jim Buckley" and Pennell was "Ted McKeever." The series helped generate interest in the sport of parachuting.

Curtis remains best known for his role as Festus, the scruffy, cantankerous, illiterate office and jail custodian in Gunsmoke. While Marshal Matt Dillon had a total of five helpers over two decades, Festus held the role the longest (11 years), in 239 episodes, and was the most colorful. Festus was patterned after "Cedar Jack", a man from Curtis' Las Animas childhood. Cedar Jack, who lived about forty miles out of town, made a living cutting cedar fence posts. Curtis observed the many times Jack would come to Las Animas, where he would usually end up drunk and in jail. Festus' character was known, in part, for his nasally, twangy, rural accent which Curtis developed for the role, but which did not reflect Curtis' actual voice.

Besides engaging in the usual personal appearances most television stars undertake to promote their program, Curtis also traveled around the country performing a western-themed stage show at fairs, rodeos and other venues when Gunsmoke wasn't in production, and even for some years after the show was canceled.

In two episodes of Gunsmoke, Carroll O'Connor was a guest-star; years later Curtis guest-starred as a retired police detective on O'Connor's NBC program In the Heat of the Night. He voiced Nutsy the vulture in Disney's 1973 animated film Robin Hood. In 1983 he returned to television in the short-lived western series The Yellow Rose.

In 1981, Curtis was inducted into the Western Performers Hall of Fame at the National Cowboy & Western Heritage Museum in Oklahoma City, Oklahoma.

Curtis' last acting role was as the aging cattle rancher "Seaborn Tay" in the television production Conagher (1991), by western author Louis L'Amour. Sam Elliott starred in the lead role, and Curtis' Gunsmoke costar Buck Taylor (Newly O'Brien) played a bad man in the same film.

A statue of Ken Curtis as Festus can be found at 430 Pollasky Avenue in Clovis, California in Fresno County in front of the Educational Employees Credit Union. In his later years, Curtis resided in Clovis.

Curtis died in his sleep of natural causes in Fresno, California on April 28, 1991. He was cremated, and his ashes were scattered in the Colorado flatlands.

Sonny Osborne alive, but retired

Sonny Osborne was born in Hyden, Kentucky on October 29, 1937 and began playing the banjo at the age of eleven on one his father bought him. With a little help from Larry Richardson, he soon found out how to play. His brother Bobby worked with the Lonesome Pine Fiddlers and Sonny had a chance to join in with them during jam sessions.

Only fourteen years old, he recorded nine tunes with the "Father of Bluegrass". Meanwhile, the same year, he recorded, on Gateway Records, together with guitarist Carlos Brock, fiddler Billy Thomas, mandolin player Enos Johnson and Smokey Ward on bass, calling themselves "Stanley Alpine". When Bobby enlisted in the Marine Corps., Sonny went on to work with Bill Monroe's Bluegrass Boys for a few months between June and September 1952. By now, his family had moved to Dayton, Ohio and Bobby returned from the Marines. Sonny and Bobby appeared together on WROL in Knoxville, Tennessee on November 6, 1953. They had a recording contract on RCA Victor and together with Jimmy Martin, the Osborne Brothers made their first recordings on November 16, 1954.

As The Osborne Brothers, Sonny Osborne and Bobby Osborne (b. December 9, 1931), were an influential and popular bluegrass act during the 1960s and 1970s. They are probably best known for their No. 33 1967 country hit song, "Rocky Top", written by Felice and Boudleaux Bryant and named after a fictional Tennessee location.

Sonny married his wife Judith on June 26, 1958. They have two children, Steven (born March 24, 1960) and Karen (born October 14, 1962).

Sonny Osborne was inducted into the International Bluegrass Music Hall of Honor in 1994 and retired in 2003.

Grandmas love their grandkids!

Gandmas are also mothers, so for Mother's Day we're featuring four of our favorite grandmas!

Left: Nadine's granddaughter, River, gives as good as she gets.

Right: This is Rio's first Mother's Day! She was born last August making Renae the waitress (or NaeNae) a grandma.

Being A Grammy
By Grammy (Luann) Black
April 2014

There is no greater love for me
than being called a Grammy.
This new name became all mine
as our family grew over time.

Deja Vu I lived on many a fun day.
Cuddling little ones - kissing baby tears away.
Reliving those memories was such sweet joy.
The memory of raising my own three boys.

I am thrilled to be called Grammy
by so many - times ten!
Blessed abundantly by
loving each one of them.
To see them grow up is an awesome treasure.
Enriching my life beyond measure.

As the years go by and my torch is passed,
I will celegrate each one always -
they are growing up fast.
Being a Grammy - the richest
of my blessings this I know -
My grandchildren are God's reward
for growing old.

Dedicated to:
Nathan, Brandon, Avery, Nicholas, Sam-Bam, Ariel, Eden, Devin, Melina, Asher

Jeannie Seely with Beth, GiAnna, Brooke holding Hagan, and Arden.

And with grandson Alex Bolinge, who isn't buying the story of Goldielocks!

Nathan, Brandon, Avery, Nicholas, Sam, LuAnn, Ariel, Eden, Devin, Melina, Asher

Gilley touring again

The original Urban Cowboy, Mickey Gilley, is hitting the road and will return to touring after recovering from 2009 tragic accident that left him paralyzed.

"I have always loved performing and I know nothing else," says Mickey Gilley. "Getting back on stage in all of these cities is something to look forward to each and every day. The outpour of love and concern from the fans, my fellow artist friends, and the music community has kept me fighting to walk back on that stage, so I am glad that time is finally here."

Throughout Gilley's career, he has released 39 Top-Ten country hits with 17 of them hitting No. 1 on country charts including, Stand By Me, True Love Ways, You Don't Know Me and A Headache Tomorrow (Or A Heartache Tonight). In 1976, he swept the ACM Awards, receiving Entertainer of the Year, Top Male Vocalist, Song of the Year, Single of the Year and Album of the Year. He has been ranked among the top-fifty country music hit makers in the 1989 book written by record research historian Joel Whitburn.

Aside from his many hits and being known as the cousin to Jerry Lee Lewis and Jimmy Swaggart, Gilley was instrumental in creating the "Urban Cowboy" era with the opening of Gilley's in 1971 – known as the World's Largest Honky-Tonk. The famed-club included mechanical bulls, pool tables, a rodeo area, punching bags, a shooting gallery and a dance floor that could hold thousands becoming the forerunner of Hard Rock Café and other theme restaurants. Esquire Magazine wrote an article "The Ballad of the Urban Cowboy" based on Gilley's, which later became the movie, "Urban Cowboy," starring John Travolta.

In 2009, while helping his friend move, Gilley became paralyzed from the neck down after a sofa landed on top of him and crushed four vertebrae. After several years of intense physical therapy he has returned to the stage and is now walking, singing and performing.

Mickey Gilley Tour Dates:
May 8-10 Jackpot, NV – Cactus Petes
May 16 Clinton, IA – Wild Rose Casino
May 17 Emmetsburg, IA – Wild Rose Casino
June 25 Pasadena, TX – Stafford Centre
June 26 Midland-Odessa, TX – Wagner Noel PAC
June 27 Greenville, TX – Greenville Municipal Auditorium
July 13 Lancaster, PA – American Music Theater
July 19 Biloxi, MS – IP Casino
July 30 Shreveport, LA – Casino

For more information, visit **http://www.gilleys.com/**

Country Questions
By Dick Boise, CMH

Send questions to:
Dick Boise, , c/o CFR News,
P.O. Box 201796, Nashville,
TN 37221.

Q. I really love Joey and Rory and watch their show each week. I know that the two older daughters refer to Joey as their mother and she refers to them as her children. Can you tell me about the girls and the real mother?

Thanks, P.S.

A. There has never been any mention of the girls' mother from Rory's previous marriage. I believe that Rory has had the girls most of the time and that Joey helped in raising them. Now, the new member has joined the family with little Indiana Boon Feek, born February 17, 2014 to Joey and Rory. I'm sure you will see her soon! Keep watching.

Q. I was watching Country Family Reunion show and saw Wilson-Fairchild duo. Have checked Wal-Mart and others in my area and cannot find their CDs. Can you tell me where I can obtain them? Thanks,

Ardyth Rice, Rushville, NE

A. I know the duo are the sons of two of the Statler Brothers and they have the CDs available at their store. The Statler address is: P.O. Box 1890, Staunton, VA 24402. You could also contact Ernest Tubb Record Shop in Nashville, and they could give you a pricing and shipping via phone. The number is (615) 255-7503.

Q. I've always enjoyed Penny DeHaven's singing. Could you tell me what she's been up to lately?

Donald Dwert, Milwaukee, WI

A. Penny DeHaven, I'm sad to say, passed away February 23, this year. She was a very talented lady and she had been battling cancer for some time. The health issue kept her from performing as much as she would have liked. Thanks for asking and she will be missed by huge amounts of fans.

Q. Can you tell me if Ricky Van Shelton is still performing? He seems to have disappeared. I enjoy his singing.

Mary Jane Finley, Milam, IL

A. Mary Jane, you are not alone in those liking Ricky Van Shelton's voice. Back in 2006, he decided to retire and spend time with his family. He had many fine records and many, many fans. I still like his version of the great Ned Miller song, "From A Jack To A King."

Courtney Cash killed in Baxter, Tennessee

A great niece of Johnny Cash was found stabbed to death and stuffed in a box in Putnam County.

Courtney Cash's body was found Wednesday, March 19 at a home in the 8100 block of Rice Road in Baxter, about 100 miles east of Nashville. She is the daughter of Mark Allen Cash, Tommy Cash's son.

Investigators said Cash was stabbed to death with a kitchen knife during a struggle at the home in the early morning hours.

Putnam County Sheriff David Andrews said her body was found in a box approximately four feet long and two feet deep similar to a cedar chest, but not made of cedar, near the front door.

Her boyfriend, Austin Johnson, was also stabbed but managed to escape the house and drive himself to a hospital.

Johnson was then transported to Vanderbilt University Medical Center in Nashville.

His injuries initially prevented him from speaking with investigators, Sheriff Andrews said.

Cash and Johnson have a young daughter who was in the home at the time of the incident. The sheriff said Johnson managed to grab her before fleeing the home. She was not injured.

Wayne Masciarella was placed into custody for the crime and charged with first degree murder. Additional charges are pending.

The sheriff described the three as friends and said they had been out Tuesday night and got into an argument after returning to the home.

"It's our understanding that at about 3 or 4 a.m. [Wednesday] morning, the three had been out together somewhere. They came home, a struggle ensued, and that's when the stabbings occurred," Sheriff Andrews said in a media briefing Thursday afternoon.

A motive was not immediately known, but when asked if drugs and alcohol were involved, Sheriff Andrews responded, "Probably."

"We live in a drug-driven society. This is a senseless, tragic death of a young lady whose life was probably taken as a direct or indirect result of drugs," he added.

Masciarella has a lengthy criminal history, with 20 entries into the Putnam County jail.

He's also been arrested in Davidson, Smith, Jackson, Cumberland and Knox counties on charges ranging from drug possession to aggravated assault.

More recently, Masciarella was arrested in May of 2013 on charges of domestic assault and vandalism.

The Cash family asked for prayers in a statement released Thursday.

"We ask for you to respect our privacy and appreciate all the support that the public and media has always offered my family. As we handle the loss of my granddaughter, pray for the father of my great grandchild and journey through the search for justice on this violent act," Tommy Cash, Johnny Cash's younger brother, said in the statement. He continued, "We are completely heartbroken. It is a time like this that we are grateful for our faith and trusting the loving guidance of God."

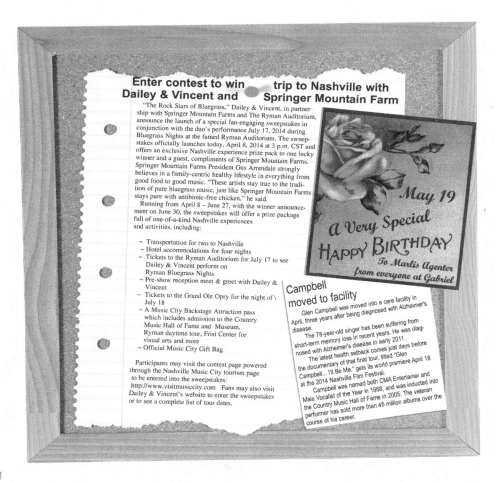

Enter contest to win a trip to Nashville with Dailey & Vincent and Springer Mountain Farm

"The Rock Stars of Bluegrass," Dailey & Vincent, in partnership with Springer Mountain Farms and The Ryman Auditorium, announce the launch of a special fan-engaging sweepstakes in conjunction with the duo's performance July 17, 2014 during Bluegrass Nights at the famed Ryman Auditorium. The sweepstakes officially launches today, April 8, 2014 at 3 p.m. CST and offers an exclusive Nashville experience prize pack to one lucky winner and a guest, compliments of Springer Mountain Farms. Springer Mountain Farms President Gus Arrendale strongly believes in a family-centric healthy lifestyle in everything from good food to good music. "These artists stay true to the tradition of pure bluegrass music, just like Springer Mountain Farms stays pure with antibiotic-free chicken," he said.

Running from April 8 – June 27, with the winner announcement on June 30, the sweepstakes will offer a prize package full of one-of-a-kind Nashville experiences and activities, including:

~ Transportation for two to Nashville
~ Hotel accommodations for four nights
~ Tickets to the Ryman Auditorium for July 17 to see Dailey & Vincent perform on Ryman Bluegrass Nights
~ Pre-show reception meet & greet with Dailey & Vincent
~ Tickets to the Grand Ole Opry for the night of July 18
~ A Music City Backstage Attraction pass which includes admission to the Country Music Hall of Fame and Museum, Ryman daytime tour, Frist Center for visual arts and more
~ Official Music City Gift Bag

Participants may visit the contest page powered through the Nashville Music City tourism page to be entered into the sweepstakes: http://www.visitmusiccity.com Fans may also visit Dailey & Vincent's website to enter the sweepstakes or to see a complete list of tour dates.

May 19
A Very Special
HAPPY BIRTHDAY
To Marlis Agenter
from everyone at Gabriel

Campbell moved to facility

Glen Campbell was moved into a care facility in April, three years after being diagnosed with Alzheimer's disease.

The 78-year-old singer has been suffering from short-term memory loss in recent years. He was diagnosed with Alzheimer's disease in early 2011.

The latest health setback comes just days before the documentary of that final tour, titled "Glen Campbell... I'll Be Me," gets its world premiere April 18 at the 2014 Nashville Film Festival.

Campbell was named both CMA Entertainer and Male Vocalist of the Year in 1968, and was inducted into the Country Music Hall of Fame in 2005. The veteran performer has sold more than 45 million albums over the course of his career.

Visiting Tennessee? Great things to do all over the state!

EAST TENNESSEE

Just like the unique beauty of each season in the Smoky Mountains, Dollywood also offers a completely different and exciting experience for guests during each season of the year. In 2014, Dollywood welcomes five festivals, each with its own atmosphere for park visitors to enjoy. International stage productions, concerts by bluegrass and Southern gospel favorites, the six-time winner for Best Christmas Event, as well as a nightly summer fireworks show provide seasons of fun at Dollywood!

Traditional cuisine and cultural activities allow guests a glimpse into the rich traditions of other countries. Dollywood's 2014 Festival of Nations lineup also includes Moscow Nights, Strings of Fire, Streichmusik Alder, Zebra Stelzentheater and many more.

A perfect way to jump start the summer, Dollywood's Barbeque & Bluegrass pairs the best barbeque in the South with the biggest names in bluegrass. This May 24-June 8 event includes free daily concerts throughout the park from artists including The Time Jumpers featuring Vince Gill, The Boxcars with J.D. Crowe, Riders in the Sky, The Bankester Family and many more. While the music serves as a treat to the ears, Dollywood's award-winning food provides the perfect complement for the taste buds. Tender and tangy ribs, pulled pork, barbequed chicken, smoked sausage and more make this the ultimate family picnic.

After a popular debut in 2013, Dollywood's Great American Summer (June 13- Aug. 3) is extended to give families more opportunities to enjoy Dollywood at night! Longer park operating hours—10 a.m. to 10 p.m. daily—and a spectacular nightly fireworks show provide the perfect atmosphere to enjoy Dollywood's award-winning rides, shows and attractions.

Dollywood's Harvest Festival featuring the National Southern Gospel Celebration presented by Humana (Sept. 22- Nov. 1) paints a spectacular palette of autumn colors throughout the park. During this festive event, the sounds of beautiful Southern gospel music echo from stage to stage thanks to multiple free concerts each day. Guests are treated to amazing demonstrations from talented crafters, and the park's menus change to reflect the offerings of a bountiful fall harvest.

A six-time winner for Best Christmas Event, Dollywood's Smoky Mountain Christmas presented by Humana (Nov. 8 – Jan. 3, 2015) features four million holiday lights and spectacular holiday performances, including Dollywood's A Christmas Carol, with Dolly Parton's hologram as the Ghost of Christmas Past. From the award-winning shows and elaborate holiday decorations to the twinkling lights and Christmas-themed menus, Dollywood captures the essence of Christmas.

In addition to five fabulous festivals, FireChaser Express, the nation's first dual-launch family coaster, makes its debut in 2014, Dollywood's 29th operating season.

For detailed concert schedules and festival entertainment lineups, please visit Dollywood.com.

MIDDLE TENNESSEE

Nashville's magnificent General Jackson Showboat, one of the largest paddlewheel riverboats in the country, added two all new shows when the 1,200 passenger vessel's 2014 cruise season began in March.

"With fun-filled performances, chef prepared cuisine and gorgeous views from the Cumberland River, there's no better place to round out a visit to Nashville," said Ron Kerere, general manager of the General Jackson Showboat. "We are proud that the

General Jackson Showboat is an iconic attraction for so many families not only here in Music City but across the country, and we're excited to introduce these new shows to our guests."

The General Jackson Jubilee invites Sunday morning guests to dine on a sumptuous Southern buffet as a vocal quartet and three instrumentalists sing "Down by the Riverside," "Good Ole Gospel Ship," "Get All Excited" and other "hand clappin'" traditional, Southern Gospel favorites. Then experience the inspirational sounds of today's contemporary Christian music with songs like "Your Grace is Enough" and "I Could Sing of Your Love Forever."

MIDDAY - SHOW

Your taste buds will flourish with the flavors of the South during our midday cruise followed by our new country music variety show, Nashville Live! The world-class cast includes two rising country artists, an internationally acclaimed trick-roper, a country comedian and features fiddle and guitar soloists, all supported by a live country band. The show's repertoire spans classic hits by Patsy Cline, George Jones and Tammy Wynette through today's chart-topping hits by Jason Aldean, Taylor Swift and Rascal Flatts.

EVENING - CRUISE

Our evening cruise boasts the full feel of the South with mouthwatering favorites, a breathtaking view of downtown Nashville and the Heart of Tennessee: A Musical Journey—

which takes you down Tennessee's Musical Highway, from bluegrass to soul, a little gospel and, of course, country music! Covering classic Elvis to the new artists of country music, the cast of seven is backed by a live talented six-piece band. The show culminates with a salute to those who proudly serve as first-responders and members of the military.

WEST TENNESSEE

Moon River Festival will be held at Levitt Shell, 1930 Poplar Avenue, Memphis, TN 38103 on June 7, 2014

Levitt Shell will come to life as the Moon River Festival takes center stage. The lineup will "Never Give In" with Will Hoge, Southern rock and alternative country singer / songwriter. Drew Holcom & the Neighbors ("Good Light") will be bringing their alternative rock along along with the rock and alternative country styling of the "Best Band in Knoxville" since 2008, the Dirty Guv'nahs. Holly Williams (granddaughter of Hank Williams, Sr.) is sure to entertain with her American folk and country music. Ellie Holcomb, known for praise & worship and folk music, joins the line up along with Rob Baird ("I Swear It's the Truth"). The spotlight will turn toward the bluegrass and folk rock music of Judah and the Lion. And don't miss Dwan Hill ("Mister Pride") who has appeared on the Jimmy Kimmel Live! show.

Tickets are: $20 for early general admission. j$55 for VIP passes which include two drink tickets, signed festival poster and wristband access. The best deal goes for $250 which is the Neighbor VIP. This pass includes the same as the VIP pass plus VIP tent access, seating options, plus a private dinner and acoustic show the night before the event.

info@moonriverfestival.com

Precious Memories;
Remembering Merle Kilgore

Born Wyatt Merle Kilgore in Chickasha, Oklahoma on August 9, 1934, but he grew up in Shreveport, Louisiana. As a teenager, he often hung around the "Louisiana Hayride" radio show, meeting numerous performers including Hank Williams Sr., whose guitar case he carried for his first job in the music business, at age 14.

When he was just 18, he wrote his first hit song: "More and More," which Webb Pierce took to No. 1 in 1954. He also worked as a disc jockey, TV show host and radio station manager in Louisiana throughout most of the 1950s. With Pierce's help, he landed his first recording contract with Imperial Records in Los Angeles; during a 20+ year singing career, he also recorded for Starday (producing a Top 10 hit with "Dear Mama"), Mercury (a Top 10 with "Love Has Made You Beautiful"), MGM, Epic, Columbia, Ashley and Warner Bros.

"Johnny Reb" was a million-seller for Johnny Horton in 1959. Following that success he moved to Nashville in 1961 to become manager of the Nashville office of Shapiro-Bernstein Music. He also became a regular performer on the Grand Ole Opry and joined the Johnny Cash road show while continuing to write. His biggest hits were Claude King's "Wolverton Mountain" and Johnny Cash's "Ring Of Fire" (written with June Carter at the beginning of her relationship with Cash). Other songs included John Anderson's "Let Somebody Else Drive," Eddy Arnold's "The Easy Way" and "The Folk Singer," Margie Singleton's "Old Records," Claude King's "Tiger Woman," and Ricky Nelson's "Old Enough To Love."

In 1964 Merle joined the Hank Williams Jr. on the road as an opening act and later turned his focus to Williams' business concerns. In 1969 he became the general manager of Williams' publishing companies, and in 1986 was named executive vice president and head of management of Hank Williams Jr. Enterprises, which relocated from Alabama to Paris, Tennessee.

He was named the Country Music Association's first Manager of the Year in 1990 at the SRO Awards and was inducted to the Nashville Songwriters Hall of Fame in 1998.

He was also a member of the CMA Board of Directors and once served as vice president of the CMA. He worked with numerous other industry organizations and was elected President of the Nashville Songwriters Association International's Board of Directors and of ROPE (Reunion of Professional Entertainers). Merle was even a member of the Screen Actors Guild, appearing in movies including "Roadie," "Coal Miner's Daughter," and "Nashville and Living Proof," the 1981 NBC movie about Hank Williams Jr. in which he played himself.

Merle died February 6, 2005 of congestive heart failure in Mexico, where he had been undergoing cancer treatments. He was 70. He is survived by his wife, Judy; sons, Steve and Duane Kilgore; daughters, Pam Compton, Kim Pomeroy and Shane McBee; eight grandchildren and one great-granddaughter.

Celebrating this Father's Day with the 'Father of Country Music'... Jimmie Rodgers

Born September 8, 1897, in Meridian, Mississippi, Jimmie Rodgers was the youngest of three sons. His mother died when he only six or seven years old, and he spent the next few years with relatives in southeast Mississippi and southwest Alabama. He eventually returned home to live with his father, Aaron Rodgers, a maintenance foreman on the Mobile and Ohio Railroad, who had settled with a new wife in Meridian.

Jimmie's love for entertaining and travel developed early. By age 13, he had twice organized traveling shows, only to be brought home by his father. The first time on the road, he stole some of his sister-in-law's bedsheets to make a crude tent. When he returned to Meridian, he paid for the sheets with money he had made from his show! He charged an expensive canvas tent to his father (without his father's knowing it) for the second trip. Not long after that, Mr. Rodgers found Jimmie his first railroad job, as water boy on his father's gang. A few years later, Jimmie became a brakeman on the New Orleans and Northeastern Railroad, a position secured by his oldest brother, Walter, a conductor on the line.

In 1924, at the age of 27, Jimmie contracted tuberculosis. The disease temporarily ended his railroad career but gave him the chance to get back to his first love, entertainment. He organized a traveling road show and performed across the Southeast until a tornado destroyed his tent. He returned to railroad work as a brakeman on the east coast of Florida, but eventually his illness cost him his job. He relocated to Tucson, Arizona (thinking the dry climate might lessen the effects of his TB), and worked as a switchman for the Southern Pacific. The job lasted less than a year, and the Rodgers family (which by then included wife Carrie and daughter Anita) settled back in Meridian in 1927.

Later that year, Jimmie traveled to Asheville, North Carolina. In February 1927, Asheville's first radio station, WWNC, went on the air, and on April 18, Jimmie and Otis Kuykendall performed for the first time on the station. A few months later, Jimmie recruited a group from Tennessee called the Tenneva Ramblers and they secured a weekly slot on the station as the Jimmie Rodgers Entertainers. A review in The Asheville Times remarked that "Jimmy [sic] Rodgers and his entertainers managed ... with a type of music quite different than the station's usual material, but a kind that finds a cordial reception from a large audience." Another columnist said, "Whoever that fellow is, he either is a winner or he is going to be."

The Tenneva Ramblers hailed from Bristol, Tennessee, and in late July of 1927, Rodgers' bandmates got word that Ralph Peer of the Victor Talking Machine Company was coming to Bristol to record area musicians. Rodgers and the group arrived in Bristol on August 3 and auditioned for Peer, who agreed to record them the next day. That night the band argued about how it would be billed on the record, which led Jimmie to declare, "All right ... I'll just sing one myself."

Jimmie Rodgers recorded two songs on August 4, "Sleep, Baby, Sleep" and "The Soldier's Sweetheart." For the recordings, he received $100.

The recordings were released on October 7, 1927, to modest success. In November of that year, Peer recorded Rodgers again at the Victor studios in Camden, New Jersey. Four songs made it out of this session: "Ben Dewberry's Final Run," "Mother Was a Lady," "Away out on the Mountain" and "T for Texas." In the next two years, "T for Texas" (released as "Blue Yodel") sold nearly half a million copies, rocketing Rodgers into stardom.

In the next few years, Rodgers did a movie short, "The Singing Brakeman", and made various recordings across the country. He toured the Midwest with humorist Will Rogers. On July 16, 1930, he even recorded "Blue Yodel No. 9" (also known as "Standin' on the Corner") with a young jazz trumpeter named Louis Armstrong, whose wife, Lillian, played piano on the track.

Rodgers' next to last recordings were made in August 1932 in Camden, and it was clear that TB was getting the better of him. He had given up touring by then but did have a weekly radio show in San Antonio, Texas, where he'd relocated when "T for Texas" became a hit.

In 1933, Rodgers traveled to New York for recording sessions beginning May 17. He completed four songs on the first take. But there was no question that Rodgers was running out of track. When he returned to the studio after a day's rest, he had to record sitting down and soon retreated to his hotel, hoping to regain enough energy to finish the songs he'd been rehearsing.

The recording engineer hired two session musicians to help Rodgers when he came back to the studio a few days later. Together, they recorded a few songs, including "Mississippi Delta Blues." For his last song of the session, Jimmie recorded "Years Ago" by himself, finishing as he'd started six years earlier, just a man and his guitar. Within 36 hours, "The Father of Country Music" was dead.

Rodgers' legacy continues though. When the Country Music Hall of Fame and Museum was established in 1961, Rodgers was one of the first three (the others were music publisher and songwriter Fred Rose and singer-songwriter Hank Williams) to be inducted.

Rodgers was elected to the Songwriters Hall of Fame in 1970 and, as an early influence, to the Rock & Roll Hall of Fame in 1986. "Blue Yodel No. 9" was selected as one of The Rock and Roll Hall of Fame's 500 Songs that Shaped Rock and Roll. Rodgers was ranked No. 33 on CMT's 40 Greatest Men of Country Music in 2003.

Since 1953, Meridian's Jimmie Rodgers Memorial Festival has been held annually during May to

The United States Postal Service issued a 13-cent commemorative stamp on May 24, 1978, honoring Rodgers, the first in its long-running Performing Arts Series. The stamp was designed by Jim Sharpe (who did several others in this series), who depicted him with brakeman's outfit and guitar, giving his "two thumbs up", along with a locomotive in silhouette in the background.

Rodgers' legacy and influence is not limited to country music. The 2009 book "Meeting Jimmie Rodgers: How America's Original Roots Music Hero Changed the Pop Sounds of a Century" tracks Rodgers influence through a broad range of musical genres, internationally. He was influential to Ozark poet Frank Stanford, who composed a series of "blue yodel" poems, and a number of later blues artists. Rodgers was one of the biggest stars of American music between 1927 and 1933, arguably doing more to popularize blues than any other performer of his time.

The 1982 film, Honkytonk Man, directed by and starring Clint Eastwood was said to be loosely based on Rodgers' life.

On May 28, 2010, Slim Bryant, the last surviving singer to have made a recording with Rodgers, died at the age of 101. They recorded Bryant's song "Mother, the Queen of My Heart" in 1932. The Union, a collaborative album between Elton John and Leon Russell, featured a song entitled "Jimmie Rodgers' Dream", which was a tribute to Rodgers.

Also in May 2010, a second marker, on the Mississippi Country Music Trail, was erected near Rodgers' gravesite, marking his role as The Father of Country Music.

In 2013, Rodgers was posthumously inducted to the Blues Hall of Fame.

Nadine
The Church Lady

Last Sunday, Homer and I went to church with our son and his wife. We always enjoy the visit however the "Minister" gave a sermon on baptism and in the course of his sermon he was illustrating the fact that baptism should take place by sprinkling and not by immersion. He pointed out some instances in the Bible.

He said that when John the Baptist baptized Jesus in the River Jordan, it didn't mean in – it meant close to, round about, or nearby. And again when it says in the Bible that Philip baptized the eunuch in the river, it didn't mean in – it meant close to, round about, or nearby.

After the service Homer, being a little contrary, came up to the minister and told him it was a great sermon, one of the best he had ever heard, and that it had cleared up a great many mysteries he had encountered in the Bible.

"For instance, "he said, "the story about Jonah getting swallowed by the whale has always bothered me. Now I know that Jonah wasn't really in the whale, but close to, round about, or nearby, swimming in the water.

"Then there is the story about the three young Hebrew boys who were thrown into the fiery furnace, but were not burned. Now I see that they were not really in the fire, just to close to, round about, or nearby, just keeping warm.

" But the hardest of all stories for me to believe has always been the story of Daniel getting thrown into the lions' den. But now I see that he wasn't really in the lions' den, but close to, round about, or nearby, like at the zoo.

"The revealing of these mysteries has been a real comfort to me because now I know when I sin I won't be going to HELL, but close to, round about, or nearby. And next Sunday, Nadine and I won't have to be in church, just close to, round about, or nearby.

Of course I gave Homer that look and knew he had gone too far !!

This Life I Live

scenes from one man's extraordinary, ordinary life

By Rory Feek

My name is Rory. I wear overalls, but I'm not a farmer, yet. I love old cars, old farmhouses, old people, and pretty much anything nostalgic or that has character. I'm 48 years old on the outside and in my early 20's down deep. I am a believer who's dreams have taken me places I've never imagined. I'm also a Believer, that has a long long way to go. I want to live a great story. I want to be a better man. I film. I write. I show up. God does the rest.

My wife: I am married to the greatest woman that I've ever known. Her name is Joey. She has the voice of an angel and the heart of a saint. She is why I'm me. We've been married 11 years and God has given us an incredible love story. Not just how we began.. but now, today. That love story is still unfolding, and hand-in-hand, we turn the pages. I want to out-love and out-serve her, but it is impossible.

My children: I have two daughters, no wait... I have three daughters. Our two oldest, Heidi and Hopie are grown and making their way in this world. Our youngest, Indiana, is brand new and making her way in this world. Indy has down syndrome. I think Hopie has up syndrome (she's always happy). Heidi's got music syndrome (she's an aspiring singer/songwriter). All my children are good and perfect gifts from above.

My life: I live on a small farm about an hour south of Nashville Tennessee. We have a cow, some chickens, some cats and a dog named Ranger. We've spent the last six years making music, traveling all over the world singing and performing for people, making a television show at home and working hard on our dreams. We are taking this year off to search for something better. To simplify, and be with our family and friends, and to homestead. We're learning how to be self-sufficient and raise as much of the food that we eat as we can. We don't have a television and don't want one. We traded our iPhones in for flip-phones and are starting to talk to people again. We love our life.

My blog: I'm a songwriter who isn't writing songs right now. Joey has been encouraging me to write about our lives instead. So at the beginning of this year, I started doing so. I don't know why. I don't have a plan or a purpose for this blog, other than to capture as much of these days and these moments as I can in posts, and share them with others.

On Fathers day last June, after eleven years of marriage, my wife Joey and I found out that we were going to have a baby. We were elated (and nervous, and hopeful, all at the same time). Soon after, Joey watched a documentary about home-birth and midwives, and was even more excited about the idea of having our baby at home, here in the farmhouse where we live and dream and share our lives.

Nine months later, on February 17, 2014, Joey and I were blessed with a beautiful baby daughter named Indiana. She was born at home at 12:03 pm with the assistance of a midwife and the birth experience was perfect. She was delivered breech, naturally, with no medical assistance and with myself and our two older daughters Heidi and Hopie by Joey's side. Joey says that giving birth at home was the single greatest thing she's ever experienced in her life. A moment later, with Indiana's first cry, we all cried tears of joy and hugged and celebrated and cried some more.

In the days that followed, there was some concern about Indy and through genetic chromosome testing done at Vanderbilt Children's Hospital, it has been confirmed that Indiana has Down Syndrome. Although that news came at first as a surprise to us, Joey and I wouldn't have changed a thing. During the pregnancy, we never did an ultrasound, or saw a doctor, nor would it have made any difference if we had. We trusted that God would give us the baby He wanted us to have… and He has. Out of all the parents in the world, He has chosen us to care for and raise this special gift.

The baby is healthy and doing wonderful and Joey and I are loving each and every minute that we have with her. We can't wait to see where this new chapter in our lives leads us and what wonderful story unfolds in the coming years. We had already cleared our 2014 schedule and committed to taking this year off to be home and simplify our lives before we got this news, and now, we think it's even more important to be here than ever. Joey encouraged me to start writing a blog at the beginning of this year to share our lives from my perspective, and so I have. It can be found at thislifeilive.com. In posts from this year's journey so far, as well as this post and future ones, you can learn more about Indiana's birth story, diagnosis and much more, from the viewpoint of a very blessed husband, father, and songwriter.

Rory's not blogging as much these days. They have decided to take a step back from technology for a while and spend time living. But he does still post some, and you can find his blogs at http://thislifeilive.com/blog/

You can also find out more about Joey and Rory at http://joeyandrory.com/

A long time coming... Marty Stuart & Connie Smith

Connie Smith was born Constance Meadows on August 14, 1941, in Elkhart, Indiana, but spent most of her early life in West Virginia and Ohio. As a result of an abusive father when she was a child, she had a mental breakdown in her teens.

She married and became a housewife in the early 1960s and occasionally sang on local tv shows around her home in Marietta, Ohio. While singing in August 1963, country music star Bill Anderson hear her and offered to help her get a contract. She signed with RCA and in July 1964 recorded several songs including "Once A Day," which Bill Anderson had written just for her.

Connie had many hits in the 1960s, but touring was hard and she slowed down to re-evaluate her life, choosing to spend more time devoted to herself, family and religion. She didn't quit music and continued to record.

John Martin "Marty" Stuart was born September 30, 1958 in Philadelphia, Mississippi, Stuart is of French, English, Choctaw, and Colombian descent.

From an early age, he was obsessed with country music and taught himself how to play the guitar and mandolin. At the age of 12, Stuart started performing with the bluegrass group The Sullivans. This was also when he set his sights on Connie. She was performing at the fair in Philadelphia, Mississippi on July 24, 1970. Marty recalls getting his mom to buy him a special yellow shirt so Connie would be sure to notice him. He says he told his mom that evening that he was going to marry Connie Smith.

By 1972, Connie was singing more gospel in her act and while her gospel recordings didn't do well on the charts, she managed to stay in the Top 20 during much of the 1970s.

During this same time, Marty met Lester Flatt bandmember Roland White. White invited Stuart to play with him and the Nashville Grass at the Labor

Day gig in Delaware in 1972. After this, White asked him to join the band permanently and Stuart accepted. This made White responsible for the rest of Stuart's education. 14 year old Stuart appeared with the band on the final episode of the fifth season of Hee Haw. Marty stayed with Lester Flatt until Flatt broke up the band in 1978 due to his failing health.

Stuart worked with fiddler Vassar Clements and with guitarist Doc Watson. In 1980, he joined Johnny Cash's backing band. The previous year, Stuart made his first solo album, With a Little Help From My Friends, on Ridge Runner Records.

Over the years Connie and Marty became friends as their paths crossed in the music business and on July 8, 1997 they finally married. It was a long time coming, but these two seem to be living the life Marty was so sure he would. They can now be seen on The Marty Stuart Show on RFD-TV.

CUTLINES: Connie recorded Where Is My Castle in October 1970.

In 1970 Marty was playing with The Sullivans when he met Roland White bandmember of Lester Flatt.

Behind the Scenes SPOTLIGHT

We have so many talented folks that work behind the scenes of our television shows and tapings that we thought you should meet them. Their talents and experience surely humble us.

Dick Boise
Country Questions

Dick Boise started his career in country music while still in high school when he entered a contest in a neighboring town and won. The next day he was on radio station WRUN in Utica, NY.

During his senior year in high school he sat in to sing a song with the band "The Trailblazers" who were playing at a school dance. They liked him so much that they invited him to become their band singer. His first job with the band was on their radio show on WRKT in Cortland, NY followed by a show at Loomis Hayloft and the next day his high school graduation.

For the next several years, Dick worked with the band playing fair dates, college shows, dances and such. In December of 1952 he got to spend two weeks in Nashville and visited the Grand Ole Opry, where he met several artists. Then in January he got to come back and audition for George D. Hay at the Opry. While he wasn't quite ready to become an Opry artist, he considered it an honor, and he went back to work with his band.

In 1959, Dick's cousin, Clayte Boise, got out of the Air Force and they decided to form their own band called "Country Cousins."

The "Country Cousins" played dates and radio shows in the New York and Pennsylvannia area. Dick had mand friends with radio personality "Barefood" Bob Kinney and when he left to take another job, Dick was offered his spot to take over his "Saturday Morning Country Style" radio show on WCHN in Norwich, NY. The radio show lasted 21 years.

During this time "Country Cousins" was named Top Country Band in Central New York, Dick and his wife, Dotty, started their own record label, and he joined a new band in the area.

It was the 1970s when Dick got the idea for a country music newspaper and he started the "Empire Country Music News." It folded after only two years, but Dick eventually found other newspapers who felt his "Country Questions" column was important including the Renfro Valley Bugle and the CFR News.

Dick and Dotty live in Lexington, KY now, near their children and grandchildren.

In 2008 he was inducted into the New York State Country Music Hall of Honor and in 2009 into the New York State Country Music Hall of Fame.

The Gibson Brothers sing in beautiful harmony

The upstate New York bluegrass group known as the Gibson Brothers is really two talented brothers and a father-and-son team who can deliver a close-knit harmony without a hitch. The brothers are writer, banjoist, and vocalist Eric Gibson, born October 23, 1970 and writer, guitarist, and vocalist Leigh Gibson who was born just less than a year later on October 11, 1971. The father-and-son team is Junior Barber on Resophonic guitar and son Mike Barber on acoustic bass. Brothers Leigh and Eric began performing when they were kids, playing gospel instrumentals in the local church. They added singing harmonies to their act when they were around 16. They did numbers by artists such as Buck Owens and Jim & Jesse. A musician by the name of Bob Fuller made sure the young brothers were exposed to the music of bluegrass greats like Red Allen, Bill Monroe, and Jimmy Martin.

They recorded their debut album, Underneath a Harvest Moon, in 1994. It was released by the independent label Big Elm Records. The album featured tunes like "Your Man in the Middle," "I Never Was Too Much," and "Tears of Yesterday." In 1995, a performance at Owensboro, KY, landed the group a contract with Hay Holler Records. A year later, the Gibson Brothers released Long Forgotten Dream. With numbers like "Good as Gold," "Little Man in the Mirror," and "I Don't Know What to Do," the album did well enough to earn a place on the bluegrass charts, holding ground there for months. The title song made it into the Top 30 Survey for the Bluegrass Unlimited chart, reaching number ten.

Their next album, Spread Your Wings, hit the stores in 1997. It did as well as the debut. In 1998, the album Another Night of Waiting was released. In October of that same year, the Gibson Brothers signed on with the Ceili Music bluegrass label, owned by Ricky Skaggs, who produced the group's next album. Also in 1998, the Gibson Brothers were named the IBMA Emerging Artist of the Year.

The band plays over 80 shows and festivals a year and has gradually building a deeply dedicated, nationwide fan base with their beautiful harmonies, which can reach the high notes of Bill and Charlie Monroe and capture the tenderness of pop/country Everly Brothers.

You can see the Gibson Brothers on the Simply Bluegrass series, which is available for sale at 800-820-5405 or online at www.cfrvideos.com.

Above: The Gibson Brothers with Bill Monroe in Waddington, NY 1988

Left: The Gibson Brothers at Smokey Greene's 1988

Country Music Hall of Fame and Museum latest expansion complete

Originally located on 16th Avenue, called Music Row, the Country Music Hall of Fame and Museum moved to a new building in downtown Nashville on 5th Avenue in 2001 and has recently completed its most recent expansion.

The Country Music Hall of Fame and Museum moved from barn shaped home on Music Row in 2001. The new building on 5th Avenue incorporates the Hall of Fame, exhibits on country stars, and an archive of country music's history in a modern interesting looking building. The spire at the top of the Hall of Fame is a replica of the WSM radio tower. Inside the Hall of Fame, the radio tower is inverted and points to the center of the Hall of Fame room. When viewed from above, the entire building is shaped like a bass cleft.

The Country Music Hall of Fame® and Museum has just revealed the final phase of its state-of-the-art expansion. The ambitious 210,000-square-foot expansion more than doubles the size of the Museum and augments the institution's ability to focus on its core mission to preserve, interpret and teach the history of country music.

Previously unveiled sections of the expansion include an additional 10,000 square feet of dynamic new exhibit space; new education, entertainment, retail and event spaces, including the 800-seat CMA Theater; the Taylor Swift Education Center; the legendary and thriving letterpress operation Hatch Show Print; and the Event Hall with breathtaking views overlooking the Nashville skyline. The expansion also includes much needed archive and library spaces, allowing for even more robust cultivation of the museum's treasured collection.

The Museum has an extensive, permanent artifact collection. This collection includes more than eight hundred stage costumes, over six hundred instruments, and hundreds of other objects-from microphones to automobiles-documenting the history of country music.

Historic instruments include a harmonica used by country music's first African-American star, DeFord Bailey; Jimmie Rodgers's 1928 Weymann guitar; the autoharp Sara Carter used at the Carter Family's first recording sessions in 1927; Les Paul's 1941 experimental "log" electric guitar; a four-necked steel guitar Barbara Mandrell played onstage as a child; Mother Maybelle Carter's 1928 Gibson L-5 guitar; and Bill Monroe's Gibson F-5 Master Model mandolin.

As with many accredited museums with large holdings, less than one-tenth of the artifacts belonging the Country Music Hall of Fame and Museum are on display at one time. The majority of the collection is accessioned, preserved, and stored using the best museum practices available.

WHAT'S NEW! – ACM Gallery

The permanent, chronological exhibition has been updated to include over 100 brand new artifacts from today's hottest country artists, including Jason Aldean, Luke Bryan, Florida Georgia Line, Brad Paisley, Eric Church, Carrie Underwood and others. Enjoy the latest chapter in country music's ever-evolving story through this hands-on immersion into the music of today.

Dinah and Fred Gretsch Family Gallery

This new interactive gallery will educate and thrill visitors of all ages. Experience country music like never before through a 40-foot guitar, replica tour bus, songwriting stations, recording booth, and dozens of technology-enhanced activities that will leave you "Certified Country."

The Design Gallery: A Window into the Collection

Go behind the scenes of the Museum as curators and archivists prepare artifacts for exhibition and carry out other tasks related to the preservation and interpretation of the Museum's collection. As they work, you can catch a sneak preview of an upcoming exhibition, get a glimpse of our latest acquisitions, or see treasures from deep within our vaults.

Taylor Swift Education Center

Seven-time Grammy Award winner Taylor Swift officially opened the education center that bears her name on October 12, 2013. The 7,000-square-foot Taylor Swift Education Center includes classrooms and a learning lab with built-in technology to facilitate distance learning and outreach programs. The Taylor Swift Education Center allows the Museum to expand its current school and family programs, as well as develop new programs and serve new audiences. Swift's $4 million gift to fund this new new education center is the largest capital contribution by an individual artist in the Museum's history.

New Home for Iconic Hatch Show Print

After 135 years in five different locations around downtown Nashville, Hatch Show Print moved to 224 5th Avenue South in October 2013. This move enabled this iconic business, another historic property of the Country Music Hall of Fame and Museum, the chance to realize more room to continue to preserve, maintain and show the collection of type, blocks, and posters. The new facility features a larger, custom-designed print shop where visitors can watch posters roll off the presses; a store with wall space to display the 100-plus posters created by the print shop and available for purchase; Hatch Show Print's Haley Gallery, featuring historic restrikes of original posters from the Hatch collection, as well as Master Printer Jim Sherraden's monoprints – contemporary interpretations and celebrations of the classic wood blocks of Hatch Show Print; Hatch Show Print Space for Design, a classroom and workshop space that will offer visitors opportunities to learn more through demonstrations, hands-on printing and more in-depth programs.

Breathtaking New Event Spaces

The Museum's new expanded event spaces, include the beautiful new 10,000-square-foot Event Hall with a sweeping view of the downtown Nashville skyline, as well as the connecting outdoor Carlton Terrace, new 800-seat, state-of-the-art CMA Theater, and more.

New Shopping Experiences

The reshaped Museum Store offers exhibition-related merchandise, a comprehensive selection of original books and music, as well as official Museum and Studio B merchandise. Circa offers unique, Nashville-made gifts, food and home decorations, classic men's and women's clothing brands and seasonal items, as well as a wide-selection of fabulous jewelry, and lifestyle apparel and accessories.

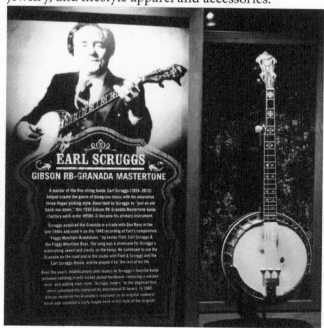

Larry's Country Diner in Branson!

Stage Clothes of the Star

By Claudia Johnson

BY CLAUDIA JOHNSON

Nudie Cohn:
From Rags to Rhinestones

Rhinestone cowboys and rhinestone cars. It seems impossible that a child born in the Ukraine in 1902 could have imagined such things, let alone create them, but that's what Nuta Kotlyarenko did. At age 11 Kotlyarenko was sent to America by his parents to protect him from widespread persecution of the Jewish community in Czarist Russia.

Nudie Cohn was born Nuta Kortlyarenko in Russia

He worked as a shoeshine boy, a boxer and at other odd jobs as he traveled America until he met and married lifelong partner Helen "Bobbie" Kruger in 1934. During the Depression the Kotlyarenkos supplied showgirls with custom undergarments, which they sold from their New York store, "Nudie's for the Ladies," giving Nuta Kotlyarenko the identity by which he was known the rest of his life – "Nudie" Cohn.

In the early 1940s Nudie and Bobbie settled in California and began creating and selling custom clothing from their garage. Drawing attention from performers like Cliffie Stone, Lefty Frizzell and Tex Williams, the business begin to flourish, and a soon a shop was opened in North Hollywood specializing in Western wear. The Cohns became tailors to Roy Rogers and Dale Evans, who epitomized the popular view of "Country-Western." A personal friend, Evans delivered the eulogy at Cohn's 1994 funeral, attended by hoards of former clients.

Perhaps the performer most consistently associated with Nudie's clothing creations is Porter Wagoner. In 1962 Cohn made an ornately embroidered and rhinestone-studded peach-colored suit featuring a covered wagon on the back and wagon wheels on the legs. He offered it to Wagoner at no cost in an effort to promote Nudie's of Hollywood's flamboyant designs, which have come to be known as "Nudie Suits."

It worked. Nudie soon moved his operation to a larger facility and renamed it Nudie's Rodeo Tailors. He also garnered a career-long customer in Wagoner, who bought 52 custom designed suits from Nudie, reportedly costing between $11,000 and $18,000.

"He could still fit into every one of them when he died," recalled Wagoner's fellow performer Jim Ed Brown.

Standing out from an extensive list of celebrities clothed by Nudie are John Wayne, Gene Autry, Cher, John Lennon, Ronald Reagan, Elton John, Robert Mitchum, Pat Buttram, Tony Curtis, Michael Landon, Glenn Campbell, Hank Snow and groups such as America and Chicago.

The $10,000 gold lamé suit Elvis Presley wore on the cover of his 1959 album, "50,000,000 Elvis Fans Can't Be Wrong," was created in Nudie's shop. Robert Redford's costume Nudie designed for the 1979 film "Electric Horseman" is now owned and exhibited by the National Cowboy and Western Heritage Museum in Oklahoma City. He created Hank Williams' white cowboy suit with music note embellished sleeves. ZZ Top band members sported Nudie Suits on their 1975 album "Fandango! album cover."

One of Nudie's more controversial creations was a suit featuring pills, poppies, marijuana leaves, naked women and a cross crafted for Gram Parsons to wear on the cover of the Flying Burrito Brothers' 1969 album "The Gilded Palace of Sin."

However, Nudie did not just tailor people. Between 1950 and 1975 he customized 18 Cadillac and Pontiac convertibles, using such bedazzlements as silver-dollar-studded dashboards, pistol door handles, rifles on the trunk and fenders, hand-tooled leather saddles and longhorn steer horns as hood ornaments. Many of these Nudie Mobiles are privately owned by collectors, but one is on display at the Country Music Hall of Fame in Nashville.

Though Nudie wore his own larger-than-life creations, the diminutive tailor often purposely wore mismatched cowboy boots, to remind himself, he said, of his humble beginnings.

Nudie Cohn, Jon Hager, Aunt Susie, Jim Hager, Tex Williams

Sons and daughters of Country Legends show at Nashville Palace

They give Larry Black and his filming of 2nd Generations credit for getting them all together and entertaining as the Sons and Daughters of the Legends!

They will share some stories about growing up with their famous parents and sing some of your favorite songs.

The 2Country4Nashville Band will accompany Robyn Young - son of Faron Young, Seldina Reed - daughter of Jerry Reed, Melissa Luman - daughter of Bob Luman, Jett Williams - daughter of Hank Williams, George Hamilton V - son of George Hamilton IV and Hawkshaw Hawkins, Jr. - son of Hawkshaw Hawkins and Jean Shepard will perform at the Nashville Palace presented by Robert's Western World on June 2. The doors open at 6:00 p.m. and the show starts at 7:00. Admission is $10 per person.

The Nashville Palace - Palace Parlour is located at 2611 McGavock Pike, Nashville, TN 37214. You can purchase tickets in advance by calling (615) 889-1540 or they can be purchased at the door.

The Mayor of Music Row, Charlie Monk will be the EMCEE. Charlie Monk is not only one of the founders of the Country Radio Seminar, (or CRS). He's also the host of the New Faces Show, the seminar's grand finale, which has helped launch the careers of Alabama, Brooks & Dunn, Mary Chapin Carpenter, Dixie Chicks, Vince Gill, Reba McEntire, George Strait and Travis Tritt, to name just a few.

Country Questions
By Dick Boise, CMH

Send questions to:
Dick Boise, , c/o CFR News,
P.O. Box 201796, Nashville,
TN 37221.

Q. I love what the Family Reunion shows are doing for the stars and the fans. I hear much talk about the Statler Brothers and Harold, Don, and Jimmy get mentioned and nobody says anything about Phil.

Ralph Maurath, Oakley, OK

A. You know Ralph, you are so right and we will do something about that. Phil Balsley was born August 8, 1939 in Staunton, VA. He was one of the first members who started singing together originally called "The Kingsmen." They were a gospel group and sand around the Staunton, VA area. Before the retirement of the Statlers, Phil   was very busy with the business and administration affairs of the group. A very talented baritone and truly an important part of the Statlers.

Q. Eddy Arnold had many number one hits and could you tell me what year he had the most? Thanks and enjoy the CFR News here at our house.

Betty and Fred Berninger

A. The late Eddy Arnold was truly a hit maker through the years. I did some research and found he had these number one hits, 10 in the 1940s, 9 in the 1950s, 7 in the 1960s, and it was written in one trade paper that he had a total of 145 weeks of number 1 songs. More than any other singer. Gone, but never forgotten, Eddy Arnold.

Q. I wondered if you could find out for me when Roy Acuff passed away. I always remembered his song Crash on the Highway when I was younger. Thanks,

Bob Myers, Kentucky

A. Thanks for your question about the great Grand Ole Opry Star everyone called Mr. Roy. He was born September 15, 1903 and passed away November 23, 1992. You know Bob, you give away your age by liking the song Wreck on the Highway, as it was recorded in 1942.

Q. I have always enjoyed Webb Pierce and wondered how old he was when he died. Miss hearing him on the radio as they don't play much good country songs anymore.

Martha Thompson, Johnstown, PA

A. Webb Pierce was 65 when he passed away, much too young. Born in 1926 and passed away February 24, 1991. His hit record, Slowly, was the very first song to use the pedal steel guitar with Bud Isaacs as the musician, 1954. I agree with you about radio today.

Comedian Jarrett Dougherty joins Billy Dean in Branson

The Starlite Theatre and Larry's Country Diner, welcomed well-known Branson comedian Jarrett Dougherty at the May shows where he had everyone in stitches.

Jarrett is creating a whole new cast of zany characters to join Grammy Award winner Billy Dean on stage as part of Billy Dean & the Steel Horses at the Starlite Theatre. "I have been having a great time performing my shows this spring at the Starlite" says Billy Dean. "It is going to be even more fun and definitely sometimes crazy adding Jarrett to the mix of entertainment we offer."

A native of the Ozarks and performing in Branson since 1995, Jarrett quickly gained popularity for his musical and comedic talents. Jarrett's side-splitting humor has rightfully earned him recognition as one of Branson's funniest comedians!

While seeking a work-life balance, Jarrett could not resist the opportunity to perform with country great, Billy Dean. Dougherty asserts, "I feel privileged to be given the chance to showcase my comedy alongside such great musical talents at the Starlite Theatre. It is definitely the hottest place for the coolest show in town!"

Linda Merkling, General Manager says, "Jarrett is a true pro and an excellent addition to our team! We are excited about his talent! Life is stressful, Jarrett is guaranteed to make you laugh and put a smile in your day!"

Show tickets and times are available by calling (417) 337-9333 or online at www.starlitetheatre.com.

Hank Jr. to become grandpa

Singer/songwriter Holly Williams and her husband, Chris Coleman, have confirmed that they are expecting their first child. The new arrival is expected this fall, giving the singer's famous father, Hank Williams Jr., his very first grandchild.

"We are so ecstatic to have this little miracle coming," said the mom-to-be in a statement. "The baby will become quite the road dog, experiencing all the amazing places we get to go as musicians on the road. Mom and Dad are unbelievably excited, and ready to spoil the little one!"

Her latest collection of tunes, The Highway, was released in 2013 on the singer's own label, Georgiana Records. Previously Holly has released three studio albums, including The Ones We Never Knew (2004) and Here with Me (2009).

Be sure to catch Dan Miller on Larry's Country Diner in July! And if you're in Cody, WY, go by and see his show, the Cowboy Music Revue!

WE HAVE A WINNER!!!

The winner in the Country's Family Reunion Ultimate Giveaway is Carolyn Sikorski of Mesa Arizona. Carolyn won over $2000 in DVDs!

New Faron Young CD to be released

Robyn Young, son of Faron Young, recently announced on his facebook page that a new CD filled with all previously un-released, digitally remastered material will be available soon. More information will be printed as soon as it becomes available.

By Claudia Johnson

Riders in the Sky, galloping on after three decades

Three decades is a long time for people to stay together. They get married, share joys and successes, have children and grandchildren, work, travel and weather life's storms.

Wait! That sounds like a marriage, but it's not. It's the career story of four men who comprise the two-time Grammy-winning cowboy quartet Riders in the Sky.

"We've been together longer than we've been married," said Douglas "Ranger Doug" Green, the group's guitarist and baritone vocalist.

Riders in the Sky also includes bassist Fred "Too Slim" LaBour, fiddler and tenor vocalist Paul "Woody Paul" Chrisman and accordionist Joey

"The Cowpolka King" Miskulin. Since first singing together in 1977, they have made more than 6,000 concert appearances in all 50 states and 10 countries, appearing in venues everywhere from county fairs to Carnegie Hall. They have performed at the White House for both Democratic and Republican administrations and at Major League Baseball's winter meetings for both American and National Leagues, but there is one venue that never ceases to inspire them.

"It is always a thrill to perform on the Grand Ole Opry stage and to be able to introduce some young artist breathless with excitement," Green said.

The quartet is the only Grand Ole Opry member to perform exclusively Western music, reviving and revitalizing the genre made famous by Sons of the Pioneers, Gene Autry and Roy Rogers.

"These were our heroes growing up – the romantic notion of the singing cowboy," said Green, explaining why Riders embraced the genre and adopted the colorfully embroidered and bejeweled costumes designed by Nudie the Rodeo Tailor for television and movie cowboys of the 1940s and '50s and now custom crafted by Manuel in Nashville.

A highlight of the Riders' career – and there have been many highlights – was a chance to work with Rogers in 1979.

"We almost could not speak," said Green recalling the first meeting with Rogers, who Green remembers as a "a real gentleman."

The quartet honors Rogers' legacy in a new album of Rogers' songs set for release in 2015, adding to their discography of more than three dozen albums. Though they have been recipients of a multitude of awards, two Grammy awards attest to their multi-generational appeal. Riders performed "Woody's Round Up" in "Toy Story 2," with the album of the same name, garnering Riders their first Grammy Award in 2001 for "Best Musical Album for Children." Two years later, Riders roped their second Grammy in the same category, for "Monsters Inc. - Scream Factory Favorites," the companion CD to Pixar's award winning movie.

To remain connected to their younger audience, these performers of traditional music communicate using Facebook, Twitter, Google+ and Blogger. Green said that one common form of technology would have been very handy in the group's early years.

"Slim got left six times at truck stops," Green admits. "Now that we have cell phones, that doesn't happen much anymore."

Apparently, the missing band member was forced to hitchhike to the next venue or all the way home.

"Once when we left him, we pulled into a truck stop later that day, and Slim hopped out of a semi he'd caught, got in with us and we went on our way," Green laughed.

Green said that for him the greatest aspect of spending half a lifetime on the road and the stage has exposure to personalities of other performers beyond their stage personae.

"I like to just sit down with them, hear them talk or crack jokes," he said. "That's why I think 'Larry's Country Diner' is such a great show. It's just a joy to be there with the others and really get to visit with them."

Precious Memories;
Remembering Jim McReynolds

Jim McReynolds was born deep in the mountains of southwest. Raised in the small community of Carfax, located near Coeburn, VA, he grew up in a family steeped in traditional mountain music. This background made it natural for them to follow in the footsteps of his grandfather Charlie McReynolds, a fiddler who recorded with the Bull Mountain Moonshiners for Victor Records on the famed Bristol sessions that launched the recording careers of Jimmie Rodgers and the Carter Family.

James Monroe McReynolds was born Feb. 13, 1927, in Carfax, Va. His brother, Jesse Lester, arrived two years later. Their harmony was exceptional, a rare quality that some say only brothers can produce. Jim's high tenor combined with Jesse's deep lead and unique mandolin style set this duo apart in the world of traditional music, now termed Bluegrass. Very early in their career, Jesse developed a "McReynolds style" technique on the mandolin, combining his invention of "crosspicking and split-string playing", which distinguished his picking from others.

Following Jim's discharge from the United States Army, he and Jesse made their professional debut a few months later in the spring of 1947 on WNVA in Norton, Va. This tenure lasted only a few months and was the beginning of a long succession of radio jobs.

They would spend close to a year in 1951 working at WPFB in Middletown, Ohio. While there, they made their first commercial recording for the Kentucky label with Larry Roll and were billed as the Virginia Trio.

Jim & Jesse moved to WVLK in Versailles, Ky., to become members of the Kentucky Barn Dance in 1952. While there, they received their first big break when they got a contract with Capitol Records. Up to this time, they had been billed as the McReynolds Brothers. At the suggestion of their producer, Ken Nelson, they changed their professional name to Jim & Jesse because there had been so many brother duos in country music, coupled with the fact that Capitol had recently signed the Louvin Brothers.

In 1960, Martha White Flour began sponsoring Jim & Jesse on television, and the following year they moved to Prattville, Ala., and also made their first guest appearance on the Grand Ole Opry. After many guest appearances, on March 2, 1964, Jim & Jesse fulfilled their life's dream to become members of WSM's Grand Ole Opry.

They continued with their own syndicated television show for a number of years and recorded a lot of material including and album of Chuck Berry tunes as well as an LP saluting their good friends the Louvin Brothers.

In 1993, the brothers received bluegrass music's highest honor when they were inducted into the International Bluegrass Music Association's Hall of Honor. They later went to the White House in 1997 to receive the prestigious National Heritage Fellowship Award from then First Lady Hillary Clinton.

In 2001, Jim started experiencing voice problems. After visiting numerous doctors and specialists, he was advised not to sing. In April of 2002, he underwent thyroid surgery and cancer was found, and it had spread to the lymph nodes. Jim was off the road until June, but resumed with Jesse and continued undergoing chemotherapy and radiation treatments. His condition worsened and he developed brain tumors.

Through it all, JIm never lost his dignity. His last appearance was at the Ryman Auditorium on WSM's Grand Ole Opry on Saturday, November 23, 2002.

He had to be helped to the stage, and even though he couldn't sing, sitting on a stool, he played rhythm guitar flawlessly. His appearance, as always, was neat, clean, and pressed to the highest degree as he smiled with pride helping to make the music he loved for the last time.

Sadly, on December 19, Jim's wife Arreta, died suddenly of a massive heart attack. Jim started hospice care the next day. His death came December 31, at 7:40 p.m. at the Sumner Regional Medical Center in Gallatin, Tenn. His daughter Janeen was by his side.

Kenny Rogers undergoes skin cancer surgery

Country Music Hall of Fame member posted an Instagram photo showing bandages on his face as he announced that he had surgery to remove some skin cancer on Wednesday, May 14.

The 75-year-old singer joked, "But you should see the other guy!" In his announcment he went on to say, "Had a bit of skin cancer removed today. I recommend everyone go get checked, especially since May is National Skin Cancer Detection and Prevention Month. Don't worry, though, I'm gonna look great in Knoxville this weekend!" Rogers performed his Knoxville concert the weekend of May 17.

JULY

Bobby Bare is truly an All American Boy

From "The All American Boy" to "God Bless America Again", Bobby Bare is truly an all American boy.

His story begins with his mother's death when Bobby was only five, followed by the split up of his family when his father couldn't earn enough money to feed his family. By 15 he was working in factories and selling ice cream to support himself. He built his first guitar and started playing music in his late teens and later moved to Los Angeles where he recorded his first record "The All American Boy," under the name Bill Parsons.

A number of labels refused the record before the Ohio-based Fraternity Records bought it for 50 dollars; the fee also included the publishing rights. "The All American Boy" was released in 1959 and it surprisingly became the second-biggest single in the U.S. that December, crossing over to the pop charts and peaking at number three. The single was also a big hit in the U.K., reaching number 22.

But success had to be put on hold when Bobby was drafted into the armed forces and while he was gone Fraternity hired someone else to tour as Bill Parsons. After Bobby left the Army he became roommates with Willie Nelson and decided to become a pop singer. This crossover into pop didn't last and he turned back to country establishing his own style. In 1962 Chet Atkins signed him to RCA Records

and by the end of the year his had his hit "Shame On You." "Detroit City" came out the following year and became his second straight single to make it in both the country and pop charts. "500 Miles from Home." was another big hit for the singer, peaking in the Top Ten on both the country and pop charts. Bobby continued to create hits in both the pop and country charts throughout the 1960s.

Bobby changed labels a couple of times in the 1970s and crossed over with pop, country and rock. He had success and tragedy as his 15-year-old daughter died in 1975.

Bobby's records were consistently critically acclaimed, but his record sales began to slip in the early '80s. In 2005, the Dualtone label coaxed Bare out of retirement and released a new album, The Moon Was Blue, produced by his son Bobby Bare Jr. Bare continued to perform concerts regularly over the next few years but he didn't return to the recording studio until 2012, when cut a collection of folk songs called Darker Than Light.

Bobby was inducted into the Country Music Hall of Fame on October 27, 2013 along with Kenny Rogers and the late Cowboy Jack Clement.

He is also on the God Bless America Again DVD series, which can be purchased for $79.80 plus $6.95 s/h at 800-820-5405.

Facts you may or may not know about the USO

Have you ever wondered how and when the USO got started? The USO stands for United Service Organizations.

In 1941, the U.S. Army made a plea for entertainment for troops preparing for the war in training camps around the country. The Citizens Committee for the Army and Navy responded and, in May1941, sent out seven traveling show buses, bringing entertainment to service men in Army camps east of the Rockies.

Meanwhile, a Hollywood committee financed by agents and producers, and with the cooperation of the Screen Actors Guild, put on several large shows at military camps in California. But the demand for entertainment continued to increase.

Later that year, the Citizens Committee for the Army and Navy, the USO and show business representatives met to come up with a solution. The result was USO Camp Shows, Inc., officially launched Oct. 30, 1941, as a separate corporation affiliated with and supported by the USO. USO Camp Shows, Inc., was designated by the War and Navy Departments as the "Official Entertainer" of the men and women of the armed forces. The USO's tradition of bringing entertainment to service members around the world was born.

Bob Hope made his first overseas tour in 1942. He went to Europe with Frances Langford, Tony Romano and Jack Pepper. At the end of the year, Camp Show units toured the South Pacific and the Middle East.

Touring Camp Shows were discontinued in 1947 but were revived in 1951 with the approach of the Korean War. Some 126 entertainment units put on more than 5,400 shows in Korea. Stars included Jennifer Jones, Jack Benny, Errol Flynn, Danny Kaye, Robert Merrill, Bob Hope, Marilyn Monroe, Marilyn Maxwell, Paul Douglas, Jan Sterling and Al Jolson. Jolson, who was warned not to make the trip by his doctor, died soon after he returned to the United States.

In 1957, USO Camp Shows, Inc. was dissolved. The USO assumed all responsibility for managing the entertainment needs of service members around the world – a tradition that continues today.

Country music has been a big supporter of the USO shows in recent years. In 1986

The Nashville Network began to air USO tours on its cable network, extending the programs to millions of viewers and also giving new publicity to USO entertainment. Loretta Lynn was one of the most popular performers.

Randy Travis made his first USO tour during a Christmas tour in 1987, to Germany and Italy. He continued to tour regularly during holidays, to the delight of his fans in uniform. This photo is from a Thanksgiving 1988 tour to Alaska, Japan and Korea.

Project Salute, Operation Iraqi Freedom's first large-scale entertainment tour to the Persian Gulf region in 2003, included Neal McCoy, Lee Ann Womack and other entertainers and athletes. Partners included MTV and Vanity Fair magazine.

Also in 2003, country music star Toby Keith went on his first of many trips to entertain troops around the world; as of 2010, he had completed eight tours. He was also instrumental in launching the USO2GO program. Here, an appreciative audience at Forward Operating Base Sharana in Afghanistan surrounded him and guitarist Scott Emerick.

Willie Nelson and Jessica Simpson treated the crowd to a duet at Ramstein Airbase in Germany in 2005, part of a performance shown on ABC that included the duo Big & Rich and others.

The USO's partnership with the country music industry is as old as the USO. The Grand Ole Opry and Gene Autry's radio show, "Melody Ranch," were popular programs during the 1940s. Country music stars from both programs traveled on several USO tours, entertaining military personnel stationed around the world. Thanks to exposure on USO tours, country music was introduced to many servicemembers from Northern regions of the United States who had considered the genre "hillbilly" music Country artists who have toured for the USO include:
Gene Autry
Red Foley
Roy Acuff
Minnie Pearl

Trisha Yearwood (left)
Hank Williams
Patsy Cline
Jerry Reed
Johnny Cash
Loretta Lynn
Conway Twitty

Barbara Mandrell
Dolly Parton
Mickey Gilley
Clint Black
Lee Greenwood
Charlie Daniels
Larry Gatlin
Ricky Skaggs
Randy Travis
KT Oslin
The Whites
Holly Dunn
Kris Kristofferson
Reba McEntire
Jamie O'Neal
Michael Peterson
Restless Heart
Craig Morgan
Darryl Worley
Mark Wills
Aaron Tippin
Trace Adkins
Neal McCoy
Chely Wright
Lee Ann Womack
Diamond Rio
Deana Carter
Merle Haggard
Sawyer Brown
Toby Keith
Wynonna Judd
The Bellamy Brothers
The Forester Sisters
Little Jimmie Dickens
Mary Chapin Carpenter
Jo Dee Messina
Rhonda Vincent
Jewel
Rockie Lynne

Fifteen facts about the USO

1. The USO traces its roots back to six other organizations . The Salvation Army, Young Men's Christian Association, Young Women's Christian Association, National Catholic Community Services, National Travelers Aid Association and the National Jewish Welfare Board all pooled resources to help start the USO at the request of President Franklin D. Roosevelt.

2. The organization derives its name from the generosity of six groups. The USO stands for United Service Organizations. (Don't forget the "s" in "Organizations."

3. A lot of people think it's a government organization. We're not. The USO is a private 501(c)(3) organization that supports America's troops and their families thanks to the support of generous donors.

4. The USO's push to help wounded, ill and injured troops isn't a new thing. The USO was sending artists – like Lila Asher – performers and musicians to entertain recovering troops during World War II.

5. You probably know the USO from the entertainment tours.

6. Particularly, those by a guy named Bob, who performed his first USO show just three months after the organization's founding.

7. Bob Hope entertained troops for 50 years, making his last overseas trip in 1990 during the Gulf War.

8. The USO center at Los Angeles International Airport bears his name today.

9. The USO worked with Congress to designate Hope as first honorary veteran of the United States armed forces.

10. The USO has more than 160 locations worldwide.

11. Country star Kellie Pickler visited several USO locations in Southwest Asia on her recent tour. Pickler's tour also linked up with the USO Christmas Convoy, which visited multiple bases in Afghanistan this holiday season, spreading gifts and cheer to troops who couldn't be home for the holidays.

12. Another little-known fact: The USO Warrior and Family Center at Bethesda, Md. was dedicated in honor of Prescott Bush, who was influential in raising funds for the USO during World War II. His son grew up to be President George H.W. Bush. And his son grew up to be President George W. Bush (who spoke at the 2008 USO Gala.)

13. Some of the simplest things we do turn out to be the most powerful. A free cup of coffee and a friendly ear when a stressed service member needs to talk. A recliner to take a nap between domestic flights. A TV break between 24-hour shifts as a base gate guard. If you've been to one of our centers, you realize food is a big part of what they do. Beyond the coffee and snacks, USO No Dough Dinners held at bases around the world keep younger enlisted troops with families to feedout of the red in the lead-up to payday.

14. The USO wouldn't be able to do any of these great things without volunteers. How many volunteers do you think the USO has? The answer: 27,000. Those volunteers gave a total of 1.35 million hours to the USO in 2013. Last June, Rear Adm. John Kirby was so inspired by watching USO volunteers take care of new sailors returning from boot camp that he wrote us an email saying, in part, "[A]ll of them were made to feel welcome and proud. All of them were treated like war heroes by the staff there. And it was the middle of the night."

15. The USO/Joining Forces campaign also hosted a care package assembly event timed for Mothers Day in 2012, where the First Lady and Dr. Jill Biden helpedCongressional spouses assemble packages for the mothers and spouses of deployed troops, including personalized notes from their loved ones serving abroad.

Nadine's Corner

Finally Homer couldn't stand it any longer. He went over to the new preacher and said "Oh, don't let that guy bother you, he's a little slow. All he does is go around repeating whatever he hears other people say".

Well Happy 4th of July! I hope you and your family has a wonderful holiday and remembers the blessings God has bestowed on our great country. We plan on having a special dinner on the grounds at our church. Speaking of our church... our pastor of 43 years passed on last month and we finally got a new preacher. He's a lot younger than all of us are use to .....but we are gonna give him a try. Last Sunday he stood at the church door greetings the members as they left the Sunday morning service. Most of the folks were very generous telling the minister how much they liked his message, except for one member who said, "That was a very dull and boring sermon, pastor." In a few minutes, the same member again appeared in line and said, "I don't think you did much preparation for your message." Once again he showed up in line, this time muttering, "You really blew it. You didn't have a thing to say pastor."

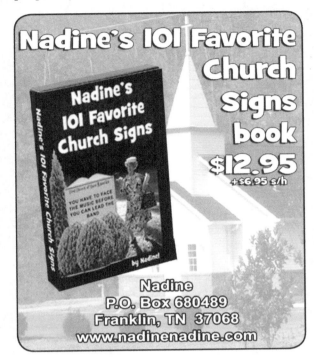
Country Songwriter Don Devaney Passes

Hit country songwriter Don Devaney died on Friday, June 6.

His friends and family will gather at Brown's Diner (2102 Blair Blvd.) to celebrate his life on Saturday, June 14, at 5 p.m.

Devaney hit the top of the charts with 1978's "Someone Loves You Honey," sung by Charley Pride and with 1988's "Cry, Cry, Cry" by Highway 101.

The songwriter also made the country charts with "Ever Lovin' Woman," recorded by both Pat Garrett (1981) and Marlow Tackett (1982), as well as with Mary Lou Turner's version of his "Yours and Mine" (1979).

He wrote the bluegrass standard "Listening to the Rain," which has been recorded by The Osborne Brothers (1970), Special Consensus (1996), Pam Gadd (1997), Doc & Merle Watson (1998), Ronnie Reno (2002), Monroe Crossing (2003) and others.

Other notable cuts include Johnny Cash's "Ain't Gonna Hobo No More" (1982), Rick Trevino's "Serious Love" (1996) and The Wilburn Brothers' "Signs Are Everywhere" (1970).

"(Drinking Beer And) Singing a Country Song" (Dick Curless, 1972), "You Keep Right on Loving Me" (Jim Ed Brown, 1972), "Comin' Home to Kentucky" (Kenny Price, 1972) and "If I Had Yesterday Again" (The Wilburn Brothers, 1968) are also Don Devaney songs.

"Someone Loves You Honey" has been revived by Brenda Lee (1982), Ronnie Dove (1996), reggae artists June Lodge (2000) and Dwight Pinkney (2002) and by Neal McCoy (2013). Devaney's songs have also been recorded by George Jones, Ray Price, Johnny Russell and Barbara Mandrell, among others.

Don Devaney was 78 years old. He is survived by daughter Heather D. Graffagnino (Chris), brother Gerald Devaney (Barbara), sisters Joy Sullivan (Brian) and Marilyn Smith and by grandsons Joseph and Zachary Graffagnino.

Behind the Scenes SPOTLIGHT

We have so many talented folks that work behind the scenes of our television shows and tapings that we thought you should meet them. Their talents and experience surely humble us.

Ingrid & the Larry's Country Diner taping catering staff

Ingrid Reed

Ingrid Reed of Reed Event Rentals and Catering cooks the chicken with potato salad and a variety of pies for the audience members to eat as they watch the musical guests perform and laugh as Nadine cracks jokes.

When it's time for the cast and musical guests to eat, Ingrid and her crew fix something great meals of items such as poached salmon, steak, Mexican entrees, barbecue ribs and other tasty meals.

"Larry left it up to me whatever I want to dazzle him with," Ingrid said. "I used to give him things good and yummy and high-calorie, now I try to look after his health."

Ingrid gets help from her staff.

Reed's culinary career includes being a personal cook for race car drivers, cooking Easter and Christmas Eve dinners for Charlie Daniels, and even styling food for music videos, including Johnny Cash's "Hurt."

"June (Carter Cash) came down the stairs in a robe and said, 'Oh, my gosh, that turkey looks so good I just want to eat it all.' And I said, 'Please don't, ma'am; it's covered in paint lacquer and it's raw in the middle,' " Ingrid said.

She has catered for "Larry's Country Diner" since the show began in 2009. She started off making traditional diner meals such as burgers, club sandwiches and more. When Springer Mountain Farms came on as a sponsor, that's when she made the switch to serving the same meal each show — 36 baskets of chicken, four shows a day.

Ingrid Grasman-Reed has spent most of her life pursuing the ups and downs of the culinary life. From her first blender as a child, to 11 years as a private chef for some of the biggest race teams in NASCAR and Indy , to food stylist for videos such as Rodney Crowell and Johnny Cash, Ingrid has been there and done it all.

Check out Ingrid's website to see what all she does at: www.reedeventandcatering.com

One of the most famous pets... and his owner; Trigger & Roy Rogers

By Claudia Johnson

Animals have long been important in the entertainment industry. Fictional animal characters such as Rin Tin Tin, Lassie, Babe the pig and the orca Willie have etched permanent memories on generations of viewers who fell in love with them. For moviegoers in the 1940s and '50s, no animal captured the hearts of children and adults more than cowboy crooner Roy Rogers' palomino Trigger.

"Trigger was without doubt the greatest horse ever to appear in motion pictures," said Joe Dortch, executive director of the Happy Trails Children's Foundation, a nonprofit that provides a safe haven for severely abused and/or neglected children, named in honor of Rogers and wife Dale Evans, who were passionate supporters.

Dortch said that before Rogers' first film, the star began his search for a suitable horse.

"As soon as he got on a big golden palomino stallion sent over by the Hudkins Brothers Stable, he knew that he had found the horse he wanted and did not need to look any further," Dortch said, observing, "In truth, it was a match made in heaven."

Smiley Burnett, Rogers' sidekick in his first two films, commented to Rogers that the big horse was "quick on the trigger," so Rogers decided that Trigger would be a good name for him.

"Trigger was very fast," Dortch said. "The beautiful golden horse was athletic and could stop on a dime and give you nine cents change. He could cut and spin so fast that a less experienced rider could be left in mid air, and yet his disposition was such that Roy could put three or four kids on his back at the same time without any worry they would be injured."

Rogers eventually purchased Trigger, who in a former movie role under his original name of Golden Cloud had been ridden by Olivia DeHavilland in the Errol Flynn film "The Adventures of Robin Hood."

For nearly two decades, Trigger appeared in 81 of Rogers' films and all 100 of Rogers' television episodes – a remarkable record unmatched by any other motion picture animal.

"Roy used doubles for Trigger in long shots and for some of the chase scenes," Dortch said, explaining that making Western pictures is very hard on horses, so Rogers was protective of Trigger's safety and health.

Trigger proved to be exceptionally intelligent, mastering tricks for bits written into the movies after being shown what was expected only a couple of times.

"He quickly learned the movie business, and when he heard the words, 'quiet on the set,' he would perk up, sometimes from dozing in the sun, ears alert, waiting on his cue, ready to work," Dortch said. "Likewise when he heard 'cut,' he would relax."

Dortch said Trigger was not only smart and professional, he was fearless, performing stunts that other horses would refuse to do. It's no wonder Trigger had starring roles in three of Rogers' films, "My Pal Trigger" (1946), "The Golden Stallion" (1949) and "Trigger Jr." (1950).

Rogers made numerous personal appearances with Trigger, who was almost as famous as his owner. More than once Rogers escorted Trigger up three or four flights of stairs at hospitals to visit with sick children, according to Rogers' autobiography "Happy Trails." Trigger was so popular, he even had his own series of Dell comics in the 1950s. After Trigger's 1965 death, Rogers had the hide professionally stretched over a foam likeness of Trigger, which was displayed at the Roy Rogers and Dale Evans Museum in Victorville, Calif., and later at Rogers' museum in Branson, Mo.

"Roy and Trigger had a true unity and partnership unmatched by any other cowboy star and his horse," Dortch said.

In 2010 Trigger's preserved remains sold for $266,500 to the television channel RFD-TV.

For more information on all of Rogers' and Evans' animals, visit www.happytrails.org

Lorrie Morgan celebrates 30th anniversary at Grand Ole Opry

In life and in art, the glamorous and gifted Lorrie Morgan is enjoying a renewed resurgence of popularity. Morgan continues to make new music, tour North America, and lat month she celebrated her 30th Anniversary as a member of the Grand Ole Opry!!! On June 9, 1984, Morgan was inducted as a member into the invitation only institution.

"You can't imagine how it felt the night I became a member of the Opry," says Lorrie Morgan. "The first time I could really call this place home. I couldn't stop shaking or trembling or crying."

Lorrie grew up backstage at the Opry, the daughter of Country Music Hall of Famer George Morgan, a 26-year member known everywhere for his smash 1949 hit "Candy Kisses."

Born in 1959, Lorrie made her Opry stage debut early, introduced at the Ryman Auditorium by her proud father. "My little 13-year-old knees were absolutely knocking," she recalls. "But Dad was standing there right beside me with big tears in his eyes, and those people gave me a standing ovation. I thought, 'This is what I'm doing the rest of my life.'"

"This was a dream of my dad's long before it was my dream," Lorrie says. "I have all of this because of Dad.

We're very blessed to be a musical family here at the Grand Ole Opry. What more could you ask for?"

George Morgan died when Lorrie was 16, but she still carries in her heart two pieces of advice he left her: "Never say, 'I can't,'" and "Always remember your manners."

Morgan's vocal style, combining country sincerity and pop sophistication, really took off in 1989 with the emotion-filled hit "Dear Me." She won a CMA Award in 1990 for her work with her late husband, Keith Whitley, the great country traditionalist who had died the year before. Her three subsequent albums — Leave the Light On, Something in Red, and Watch Me — all sold more than a million copies.

She has released hit after hit in a distinctive style steeped in passion and believability — "I Guess You Had to Be There," "What Part of No," "Except for Monday," "Something in Red," "I Didn't Know My Own Strength," "Half Enough," and others.

Throughout her career, Morgan says, she has thought of the Opry as home.

"The Opry gave me my start in country music," she says. "It's a place we all need to go from time to time to remember why we're here and what gave us the opportunity to be here."

Our fans and their Model A cars!

This Model A has been in Jerry Bergt's family for as long as he can remember. The above photos are what the car looked like when he brought it into his shop. The car belonged to his uncle until he passed away then Jerry bought it from his cousin.

"I worked on it for about two and a half years. We had a lot of shows and parades. I worked in sales for Jacob & Decker & Sons Packing Co. Roger Miller sang the Decker Hot Dog jingle for us," he wrote.

Jerry, who lives in Texarcana, TX loves showing his Model A.

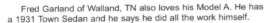

Fred Garland of Walland, TN also loves his Model A. He has a 1931 Town Sedan and he says he did all the work himself.

Do you have a Model A, or any other car that you have restored, and you would like to share it with the CFR NEWS and readers? Send photos and info to CFR NEWS, P.O. Box 210796, Nashville, TN 37221 or email them to: paula@gabrielcommunications.com!

The Roys release new music & tour schedule thru September

The award-winning bluegrass duo, THE ROYS, released the first single, "No More Lonely," from their highly-anticipated album The View, set to be released in September. The song celebrates a fresh, optimistic look at life and the dismissal of former anguish with the discovery of one's "true love." This upbeat track was penned by Lee and Elaine Roy, along with multi-BMI-Award-winning songwriter Steve Dean. Dean is responsible for writing songs for such icons as Conway Twitty, Barbara Mandrell, Lee Ann Womack, Reba McEntire, George Strait, Alabama, and many more

"No More Lonely" is a sampling from THE ROYS' upcoming fourth album The View, following last year's top-5 album, Gypsy Runaway Train, which also earned the #1 spot on Sirius XM Bluegrass Junction's Most-Played Albums Chart (Oct. 2013). As on Gypsy, The View will once again feature THE ROYS' band members Clint White on fiddle, Daniel Patrick on banjo and Erik Alvar on bass, giving listeners a chance to enjoy the same authentic sound that ROYS fans hear live and on tour.

The upcoming album comes on the heels of an amazing year of accomplishments, including THE ROYS' debut on the Grand Ole Opry, performance at "George Jones' Final No Show" tribute concert, being named the Inspirational Country Music (ICM) Awards Bluegrass Artist of the Year for the third straight year and #1 Bluegrass Artist at the 2014 International Acoustic Music Awards (IAMA). The Roys look to carry this momentum with them for the release of The View this fall.

THE ROYS are currently splitting their time in the studio with an active touring schedule this summer and fall. Festival appearances include Bean Blossom, Blistered Fingers, Rockahawk, Gettysburg, Poppy Mountain and Outer Banks Island Bluegrass Festivals and their back-by-popular-demand return to Country Thunder Wisconsin! Hope to see you there!

You can catch The Roys at the following locations/venues:

Jul 15 Mineral Wells, WV – West Virginia Interstate Fair & Expo

Jul 24-27 Twin Lakes, WI – Country Thunder

Aug 03 Athens, OH – Athens County Fair

Aug 07-08 Richmond, MN – Minnesota Bluegrass & Old-Time Music Festival

Aug 16 Gettysburg, PA – Gettysburg Bluegrass Festival

Aug 20 Staunton, VA – Bluegrass in the Park

Aug 22-23 Rogersville, NB, Canada – Rogersville Bluegrass Festival

Aug 25-26; Aug 28-29 New Richmond, Quebec, Canada – New Richmond Bluegrass Festival

Sep 20 Morehead, KY – Poppy Mountain Bluegrass Festival

Sep 21 Lyons, PA – 31st Annual Lyons Fiddle Festival

Sep 27 Manteo, NC – Outer Banks Island Bluegrass Festival

Oct 01-04 Raleigh, NC – IBMA Convention

Oct 10 Rio Grande, OH – Bob Evans Bluegrass Festival

Oct 19 Orange Park, FL – Orange Park Fall Festival

Nov 01 McKinney Performing Arts Center

Nov 14 Crystal River, FL – St. Timothy Lutheran Church

Nov 22 Dunnellon, FL – Withlacoochee River BGF

Dec 13 Pigeon Forge, TN – Christmas in the Smokies - Smoky Mountain Convention Center

Country Legends of the Past and Present

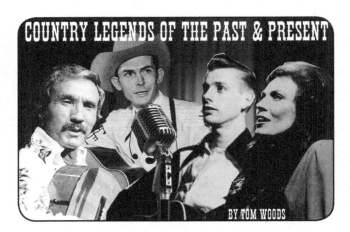

BY TOM WOOD

George Morgan

Of all the tributes accorded singer George Morgan during his illustrious four-decade career, perhaps none states the measure of his impact on country music than this:

On March 9, 1974, the country crooner was the closing act for the Grand Ole Opry's 31-year run at Ryman Auditorium in downtown Nashville.

A week later, on March 16, 1974, Morgan was opening act when the show moved into its sprawling new Grand Ole Opry House nine miles outside the city, kicking off a star-studded performance that included then-President Richard M. Nixon.

In being chosen for this singular honor, it is abundantly clear in what high esteem the Opry held for George Morgan. Truly a class act, often compared to contemporaries of his day such as Eddy Arnold, Perry Como, Mel Torme and Bing Crosby.

His first hit was his biggest. In fact, "Candy Kisses", released in early 1949, was Morgan's only chart-topping hit. It reached No. 1 in April of that year and spent three months atop Billboard's country music chart.

And when you start out on top, usually the only way is down.

But that wasn't true for Morgan, who remained No. 1 in the hearts of his legion of fans until his untimely death in 1975 at age 51.

Following "Candy Kisses," George had six more songs rated in the top 11 that year, with "Please Don't Let Me Love You," "Room Full of Roses" and "I Love Everything About You" all peaking at No. 4.

The silky smooth singer almost had another No. 1 in 1951 when "Almost" climbed to No. 2.

In all, 17 of his songs made it to the Top 25.

George had a thing for roses, at least his song catalogue suggests he did. In addition to "Room Full of Roses," he also had hits with "One Dozen Roses (And Our Love) in 1963, "Tears and Roses" (1964), "Red Roses For a Blue Lady" (1965), "Rose is Gone" (1971) and "Red Rose From the Blue Side of Town" (1974).

George was a member of the Grand Ole Opry from 1948 until his death, except for a three-year hiatus from 1956-59 when he hosted a country music show on one of Nashville's television stations. He was inducted into the County Music Hall of Fame in 1998.

He never got to see the success daughter Lorrie Morgan enjoyed, but he did sing — posthumously dubbed in — a pair of duets with her. In 1979, Lorrie released "I'm Completely Satisfied," and she followed up in 2006 with "From This Moment On."

Stage Clothes of the Stars

By Claudia Johnson

Manuel: Fringe and the Future

The sign simply states "Manuel" on the deceptively nondescript storefront at 800 Broadway. It might go unnoticed altogether if this wasn't Nashville and Manuel wasn't a legend.

Inside, it's all color and sparkles. A band is warming up. It's the first Thursday, and Manuel is hosting his monthly charity event, this one for Save the Music America.

"I am so grateful for the life I've had, and I want to give something back," Manuel said, watching as an eclectic crowd gathers.

Guests try on embroidered jackets – roses and rhinestones – or shirts of satin and silver, look at buttons, belts, boots. Framed prints show stars from Porter Wagoner to Elvis Presley to Elton John wearing custom designed clothing crafted by Manuel. There is history here, and Manuel has made it.

Born in a small Mexican town in 1938, Manuel Cuevas was taught to sew at age seven by an older brother. He learned to work with leather and silver. Armed with technical expertise, an artistic eye and youthful passion, Manuel moved at 21 to Los Angles, Ca. There he worked for "tailor to the stars" Sy Devore, where he crafted suits for style-setters like Frank Sinatra, Dean Martin, Sammy Davis Jr. and Bobby Darrin.

By the late 1950s he was seeking a new challenge, which he found at Nudie's Rodeo Tailors, the premier Hollywood outfitter for the Western-themed television and movie industry, country music performers and rock and roll giants. Having worked

with master embroiderer Viola Grae, Manuel was well-prepared to merge his skills and creativity to incarnate not only Nudie's designs but his own. He soon became head tailor and designer, contributing, during his 14 years with Nudie, some of fashion history's most iconic looks and making lifelong friendships. For example, it was Manuel whose fashion intuition helped shape Johnny Cash's identity as "The Man in Black."

"Johnny was one of my best friends," he said, noting that many of those he dressed across his long career are gone. "Presidents, athletes, dancers, artists, movie stars, singers… there are too many to name."

Standing out from among them all is Clayton Moore, who portrayed The Lone Ranger, a hero of Manuel's, on television and later in public appearances following the show's eight-year run. During Manuel's tenure

as Moore's costume designer the two became close personal friends – a friendship that lasted until Moore's death in 1999.

In the mid-1970s Manuel opened his own costume design studio in North Hollywood, finally settling in Nashville in 1989. Here he has racked up a multitude of awards and recognitions, created a traveling exhibit of embellished jackets honoring each of the 50 states, taught a number of young designers and tailors through an acclaimed internship program and costumed everyone who's anyone in the country music industry and beyond.

He said he is humbled at the support her has known from the Nashville community and its stars, from the clients he has long served to the ladies he calls the "queens of country" to the fresh young performers who have redefined the country music genre.

Manuel sees his current location on a major tourist thoroughfare as a gateway to sustaining his business, which in turn is good for Nashville's economy. He envisions expanding his lines, adding employees, partnering with accessory designers, training new tailors and attracting new types of customers.

"I want regular people who are not stars to feel they can come into the shop and look around, to try on the clothes… have the chance to buy something from the same place as the stars they love," he said. "I want them to feel like they are part of history."

Letter from one of our readers

"HEROES ALL AROUND US"

I wish to share a touching moment with all the readers. Friday night I was tuned into the TV channel for Country Family Reunion Program with Bill Anderson. There is a special running entitled "God Bless America Again."

I learned there is more to television than news, soaps, westerns, mysteries, and commercials. During this program, Bill Anderson told a story of a newspaper article he read years ago and got a gentleman from Alabama to help write a song about the article. The story he told about his song, "Old Army Hat," really touched my heart.

I would like to share this moment! It seems a 90 year old World War II veteran was told about the World War II Monument, and his son flew with him to Washington, DC to see this monument. When he came home from the war, he placed all his equipment in a cedar chest except his hat. He wore this hat to DC, and when he got out of the taxi cab at their hotel, the people saluted him and thanked him for his service.

When this hero got to the Washington Mall and came upon the World War II Monument, there were

two soldiers and a small boy present. One of the soldiers thanked him for his service, and the other soldier stated: "Amen." The little boy came up to him and shook his hand and told him of his father's service to our country and told the gentleman that his father did not make it home. He asked the gentleman if he would stand beside him and let him get a picture of him by the monument and would he please let him wear his "hat." This was so touching for the hero let the little boy wear the "hat," and he gave him the "hat" because every little boy with his courage should have a "hat".

This song "Old Army Hat" by Bill Anderson tells this story and was so very touching to my heart. My heart goes out to all our servicemen and women and their families for I personally know what they endure serving our Nation's Finest.

We live in the finest Nation because of God and these heroes that serve and have carried our "Old Glory" to many, many countries.

Thank you for allowing me to share this heart stricken moment with each of you.

Shelia Winsett, Parrish, AL

Country Questions
By Dick Boise, CMH

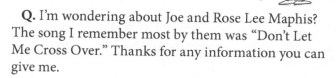

Send questions to:
Dick Boise, , c/o CFR News,
P.O. Box 201796, Nashville,
TN 37221.

Q. I'm wondering about Joe and Rose Lee Maphis? The song I remember most by them was "Don't Let Me Cross Over." Thanks for any information you can give me.

Wilma Christopher, Turney, MO

A. Thanks for asking about one of country music's man and wife teams. Joe Maphis was born in Suffolk, VA May 12, 1921 and was one of music's finest guitarists. He was noted for playing a double neck guitar that was created by Mosrite Guitars. Joe passed away June 27, 1986. Rose Lee was born in Baltimore, MD December 29, 1922. They were married in 1953 and Rose had a big birthday celebration in 2012 for her 90th birthday. Fine country music entertainers.

Q. I really liked George Jones' song "She Thinks I Still Care." What year was it a number one and who wrote it? Special thanks.

Betty Jean Huskins, NC

A. George had a hit with that great country song in 1962. It was written by Dickie Lee Lipscomb and Steve Duffy. THat truly is an easy song to enjoy and "Jones" gave us many fine country memories.

Q. I have enjoyed seeing Leroy Troy playing his banjo on the Marty Stuart show and my question is, wasn't there another old time banjo player who used to spin his banjo around when he sang? Leroy does a great job with Grand Fathers Clock. Most entertaining.

Bill Samuels, Dover, DE

A. I believe the old timer that you have heard of was "Uncle" Dave Macon. He was one of the early Grand Ole Opry entertainers and was there until his passing in 1952. I agree that Leroy plays and sings Grand Fathers Clock very well. Controls that banjo in a "timely" manner.

Q. I have been trying to remember what year Hank Williams had the hit song, Lovesick Blues. Hope you can aid me with this question. Thanks,

Cindy Collins, PA

A. Hank first sang that song to several encores on the Louisiana Hayride and later on the Opry with a similar effect. Many folks believe that it was one of Hanks greatest song writing efforts, however, it was written by Irving Mills and Cliff Friend. Others had recorded it before Hank Williams, but his version was the most successful one. The year Hank was first singing it was 1949.

The photo below is from Shelba O'Neal who sent it for us to pass along to Jimmy Capps. He is the one grinning from ear to ear, third from the right. The letter says:
"I am sending you a picture of Jimmy Capps travel on the road to Nashville and all the music he has played over the years for us to enjoy. Without the music behind the singers, there's not a song. I really enjoy what you are doing for Country Music. "
Shelba O'Neal,
Darlington, SC

Kids Corner

Max Munna, great grandson of Rosell & Wallace Brewer, Richton, MS.
Do you have a cute or funny baby or kid pic? Send it to us at CFR NEWS, P.O. Box 210796, Nashville, TN 37221.

Sons & Daughters of Country Legends packs housepacks house

The Sons and Daughters of Country Legends concert at the Nashville Palace on Monday, June 2 proved that traditional country music can still pack a house. The show was filled with the best crowd they had seen there in quite a while.

Charlie Monk was the show's emcee which featured the 2Country4Nashville band to back up the artists.

Robyn Young and Jett Williams sang first so they could get to a fundraiser held the same night by Georgette Jones. Seidina Reed and Melissa Luman Phillips represnted their dads well.

As a special treat, Hawkshaw Hawkins, Jr. sang with his mom, Jean Shepard and George Hamilton V sang with his dad, George Hamilton IV.

LeAnne and Jo-el Ulmer of the
2Country4Nashville Band

Jean Shepard and her son
Hawkshaw Hawkins, Jr.

Robyn Young

Radio personaility
Charlie Monk

Jett Williams

Seidina Reed

Melissa Luman
Phillps

George Hamilton
IV and V

Charlie Daniels' new recording set for Macy's July 4th celebration

On Friday, July 4th, The Charlie Daniels Band will help celebrate Independence Day as his newly recorded performance of "My Home," written by the Emmy Award winning songwriting team of Doug Katsaros and William Schermerhorn, will be synced to dazzling pyrotechnics as the 38th Annual Macy's 4th of July Fireworks® ignite the sky over New York City – Live from the Brooklyn Bridge. Set to deliver the nation's largest display of patriotic firepower and ready to dazzle more than 3 million spectators and millions more on television nationwide, Macy's Fireworks this year will be launched from barges positioned on the lower East River and from the world-famous Brooklyn Bridge.

"It's an honor to be a part of celebrating the birthday of the greatest nation on earth and an honor to be chosen to record this patriotic song that is going to be choreographed with one of the most spectacular fireworks displays that our country will see this year," says Charlie Daniels.

"As the song was being written for the fireworks score, we knew it had to be performed by an iconic American band that can get this country up on its feet!" says William Schermerhorn, creative director for Macy's 4th of July Fireworks. "It was thrilling to have Charlie and his band take this song and make it their own. And nothing could add to our pyrotechnic celebration like the sound of Charlie Daniels' fiddle!"

Beginning with the score, the musical blueprint to the high-flying explosions will be a patriotic wonder. The 25-minute display will be choreographed to dynamic new arrangements of both classic patriotic favorites and new musical selections. From "God Bless America" to "This Land Is Your Land," the score will feature the talents of the all-female musicians of The DIVA Jazz Orchestra; with vocal artistry featuring Tony Award® winner Billy Porter helming the new song "It's a Patriotic Kind of Day;" the world-famous Charlie Daniels Band on the patriotic "My Home;" and the acclaimed vocal ensemble Judith Clurman's Essential Voices USA putting their special touch on "America the Beautiful." In honor of the 200th Anniversary of "The Star Spangled Banner," Broadway superstar and Tony Award winner Idina Menzel will inspire the entire nation with her heartfelt rendition of the National Anthem.

Macy's explosive spectacle is made possible in part by Cracker Jack®, FYI™ Network, The Howard Hughes Corporation's South Street Seaport, Kool-Aid®, Planters®, South Street Seaport Museum, and is presented in partnership with the City of New York.

Fans joining the revelry in person along viewing points on the water will be in for extra special treats as the fun begins with two rumbling flyovers from United States Navy F-18 jets at approximately 7:30 PM and a patriotic flight from the NYPD Helicopter unit at approximately 7:45 PM. In addition, the FDNY will return with their famed 4th of July water show beginning at 8:00 PM. Public viewing locations and dedicated entry points will be set up along various streets in the South Street Seaport historic district for FDR Drive viewing in lower Manhattan and from various streets in Brooklyn for access to Brooklyn Bridge Park Piers 1-6, as well as the Brooklyn Heights Promenade.

Spectators from coast-to-coast will also have a front row view of the pyro in the sky by tuning to NBC's national broadcast of "Macy's 4th of July Fireworks Spectacular" at 8:00 PM ET (check local listings). In addition to the pyrotechnics, the 4th of July's most popular entertainment special will be hosted by Nick Cannon and feature performances from Ariana Grande, Hunter Hayes, Miranda Lambert, Lionel Ritchie, and more of the nation's hottest musical acts.

For more information on the 38th annual Macy's 4th of July Fireworks including detailed public viewing entry points and spectator tips, please visit www.macys.com/fireworks or call the Macy's Fireworks Hotline at (212) 494-4495. For marine viewing information please call 212-494-5243.

BY CLAUDIA JOHNSON

Ray Stevens - Play Misty for Ray

An impromptu jam session transformed a jazz standard into a Grammy-winning country song.

Written in the 1950s, "Misty" became the signature song of Johnny Mathis. It was covered a dozen times by singers from pop to gospel before it became an integral component in the plot of Clint Eastwood's 1971 movie, "Play Misty for Me." In 1975 "Misty" became a country classic, and Lisa Silver was in Ray Stevens' studio the day it happened.

Silver is a vocalist, musician and songwriter who for four decades has made a career as a backup singer, studio musician and fiddle player in Nashville. She's earned more than 20 gold and platinum albums for her contributions to thousands of recordings by hundreds of artists. More than 50 of her original songs have been recorded, and her number one song, "Forty Hour Week," recorded by the group Alabama, earned her a Grammy nomination.

Back in 1975, however, Silver was a relative newcomer in Nashville when Stevens invited her to his studio to play fiddle and sing for possible inclusion in a tour band he was assembling. Among the stops would be performances at "Disneyland" and on "The Tonight Show" with Johnny Carson. Stevens offered her the gig, and Silver was thrilled when rehearsals began at Stevens' studio adjacent to his Nashville office.

"Everything was set up, then the steel [guitar] player began jamming on the song "Misty," Silver recalled. "We all just chimed in, and when we got to the line where it says 'and a thousand violins began to play' I started sawing on the country fiddle."

Stevens quickly called in his engineer.

"Ray worked up this really fun, cool arrangement," said Silver, who can be heard playing the fiddle and singing with Stevens on the background vocals. "We recorded it, we overdubbed the vocals and it was done in about an hour."

"Misty" garnered a Grammy Award in the Best Arrangement category for Stevens that year.

"It was spontaneous," Silver said. "Ray had this flash of inspiration. He hears things in his own way, and he puts his own stamp on it. He knew this would be great, and it just took off."

Silver has maintained a professional relationship with Stevens since that day.

"He has always been fun to work with," Silver said. "Even though he seems wacky, he is very serious about getting the music right. He would often write out the musical notation of what he wanted us to sing and play. He is a brilliant guy."

A recent project in which Silver participated was Stevens' eight-volume CD set, "Encyclopedia of Recorded Comedy Music," which features 12 tracks of Stevens' comedy songs and 96 new recordings of classic comedy songs, all performed by Stevens.

"When we were working on it, we would listen to the original, then we would listen to the way Ray wanted to do it," Silver explained. "There were elements of the original, but we did them in his own unique, Ray Stevens way."

Silver said that since first touring with Stevens from 1975 through 1981, she has been asked to work with him in some manner almost every year since – public performances, television appearances, studio sessions – and she does.

"He's consistently professional. He knows what he wants and knows how to do it," Silver observed. "He is also very loyal. There are not that many people who would be calling the same folks 40 years later. It has been a great association with him."

Precious Memories; Remembering Hank Locklin

When Hank Locklin sang a tear-jerker like "Danny Boy," the tone of his sorrowful voice could make people shiver

Lawrence Hankins Locklin was born on February 15, 1918, just south of Brewton in McLellan, Fla., a village so small it is not shown on most maps. Hoedowns with guitars and fiddles were a common occurrence in the family living room.

Hank was hit by a school bus when he was 9. "It almost mashed me flatter than a fritter," he said in an interview.

During his recuperation, he learned to play the guitar. He had already begun singing at the local church, where his mother played the piano. He won amateur contests and by his teens was a featured performer on a radio station in Pensacola, Fla. He dropped out of high school to become a traveling musician, often taking jobs on farms or at shipyards to supplement his income. He sometimes shared a stage with Elvis Presley.

His style was influenced by Roy Acuff and Ernest Tubb, he had one of his first hits in 1949 for 4 Star Records with "Send Me the Pillow You Dream On," which he both wrote and recorded. He took the title line from a song written by Claude Casey and had a much bigger hit when he re-recorded it for RCA in 1958.

"Please Help Me, I'm Falling", his 1960 hit, was Billboard's No. 1 country song for 14 weeks and spent 36 weeks on the country charts. It also climbed to No. 8 on the pop charts. Other hits included "Geisha Girl," "Let Me Be the One," "It's a Little More Like Heaven," "Happy Birthday to Me" and "Country Hall of Fame."

He was one of the first to travel the globe playing country music and is particularly credited with helping popularize the genre in Ireland.

Pianist Floyd Cramer developed his celebrated version of the "slip-note" piano style, in which the piano seems almost to slur notes, in "Please Help Me, I'm Falling.". That style became Hank's signature backup sound in many more recordings.

Later, Hank found his way to Houston, where he hosted his own radio show. After his first broadcast of the "Pillow" song, which he had written in 20 or 25 minutes, the station was deluged with 200 pillows. After recording for several smaller labels, his career took off when he signed with RCA in 1955. He stayed with the label for 19 years.

His marriage to Willa Jean Murphy ended in divorce. He then married Anita Crooks and was married for 39 years, until his death on March 8, 2009. He had two sons and three daughters, as well as 12 grandchildren and 8 great grandchildren.

For the country music establishment, Mr. Locklin's death represented the loss of "the fourth Hank," said Bart Herbison, executive director of the Nashville Songwriters Association International. The other three were Hank Williams, Hank Snow and Hank Thompson.

At his death, Hank Locklin was the oldest member of the Grand Ole Opry, where he performed for nearly a half-century. He recorded 65 albums and had 70 charted singles, including six No. 1 songs on the Billboard country chart. He sold 15 million records worldwide. His songs were recorded by hundreds of artists, including Willie Nelson, Dolly Parton and Roy Rogers. Little Jimmie Dickens has now surpassed him.

Jimmy C. Newman, gone but never forgotten

Jimmy C. Newman was 86 when he passed away Saturday night, June 21, in Nashville after a brief illness. His wife of 66 years, Mae Daire Newman was one of his greatest fans.

Born Jimmy Yeve Newman on August 29, 1927 in High Point, Louisiana just outside Big Mamou, he is known world wide as Jimmy C. Newman (C stands for Cajun.) Though raised true Cajun, it was the cowboy music of his boyhood hero Gene Autry that got him started singing with bands and performing throughout Southwest America. and in his youth with his brother Walter, helped support his mother and father on their family farm. His lifelong dream was realized when in 1956 he was invited to join the Grand Ole Opry. He gave his last Opry performance on Friday, June 6, 2014 with his band, Cajun Country. The legendary Jimmy C. Newman was an absolute pioneer in Cajun-Country music history! He charted 33 songs on the Billboard Country Chart from 1954-1970

He was inducted into the North American Country Music Association's International Hall of Fame in 2000, the Cajun Hall of Fame in 2004, and the Louisiana Music Hall of Fame in 2009; Grammy nominated, Jimmy C. Newman is undoubtedly a true legendary music pioneer.

As a member of Chuck Guillory's Rhythm Boys, a band he joined while still a teenager, he was adding several Cajun songs to his repertoire. Jimmy recorded songs in the late 1940s for J.D. Miller's Feature label. J.D. was later instrumental in convincing Nashville legend Fred Rose to give Jimmy a chance in Nashville.

As a singer, songwriter, and guitarist he signed a record deal with Dot Records in 1953 and scored a hit the following year with a song he co-wrote "Cry, Cry, Darling". It reached #4 on the Billboard country charts. This was to become the first of 33 career hits to land on Billboard charts.

His next 4 songs all hit the top 10..."Daydreamin'," "Blue Darlin'," "God Was So Good" and "Seasons Of My Heart". Jimmy became a member of the Grand Ole Opry in 1956 and released "A Fallen Star" the following year. The single spent a total of 21 weeks on the country chart, including two weeks at #2 and also entered the pop Top 25. After 7 hits on Dot records, he signed with MGM Records in 1958.

"You're Makin' a Fool Out of Me" was the first of 8 hits on MGM before moving on to Decca Records. He began to integrate Cajun influences into songs like the 1961 release of "Alligator Man" and a year later, "Bayou Talk."

His 1963 album FOLK SONGS OF THE BAYOU COUNTRY is considered a historic milestone in the popularization of Cajun music. It included the talents of accordion player Shorty LeBlanc as well as Rufus Thibodeaux on fiddle. The album produced songs like "Jolé Blon", "Louisiana Moonlight", "Pretty Mary Ann" and "Grand Chenier" which he wrote.

Among his 14 hits on Decca was "D.J. for a Day", released in December of 1963, it went to #9. The song was written by an "unknown" songwriter signed to Jimmy's song publishing company. The writer was Tom T. Hall and the song was his first recorded hit. Other songs to note on Decca were "Artificial Rose" a #8 hit released in October 1965, and the top 10 hit "Back Pocket Money" from spring of 1966 (both Tom T. Hall songs).

Other labels he has recorded for include Rounder, RCA, Plantation, La Louisiane, and Delta.

In his later years, he enjoyed spending time with his wife Mae on his ranch in the Big Spring Community just south of Nashville.

He is survived by his wife; his son Gary Newman and his wife Sharon of Broussard, LA; granddaughter Natalie Newman Valdes and husband John of

Pompano Beach, FL; step-grandchildren Neil Simon of Houston, TX, and Jacy LeBlanc and her husband Mike of Lafayette, LA; step-great grandchildren Michael and Emmy LeBlanc.

A memorial service was held Wednesday June 25, 2014, 10:00 am at The Ryman Auditorium

A little about some upcoming artists on Larry's Country Diner

Jamie O'Neal was born Jamie Murphy in Sydney, Australia, to parents Jimmy and Julie Murphy, who were also professional musicians. In the early part of her career she was a backing singer in Australia, appearing on Kylie Minogue's Enjoy Yourself Tour of Australia, UK, Europe and Far East Asia in 1990. She rejoined Minogue's tour in 1991 for the Rhythm of Love Tour (Australia and Far East Asia) and the Let's Get To It Tour of the UK and Ireland.

She was signed to Mercury Nashville in 2000, and soon after she began to work on her first album. Her first single, "There Is No Arizona", debuted at No. 69 on the Billboard Hot Country Singles & Tracks (now Hot Country Songs) chart, reaching number one in February 2001.

In 2002, she and the country singer Mark Wills recorded a duet together, titled "I'm Not Gonna Do Anything Without You". It was released as the second single from Wills' album Loving Every Minute. The song only reached No. 31 on the Hot Country Singles & Tracks chart.

Jamie O'Neal is married to Rodney Good, who is a songwriter, record producer, engineer, and guitarist in O'Neal's road band. They have one daughter, Aliyah, born in 2003.

Tim Menzies

Timothy Ray Menzies, born August 25, 1959, in Mechanicsville, Virginia, known as Tim Mensy, is a country music artist who debuted as a performer at age three, with a band his mother was a member of. He was born to a musical family. He, his two brothers, two sisters, and parents performed throughout Virginia. They opened shows for Dolly Parton, Johnny Cash and other country music stars. At age eight, he was playing mandolin in the band. Mensy suffered a hearing disorder as a child, which he overcame at age sixteen following seven operations.

He was also a member of the band Bandana. The band charted several singles on the Hot Country Songs charts in the 1980s. After leaving Bandana, Mensy began a solo career on Columbia Records in 1990, releasing his debut album Stone by Stone that year. A second album, This Ol' Heart, followed in 1992 on Giant Records. Overall, these two albums produced six singles for Mensy on the country charts as well.

In addition to his work as a musician, Mensy has written songs for several artists, including Mark Chesnutt, Shelby Lynne, Trisha Yearwood, and Reba McEntire.

Nadine's Corner

Father Brian, an elderly Catholic priest, was speaking to Father Karl, a younger priest, saying, 'You had a good idea to replace the first four pews with plush bucket theatre seats. It worked like a charm. The front of the church always fills first now.'

Father Karl nods, and the old priest continues, 'And you told me adding a little more beat to the music would bring young people back to church, so I supported you when you brought in that rock 'n' roll gospel choir. Now our services are consistently packed to the rafters.'

'Thank you, Father Brian,' answers the young priest. 'I am pleased that you are open to the new ideas of youth.'

'All of these ideas have been well and good,' comments Father Brian wisely. But I'm afraid you've gone too far with the drive-thru confessional.'

'But, Father Brian,' protests the young Father Karl, 'My confessions have nearly doubled since I began that!'

'Indeed,' replies the elderly priest, 'And I appreciate that. But the flashing neon sign, "Toot 'n Tell or Go to Hell" cannot stay on the church roof.'

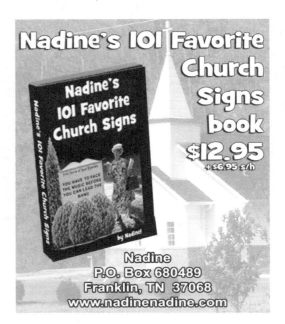
Larry's Country Diner RFD Show Schedule

JOHNNY RODRIGUEZ
Saturday, August 2
10:00 p.m. Central
Sunday, August 3
6:00 p.m. Central

JAMIE O'NEAL
Saturday, August 9
10:00 p.m. Central
Sunday, August 10
6:00 p.m. Central

TIM MENZIES
Saturday, August 16
10:00 p.m. Central
Sunday, August 17
6:00 p.m. Central

HOT CLUB OF COWTOWN
Saturday, August 23
10:00 p.m. Central
Sunday, August 24
6:00 p.m. Central

GEORGE HAMILTON IV
Saturday, August 30
10:00 p.m. Central
Sunday, August 31
6:00 p.m. Central

Joe Bonsall: Sharing One Life with Many Cats

By Claudia Johnson

A house full of cats and a heart filled with compassion led one member of a beloved quartet to establish a charitable foundation serving animals in need.

Joe Bonsall, tenor for the Oak Ridge Boys since 1973, along with his wife, Mary, established the Joseph S. and Mary Ann Bonsall Foundation support to animal-related causes.

Bonsall said his family had dogs while he was growing up in Philadelphia, Pa., and for the past 15 years he's kept donkeys named Blondie and Truffles at his 400-acre farm in Macon County, Tenn. However, it was when a big, orange cat named Pumpkin entered the Bonsalls' lives in 1982 that pet ownership became a passion. Soon Omaha, Molly and Gypsy joined Pumpkin.

"We so enjoyed watching and relating to them," Bonsall said, recalling how the cats inspired him to write Molly, The Home, Outside and Brewster, a series of children's books starring his own cats and capturing their distinctive, even human-like qualities. "Cats are like people. Every cat is different, so I gave them their own language, their own personality and their own story line."

The money from these books, which remain available for purchase, was used to start the foundation, which is funded primarily by the couple's personal contributions as well as through donations from friends, family members and fans. Bonsall said that 100 percent of every donation goes directly to charities and that no administration fees or salaries are paid.

"The foundation has provided funds for animal shelters and rescue centers," Bonsall said, adding that education about pet ownership is another area of focus. "Adopting a pet is a lifelong commitment, and it is important that owners act responsibly and have their animals spayed and neutered, take them to the vet and care for them. They are a part of your family, and they add to your home."

Bonsall said the foundation also provides direct assistance when needed. Recently, a donation was made to Walden's Puddle in Sumner County, Tenn., after a fire killed dozens of rescued animals and devastated a portion of the nonprofit's facility. Other Nashville-region recipients of foundation assistance are the Freedom Farm Animal Sanctuary and the Sumner County Human Society.

A dedicated writer, Bonsall's popular "Molly" books are not his only literary contributions. He's had nine books published. In 2003, he released a biographical book, G. I. Joe and Lillie: Remembering a Life of Love and Loyalty, about his parents, who met during their service in World War II.

"The book still sells," he said. "It's touched a lot of people's lives because so many people relate to that period of history."

An accomplished songwriter, he wrote the title song for the Oaks' "The Journey" album, as well as the text for the Oaks' 2004 coffee table book, An American Journey. Also in 2004, he published a children's Christmas book, An Inconvenient Christmas.

A collection of commentaries, stories and other writings, From My Perspective, was released in 2010.

He is currently writing a new book for release in 2015 that offers an inside look at the history of the Oak Ridge Boys, who continue to perform 150 or more engagements annually and have sold some 41 million albums in their four decades together. In April, the Boys' released their first-ever live album, "Boys Night Out," in three formats, CD, vinyl and digital download. The talents of Bonsall and each of the other quartet members, Duane Allen, William Lee Golden and Richard Sterban, are collectively and individually showcased in the 14 cuts chosen from more than 60 recordings of several live performances.

The original Oak Ridge Boys began as a gospel quartet during World War II, and throughout the years, gospel music has remained important, with religious songs performed alongside pop and country. In 2012, the Oaks recorded "Back Home Again," an album of gospel favorites for the Gaither Gospel Series. Bonsall said they have been invited by Bill Gaither to record a new album of hymns this fall, which should be released in early 2015.

Busy as he is with writing, performing and recording, Bonsall is never too busy to appreciate his daughters and grandchildren and to savor the life and home he shares with Mary and their seven felines.

"I love having cats around," he confessed, laughing, "They are like beautiful pieces of artwork that have the capacity to throw up on your computer."

Behind the Scenes SPOTLIGHT

We have so many talented folks that work behind the scenes of our television shows and tapings that we thought you should meet them. Their talents and experience surely humble us.

Jan Reams - Makeup Artist

JAN REAMS is a licensed Massage Therapist, Instructor/ Aesthetician, Cosmetologist, professional make-up artist, Certified Clinical Aromatherapy Practitioner and Owner of Ageless Journey Salon, Murfreesboro, TN.

It has been Jan's goal to stay abreast of new modalities and information that could benefit her clients. This quest resulted in seeking out certifications in Clinical Aromatherapy, through Jane Buckle and Associates, Dr. Vodder Lymphatic Drainage of the Head, Face and Neck, Bellanina ®Facelift Massage Dinair® Airbrush Cosmetics, and Face Sculpting Micro Current.

Jan has been active in the professional makeup arena since 1989.

"I started my career, as a professional make-up/ Hair Stylist, at a time when videos were beginning to break in Nashville. I have been blessed to work with those just starting their careers, to major stars.

I have worked on video projects with numerous celebrities like Vince Gill, George Jones, Billy Ray Cyrus, Judy Collins and others. I have worked numerous award shows, television shows and photo sessions as well.

I met Larry Black on a project with a local production company and was asked to work on the CFR shows. When Larry decided to do the Diner, I was blessed to be asked again to be a part of a new show. You couldn't ask for a better boss than Larry Black. I look forward to every taping of Larry's Diner and the CFR shows. I love the music, the guests and the crew. What a wonderful thing to be doing something I truly enjoy!"

Buzz Cason: A great songwriter you may not know you know!

The book, Living the Rock 'N' Roll Dream: The Adventures of Buzz Cason, is about freedom, adventure and, above all, music and the fun Buzz Cason has had being an integral part of it for almost 50 years. This book is an insider's view of the early days of rock'n'roll, from a man whose experiences influenced music history. Buzz's story is for everyone, from the aspiring young musician looking to break into the business as a performer or songwriter, to the fan, reflecting on life, music and dreams.

One of the most interesting things about this book, is the great crossover there was between Rock 'n' Roll, Rockabilly and Country music during the 1950s and 1960s. Buzz worked and toured with some of the great country and rockabilly legends. His book tells the stories of performing on shows with Brenda Lee and Carl Perkins, writing songs with Bobby Russell and living the life of a musician.

From his early days as a teenager in 1957, when Buzz formed The Casuals, one of the first rock bands in Nashville and over the next four decades as he worked successfully as a performer, songwriter, producer, actor and recording studio pioneer, his book covers it all.

He wrote the hit song "Everlasting Love," published the award-winning songs "Honey" and "Little Green Apples," sang with Roy Orbison, Kenny Rogers, Brenda Lee and Jimmy Buffet, and recorded with such artists as Olivia Newton-John, Emmylou Harris, Merle Haggard and The Gatlin Brothers.

Buzz was also one of the guests on Rock 'N' Roll Grafitti, a DVD series produced by Larry Black and Country's Family Reunion, which he mentions several times in his book.

Buzz Cason is someone you may have never heard of, but I'm sure you've heard and enjoyed many of his songs.

The book can be purchased at www.amazon.com

POETS AND PROPHETS
SALUTE TO LEGENDARY SONGWRITER
BUZZ CASON

Photo by Garth Shaw

Wayne Moss, Chip Young, Scotty Moore, Sonny Curtis, Jerry Chesnut, Buzz Cason, Bob McDill, Allen Reynolds, Dickey Lee, Michael Gray, Dallas Frazier, and Bergen White

This Life I Live

scenes from one man's extraordinary, ordinary life

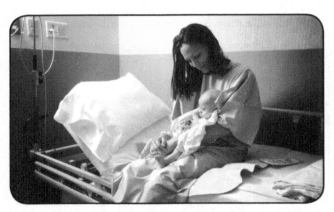

Home of the brave – Joey, courage and cancer

by Rory, Wednesday, Jun 25, 2014

It's been almost a month since my last post. And though I had planned, and even written, some entries to share (like my trip in May to the Amish with my sister Marcy and the day I spent making homemade strawberry jam with Joey), it didn't seem right to post stories like that right now…. not with the story that has been unfolding in our lives for the last six weeks.

In May, at a routine appointment with her gynecologist, Joey's doctor discovered something that concerned her. She said there was a mass on Joey's cervix and that she wanted do a biopsy, and would let us know the results when she got them back. A few days later, Joey woke up from a nap with a message from the doctor, asking that we come in and talk with her that afternoon. When we walked into the her office, the doctor was clearly upset. Before she could even say the word "cancer", her eyes welled up with tears and sobbing she said, "I'm so sorry Joey…". My wife bravely smiled and said, " it's gonna be okay, just tell us". And so she did.

Joey has cervical cancer.

It's a strange thing when your doctor starts crying before you do. Especially when it's a doctor you don't really even know. This was only the second time we had ever seen her. Strangely, the first time was when we were at the hospital after the birth of Indiana, and she is the one who took me out into the hall and told me that she believed that our baby had Down Syndrome. I was completely caught off guard. In the excitement and joy of Indy's birth, none of us had even given her little almond eyes a thought. But from that moment on, I knew our lives and our story would forever be different. And once again, as we heard this sweet doctor say "it's just not fair" through her tears… we knew that our lives and our story was taking another unexpected turn.

When we got home and the news finally sank in, Joey only worried about one thing. It wasn't "why did this happen to me" or "am I going to be okay", or a hundred other questions that I would've had. Joey only thought of our baby. She cried and cried worrying about Indiana, and what this might mean to her… what if she couldn't continue breastfeeding her, or will Indy's sleep schedule be interrupted, or worse yet…what if she won't get to watch this precious gift grow up?

I can honestly say that in the six months that we've been off the road and taking a break from the music business, I haven't picked up a guitar once and Joey and I haven't sang a single song together. But when I came in the house that day and saw Joey holding Indiana in her arms, singing "I Need Thee Every Hour"… I went into the closet, pulled out a guitar and came and sat beside her. For a half-hour straight, we held our little one and we cried and we sang these words over and over.

I need Thee every hour, in joy or pain

Come quickly and abide, or life is in vain

I need Thee, O I need Thee

Every hour I need Thee

O bless me now, my Savior

I come to Thee

And then, like turning off a faucet,… we said a prayer, dried our tears and decided to put our trust in Him.

A few days later we were in another office seeing a gynecology/oncology specialist in Nashville and he told us that though the mass was already 4 cm and growing aggressively, we had caught it early. He recommended that Joey have a radical hysterectomy right away to remove the cancer and surrounding areas.

And so, this past Friday, we loaded up our four-month-old baby, and along with our older girls and Joey's mama… drove to Centennial hospital in Nashville. And soon after, my brave little wife, kissed us all goodbye and smiled as they wheeled her away to surgery.

About 6 hours later, they wheeled her out of the recovery room and though she was still groggy and in some pain, she waved to us and smiled again and we walked with her as they wheeled her to her room.

The next morning about 11 am, she got to come home to our farmhouse.

It's been five days now, and Joey's getting stronger every day. Her swelling is going down and spirits continue to go up. We had a follow-up appointment with the oncologist yesterday and he said that the margins and the lymph nodes he removed came back clean, so there's no more cancer in her body and she won't need chemo or radiation. There in the waiting room after the appointment, we held each other and our baby, and we cried once more.

I heard a preacher tell a short story one time about God and a tandem bicycle. I'm reminded of that story today. It's only 3 minutes long, but the lesson has stayed with me for years.

Yes, it has been quite a year for us so far. In the past six months, God has taken us places we never dreamed we would go. It's been terrifying and thrilling all at the same time. We never know what tomorrow will bring…none of us do. But what an incredible journey life is. We are just going to continue to trust Him and hold to each other and… pedal, pedal!

You can also find out more about Joey and Rory at http://joeyandrory.com/

Our hearts and prayers go out to Joey and Rory and their families, happy that she does not need chemo or radiation, but sad for what they have had to go through in the past few months. -- ed.

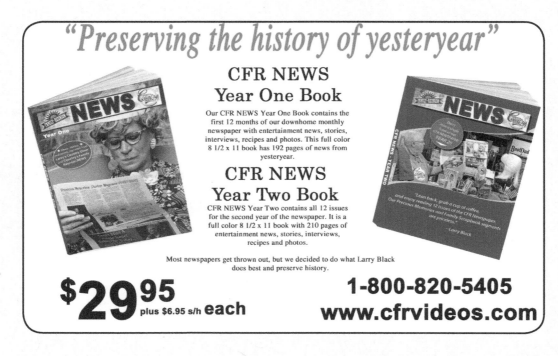

Nashville in danger of losing historic RCA studio A

Ben Folds, a tenant at the historic RCA recording studios building, sent an open letter out to the residents of Nashville this past June. It was to give them a heads up about the prospect of losing another of Nashville's music legacies. According to Folds' open letter, the building is set to be sold to a Brentwood development company. In the letter, Folds said he is unaware of the developer's future plans for the building.

Folds said he has leased the studio for the past 12 years and pumped more than $1 million into rent and upgrades.

"I could have built my own space of the same dimensions with that kind of investment," Folds said. "But I'm a musician with no interest in development or business in general."

"I only want to make music in this historic space, and allow others to do the same."

His letter said, "On the day that would have been Chet Atkins' 90th birthday (June 20), my office received news that the historic RCA Building on Music Row is set to be sold. This building, with the historic Studio A as its centerpiece, was Atkins' and Owen Bradley's vision and baby, and had become home to the largest classic recording space in Nashville. Word is that the prospective buyer is a Brentwood TN-based commercial development company called Bravo Development owned and operated by Tim Reynolds. We don't know what this will mean to the future of the building."

Folds gave kudos to the estates and descendants of Atkins and Bradley "for doing their best to keep the building alive. They've owned the property all these years and could have at any point closed it up or mowed it down. Sadly, it's what happens in the name of progress. Studio A, which turns 50 years old next year, has a rich history."

Some of the artists who have made hits at the RCA building are:

Asleep at the Wheel, Steven Curtis Chapman, Faith Hill, Alan Jackson, Jim Lauderdale, Ronnie Milsap, Willie Nelson, The Oakridge Boys, Phil Vassar, Hank Williams Jr., and LeeAnn Womack, to name just a few.

Folds went on to say, "I had no idea of the extent of legacy of this great studio until I become the tenant of the space 12 years ago. Most of us know about Studio B. Studio A was its grander younger sibling, erected by Atkins when he became an RCA executive. The result was an orchestral room built to record strings for Elvis Presley and to entice international stars to record in one of these four Putnam-designed RCA spaces in the world. The other three RCA studios of the same dimensions – built in LA, Chicago and New York – have long since been shut down. I can't tell you how many engineers, producers and musicians have walked into this space to share their stories of the great classic recorded music made here that put Nashville on the map. I've heard tales of audio engineers who would roller skate around the room waiting for Elvis to show up at some point in the weeks he booked, stories about how Eddy Arnold recording one of the first sessions in the room and one of the songs was "Make The World Go Away," Dolly Parton (Jolene) and The Monkees recorded here, and so on. Legendary songwriter John D. Loudermilk and his bride were serenaded by a session orchestra hired by Atkins who were recording here for an artist. He recalled that they danced all the way to the loading doors and into their limo, reminiscing about the beautiful floor tiles which still line the entire space. He co-wrote countless numbers of songs with Atkins and many others in this studio."

To this day, Studio A remains a viable, relevant and vibrant space.

"Before the news of the sale I had been in recent talks with other entities on how we could collaborate on allowing visitors to Music City to see the space firsthand and hear its rich history, while also making sure that it stays busy making music history of tomorrow. No one can say now what will become of that idea."

"Selfishly I'd love to remain the tenant and caretaker of this amazing studio space. I love it dearly. But if I must let it go in the interest of change, my only hope is that it remain intact and alive. A couple of years ago my co-manager, Sharon Corbitt House, promised the late, great producer Phil Ramone, while he was in town recording Tony Bennett and an orchestra LIVE in this space, that she would do what she could to keep the studio doors open. Ramone had watched the former New York RCA studio transform into office space for the IRS and couldn't bear to see the last of this incredible acoustic design fade away."

Folds, as well as many other musicians in Nashville wonder what will the Nashville of tomorrow look like if we continue to tear out the heart of the Music Row that made us who we are as a city? Ultimately, who will want to build new condos in an area that has no central community of ideas or creatives?

"My simple request is for Tim Reynolds or whoever the next owners might be of this property, before deciding what to do with this space, to take a moment to stand in silence between the grand walls of RCA Studio A and feel the history and the echoes of the Nashville that changed the world. I'd like to ask him and other developers to listen first hand to the stories from those among us who made the countless hit records in this studio – the artists, musicians, engineers, producers, writers who built this rich music legacy note by note, brick by brick."

"I don't know what impact my words here will have on anything. But I felt the need to share, and to encourage others who also care about preserving our music heritage to speak up as well.

I believe that progress and heritage can co-exist in mutual respect. Maybe this time we can at least try to make the effort.

A crowd of Music Row artists, songwriters, technicians and other concerned citizens gathered at a rally inside the famed RCA Studio A in Nashville to rally support for the studio and other historic buildings, June 30. The rally was planned when news reports noted that the studio building was being bought and would possibly

be demolished by a Nashville developer.

Preservationists were able to breathe a little easier when the developer shared that the company intends to save the studio, should the impending purchase go through. But the rally continued as planned, taking on the bigger picture issue of preserving other buildings in Nashville's iconic Music Row area

On the flip side of this story, a letter was sent to the Metro Council from Harold Bradley, The Owen Bradley Family, and The Chet Atkins Family Trust is concerned that a zoning overlay could prevent the sale of the property that they say was intended to be an investment for the future.

The letter goes on to say, "When a tenant, with no ownership in the property, requests restrictions to a property without the owners' consent, he effectively hijacks the owners' original risk and the possibility of a good return on their investment."

This is a complicated issue, which has many upset, but hopes from everyone seem to be that the property can be sold to appease the families, and that whoever purchases the building will be able to keep the historic Studio A intact.

What Musicians Are Saying

Robyn Young's thoughts give an insight into the frustration of the traditional country artists when he says, "Why should a building survive when the careers & the music have not? It is just the latest victim of Murder on Music Row. At least it doesn't have feelings, unlike the artist who were made then cast away there."

When told of the rumored sale, Jimmy Capps was surprised and said, "Oh no! History must mean nothing anymore. We must respect our history."

Deana Carter attended the rally and recalled how fond her father, musician and producer Fred Carter Jr., was of the studio. "Dad worked here a lot. He was part of the A-team crew of session musicians," Deana said. "The history here means everything. It's so important that we don't lose this place."

John Anderson among those to be inducted into Nashville Songwriters Hall of Fame

Nashville Songwriters Hall of Fame inductees were revealed on Tuesday, July 8 at a press conference at Music City Center in Nashville. Joining John Anderson are celebrated songwriters Paul Craft, Gretchen Peters and Tom Douglas. All four will be officially inducted during the 44th Anniversary Nashville Songwriters Hall of Fame & Induction Ceremony, October 5, at Music City Center. The awards are presented in conjunction with Nashville Songwriters Association International.

John Anderson

John wrote many of his best-known hits, including the award-winning "Swingin'" and "Seminole Wind." He will be inducted in the Songwriter/Artist category. John told Country Weekly following the announcement that he was pleased to be recognized for his songwriting.

"That means an awful lot to me because we fought so hard for many of the songs I'd written," John said. "I figured out early on that writing your own songs could be very helpful to your career. I was fortunate to have great writers around me who would help and advise me."

Paul Craft

Paul Craft has written an eclectic mix of hits, including "Dropkick Me, Jesus" by Bobby Bare and "Brother Jukebox" by Mark Chesnutt. He has also had songs recorded by such bluegrass greats as Earl Scruggs and Dr. Ralph Stanley.

Gretchen Peters

Gretchen Peters first found songwriting success with "The Chill of an Early Fall," recorded by George Strait. Her most widely known song is the anthemic "Independence Day" by Martina McBride, which won the 1995 Country Music Association award for Song of the Year.

Tom Douglas

Tom Douglas scored one of his early songwriting hits with "Little Rock" by Collin Raye. He also co-penned Lady Antebellum's "I Run to You" and "The House That Built Me" by Miranda Lambert, the 2010 Country Music Association award winner for Song of the Year.

(Clockwise from top left) Nashville Songwriters Hall of Fame Board Chair and Hall of Fame member Pat Alger, John Anderson, Gretchen Peters, Hall of Fame executive director Mark Ford, Tom Douglas and Paul Craft photo courtesy Alliance Media Relations

Country Legends of the Past and Present

BY TOM WOOD

Kitty Wells

There's a honkytonk angel singing in heaven now.

Kitty Wells had plenty of hits during her long and productive career — but just three No. 1 records.

And that first smash hit was exactly that—knocking down barriers and opening doors for female country singers that had previously been shut.

When the ground-breaking "It Wasn't God Who Made Honkytonk Angels" burst onto the scene in 1952, it struck a chord with the national consciousness and its serious message. But the song — written by a man (J.D. "Jay" Miller) — was also controversial at the time, banned from airplay. Still, it quickly sold more than 800,000 records and became a treasured anthem for women.

With its success, Kitty Wells became the first woman to reach the pinnacle of the U.S. country charts. She was dubbed the Queen of Country Music, a title that stuck with Kitty until her death in 2012 at age 92.

Unbelievable as it may sound today, until Kitty came along, record companies just did not believe that an album made by a woman could successfully be marketed. But her record company believed in Kitty as she was the first woman to issue a country album, a collection of her greatest hits in 1956, followed by her first studio album a year later.

Kitty proved them wrong and she became the standard-bearer for generations of female artists, a true inspiration.

Combined with her string of other chart successes, "It Wasn't God Who Made Honkytonk Angels" earned Kitty a lifetime membership in the Grand Ole Opry and induction into the Country Music Hall of Fame (1976).

Her other No. 1 songs were "One By One" (1953), a duet with Red Foley, and "Heartbreak USA" (1961). And while great songs that cemented her place in history, neither had the impact of her first smash hit.

Nearly 40 years after the song came out, "It Wasn't God Who Made Honkytonk Angels" earned Kitty a Grammy Lifetime Achievement Award in 1991. She was the first female country artist to earn that recognition (and only the eighth woman so honored). Previously, only two country music stars, Hank Williams and Roy Acuff, had received Lifetime Achievement honors from the Grammys.

And another honor was accorded to Kitty's life-opening anthem in 2008 when the Library of Congress added "It Wasn't God Who Made Honkytonk Angels" to the National Recording Registry along with "Oh Pretty Woman" by Roy Orbison.

Born Ellen Muriel Deason in 1919, Kitty lived all her life in Nashville. At age 18, she met and married Johnnie Wright in 1937 and they remained together until Johnnie's death in 2011 at age 97, just 33 days before the couple's 74th wedding anniversary.

Stage Clothes of the Stars

By Claudia Johnson

Stringbean's Style Unduplicated on the Country Stage

Amid the fringe and rhinestones, Stetsons and boots, bouffants and calico, David Akeman's stage style is unduplicated in the annals of country music history.

A banjo player and comedy musician, Akeman was best known by his stage name, Stringbean, alluding to his thin 6'5" frame. Stringbean admitted that his stage costume was inspired by Renfro Valley Barn Dance fiddle player Homer "Slim" Miller, who wore a plaid or striped shirt with grossly oversized pants held up by suspenders.

Stringbean's interpretation of the look combined Miller's choice of shirts but made with an exceptionally long waist and tail. These were tucked into a small pair of pants belted around his knees, making Stringbean appear to have very short legs. Tradition holds that fellow performer Little Jimmy Dickins loaned Akeman the first pair of Lilliputian-length pants to create the costume. Sometimes the pants were tucked into tall boots creating an even more distorted body shape.

Photos of Stringbean made prior to adoption of his signature costume show a tall, well-groomed but not especially handsome man in a variety of clothing styles. Born in 1916 in rural Kentucky, Akeman began playing music in childhood and performed as a musician at local dances while still a youth. To make a living during the Depression he built roads and planted trees with the Civilian Conservation Corps.

Winning a contest judged by musician Asa Martin gave Akeman a chance to work as a singer, comedian and musician when he was invited to join Martin's band, also playing with other groups as the 1930s progressed. A photo of the Bar X Boys, a group comprised of Adair County, Ky., musicians, appeared in the local paper on Feb. 1, 1939, during the time the band had been playing on WLAP-AM radio in Lexington, Ky. His four band mates are wearing dark tailored slacks, crisp white shirts, narrow ties and tall-crowned hats. Akeman, who had already been dubbed Stringbean by Martin, wears a plaid shirt, overalls, a boxy casual jacket and a flat-crowned hat. Prominent in the old photo is Stringbean's long, narrow, very pale bare foot.

In the 1940s, Akeman played semiprofessional baseball and was captured in a photo with other musicians who played for the Bluegrass All-Stars, including Bill Monroe. Stringbean became Monroe's first five-string banjo player, playing in an old-time clawhammer style, as well as the two-finger method, working with Monroe from July 1942 to September 1945. In a promotional picture of Bill Monroe and his Bluegrass Boys, Akeman, like the rest of the band, wears a white shirt, wide necktie, black slacks and a cowboy hat.

After leaving Monroe's band, Akeman married Estelle Stanfill. The smiling couple posed for a 1940s-era portrait with Akeman wearing a suit and tie and uncharacteristically exposing his thick crop of wavy brown hair. Estelle, too, wears a suit, tinted powder blue in the portrait, with an elegant silky blouse tied elaborately at the throat. A 1960 candid of the couple snapped at a WSM breakfast shows both of them wearing conservative tailored suits.

Akeman performed regularly on the Grand Ole Opry from the late 1940s until his death in 1972.

He and his Opry co-star, neighbor and best friend Louis "Grandpa" Jones were founding cast members in 1969 of the long-running comedy variety show, Hee Haw, where Stringbean wore bibbed overalls instead of his Opry costume.

Overalls were also his attire of choice in his personal life. In fact, they were fitted with a special compartment that substituted for a bank account. Having lived through the bank failures of the Hoover years, Stringbean distrusted banks and did not hide that he often carried thousands of dollars in his clothes. Rumors also swirled that Stringbean had a fortune in cash stashed at his Ridgetop cabin.

When Stringbean and his wife returned from a performance at the Opry on the night of Nov. 10, 1973, they encountered cousins John and Marvin Brown,

who had broken into the cabin and searched without success for hidden money. Akeman was shot dead as he entered his home, while Estelle was killed outside. Both men went to prison for the murders.

Twenty-three years later in 1996, $20,000 was discovered within the cabin's brick chimney. Time and rodents had turned the cash to confetti.

Country Questions
By Dick Boise, CMH

Send questions to:
Dick Boise, , c/o CFR News,
P.O. Box 201796, Nashville,
TN 37221.

Q. My Uncle Fred used to mention a song about a shirt the mother made. Could you tell me something about it? Thanks and we enjoy the CFR News at our home.

Betty Ann, New York

A. Your Uncle Fred was probably speaking of "The Little Shirt My Mother Made for Me." It was believed to have been written in England and Bradley Kincaid, "Radio's Kentucky Mountain Boy" learned it in Chicago. He sang it often on the WLS Saturday Night Barn Dance show. I learned that great old song from my late friend "Barefoot" Bob Kinney who entertained with Bradley Kincaid back in the early 1940s. Little note of interest, Bradley gave Louis Marshall Jones his nickname "Grandpa," while playing a WBZ in Boston in the mid 1930s.

Q. My Mother had a favorite song called "Young Love." Could you tell me when it was recorded and by whom it was recorded? Thanks.

Jon Harrison, Farfax, VA

A. That was a 1956 Capitol record by Sonny James. His real name is James Loden, born May 1, 1929.

He had 22 number one hits in his years of singing. Sonny was inducted into the Country Music Hall of Fame in 2006.

Q. I was sad to hear the passing of Jimmy C. Newman. I would like to ask where was he born and what was his middle name. I always liked his song "A Fallen Star." Thanks,

Mike, Broken Bow, OK

A. Yes, a sad day for country music when we lost Jimmy. He was born Jimmy Yves Newman on August 27, 1927 in High Point, Louisiana. The C. that he used in his show name stood for Cajun. Your favorite "A Fallen Star" was his biggest hit and in 1957 it was #3 on the country charts and #25 on the pop listings. He was a favorite of many.

Q. Could you find out for me where Freddie Hart was born. I know he was in California in his early music times. We enjoy him on the Reunion TV shows. Thanks,

Billie Williams, Dayton, OH

A. Freddie Hart, whose real name is Fredrick Segrest, was born in Loachapoka, Louisiana, December 21, 1925. Most folks believe that he got started in music in California, however, long before that he came to Nashville in 1949. And then next year, Lefty Frizzell had Freddie on the Lefty tours. He wrote many hit songs that other recorded and "Easy Loving" was the first of five number one hits for him.

From the Six Hoosiers to Captain Stubby & the Buccaneers

Tom C. Fouts, nicknamed Stubby for his stature, left Indiana Central University after a year, and in 1938 formed a band with five friends. The Six Hoosiers specialized in comedy, Fouts playing novelty instruments like a "tuned toilet seat" he called the "gitarlet."

WDAN radio in Danville, Illinois signed them to a contract, and in 1940 held a contest to rename the Six Hoosiers. The $100 prizewinner suggested Captain Stubby and the Buccaneers. (During performances, Fouts would sometimes refer to them as "Captain Stubby and the bucket of tears."

Several of the band members joined the U.S. Navy in 1944, Entertainment Division, going overseas to entertain sailors. Tom chose to return home to the family farm to stay out of the war. The other band members eventually convinced him that joining the effort was the right thing to do. After World War II they signed with WLS Radio in Chicago and performed on the popular National Barn Dance, heard throughout the Midwest.

Captain Stubby and the Buccaneers first performed the original Roto-Rooter jingle on WLS in the early 1950s, and the recorded version became one of the longest-running tunes in the history of advertising, featuring Tom Fouts' bass voice in "Away go Troubles Down the Drain." Shortly before his death at 85 in 2004, he contributed to nostalgic radio spots for Roto-Rooter.

Captain Stubby and the Buccaneers also sang the 1959 Chicago White Sox fight song, "Let's Go, Go-Go White Sox", and Tom Fouts was the voice of Green Giant's Little Sprout.

Captain Stubby and the Buccaneers eventually became regulars on the ABC-TV program Polka Go-Round. They also recorded with five labels, performing many of Fouts' songs. With singer Lola Dee, they recorded the Mercury Records single "Padre" and "Takin' The Trains Out". Fouts was host of a syndicated talk show called Captain Stubby's Special Delivery. He also wrote for and performed on the national Don McNeill's Breakfast Club from 1968 until 1971.

Curly Myers and Tiny Stokes performed for a while as the Two Bucs. For a period of time in the late seventies and early eighties all five buccaneers worked for Martin Buildings, a farm pole building company, performing at state fairs throughout the Midwest, on Caribbean cruises and even one trip to London. In the mid 1980s the Two Bucs were performing Wednesday through Saturday at a Best Western.

The band continued to perform together under an agreement of equal pay. When it was discovered Tom Fouts was performing quietly with a band of his own making called "Captain Stubby and His Buccaneers" using musicians that were not part of the band and without compensating his fellow band members, the original Buccaneers demanded he halt using their name for his own personal gain. He cancelled future shows.

Larry's Country Diner returns to Branson's Starlite in September

Don't miss your chance to see Larry and his cast of characters including the wisecracking church lady Nadine September 23 through 28, 2014. Starlite Theatre is proud to present the live production of the popular hit series. for tickets and information please visit starlitetheatre.com or call the box office 866-991-8445.

Rhonda Vincent & The Rage - September 23

The undisputed Queen of Bluegrass brings her hot-pickin band The Rage back to The Starlite for an evening of fun and music with the cast of Larry's Country Diner on September 23. Rhonda Vincent & the Rage have gained popularity since their formation, playing hard-driving, high-energy contemporary bluegrass music. Her 2001 album, The Storm Still Rages, was nominated for seven International Bluegrass Music Association awards, including Female Vocalist of the Year. She also won 3 consecutive IBMA Female Vocalist of the Year awards.

Gene Watson - September 24

Watson's long career has notched two number ones, 23 top tens and over 75 charted singles, including his big hits "Love In The Hot Afternoon" and his signature song "Farewell Party." Gene Watson was inducted into the Texas Country Music Hall of Fame in 2002 and inducted into the inaugural class of the Houston Music Hall of Fame in August 2014. Always a stupendous vocalist, his voice has only gotten better. This show will sell out so get your tickets early!

Dailey & Vincent - September 25

Dailey & Vincent are favorite visitors to the Larry's Country Diner stage. The group has released six albums for Rounder Records, with five of the six albums having charted on at least one Billboard albums chart. They have also won thirteen awards from the International Bluegrass Music Association and twenty-three awards from SPBGMA (The Society for the Preservation of Bluegrass Music of America) . In 2011, they received a Grammy Award nomination for Best Country Performance by a Duo or Group with Vocal, and won the 2011 Dove Award for Best Bluegrass Album with "Singing From The Heart." In 2013, Dailey & Vincent received their 2nd Grammy Award nomination for Best Bluegrass Album for their album "The Gospel Side Of Dailey & Vincent".

Mandy Barnett - September 26

Mandy starred as country music legend Patsy Cline in the stage show Always...Patsy Cline at the celebrated Ryman Auditorium in Nashville, Tennessee. The performances were sold out nightly and received rave reviews across the country. Mandy, in role as Patsy appears on the Decca Records cast recording. Her album "I've Got A Right To Cry" was a huge critical success. Rolling Stone magazine named the project the top country album of 1999. She is a frequent guest on the Grand Ole Opry, as well as Larry's Country Diner. One listen and you'll see why.

Bill Anderson and Mo Pitney - September 27

Larry's Country Diner brings you the bright future of country music and it's glorious past with this pairing. Mo Pitney delivers true country music with a unique style all his own, singing with a deep baritone and skill surprising from someone so young. He taught himself to play several instruments, perfecting his guitar playing while being heavily influenced by bluegrass music. Whispering Bill Anderson scarcely needs an introduction: He has released more than 40 studio albums and has reached No. 1 on the country charts seven times: "Mama Sang a Song" (1962), "Still" (1963), "I Get the Fever" (1966), "For Loving You" (with Jan Howard, 1967), "My Life (Throw It Away If I Want To)" (1969), "World of Make Believe" (1974), and "Sometimes" (with Mary Lou Turner, 1976). Twenty-nine more of his singles have reached the top ten. Anderson has been voted and nominated Songwriter Of The Year six times, Male Vocalist Of The Year, half of the Duet Of The Year with both Jan Howard and Mary Lou Turner, has hosted and starred in the Country Music Television Series Of The Year, seen his band voted Band Of The Year, and in 1975 was voted membership in the Nashville Songwriters Hall of Fame. In 1993, he was made a member of the Georgia Broadcasters' Hall of Fame. In 2001, he received the ultimate honor, membership in Nashville's Country Music Hall of Fame.

Jimmy Fortune - September 28

Fortune sang tenor for the Statler Brothers for 21 years. Fortune wrote several number one songs that were recorded by the Statler Brothers, including Elizabeth, Too Much on My Heart, My Only Love, and More Than a Name on a Wall. "Elizabeth" recently was a top bluegrass release for Dailey & Vincent. He spent 21 years touring, singing, and performing with them until Don, Harold and Phil, the other three members of the group retired in 2002. He is a successful solo musician and frequent guest on Larry's Country Diner, as well as a top-flight musician and vocalist and all-around nice guy.

Sweet Dreams of Mandy Barnett

Mandy Barnett's career has been a sweet dream.

"I've been performing since I was a kid, so I've had so many wonderful, funny and memorable experiences out on the road and on stage," said Barnett, who began singing at age five.

As a 12-year-old, Barnett won a singing competition at Dollywood and made her first appearance at the Opry.

"I've been blessed to be a frequent guest on the Grand Ole Opry for many years," said Barnett. "I've shared the Opry stage with an amazing group of true legends such as Porter Wagoner, Loretta Lynn, Jean Shepard, Jeannie Seely, Jan Howard, Bill Anderson, Jim Ed Brown, Connie Smith, and of course, Little Jimmy Dickens. There's no place as special as the Opry stage."

While still in her teens, the Crossville, Tenn., native gained international accolades by portraying country music legend Patsy Cline in the stage show "Always . . . Patsy Cline" at Nashville's Ryman Auditorium.

"I always considered it an honor to step into Patsy's (high-heeled!) shoes and bring her music and style to audience members, who in all likelihood never got to see Patsy herself perform, as Patsy was tragically young when she died," Barnett said.

Barnett said she's been proud to keep Cline's memory and songs alive, even releasing "Sweet Dreams" in 2011, an album featuring her renditions of songs previously recorded by Cline. However, Barnett has also forged ahead with her own successful recording projects and concerts.

Her album "I've Got a Right to Cry" was a huge critical success, named by Rolling Stone magazine as 1999's top country album. Barnett's songs are featured movie soundtracks for "Drop Dead Gorgeous," "A Walk on the Moon," "Space Cowboys" and others. Her rendition of "Have Yourself a Merry Little Christmas" from her 2010 Christmas album "Winter Wonderland" was used in USA Network's drama "Political Animals."

Barnett said that her fondest career memories, however, are of performing with artists whose work she's admired.

"Country Music Hall of Fame member and renowned guitarist Harold Bradley used to be in my band, and he still sits in with us once in a while," she said, adding, that Bradley played with her at her Nashville Symphony Orchestra debut last year. "When Harold's with us, sometimes while I'm singing on stage, I'll turn and just watch him and listen to him play. It's a treat that always makes me smile."

Bradley was among the stellar lineup of musicians who played on Barnett's 2013 album "I Can't Stop Loving You: The Songs of Don Gibson," which she recorded in keeping with a promise to legendary songwriter and her close friend, Gibson, before his death.

"Besides my memories of performing with amazing artists and musicians, I also cherish memories about fans I've met," Barnett said, calling them "welcoming and loyal."

She muses that every so often, things happen out on the road that illustrate how truly loyal country music fans are.

"Years back, I was playing an outdoor festival during the day, and it was sweltering hot," she recalled. "I could feel my make-up melting, and audience members were using their hands as fans to try to cool themselves down. A woman at the show was a die-hard country music lover and was so excited to be there, but at some point, she got terribly overheated and had to be taken by ambulance to get medical attention. About three hours later, though, she was back in the audience because she didn't want to miss Marty Stuart's performance that came after mine. That was one devoted country music fan!"

Barnett continues to maintain a rigorous monthly performance schedule that includes stage, radio, theater and television, and she has no intention of stopping.

"I wouldn't trade my performance and road memories for anything," she said. "Singing for an audience is what feeds me. When I'm on stage, there's nowhere else I'd rather be. It's been a dream come true."

Precious Memories;
Remembering Walter Bailes

Walter Bailes was part of the Bailes Brothers , who were among the most popular harmony duets in the 40s and 50s. The four brothers, Kyle, Johnnie, Walter, and Homer, seldom worked together as an entire group, but instead paired up for their performances. They were born and raised in West Virginia, near Charleston. Their father, a minister, died with they were young and their mother struggled to keep them together.

Roy Acuff gave them their big break when he suggested the brothers perform on the Grand Ole Opry. Walter and his brothers made their debut on the show in 1944. They made their recording debut in 1945.

A talented writer of both secular and sacred songs, Walter penned the Bailes Brothers' best known works, "Dust on the Bible," later recorded by Kitty Wells, and "Give Mother My Crown," later covered by Flatt & Scruggs.

Walter and John went to KWKH in Shreveport, La in 1946., where they helped initiate the Louisiana Hayride and gave support to the fledging career of Hank Williams.

Walter joined the ministry a year later and was replaced by Homer in the duo. Walter pastored evangelical churches and preached at numerous revivals in the U.S. and overseas.

In the 1960s Walter did team up with Kyle and Homer at different times. Walter also became an evangelical preacher.

In 1976 Walter and Kyle made an album; and in 1977, all four brothers reunited for a record, joined by their sister Minnie on a few cuts.

The Bailes Brothers were inducted into The Walkway of Stars of the Country Music Hall of Fame and Museum, in Nashville, TN on June 8, 1983. Johnnie, Walter and Kyle attended the installation ceremony and reception.

Walter died November 27, 2000 in Sevierville, Tennessee at the age of 80.

There could be a new U.K. dog in Dolly Parton's life

During her first ever visit to the Glastonbury Music Festival in the U.K., Dolly Parton won the hearts of the audience, and she lost her heart to a dog that was left behind after the event was over. Now, that dog may be traveling to the U.S. and into the home of the country artist.

The fluffy white dog made its way out of a tent as workers were cleaning the outdoor fields where the event is held and was quickly named after the iconic singer because "it characterized Dolly's beauty, love, peace and sweetness, just as she had shown fans a few days before," a rep for Parton said in a statement. The dog quickly became known as "Doggy Parton" or just plain "Dolly."

Parton immediately had her manager get in touch with a local animal shelter to make sure the dog was taken care of. "At this time, nobody has claimed the dog and the dog is in great hands at the shelter," she said in a statement. "I will take the dog home to America if nobody claims her within a reasonable amount of time."

She posted on Twitter, "Heard about the abandoned dog at @GlastoFest? If nobody claims her, I'll take her home to America! Ain't she cute?"

SEPTEMBER

★

Johnny Rodriguez, the rise of a small town boy

Born December 10, 1951, Johnny Rodriguez was the second youngest of 10 children living in a four room house in Sabinal, Texas, a small town about 90 miles from the Mexico Border.

Johnny was an A/B student, captain of his Junior High School Football team, a high school letterman and an altar boy at church. But he wasn't always an angel. In 1969, he and some friends were caught stealing and barbecuing a goat for which Rodriguez took the rap. It was this jail visit that gave Johnny his first break.

His jail house singing enthralled Texas Ranger, Joaquin Jackson, who told a promoter about Rodriguez. The promoter, Happy Shahan, hired Johnny to perform at the Alamo Village, a popular south Texas tourist attraction and location of many well know movie sets. It was here that Johnny was heard by Nashville artists Tom T. Hall and Bobby Bare who both encouraged Johnny to fly to Nashville. So, in 1971, 20-year old Rodriguez found himself stepping off the plane with nothing more than his guitar in hand and $14 in his pocket. Soon he was fronting Tom T. Hall's Band and writing songs.

Mercury Record's Nashville operation heard him audition the next year and offered a contract on the spot after hearing "I Can't Stop Loving You" and "If I'd Left It Up To You".

Fifteen of his singles rose to top ten, six of which were #1 hits. The first of the singles to reach number one was "Pass Me By".

His debut album, Introducing Johnny Rodriguez, went to #1 on all three major trade charts and by 1973 he was nominated by the Country Music Association for "Male Vocalist of the Year" and won

the Billboard Trend Setter Award for first Mexican-American to capture a national audience

In 1979, Johnny moved from Mercury to Epic Records, where he worked with producer Billy Sherrill. His debut album with Epic, "Rodriguez", contained with one exception, songs written by Johnny. His successes included: "What'll I Tell Virginia", "Love Look At Us Now", "North Of The Border", "Foolin", "How Could I Love Her So Much", and "Rose Of My Heart".

He moved to Capitol Records in 1987, which resulted in Rodriguez' album titled "Gracias", which contained such hits as "I Didn't (Every Chance I Had)", "I Want To Wake Up With You" and "You Might Want To Use Me Again".

In 1993, Johnny recorded "Run For The Border" on Intersound and in 1996 he reunited with the Dea/Kennedy team from his Mercury days, to truly capture the fire and magic of their past collaborations with the creation of "You Can Say That Again".

Johnny was inducted into the Texas Country Music Hall of Fame in Carthage, TX in 2007, an honor well deserved for his contribution to country music. In 2010, Johnny received the Pioneer Award from the Institute of Hispanic Culture.

Now, almost 40 years after he first arrived in Nashville, Johnny Rodriguez is right back where he started coming full circle back to making the kind of honest country music that he and his fans always enjoyed.

Nadine's Corner

Homer did almost get in some trouble on the Cruise. He overhead another passenger talk about Candy and followed him all the way to his cabin. Just to find out the guys wife's name was Candy.

I reckon what happens on the ship....stays on the ship.

Have a nice day.

Food was the key component to get Homer on the Cruise.

Of course I gotta say the spectacular dining room and exotic ingredients and the array of savory cuisine and beautifully crafted menus went to waste with Homer. He didn't care that the food was cooked from some of the world's top chefs. What he liked was the freedom and flexibility of Freestyle Dining with no fixed dining times or pre-assigned seating   He headed straight for the buffet and all he had to do is get passed the ship employees that constantly stand at the entrance singing…. "Wishy Washy Good For You, Good For Me" as they squirt antibacterial in your hands. I swear Homer tried his best to get past them without a squirt just to see if he could. One morning he ducked and almost got it in the eye.

Once inside he enjoyed grazing the huge buffet. He usually balanced 2-3 plates heaped full of his favorite foods. Fried Chicken, Pot Roast, Catfish. Mashed Potatoes, Green beans, Gravy and buttered Rolls. I am sure Homer thought food just magically appears…just like at home. He wouldn't even think about leaving that area of the ship until he had eaten 2-3 desserts. Now I do join him for the desserts. Homer and I usually don't eat dessert three times a day at home unless I am at the Diner of course, but on these cruise ships they are just too hard to pass up.

The Grandkids

Renae and Nadine's granddaughters came by Larry's Country Diner recently. Renae is holding Rio and Nadine is holding River.

New column on decorating by Carol Bass (Luann Black's sister!)

Carol Bass, and Luann Black (Larry Black's wife) sisters and southern girls went from playing house pretend, to playing house for real. As little girls they loved rearranging furniture and making doll houses look great. In 2001 they decided to turn their love for decorating into a real business, even though one lived in Nashville and one lived in New Jersey at the time. But together, yet apart, they started an interior redesign decorating and staging business.

Luann went on to use her knowledge and certification as a ministry to help young mothers create beautiful homes for their families. Carol built a business with her certification and is now a master professional trainer with The Decorating and Staging Academy (The-dsa.com) and owns her own training business The Practical Decorator (Thepracticaldecorator.com). She uses her energy teaching, training and certifying others who have a talent for decorating in how to build a business.

Carol has offered to pen a monthly tips and tricks for us called "Down Home with Carol". In these articles Carol will share practical decorating tips. Also if any of you are planning to sale your home soon she will share practical staging tips to get you home ready for the market.

Carol's decorating tips will start in the October issue.

Carol and Luann went from playing house to decorating them.

Carol and Luann went from playing house to decorating them.

RAY STEVENS
Saturday, Sept. 6
10:00 p.m. Central
Sunday, Sept. 7
6:00 p.m. Central

MARGO SMITH
Saturday, Sept. 13
10:00 p.m. Central
Sunday, Sept. 14
6:00 p.m. Central

EXILE
Saturday, Sept. 20
10:00 p.m. Central
Sunday, Sept. 21
6:00 p.m. Central

RHONDA VINCENT & Mike Johnson
Saturday, Sept. 27
10:00 p.m. Central
Sunday, Sept. 28
6:00 p.m. Central

Byron Hill keeps the hits coming

Many times we fall in love with the performers, but the songs are sometimes what makes us fall for them. And it's the songwriters who know how to tug at your heartstrings, or make you want to dance. It's the song that brings back the memories. So many times, we don't know who the songwriter is, but we know their songs.

This is the case with Byron Hill. Some of the songs he wrote that you will recognize are:

PICKIN' UP STRANGERS (Hill), Johnny Lee, FOOL HEARTED MEMORY (Hill/Mevis), George Straite, NIGHTS (Hill/Hiller), Ed Brucee, BORN COUNTRY (Hill/Schweers), Alabamae, LIFESTYLES OF THE NOT SO RICH AND FAMOUS (Hill/Tester), Tracy Byrde, HIGH-TECH REDNECK (Hill/Turner), George Jones , IF I WAS A DRINKIN' MAN (Hill/Rudd), Neal McCoye, NOTHING ON BUT THE RADIO (Hill/Blackmon/Long), Gary Allane

Byron Hill is from Winston-Salem, NC. Byron is the eldest of four children. When Byron was about 10 years old, his parents bought him his first guitar, a Kay arch top. His father then began teaching him some old Carter Family songs. Later, a neighbor named Paul Huff, introduced Byron to some basic "Rock and Roll" chords and riffs on the guitar.

"When I was about 16 years old, we wore Johnny Cash's records out around our house. My Dad sat me down one day and asked me to listen to the great Kris Kristofferson song "Sunday Morning Coming Down" from Johnny Cash's The Johnny Cash Show album. That is the song that started me on the path of being a professional songwriter. I loved the song. Kristofferson's description of that Sunday morning showed me that a song could be far more than something for people to sing along with, that you could actually paint a picture with words."

He moved to Nashville in May of 1978 and signed his first songwriting contract with ATV Music Group in September of 1978.

During his thirty-six years as a professional songwriter, Byron's songs that have generated more than 700 recordings, earned seventy-seven RIAA certified Gold and Platinum awards, ten ASCAP awards, thirty-two U.S. and Canadian top-ten chart hits, and numerous hits in other worldwide markets. His songs have been recorded throughout the world.

Byron performs as a singer/songwriter in Nashville and on the road. Byron's own albums are available online at www.cdbaby.com, at Byron's website at www.byronhillmusic.com,

WORD SEARCH

```
B P R P E N C O U N T E R
R A I G O M O N A R C H S
O N N O R K D B I S O N H
O I C A L O E W K R M N E
K C U T E S P A T E M M E
L F R A C A S E S I O U P
I N S E R T P P M G T L K
Q M Y G W O A Y V N I L S
U L E O L L E A K B O L T
O F L E E C A N O N N I R
R F T A T S H M C O M B A
A N C A M E L E R O L L N
A R E G N A N T W Y A R D
```

antelope	**bill**	**bison**	**bolt**
brook	**camel**	**canon**	**chew**
code	**clot**	**comb**	**commotion**
crew	**cute**	**elapse**	**encounter**
flee	**flow**	**fracas**	**goat**
grope	**incur**	**insert**	**king**
leak	**liquor**	**llama**	**meet**
monarchs	**mull**	**omit**	**panic**
poke	**regnant**	**reign**	**roll**
sheep	**spate**	**strand**	**yard**

Kellie Pickler and her country roots

Kellie Dawn Pickler was born June 28, 1986 in Albemarle, North Carolina, a small town near Charlotte. Her life reads like a country song. Her mother left when she was only two, her father was an alcoholic and drug addict who spent time in prison. She was raised by her grandparents and she dreamed of being a country singer.

In a recent interview she stated, "My grandpa Pickler had a big role in raising me. He was an electrician and after he retired from the Marines, he got his electrical license. I'd go on jobs with him and help him run wires up houses. I was tiny. I was like 5. We'd sing Hank Sr. songs. And 'My Bucket's Got a Hole in It' was of the first song I ever learned."

She was raised in a home with music and has said, "My grandma is the woman that I called 'mom.' She raised me. She had these little children's books and hymns and we'd sit on her front-porch swing and I'd sing her favorite hymns, like 'Old Rugged Cross.' A lot of my musical background came from being a little girl with big dreams in a tiny town with grandma and grandpa."

Kellie gained fame as a contestant on the fifth season of American Idol, and finished in sixth place. In 2006, she signed to 19 Recordings and BNA Records as a recording artist, releasing her debut album, Small Town Girl, later that year. As of 2009, it has sold over 800,000 copies.

Even though many of her songs have the tempo of the 'new' country sound, she seems to always go back to her traditional country roots in her vocals. "I've always been a fan of traditional country music," says Kellie. "Country music is wide. There's room for all of it and everyone's definition of country music is different and that's OK."

She has written songs with her friend Taylor Swift that were more commercial, "But I want banjo and spoons and steel," she continues.

Some of Kellie's best country songs can be found on her 2012 release 100 Proof. Songs such as, "Mother's Day," "Where's Tammy Wynette," "Unlock That Honky Tonk," and "Stop Cheatin' On Me" are examples of just how country Kellie really is....and she's country right down to her soul.

Kellie on Country Artists

Tammy Wynette " is one of the reasons I fell in love with country music. I have sat on my bus and YouTubed videos of her singing. I just close my eyes and I feel like she's right there with me, singing. I'm hanging on to every word. And I love that she just stood there and sang her songs."

"We did a show a few years ago with Loretta Lynn in Canada and it was just her, her band and her big sparkly dress. She stood there, behind that microphone, and just sang hit after hit, and everyone was hanging on every note, every lyric. She didn't need people swinging from the rafters to get their attention. She had the power of a great country song. Tammy and Loretta both did."

Dolly Parton "is another big reason I fell in love with country music. For me, her life is a country song. And she is a true…I don't like to say 'Cinderella story,' because she made it on her own. She didn't depend on a man on a white horse to come save the day. She did it herself. She is just a true rags-to-riches story."

"I love Patsy Cline's voice. And 'I Fall to Pieces' is one of my favorite songs. Most everything was predominantly country in our home. I really wasn't educated on a lot outside of traditional country music until I did American Idol and had to sing Rod Stewart songs or a Queen song, which I knew. Everybody knows Queen."

Country Legends of the Past and Present

BY TOM WOODS

Webb Pierce

It would not be an understatement to say that Webb Pierce grabbed life by the horns and hung on for one wild ride.

Before the advent of the www acronym that stands for World Wide Web, there was another: Wild, Wooly Webb.

In an era of gaudy, rhinestone-covered clothes, few country music superstars stood out quite like Webb Pierce. His garish suits and flamboyant cars were custom-made, and his guitar-shaped swimming pool drew thousands of gawkers. Webb's white Bonneville — replete with Longhorn steer horns up front, six-gun door handles, a leather saddle between the seats, the leather interior inlaid with silver dollars — is still a top attraction at the Country Music Hall of Fame.

And the funny thing, with 60-something years to reflect, Webb Pierce didn't need any of the sideshow clothes and bedazzled cars to call attention to his songs.

Webb Pierce's music has withstood the test of time and still resonates with many die-hard, pure country fans today.

The honky-tonker first hit No. 1 with "Wondering" in 1952, and he topped the Billboard country chart a dozen more times between then and 1956 for a grand total of 113 weeks at No. 1. Some of his other chart-toppers in that stretch included "There Stands the Glass (1953), "Slowly" (1954), "More and More" (1954), "Love, Love, Love" (1955) and "I Don't Care" (1955).

And it wouldn't be too much of a stretch to say the entire decade of the 1950s belonged to the Webb-spinner with 48 singles hitting the charts. Thirty-nine made the top 10 and 26 zoomed to top 4 status.

Perhaps none of Webb's hits stood as tall as his version of "In The Jailhouse Now," first recorded by the great Jimmie Rodgers in 1929 and covered by many other artists over the decades, most recently by Tim Blake Nelson on the 2001 "O Brother Where Art Thou" soundtrack.

"In The Jailhouse Now" spent 21 weeks at No. 1 for Webb and remained on the charts for a whopping 37 weeks. That matched the longevity record for most weeks at No. 1, tying only Eddy Arnold's 1947 smash "I'll Hold You in My Heart (Till I Can Hold You in My Arms) and "I'm Movin' On" by Hank Snow in 1950. Those three artists held the record for 58 years until Florida Georgia Line spent 22 weeks at No. 1 in 2013 with "Cruise."

Webb was selected to join the Grand Ole Opry in September 1952, but he quit in early 1957 in a dispute with management. Pierce continued to churn out chart-making hits over the next three decades before his 1991 death. He was elected to the Country Music Hall of Fame 10 years later in the Class of 2001.

Indeed, the 1950s were heady days for Webb Pierce—and might have gone to his head, truth be told. But as the old sports adage goes, "It's not bragging if you can really do it."

And Webb Pierce really did it.

The Songwriters is a great series for serious music lovers

Did you know that Bill Anderson's songwriting career has spanned over 50 years with over 132 singles on the country charts…more than any other songwriters except Harlan Howard and Bob McGill.

Hank Cochran had huge hits and won a BMI award for two million performances of Patsy Cline's "I Fall to Pieces." He wrote "Make the World Go Away" when he was inspired by a line in a movie.

Larry Cordle's "Murder on Music Row" has been an anthem for all that has gone wrong in country music in recent years.

Vince Gill has written some of the most beautiful and haunting songs, including "Go Rest High on That Mountain."

Country's Family Reunion: The Songwriters is a 6 hour, 5 DVD series features these songwriters as well as 20 more of the best country music songwriters of all time… You'll hear how songs like "The Gambler," "Always," "All My Exes Live in Texas," "When You Say Nothing at All," "Don't It Make My Brown Eyes Blue," and many more. You'll hear the stories of how these great writers were inspired to write the songs.

Each songwriter has the opportunity to tell some stories and sing a song. They tell stories about the songs and they tell stories about each other. Some of the writers who have been around for a long while talk about the way it used to be and the younger ones talk about how the more experienced writers took them under their wing to mentor them.

You also get a book that has each songwriter's photo and lists some of the songs they have written along with information about that writer.

If you're truly interested in where the music comes from, this series is one you'll want to own because without the songwriters, there would be no music.

The series is $79.80 + $6.95 s/h. To order this series, call customer service at 800-820-5405.

New CD of unreleased songs by Faron Young

No one expected a new CD release from Faron Young. After all, he died in 1996. But with the help of Country Rewind Records, new music by the great Faron Young is now available.

Titled "Faron Young You Don't Know Me," this wonderful CD is made up of a collection of very rare one-of-a=kind recrodings that most people didn't even know existed. It is made up of live performances, old radio shows and, studio cuts that Faron made many years ago. Faron's son, Robyn Young, has authorized these for release and has written the liner notes.

Country Rewind Records, a division of Hindsight Records is responsible for taking these recordings, many of which had suffered the ravages of time, and updated them by adding additional instrumentation, vocal backing tracks, and orchestration.

Scott Oliver, the producer, was charged with taking these songs and modernizing them. The original recordings were one –track mono which Oliver then added additional tracks to bring them to 2014 standards.

"The main goal throughout the project was to honor and maintain the flavor of the original style of Faron Young," says Oliver. "The most amazing thing I noticed was what an incredible artist Faron Young, and his group of players were. "

With classics such as "Hello Walls," "Sweet Dreams," and "Live Fast, Love Hard, Die Young" this CD is sure to be one ever collector of traditional country music will want in their collection.

"The title song, "You Don't Know Me" is possibly the rarest gem of them on this album," says Robyn. "Had this song ever been released as a single I have no doubt that it would have become a hugh hit for my Dad."

Faron Young was one of the great legends of country music who died too young.

Other artists with CD released, or soon to be released, through this company are Ferlin Huskey, Waylon Jennings, Skeeter Davis, Bob Luman, Johnny Russell, Connie Smith, Barbara Fairchild, Mickey Gilley and Cal Smith.

This CD can purchased for $10.00 (includes nshipping) at www.countryrewindrecords.com or by sending a check to Hindsight Records, Box 566, Massena New York 13662.

Country's Family Reunion &
Larry's Country Diner Alaska Cruise

Signing autographs with the Diner cast ...

and the artists.

Nadine!!

Joey & Rory introduce Indiana

Showing their love for Larry with heart shaped tattoos with Larry's face!

Larry's Country Diner with cast and guests!

Larry and Luann Black and the entire Black family!

Bill Anderson

Gene Watson

Jeannie Seely

Jim Ed Brown

Jimmy Fortune

Joey & Rory (with Heidi)

Dailey & Vincent

Sweethearts of the Rodeo

Moe Bandy

Rhonda Vincent

Pirate Bill

Stage Clothes of the Stars

By Claudia Johnson

Patsy Cline

As the daughter of a seamstress, Patsy Cline began her country music career in the cowgirl-style clothing lovingly and expertly sewn by her mother. Vintage photographs show Cline in elaborately fringed and embroidered skirt and shirt costumes with coordinating boots, hat and scarf.

That's exactly what she was set to wear on Jan. 21, 1957 when her mother, Hilda Hensley, secured Cline a spot on Arthur Godfrey's Talent Scouts television show. However, the show's staff insisted Cline appear in a cocktail dress instead and perform her recent release of "Walkin' After Midnight." The performance was a hit with the audience, and the song soon reached No. 2 on the country chart and No. 16 on the pop chart, making Cline one of the first country singers to have a crossover pop hit.

The country music industry in the 1950s was no place for a weak woman, and by all accounts, Cline was very strong, commanding respect from her employers and peers and garnering absolute devotion from her fans. She was the first woman in country music to perform at New York's Carnegie Hall; the first female country music star to headline her own show and receive billing above the male stars with

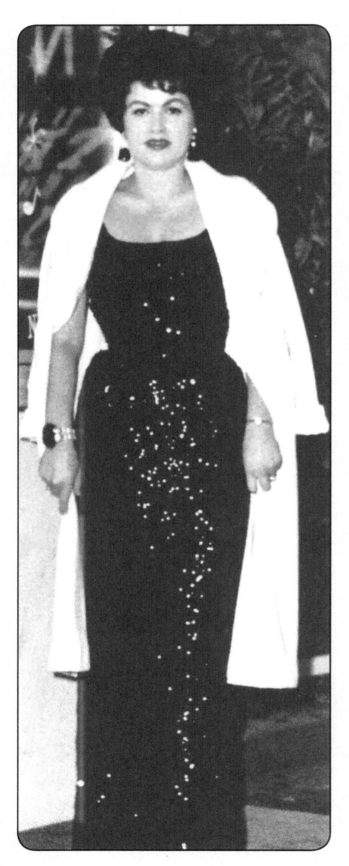

whom she toured; the first woman in country music to headline her own show in Las Vegas; and the first female solo artist to be inducted into the Country Music Hall of Fame.

From the late 1950s through the time of her death, promotional photos, stage and candid shots and album covers show Cline as a beautiful, sophisticated woman dressed in feminine, sometimes sexy clothing, red lipstick and dramatic jewelry and accessories, which were in direct contrast to the image of the female country music performers and singing cowgirls of the time.

In 1961, Cline survived a near fatal automobile accident that left her forehead visibly scarred. She wore wigs and makeup to hide the scars for the rest of her life. She also incorporated headbands into her dark coif, as they applied pressure that helped relieve her headaches.

Since her death in 1963, private collectors have acquired some of Cline's attire. On June 24, 2004, several pieces were sold at auction by Christie's at New York's Rockefeller Plaza.

A sleeveless black sequined gown together with a matching black sequined clutch purse and a pair of sheer elbow-length gloves sold for $2,151. Cline was photographed wearing the dress in front of the Mint Casino in Las Vegas, Nev., where she performed in November and December 1962. Another piece from the Mint Casino performances, a two-piece outfit consisting of a capped sleeve top adorned with iridescent sequins and faux pearls together with a matching skirt, sold for $1,554.

Selling for $1,912 was a three-quarter-length sleeve black sequined dress with a front and back v-neckline that was worn by Cline on the album cover 'The Legend of Patsy Cline' as well as for numerous performances. A tan leather fringed jacket and a faux fur coat brought $5,139. Fetching $2,390 was a collection of Cline's accessories, including a faux-leather handbag, three clutch purses, a faux fur collar, a pair of black high heels, two gold-colored belts, a hairpiece and seven hats of varying styles and materials. Some of the singer's costume jewelry sold for $1,016 and included a necklace, two bracelets, two brooches and two rings all made of rhinestones, three bead necklaces, four pucca shell necklaces, one Bakelite necklace, two sweater clips, three pairs of clip earrings, three brooches, one pendant and one Timex watch without a band.

One group of clothing primarily worn by Cline offstage selling for $2,629 included a pair of black cotton Capri pants and a beige cotton skirt hand sewn by Cline's mother, who frequently made clothes for her daughter throughout her life. Other items of interest were a cotton shirt with a black, gold and red Asian motif and a green cotton two-piece skirt and jacket with a "Rothmoor, Cain-Sloan Co., Nashville, Tenn." label. Most recognizable was a simple shirtwaist cotton dress printed with whimsical images of posters, which Cline wore during a 1960 Grand Ole Opry performance.

A collection of four sleeveless, black silk chiffon cocktail dresses worn during the time Cline was performing in Las Vegas sold for $1,195, and another set of four cocktail dresses also brought $1,195 as well. One of these was designed by Helen Rose, an Academy Award-winning Hollywood costume designer. A black cotton dress with three-quarter-length sleeves and a leopard print attached sash was created by Cline's mother.

A sleeveless tangerine-orange silk chiffon dress by Ceil Chapman, one of Marilyn Monroe's favorite, designers brought $956, while a sleeveless peach-colored cotton dress hand sewn by her mother sold for $3,107.

It seems fitting that the daughter of a seamstress would become a style setter on the performance stage, and it's a compliment to Cline's beloved mother and closest friend that the clothes she created for her daughter were among the highest valued at auction.

"If I made a list of the people I admire," Cline once said, "Mom would probably fill up half of it."

The beautiful music of husband/wife team T.G. Sheppard and Kelly Lang

Kelly Lang was born the youngest of 4 children in Oklahoma City, Oklahoma. Her father, Velton Lang, was the road manager of Country superstar, Conway Twitty for over 25 years. Kelly recorded her first Billboard single, "Lady, Lady" at the age of 15, filmed a video that came to the attention of CMT—, and in rapid fire time was soon appearing as a regular on Nashville's popular Ralph Emery Morning Show.

T. G. Sheppard was born Billy Neal Browder, 20 July 1944, in Humboldt, Tennessee. Sheppard dropped out of high school and at the age of 15 ran away from home to become involved in the music industry in Memphis, Tennessee. He had 15 number one hits during the 1970s and 1980s.

Sheppard first recorded for Atco Records as Brian Stacy in 1966. In 1974, Sheppard signed with Melodyland (later Hitsville) Records.He recorded the song "Devil in the Bottle", which became a No. 1 hit. The follow-up, "Tryin' to Beat the Morning Home", also went to No. 1 and cracked the Top 100 during the summer of 1975. Several subsequent releases during 1975-1977 also made the Top 10 like "Motels and Memories" and "Show Me A Man".

Sheppard signed with Warner Bros. Records in 1977. Starting with that summer's "When Can We Do This Again", he had a series of fifteen consecutive Top 10 releases. His success continued until about 1988, when rootsy neo-traditionalist artists began to eclipse more polished pop-country artists like Sheppard on the country charts.

Kelly's teen years were a whirlwind.. She moved to national attention as a frequent guest on the highly popular Music City Tonight, with Crook & Chase, televised on TNN. Kelly next made the finals of Ed McMahon''s popular weekly televised Star Search.

Kelly became a semi-regular artist on Ralph's Emery''s popular "Nashville Now" on TNN, pulling in major viewer mail and a large national fan base. On the road in concert, Kelly shared billings with legends such as Barry Gibb, Ronnie Milsap, Brenda Lee, George Jones, Lorrie Morgan, Ricky Skaggs, TG Sheppard and many of the hot new artists from her own peer group. Kelly has made music her true passion.

Along with balancing a busy career as a performing artist, Kelly is a highly sought after and accomplished songwriter and producer. Kelly's songs have been featured on the major motion picture screen and have been recorded by artists such as Lorrie Morgan, Jerry Lee Lewis, Crystal Gayle, George Jones, BJ Thomas, The Oak Ridge Boys, and Janie Frickie to name a few.

TG and Kelly had been together for several years before they married in August of 2007 and in 2013 they released the album "Iconic Duets." Lang was quick to say they weren't trying to repaint the Mona Lisa. "We did not cut these with any intention of trying to improve them or make them better than the originals. You can't. It's impossible. But, we went into the project with the hope that we would be honoring who came before us."

T.G. and Kelly will be joining Country's Family Reunion and Larry's Country Diner for the 2015 Caribbean Cruise. They have previously been guests on Larry's Country Diner and are looking forward to being on the cruise with everyone.

Daily & Vincent pranking to pass the time

Life on tour with Daily and Vincent vacillates between the absurd and the sublime.

First, the absurd.

With 11 men living on a tour bus a major portion of each year, absurd is to be expected. One of the top Bluegrass bands in America, the award-winning duo of Jamie Dailey and Darrin Vincent, along with their entourage, play more than 115 shows per year to sold out crowds, so breaking the monotony and easing the pressure manifests in some harmless pranks. Well, they're harmless depending on who's pranking and who's being pranked.

"We have a lot of fun," Vincent said, adding conspiratorially, "but it's awful what we do."

One example that Vincent and perhaps nine other people found uproariously funny was the time they froze bottles of water, and while their audio engineer innocently showered, he was subjected to possible frostbite as his buddies attacked him with the glacial water.

"He had no where to go," Vincent laughed before launching into a story of mayhem and revenge sparked by the placing of ice cubes under Daily's pillow by Jeff Parker, who plays mandolin and guitar and provides vocals for the band.

There seems to be a theme here or else frozen water is the groups' weapon of choice. Whatever the case, Daily planned an elaborate retaliation hinging on Parker's ritual of putting on his pajamas and diving into his curtained bunk. On the night of revenge, Daily removed and hid all the bedding from the bunk, including the mattress. Everyone went to bed early, making sure the lights were out. Parker took his usual approach, then THUD! and OUCH! Parker did not think it was funny, and the only way to placate him was to stop the bus and retrieve the mattress so he could get some comfortable sleep.

Now for the sublime.

In April 2014, Vincent, Daily, Parker and guitar player/vocalist Christian Davis performed a traditional gospel number, "When the Roll is Called Up Yonder," on "Country's Family Reunion: God Bless America Again," after which Vincent testified about his belief that the blood of Jesus washes away sin. Soon after, following an appearance at Stoughton Opera House in Wisconsin, a woman approached Vincent in tears.

"She had driven more than four and a half hours to tell us that [after hearing Vincent's testimony] she had rededicated her life," he said. "She wanted us to know what this had meant to her. This just goes to show that the lost are not sitting in a church pew. We have a real opportunity to sing and share the gospel. The [Country Family Reunion] gives us a chance to have an impact."

Vincent noted that the group's first song was "By the Mark," an expression of deep faith in a heavenly reward. In the seven years they've been together, the band has developed a fan base across three musical genres – bluegrass, country and gospel. They've also garnered numerous awards, including multiple Grammy nominations and several Dove Awards. They've won 13 IBMA and were named Entertainer of The Year and Vocal Group of the Year three times each.

In addition to Vincent, Daily, Davis and Parker, the band includes multi-instrumentalist B.J. Cherryholmes and guitarist Jessie Baker. A continent-hopping annual schedule has the group performing at festivals, hosting a radio show, appearing on television and giving concerts at prestigious venues like Carnegie Hall, Ryman Auditorium and the Grand Ole Opry.

If that's not enough to keep them occupied, they host the Daily Vincent Land Fest, heralded as "three days of great music, laughter and fellowship" for their fans each September in Denton, N.C. New for 2015 is Daily Vincent Water Fest, a Western Caribbean cruise promising a week of sun, beaches and, according to Daily and Vincent, "playing pranks on Parker.

Country Questions
By Dick Boise, CMH

Send questions to:
Dick Boise, , c/o CFR News,
P.O. Box 201796, Nashville,
TN 37221.

Q. I do not hear much music from Hank Snow these days on the radio. He was one of my favorites and I miss him. Was he the first country entertainer to come to America from Canada? Thanks for your find newspaper,

Loretta, Oneonta, NY

A. Yes, Lorettta, it's true that "so called" country radio does not play many of the fine older country legends. Hank came to the States early in the forties, around 1945. He tried his talents in many places before gaining a spot on the Opry in 1950. However, the first -known Canadian country entertainer to come to the states in 1941 was "Montana Slim," real name Wilf Carter. A friend of mine, the late Lynn Strauff, in his later teenage years, played all across the northern states and Canada with Slim. Lynn was a fine steel guitarist in the days "BPS" (Before Petal Steel).

Q. I'm a "Little" Jimmy Dickens fan, and have a question that goes back a few years. I saw his show in the mid 50s and at that time he had a bass player who was playing electric bass. Possbily the first one I ever saw. Could you in any way be able to tell me who that might have been? Thanks.

A big Tater fan in Arkansas

A. I'll bet that there are a lot of "Tater" fans in that state. He has been such a favorite entertainer for all those many years. Back in the mid 50s "Little" Jimmy had one of the top bands traveling the country music trail. It included, Howard Roetan and "Spider" Wilson on the twin lead guitars, teenage "Buddy" Emmons on pedal steel and Joel Price on electric bass. They were a find group and worked well with Jimmy.

Q. I have always like the song Sixteen Avenue and have some questions. What is the singer's name and did she write the song?

Elroy Goodrich, Mississippi

A. The song "16th Avenue" was written by Thom Schuyler (who can be seen singing that song on The Songwriters by Country's Family Reunion) and it was a big hit in 1982. The singer is Lacy J. Dalton, born Jill Byrem in Bloomsburg, PA, October 13, 1946. A great song about the inner workings of Nashville, Music City USA.

Precious Memories; Remembering Roy Drusky

Roy Frank Drusky Jr. was born June 22, 1930, in Atlanta, Georgia. His mother, a church organist, had tried for years to get her son into music as a child, but he was more into sports. He originally planned to become a baseball player. His music career began in the early 1950s performing on a Decatur, Georgia radio station, but he actually began singing while in the US Navy during the 1940s, and later attended Emory University and studied veterinary medicine. During this time, he also played country music with a group he founded, the Southern Ranch Boys.

Drusky had a beautiful baritone voice. He was known for incorporating the Nashville sound and for being the first artist to record a song written by Kris Kristofferson ("Jody and the Kid"). His highest-charting single was the No. 1 "Yes Mr. Peters", a duet with Priscilla Mitchell.

Drusky also worked as a disc jockey. In 1953, he signed with Starday Records; the first single he released was called "Such a Fool". That same year, he joined the Grand Ole Opry. A couple of years later, he recorded for Columbia Records, but none of his work gained much success.

Faron Young helped Drusky's career by recording his songs. Two songs he wrote, "Alone With You" and "Country Girl", Young turned into No. 1 country hits. After that, Drusky moved on to Decca Records.

In 1960, Drusky finally made it big. At Decca Records, where he worked with producer Owen Bradley, he released a single called "Another", which he co-wrote. Bradley helped smooth out Drusky's orchestral tones and the next year, Drusky reached the Country Top 10 with the single "Second Hand Rose".

Drusky appeared on most of the country music television programs of the era; and in 1965, he appeared in the movie White Lightnin' Express and two other films as well, The Golden Guitar and Four Acre Feud.

Drusky's last top 40 country was a remake of "A Satisfied Mind" in 1973 which had earlier been a hit for both Porter Wagoner and Jean Shepard. He made his last appearance on the Billboard charts in 1974 but occasionally recorded on smaller record labels into the 1990s. He also recorded a number of gospel albums for Chapel Records during this period. He also returned to writing and producing music, the latter of which he had done since the 1960s.

Drusky's membership with the Grand Ole Opry ensured him exposure for decades long after the radio hits stopped coming. He appeared regularly on the program until the year of his death, singing the hit songs he had racked up in the 1960s and 1970s in addition to performing country standards from other artists, which became a tradition at the Opry.

On September 23, 2004, Drusky died at age 74 from complications stemming from lung cancer, which he fought for several years. A memorial service was held at the Highland Seventh-day Adventist Church, in Portland Tennessee. The service was attended by many of Drusky's long time friends, musicians, recording artists and family.

Sam Moore & Nu-Blu Set to Perform Sept. 20th on Fox News' Huckabee

The legendary "Soul Man" Sam Moore, and the fastest rising act in bluegrass, Nu-Blu continue to generate buzz, as they gear up to perform their brand new George Jones inspired single, "Jesus and Jones" on Fox News' Huckabee show on September 20th. This must-see performance will be both soulful and bluegrass-flavored. "Jesus and Jones" is the first offering from Nu-Blu's upcoming album All The Way, which is set for release on September 16. The song was written by Cheri Hefner and Rick Tiger and is NOW AVAILABLE at iTunes, Amazon, Google Plus, Rhapsody and eMusic. "Jesus and Jones" is also available for D.J. download on AirPlay Direct RIGHT NOW by clicking HERE. Also, check out Billboard's interview with Sam Moore discussing the new single HERE.

This single takes Sam Moore on his first venture into the bluegrass realm, noting that he has already recorded songs in rhythm & blues, jazz, big band, pop, and country. Reaction from bluegrass radio to Moore's debut performance is already garnering positive reviews.

"You pair one up and coming bluegrass band with one R&B legend, then add a song pairing country music icon, George Jones, with Jesus and you have what has to be the most unique sound in bluegrass today! Nu-Blu's Carolyn Routh vocally sets up the song "Jesus and Jones" as a mainline bluegrass salute to the late Mr. Jones. Rock and Roll Hall of Fame member Sam Moore then shows why he is still a "soul man" with his turn at the mic. When their voices blend on the finale it is magic! Totally bluegrass…. No….Totally soul….No….Totally great music….YES!," says Gene Skinner of Great Stuff Radio.

"Carolyn's vocals align perfectly with Sam Moore's soulful sound on "Jesus and Jones" as Nu-Blu carves a new notch in their musical achievements." – Bob Cherry, Cybergrass

"The song is massive!" – Gary Henderson, WAMU-FM – BluegrassCountry

"Sam was a pure delight, and the sincere joy he takes in music, and in having a chance to remember his friend, George Jones, was palpable." – John Lawless, Bluegrass Today

"This is TOO COOL, … well done!" – Buddy Merriam, Blue Grass Time

"…we have the song in rotation as of today." - Paul Marx, KBON-FM

After garnering multiple showcase performances, including CMA Fest, MerleFest, NAMM, and Folk Alliance, 2014 has already been a momentum-building year. With several new collaborations, including a special feature with the 'queen of bluegrass' Rhonda Vincent, this album is sure to go all the way to the top of fan playlists!

OCTOBER

★

Tribute to Ray Price & Honky Tonk Reunion delivered by Christmas if you order by Dec. 1

Rarely in life do we get to honor someone whose singing style ushered in a new way to do it. Ray Price passed away December 16, 2013 and we here at Country's Family Reunion are honoring Ray's memory by getting together those who knew him best with a CFR Ray Price Tribute, and I want to tell you about it.

Janie Price, Ray's widow, joins Bill Anderson and a room full of Ray's friends, band members and Country artists who all want to pay tribute to his songs, his style and his life. Here are some of the people who came to the taping: Johnny Bush, Darrell McCall, and friends like John Conlee, Larry Gatlin, Gene Watson, Jeannie Seely, Moe Bandy, T. Graham

Brown, Wade Hayes, Johnny Lee, Ray Pillow, Curtis Potter, Bill Mack, Linda Davis, David Ball, Teea Goans, Jim Lauderdale, Jim Ed Brown, Mo Pitney, Jan Howard and Roy Clark.

It truly is a tribute to the man who brought us songs like City Lights, Release Me, Crazy Arms, Heartaches by the Number, For the Good Times, Night Life and so many more-- Songs that were sung by his friends to honor his memory during our taping.

AND… since we had all these great artists around, we had a HONKY TONK REUNION as well! And it was a GREAT Reunion. In addition to the list above, we had Rhonda Vincent, The Whites, Dale Watson, Paul Franklin, Becky Hobbs, Junior Brown, Eddy Raven and David Frizzell. Incredible artists celebrating the legacy of Honky Tonk!

So… we've got 2 new reunions that are being finished right now and they WILL be out in time for Christmas gifts. That's right. You'll have these in your hands before Christmas morning! The tapings were wonderful, and we want you—the fan of TRUE country music—to be the first to know about it.

More Tribute & Reunion photos

Dale Watson

David Ball

Bill Anderson & Janie Price

Roy Clark

Nadine's Corner

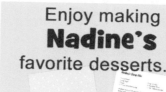

First Church of Hard Knocks

PRAYER IS LIKE WIRELESS ACCESS TO GOD, WITH NO ROAMING FEES

1 Thessalonians 5:16-18--Rejoice always, pray continually, give thanks in all circumstances; for this is God's will for you in Christ Jesus.

...and unlimited messages!

Down Home
with Carol Bass

You have heard the saying, "You can tell the year a woman graduated from high school by the way she wears her hair and makeup!" Just like hair and make-up, a home can show its age too. Here are some dead give-a-ways known as age spots, see if you recognize any. But more importantly, here are some simple practical fixes.

Is Your Room Showing Its Age Spots

Age Spot "Artwork"

Are there clusters of little bitty pictures covering your walls? Was your artwork purchased from a Home Interiors party circa 1989? Or perhaps your art is not art at all but school photos of your kids. I can't tell you how many homes I see those 'age spots.' Family photos are just that – people not art. And better yet most photos are of the kids who now have kids of their own. You need to be aware of both the subject matter, and how you hang the artwork, so you don't reveal more 'age spots.' Is the art staggered? Is it hung too high? Is it too small? Is it really artwork?

Simple Practical Fix

The way we display art is as trendy as a hemline, going up and down. Today the look is a few big pieces. Just like there was a time when big hair was all the rage, today in décor it is big art, big accessories and even big furniture. Groupings are larger in scale today too. The current on-trend way to display more than one piece of art is side-by-side or straight up and down, not staggered or stairstepped. Move the school photos upstairs into the hallway and make way for larger and current style artwork. We decorate from the floor up, not the ceiling down, so art needs to relate to the furniture it's hanging over. If it's on a wall by itself, the rule is 54" from the floor to the center of the art. Notice in the Before and After photos below the size of the art and the height of the art. In the photo on the right the center of the two pieces is 54" above the floor.

Behind the Scenes SPOTLIGHT

We have so many talented folks that work behind the scenes of our television shows and tapings that we thought you should meet them. Their talents and experience surely humble us.

Jamie Amos & Patrick Kennedy

Jamie and Patrick are both natives of west Texas who met at a film meeting in Nashville and realized they had grown up two hours away from each other in Texas.

They have been in the film production business for over 25 years - both began by working on movies. Jamie then began producing music videos and worked with many different types of artists - country, rock, pop, Christian - and on many commercials. She hired Patrick to be her production coordinator and ended up marrying him!

They have worked on every CFR production since the beginning and "totally enjoy the work," Jamie says. "It really is like a family reunion for many of the crew as well as the artists."

Jamie's job for CFR and Larry's Country Diner is do the budgets, hire the crew, handle all the travel for the artists, make sure everyone is paid, manage the productions, and handle any problems that come up.

Patrick does most of the scheduling and arranges for and manages the technical and equipment needs for the tapings.

We get great gifts from our fans...thanks to Sharon Kehrer from Michigan who sent the dolls to Michele, Nadine and Renae!

Some of the chickens at Springer Mountain Farms were working overtime producing eggs that looked like the cast of Larry's Country Diner. Thanks Gus, for bringing them to the show!

Glen Campbell documentary due for release in October

"I'll Be Me," the documentary about the life of Glen Campbell, is an award-winning film that will be released nationally in theaters this coming October 24, 2014. Volunteers of America is proud to be a sponsor. The film depicts music icon Glen Campbell as he and his family crisscross the country on his farewell concert tour following his diagnosis of Alzheimer's, to share his experience with fans and to raise awareness about the disease. View the trailer now. http://t.co/aFLFbIYKbQ

I'll BE ME tells the story of music legend Glen Campbell; his life, his music, and the extraordinary 151-city "Goodbye Tour" de force that's made him a hero.

The film features those who know and love Glen, including Bruce Springsteen, Bill Clinton, The Edge, Paul McCartney, Jay Leno, Vince Gill, Jimmy Webb, Blake Shelton, Sheryl Crow, Keith Urban, Brad Paisley, Steve Martin, Chad Smith and Taylor Swift among many others.

This powerful portrait of the life and career of great American music icon Glen Campbell opens us to the world of the singular talent who created hits such as Rhinestone Cowboy, Wichita Lineman and Gentle on My Mind.

Winner of the Grammy for Lifetime Achievement and member of the Country Music Hall of Fame, Glen was the first country music star to cross over to the pop charts, opening a new realm of opportunity for generations of country musicians.

The film is directed by James Keach, produced by Trevor Albert and James Keach.

Country Legends of the Past and Present

BY TOM WOODS

Patsy Montana

Let's play a quick version of Larry's Country Jeopardy.

The answer: She was the first female country music star to sell a million copies of a record.

The question: Who was Patsy Montana?

It might not be a Gold Star piece of trivia, but at least give yourself a pat on the back if you got it right.

First recorded in 1935, "I Want to Be a Cowboy's Sweetheart" quickly transformed Patsy into America's Sweetheart.

Her good looks, combined with a perky spirit and a lilting yodeling sound, took the country by storm. "I Want to Be a Cowboy's Sweetheart" became the signature hit for Patsy, who soon became known to her legion of fans as The Girl With the Million Dollar Personality.

Patsy was inducted into the Country Music Hall of Fame in 1996 for her influence on the genre. She's also in the National Cowgirl Museum and Hall of Fame, accorded that honor in 1987.

And Patsy's charisma didn't stop with her songs, radio show gigs and personal appearances.

A friendship she developed with Gene Autry and Pat Buttram led to her being cast as an actress in

Autry's Colorado Sunset in 1939. Five years later, in 1944, she had a role in the short movie The Chime Bells Ring.

Her other hit songs included "Montana Plains," "Rodeo Sweetheart" and "I Want to Be a Cowboy's Dream." Her music has appeared in nine films, most recently in 2009's All About Steve, starring Sandra Bullock and Bradley Cooper. "I Want to Be a Cowboy's Sweetheart" was played over the closing credits of Lone Star (1996).

Quite a legacy for a colorful woman who lived life to the fullest until her death in 1996, just prior to her Country Music Hall of Fame induction ceremony.

Here are a few other fun facts and trivia you may or may not know about Patsy Montana:

Patsy's given name was Ruby Rose Blevins. She later added an 'e' to Ruby as a teen-ager, thinking it made her name look more grown-up.

She was born in 1908 in Arkansas, not Montana. The 'Montana' part of her name was a tribute to Montie Montana, a champion roper and yodeler from that era. She changed her first name from Rubye to the stage name Patsy at the suggestion of western star Stuart Hamblen.

Hamblen and Montie Montana were headlining a radio show in 1935 and Rubye was part of a trio backing them, called the Montana Cowgirls. One

of the other singers was named Ruthie and Hamblen thought the names too similar.

Her husband was Paul E. Rose, a stage manager for Autry when they met. They had two daughters who later performed with their mother.

Outlawfest in KY has mixture of music to please all sorts of fans!

Outlaw Fest 2014 will be held October 9 – 12 at Edgehill Farm in Oakland, KY. This year it is honored to announce the addition of Gordon Ames, better known as Big G, as the voice of Outlaw Fest 2014. Gordon will host all four days of the festival. With a worldwide fan base, Big G is considered a living legend within outlaw country music circles. Appearing on Gordon's radio program, Big G's Texas Roadshow, is a huge honor.

With the addition of Willie Nelson's Granddaughter and Outlaw Country Music Legend Billy Joe Shaver.. THIS FESTIVAL WILL BE A MAJOR DEAL in 2014.

It's a history-making event when you have the Raelyn Nelson Band opening for Grandpa Willie's friend and music legend Billy Joe Shaver. When the up-and-coming Josh Morningstar opens for the Grammy winning members of Steel Driver...the event has to be special.

Free primitive camping is included with your paid admission...bring your tent or RV and stake your claim early. Outlaw Fest also offers tent packages for those of you flying in, or maybe you just don't own a tent. The Outlaw Fest staff will have your tent, air mattresses and sleeping bags in your tent waiting on your arrival.

The Bryce Inn at Smith's Grove has been chosen as the OFFICIAL hotel of Outlaw Fest and we have reserved the entire hotel for that weekend. You can get a discounted room at $61 per night plus tax. YOU MUST MENTION Outlaw Fest in order to take advantage of this deal.

For more information or to purchase tickets, call, (615) 745-9227 or email, Info@OutlawFest.com or ShineSauce@Gmail.com or visit www.outlawfest.com.

THURSDAY, October 9

6:00 PM 2Country4Nashville

7:00 PM Urban Pioneers

8:00 PM Josh Morningstar

9:00 PM Break / Special Presentation

9:30 PM The Steeldrivers

FRIDAY, October 10

10:00 AM Only Threads Left

11:00 AM Bo Chadly

12:00 PM Brandon Self & Outlaw Revival

1:00 PM Rye Davis

2:00 PM Billy Sidwell

3:00 PM P.J. Steelman, James Austin, RC O'leary

5:00 PM The Buzz Band

6:00 PM Brandon Lee Tallent

7:00 PM Whey Jennings & The Unwanted

8:00 PM Raelyn Nelson Band

9:30 PM Billy Joe Shaver

SATURDAY, October 11

10:00 AM Clarence Light Orchestra

11:00 AM Brandon Atwell & Broken Ground

12:00 PM Ross Key

1:00 PM Hanging Judges

2:00 PM Taylor Shannon Band

3:00 PM Tom Ghent

4:00 PM Hal Bruni

5:00 PM Kyle Wilson

6:00 PM J.B. Beverley & Buck Thraikill

7:00 PM Pure Grain

8:00 PM Billie Gant

9:00 PM Hatfield & McCoy Tug-O-War

9:30 PM Dallas Moore Band

SUNDAY, October 12

10:00 AM Rooney Sisters

11:00 AM Terry Jennings-Between Father's & Sons

12:00 PM Cley Reynolds

1:00 PM Chris Corkery

2:00 PM Travis Egnor & The Horse Traders

3:00 PM Otis

4:00 PM Left Hand Voodoo

5:00 PM Sinners & Saints

Eva unaware she is a pet, not a person

BY CLAUDIA JOHNSON

It is altogether possible that Eva does not realize she is a dog. And why would she?

She is the owner of this beautiful human named Elana James. She's a member of the group Hot Club of Cowtown. She's traveled throughout most of North America. She's even toured with Bob Dylan and Willie Nelson.

Oh, and she'll soon be a published author. At 11, Eva, a Welsh corgi-Australian Shepherd mix, has plenty to write about. Her book, "My Life on Tour with The Hot Club of Cowtown," isn't quite a tell-all, but it does offer a dog's eye view of the journeys of the Austin-based group that includes Jake Erwin, Whit Smith and James.

"She really knows how to be one of the band," James said. "She simultaneously guards us and allows herself to be petted. She rides the razor's edge."

The lifelong and life-altering relationship between James and Eva began with what James calls a "failed" attempt at fostering Eva, who was still a puppy.

"I guess we were a failed foster family because I kept her," James said. "I'd had several other foster dogs, but I'd never felt the same connection."

Eva's first experience on the road was a tour of minor league baseball parks with Cowtown opening for Nelson and Dylan. When Eva's idyllic summer of plush, green fields and adoring fans ended, she and Nelson were photographed together – she wearing her Willie braids and the pair wearing matching smiles.

"She's adapted well," James said. "She understands 'the hang'. If we play at a performing arts center, she's like a little hostess. She brings people together, gives them a little kiss on the ankle. She evokes this sweet, earthy vibe that is so precious."

Sometimes Eva sleeps onstage, completely at peace, despite the excitement and passion of Cowtown's lively music, but sometimes she's offstage, working the crowd, allowing fans to pet her.

"I see people go into this meditative state," James observed. "You go see a band and have no idea you're going to get to pet a little Buddha dog."

Sometimes Eva draws as much attention as the human members of Hot Club of Cowtown.

"I never mind that," James said. "I am as enamored by her as much as everyone else. Besides, I don't think you can be upstaged by a dog. If I am, I need to practice more!"

James said Eva's presence with the group "deepens what we do."

"We're a rustic act," James said. "We do hot jazz, 1930s and '40s vintage Parisian hot swing, but we also do western music. Animals are part of Western life, and who would not want them to be?"

Despite Eva's star status, personally for James, Eva is a companion and a friend. With many of her nights spent far from her Austin, Texas, home, James has learned to create a peaceful space in an unfamiliar room through use of her own pillow, quilt and other personal items strategically placed. And, of course, there's Eva.

"I always appreciate what this sweet, loving, constant creature brings," James said. "It is hard for me to ever articulate her influence in my life."

The Nashville BratPack Kids of the Country Stars!

Hey, That's My Dad's Friend!

By Alison Clement, daughter of Cowboy Jack Clement

Somewhere around 1976, I went to Memphis to live with my grandmother, my dad's mother, for a few years. She had been a widow since 1974 and she lived alone. My dad thought it would be a good idea for her to have me to look after and be with, so it was decided that I would enroll in school in Memphis and live with her for a bit. I was all for the idea and loved that time with her. I was a student at LaBelle Haven Christian Academy, which I also loved. I sang in the choir at school, I played on the volleyball team and we attended Bible Baptist Church, which just happened to be on Clement Road. The road wasn't named after US but I do love a good coincidence. My grandmother, Angela, was the church pianist there and I often sang solos. I loved belting out the old hymns that my grandfather had taught me growing up. She had accompanied him for years as he was the music minister and soloist at their church. Those were good times.

I can remember having the whole living room in our house to myself. That's where I would have hairbrush concerts. Most girls and some boys know what I mean by this, but to clarify, it's where you stand in your room and sing along to all of your favorite 45 records and cassettes, into your hairbrush. They make splendid microphones. If you don't have a hairbrush handy though, don't panic, you can use a wooden spoon or a ping pong paddle, whatever is handy.

My music collection consisted of a pretty good assortment of 45's but an even better assortment of cassettes that I had collected from my dad. He had done a lot of recording in Nashville during my earlier years. He would leave to go to "work", which in my eyes, at eight and nine years old, seemed to mean that he went and met Mr. Cash and Mr. Pride at his studio and they made up songs, then played them and put them on tape. He would bring home rough mixes and listen to them at night. I would love them and he would give me copies. I know now that some of that music never even made it to the album. I was getting to hear the stuff that nobody else got to hear. And as it turns out, in some cases, never would. My Dad was married to Jessi Colter's sister at the time and I remember when he brought home a rough version of Jessi's song, I'm Not Lisa. My hairbrush would never be the same after that. For those of you unfamiliar, Jessi was Waylon Jennings wife. My dad did some "work" with Mr. Jennings during this time also.

My cassettes weren't slick in packaging, they might be marked with a marker "Cash Ruff mix #5" or "Pride Outtakes", something like that. All I knew was that they played on my little player and I liked them. I guess I didn't realize that the music my dad was making would later turn into 45's or LP's. The 45's that I had, I bought at Kmart for 99 cents. Among the couple of dozen of them was Donny Osmond's version of Puppy Love and Terry Jacks singing Seasons in the Sun. Then I had my cassettes. My one of a kind work tapes. The stuff my dad made at his work. When I moved to Memphis, I took my little suitcase full of music with me.

My first year at LaBelle, I was invited by my friend, Caroline, to a slumber party at her house. The theme of the party was to share your music. The idea was to bring all of your favorite 45's and cassettes and we would gather in a gaggle and listen and share and sing into our hairbrushes. I was ready. I had my suitcase of tunes, my best hairbrush, my pajamas and I was off. The party was fun. Cake, piñata, boys, punch and then finally after all of the guests left, we rolled out our sleeping bags and put on our pj's and settled in for a long night of music, popcorn, prank phone calls and warnings from Caroline's mother in the wee hours to shut up or she was going to separate us. We did each other's hair, painted our nails and then we hit a lull. That's when we got out our music.

It's just me. My hair was ahead of it's time! My brother Niles, my dad and Me (age 9 or 10)

I watched as Caroline and Margaret H. sang Torn between Two Lovers and sang along as Maude B. belted out Cherish along with David Cassidy. We took a break to look at all of our TIGER BEAT magazines and ooh and ahh over Donny Osmond in his purple jumpsuit and David Cassidy in his. Then it was my turn. I said "you're gonna love this" and I played my cassette crudely marked: Johnny Cash Mixes. I can't remember the exact songs but I can remember the looks on their faces as they played. They did NOT get it. "Who IS that?", one of them asked. My retort was, "that's some music that my dad gave me that he made at his work." "Well, it's weird" and "it sounds so country" and "you can't even skate to it" were a few of the comments that followed. As much as they didn't get it, I didn't get them. I mean I love Cherish as much as the next person but this is really cool music we were listening to here. I mean, just listen to Jessi singing… have you ever heard anything like that? THAT'S what I was thinking. It was like someone had let the air out of some big music balloon and it was just about to be empty and land in a little pile on the floor. What else could I do but turn it off? So I did. I quickly relinquished my DJ rights and kind of lost interest at that point. I decided to go in the living room and watch TV. I could hear their voices faintly singing "Ah Sugar, Ah Honey Honey, You are my candy girl….." as I left the room.

In the living room, Caroline's parents had a very large collection of LP's. Among them I came across a Johnny Cash record. I was shocked. There he was, my dad's friend and co-worker, Mr. Cash. Hey, wait a minute. Does my dad have something to do with making "real" records? I thought they just made crudely marked cassettes. And went to lunch. And wrote funny stuff down on big legal pads. And picked guitars and hung out. Have other people

heard of Mr. Cash and bought his records just like I bought Donny Osmond's? It was a revelation for me. I flipped the record over and there in print were the words Producer: Jack Clement. Back in those days, you had to be a big deal to have your own record. I guess this Mr. Cash, with his really sweet wife and neat daughter named Roseanne was a big deal. Who knew?

I marched back into the slumber party and I said, "Look, there he is, my dad's friend, the one on the cassette." "Yeah, sure, you know somebody on a record" were the next words I heard. "Well, as a matter of fact, I do. His wife, June, and I made an easy bake oven cake last Sunday while my dad and Mr. Cash worked in the studio. I guess somebody liked it, cause they made a record of it, just like they did of David Cassidy" was all I knew to say to THAT.

Well, as girls are resilient, we moved on, merrily and giggling about something else without a hitch. But, on that day, I realized that what my dad did was much more than just leave the house and come home with cassettes. And on that day, it turns out that I was right about the music. I'm sure that there are more Johnny Cash posters on walls in the world than there are ones of Donny Osmond and the like. I was too young to realize that musical history was being made all around me. I just knew that I liked what I heard.

Turns out I was right about Jessi Colter, too.

Be sure to read next month when we'll have more stories from one of the kids of 'The Nashville Brat Pack'.

Stage Clothes of the Stars

By Claudia Johnson

BY CLAUDIA JOHNSON

Jim Ed Brown: Dapper and Distinguished

The black and white video features two very attractive young women flanking a drop-dead gorgeous man. It's 1965, and The Browns are at the Grand Old Opry singing "The Three Bells," their 1959 number one hit. Maxine and Bonnie Brown don matching sleeveless, street-length dresses adorned with just enough sparkles to attract interest but remain elegant. Their brother, Jim Ed, looks dapper in a shiny, fitted jacket and a black bolo.

Some of Jim Ed Brown's early performance attire was designed by Nathan Turk, owner of Turk of Hollywood, who fashioned clothing for Gene Autry, Roy Rogers and other notable musicians of the 50s. Iconic designer Manuel, known for his elaborate creations, has also crafted a number of costumes for Brown.; however, album covers, publicity shots and videos from across the decades attest to Brown's sartorial restraint.

Sure there are embellished collar points and jacket lapels, beaded bolos, skinny ties, leather vests and even some brightly colored suits with contrasting piping, but the venerable singer has remained clean cut, impeccably groomed and conservatively attired.

"If you are going to be in the public eye, you must respect the public enough to show up looking respectful," he said.

At age 80, Brown is still a handsome man with a commanding presence. The cover for a recent single, aptly titled "In Style Again," has Brown dressed in a bright red jacket with beaded cuffs and lapels, a crisp black shirt, tailored black slacks, shiny black leather cowboy boots and a silver-clasped bolo.

"I never went for the bad-boy look," he said. "Women love a rebel, but for some reason, when all is said and done, they choose the other."

Apparently, the "other" is the boy-next-door, which the rural Arkansas native was. Jim Ed's father was in the logging industry, and he and sisters, Maxine, Bonnie, and Norma, and brother, Raymond flourished in a home filled with love and guided by wisdom.

After a logging accident in which the elder Brown lost his leg, Jim Ed was groomed to take command of the family business, even majoring in Forestry in college. Throughout his 20s he managed a dual career as a radio, stage and television performer and as a businessman in Pine Bluff, Ark., where he actively participated in the community. It was during his stint as organizer of the Pine Bluff Jaycees annual beauty pageant he met Becky, the woman who has been his wife for more than five decades. Together the two have raised a daughter and son.

"After our first child was born, Becky insisted we move to Nashville," Brown said, explaining that his performance obligations kept him gone most weekends, flying out on Friday and returning in time to work at the sawmill during the week. "It was the right thing to do."

Brown is working on a new album for release this year, continuing to host his Country Greats Radio Show and performing in concert.

"It's been a great career," he said with satisfaction. "My wife and I are so happy. My children are successful and happy. God has always blessed my life and shown me the way."

The radio history of Doc Williams and the Border Riders

The CFR News received a letter stating the following:

"We found this photo in an old frame at a yard sale. Can you tell us who they are and if any of them are still alive?

Sincerely, Ginny Mowers and Jim Coffin"

The following is what we were able to find out for you.

Doc Williams was born as Andrew John Smik, Jr., on June 26, 1914, in Cleveland, Ohio, and raised in Kittanning, Pennsylvania. He was the son of parents who immigrated to the United States in the early 1900s. Andrew Sr. and Susie would have five children--Doc the oldest.

Doc's father taught him about music and there was always an old fiddle, a cornet, and other instruments around their home. By age 12, Doc had learned to play the cornet by note, and could play many songs from the family hymnbook. He also played the trumpet, accordion, and guitar and had a natural love for music. His father bought him a guitar for $3.00 at a pawnshop, and brother Cy, who was six years younger than Doc, got a fiddle.

In 1929, as he was going into the 10th grade, Doc had to quit school so that he could help support his family. He worked with his father for a couple years in the coal mines; however, during those years, Doc still pursued his love for music. He played guitar and sang vocals, brother Cy played fiddle and helped out on vocal harmonies, and neighbor, Dale Kuhn, played the tenor banjo. The band worked weekend dances for free.

Doc left the mines to follow his dream of becoming a country music entertainer, moving to Cleveland, Ohio, to live with his maternal grandmother, Suzanna. When she saw that her grandson was serious about music, she gave him a small professional guitar, which she had purchased for $45. Doc began rehearsing songs with neighbor Joe Stoetzer, and they called their duo the Mississippi Clowns. Doc played guitar and harmonica, and Joe played the musical spoons and the kazoo with a horn attached.

Doc and Joe started broadcasting on an amateur program, the Barn Busters, at WJAY in Cleveland. The emcee of the program was Morey Amsterdam, who would become a famous comedian.

When Joe left the act, Doc and Curley Sims (on mandolin) formed the Allegheny Ramblers, along with brother Cy Williams on fiddle and vocal harmonies. In 1935, the group moved to KQV in Pittsburgh, Pennsylvania, where they renamed the group the Cherokee Hillbillies, borrowing from the fact that Curley was part Cherokee Indian. In 1936, they were offered a contract with Miss Billie Walker and her Texas Longhorns, who were also broadcasting over KQV. Big Slim, the Lone Cowboy, was a member of that group. When Miss Billie moved to WLS in New Orleans, Louisiana, Doc formed his own group, the Border Riders. The group moved to WJAS in Pittsburgh, on a three-station hook-up with KQV and WHJB in Greensburg, Pennsylvania, for a daily 8:30 a.m. broadcast, sponsored by the ABC Washing Machine Company. This marked the first time the name Doc Williams and the Border Riders was used over the airwaves.

In 1937, Doc and the Border Riders auditioned for a spot over WWVA in Wheeling, West Virginia, located about 57 miles west of Pittsburgh. The group was immediately given a 2:45 p.m. daily show over WWVA. Their first broadcast was on May 1, 1937.

The group also became members of the Saturday night "World's Original WWVA Jamboree" (later called Jamboree USA)--which was the second oldest surviving live country music "barn dance" at the time of its closure at the end of 2005. Although Doc Williams and his Border Riders were newcomers to WWVA, they won the Silver Trophy as the most popular act during the radio station's on-air popularity contest from March 14-19, 1938, with 15,877 votes. The group at that time was composed of Doc, as leader of the band, Brother Cy, Big Slim, Sunflower (female vocalist), and Rawhide (comedian).

Doc met his future wife and singing partner, Chickie Williams (Jessie Wanda Crupe), at the Reawood Dance Hall in Hickory, Pennsylvania, when Chickie wrote to him requesting a personal appearance there. It was love at first sight for Doc. They married in 1939 and made their home in Wheeling.

Doc has spent most of his long country music career at WWVA, except for brief periods at WREC, Memphis, Tennessee, and WFMD, Frederick, Maryland in the 1940's. On the Border Riders' return to Wheeling after their short tenure at WREC in 1940, Doc stopped off to see Harry Stone at WSM in Nashville. Mr. Stone offered Doc a job at the Grand Ole Opry, but Doc had to take a "rain check," as his wife, Chickie, was expecting their first child and she wanted to return home to Wheeling. They went on to have three daughters, Barbara, Madeline, and Karen. The girls were known over the radio and on stage as Peeper, Pooch, and Punkin, and made their debut on the Jamboree at ages, 7, 5, and 4. They also traveled with their parents' show during school vacations.

Doc never picked up the rain check, as WWVA increased its power from 5,000 watts to 50,000 watts in 1941, and Doc and Chickie Williams would continue as two of Jamboree's most popular and enduring entertainers.

Doc Williams passed on at the wonderful old age of 96 in January 2011. His was a life filled with devotion to his family, his fans and friends, and to his life's work as a country music entertainer and business person. He credited a great deal of the success he enjoyed over the years to the lady who had been at his side all those years, his wife and singing partner, Chickie Williams, "The Girl with the Lullaby Voice."

THE DOC WILLIAMS SHOW — WWVA — WHEELING. W. VA.

A copy of the photo found at a garage sale or Doc Williams and The Border Riders

Group Members of Th Border Riders

Group members, 1937 (Pittsburgh, PA):
* Doc Williams
* Hamilton "Rawhide" Fincher
* Mary Jane Mosier
* Cy Williams

Group members, 1937 (Wheeling, WV):
* Doc Williams
* Hamilton "Rawhide" Fincher
* Cy Williams
* Sunflower (Mary Calvas)
* Curley Simms

Group members, 1938-40 (Wheeling, WV and Memphis, TN)
* Doc Williams
* Curley Simms
* Cy Williams
* Froggie Cortez
* Sunflower (Mary Calvas)

Group members, 1942 (Wheeling, WV):
* Doc Williams
* Smokey Davis
* Jesse Porter
* Cy Williams
* Sunflower (Mary Calvas)

Larry's Country Diner RFD Show Schedule

CHARLIE MCCOY
Saturday, Oct. 4
10:00 p.m. Central
Sunday, Oct. 5
6:00 p.m. Central

DEANA CARTER
Saturday, Oct. 11
10:00 p.m. Central
Sunday, Oct. 12
6:00 p.m. Central

MOUNTAIN FAITH
Saturday, Oct. 18
10:00 p.m. Central
Sunday, Oct. 19
6:00 p.m. Central

COLLIN RAYE
Saturday, Oct. 25
10:00 p.m. Central
Sunday, Oct. 26
6:00 p.m. Central

Sometimes you have to wonder why they still love us!

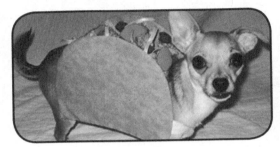

Country Questions
By Dick Boise, CMH

Send questions to:
Dick Boise, , c/o CFR News,
P.O. Box 201796, Nashville,
TN 37221.

Q. I have been a long time classic country music fan. Hope you can help me with my questions. Is former school teacher Donna Fargo still alive?

Bea Aust, Camano Island, WA

A. Donna Fargo was born Yvonne Vaughn in Mount Airy, NC on November 10, 1945. She had a couple of number one hits with "Happiest Girl In The Whole USA" and "Funny Face." In 1978 she was diagnosed with multiple Sclerosis and returned to limited schedule in '79. She has written four books and is a self created greeting card lady at this time. Yes, that talented "teacher" is still alive.

Q. I watch Midwest Country and want to ask if Bobby Darren and Shelia Marie are married?

Dorothy Held, Coloma, WI

A. Dorothy, thank you for your inquiry here to Country Questions. Bobby Darren is married and he and his wife, Debbie, have two sons and a daughter. Possibly more future singers coming along. Shelia Marie is part of Bobby's show and he is her uncle. I have not heard that she is married.

Q. Have not seen Little Jimmy Dickens or heard anything about him in a while. Enjoyed him on the Family Reunion shows. Can you tell me anything about him? Thanks.

Jean Snook, Kimberling City, MO

A. Jean, Little Jimmy is just about everyone's favorite on those shows. With his advanced age (he is going to be 94 on December 19) and some recent health issues, he might tend to slow me down a bit. He had radiation treatments on his vocal cords in June of 2013. At this time he is the oldest living Opry member. I hope to see him on TV again soon also.

Q. I seem to remember a song years ago with the title, "Today." Can you find me any information about that?

Kirk Cooper, Clifton Springs, NY

A. Hank Thompson recorded that song with his great western swing band sound. You got me to thinking and he also recorded a song called "Tomorrow Night" and one titled "Yesterday's Girl." He is probably the only singer to work in Yesterday, Today and Tomorrow into his fast song selection. He was also the first entertainer to record a live show album at the Golden Nugget.

Look what's happening at the Starlite Theatre!

What's happening at the Starlite Theatre? Lots of shows, that's what. Some of your favorite artists and shows are at the Starlite, so if you're in town to see Larry's Country Diner, you might want to check out some of the other great shows they have there. Here's the scoop!

The Texas Tenors bring back their unique blend of Country, Gospel, Classical and Broadway style to their award-winning Branson show at the Starlite Theatre.

Over 100 million people from around the world tuned in to see The Texas Tenors become the #1 vocal group in the history of "America's Got Talent." Winning the hearts of millions, The Texas Tenors burst onto the national scene and never looked back. Since then, the group has performed more than 600 concerts around the world.

In their first PBS special, "You Should Dream", which aired nationwide December 2013, The Texas Tenors brought their own signature blend of breathtaking vocals, humor, harmony and cowboy charm. This charismatic and talented trio — Marcus Collins, John Hagen, and JC Fisher — smoothly blend great music from the worlds of country, classical, gospel and Broadway. "You Should Dream" PBS special will continue to air through 2014, so check your local listings.

The Texas Tenors will be performing select dates through December 4, 2014.

Billy Dean Live featuring comedian Jarrett Dougherty is all new in 2014! Join Billy and Jarrett for a show filled with country and comedy, lyrics and laughter! Grammy Award Winner Billy Dean has sold over four million albums with 11 Top Ten singles and five number one hits! CMA voted him Top New Male Vocalist of the Year and he won song of the year for his self penned "Somewhere In My Broken Heart."

Dean first gained national attention after appearing on "Star Search" and has recorded eight studio albums since 1990, of which four have been certified "Gold ." He has generated more than 20 hit singles on the Billboard country charts including 11 Top Ten hits.

After traveling the country as the drummer for various award-winning musical groups, Jarrett Dougherty settled in the Branson area in 1995. He quickly gained popularity for his musical and comedic talents – performing with Barbara Fairchild, Sons of the Pioneers, and Pierce Arrow. Jarrett's side-splitting humor has earned him recognition as one of Branson's funniest comedians.

Come see the new Billy Dean Live through selected dates to November 19.

Larry Gatlin is perhaps best known for teaming up with his brothers Steve and Rudy in the late 1970s, becoming one of country music's most successful acts of the 1970s and 1980s. Gatlin has had a total of 33 Top 40 singles (combining his solo recordings and those with his brothers). As their fame grew, the band became known as Larry Gatlin & the Gatlin Brothers.

In 1979, they released their album, Straight Ahead. It spawned the classic single "All the Gold in California," which became their biggest hit together, taking the No. 1 spot on the Hot Country Songs list. This was Larry Gatlin's second number one hit, and led to his being awarded "Top Male Vocalist of the Year" by the Academy of Country Music that year. On June 6, 1980, Straight Ahead was certified gold. The Gatlin

Brothers were also one of the first country groups to have music videos, like 1984's "The Lady Takes the Cowboy Every Time". In 1985, Gatlin wrote the song "Indian Summer" with Barry Gibb, which he recorded as a duet with Roy Orbison.

In 1989, the Gatlin Brothers sang the National Anthem before game three of the 1989 World Series, played at Candlestick Park in San Francisco, California.

Larry Gatlin and the Gatlin Brothers show will be playing select dates starting March 6 – December 3, 2014.

Gene Watson is most famous for his 1975 hit "Love in the Hot Afternoon," his 1981 hit "Fourteen Carat Mind," and his signature song "Farewell Party. Watson was nationally successful throughout the late 1970s and early 1980s, as he recorded several Billboard top-40 hits. In February 2012, Watson, celebrated his 50th year in the music business with the release of Best of the Best, 25 Greatest Hits (his very first single on radio "If It Was That Easy" was released in 1962).

Gene Watson was inducted into the Texas Country Music Hall of Fame in 2002 and inducted into the inaugural class of the Houston Music Hall of Fame in August 2014.

Gene Watson's appearance on the Sept 24th with Larry's Country Diner was SOLD OUT, but he will be back by popular demand for 3 NIGHTS OF HIS OWN SHOW October 21-23!

Country's Family Reunion with Bill Anderson will be at the Starlite inOctober.

• OCTOBER 21 (2:00pm):

Bill Anderson, Jeannie Seely, Barbara Fairchild, Buck Trent & Mickey Gilley

• OCTOBER 22 (7:30pm): Bill Anderson, Jeannie Seely and Mary Lou Turner

• OCTOBER 23 (2:00pm): Bill Anderson, Jeannie Seely, Mickey Gilley and Leona Williams

• OCTOBER 24 (2:00pm): Bill Anderson, Jeannie Seely, Barbara Fairchild and Buck Trent

• OCTOBER 25 (7:30pm): Bill Anderson, Jeannie Seely, Mary Lou Turner and Larry Gatlin

• OCTOBER 26 (2:00pm): Bill Anderson, Jeannie Seely, Leona Williams and Larry Gatlin

Paul Harris, an Arkansas native, is widely known as a comedian, singer and musician, with tastes ranging from rock to bluegrass, and has been performing in Branson for nearly 20 years.

Having such a long career in the area, Harris has gotten his shows down to a science.

The Cleverlys

"The 2014 Branson show, will still be the same format, but there's going to be some new material," he said. "I do stand-up comedy, so I'll do a 40-minute comedy set of some of my best old stuff and a lot of new stuff I've been writing this winter."

Much like Jeff Foxworthy, for whom Harris has opened in the past, he uses his southern charm to tackle nearly every subject there is, but he always walks the line and keeps his show clean.Once his stand-up is done, Harris is joined by his band to play a few bluegrass tunes before the Cleverlys take over in the second half.

The Starlite is located at 3115 W. Hwy 76 Branson, MO. For tickets or more information, call 417-337-9333.

Jimmy Fortune's career made by serendipity and talent

A combination of serendipity and talent best explains how country music's beloved tenor, Jimmy Fortune, wound up with the Statler Brothers. Fortune was handpicked by the group's original tenor, Lew DeWitt, as a temporary replacement for himself while he fought a debilitating medical condition. In 1982 when DeWitt opted not to rejoin the group, Fortune became a permanent "brother," joining lead singer Don Reid and his real-life brother, bass singer Harold Reid, along with the group's baritone Phil Barsley.

That turn of fortune, so to speak, resulted in a 21-year stint with the Statler Brothers, but an early case of mistaken identity remains one of Fortune's comic memories. The group had arrived at a venue, and "the Brothers," as Fortune refers to his band mates, had gone ahead to conduct sound check while Fortune retrieved his guitar from the bus. When he approached the guard for entry, he was stopped.

"You're not one of the Statler Brothers," the guard told Fortune. "I know what they look like, and you are not one of them."

"I am," Fortune argued and continued to try to convince the guard. "You'll find out."

Not budging, the guard made Fortune wait until help arrived.

"The road manager really crawled all over that guard," Fortune laughed. "I said, 'I told you,' but I guess he was just doing his job."

Fortune said that the Statlers' hit "Elizabeth" was rumored at the time of its release to have been penned about Elizabeth Taylor, but he did not write the song specifically for the actress. He does believe, however, that Divine intervention inspired him to write it. Not only did he begin the song while watching Taylor's movie "Giant" on the tour bus headed for Tulsa, Okla., but as the Statlers performed there, a young woman grabbed Fortune's hand, yelling repeatedly, "I'm Elizabeth." When he finally pulled away, he lost his balance and fell into the drums.

"I told myself that I'd better put that name in a song," he said, adding, "It became my first number one song and one of the biggest songs I've ever had anything to do with."

Fortune treasures the memory of the Statlers singing to Elizabeth Taylor on her 52nd birthday while she was shooting "Poker Annie" in Old Tucson, Ariz., and the Brothers were performing there.

"She came to our bus, and first we sang "Happy Birthday," Fortune said. "When we finished, Harold stepped up and said, 'We wrote "Elizabeth" just for you.' So we sang it, and I guess she thought it was written just for her."

Fortune said that as the tour bus traveled the long roads between concert sites, Don Reid would often start craving candy, announcing, "I'd give $100 for a Three Musketeers," which no one had readily available.

"Don would change it up, but he'd still say he'd give $100 for this or that," Fortune said. "Well, I bought one of every candy bar so the next time I'd be able to say 'here it is buddy, pay up'."

Not long after, Reid said, "I'd give $500 for a Three Musketeers."

"I took off to the back of the bus, and I was digging in my candy bar bag," Fortune said. "I had the candy bars torn out, laying everywhere. I knew I had a Three Musketeers, but I couldn't find it."

The he heard it – the laughter. Unfortunately, Fortune confided his plan to Barsley, and Fortune's brilliant candy joke was on him.

The Statler Brothers' hit "Count on Me" was used as the theme song of the DARE (Drug Abuse Resistance Education) program initiated by the Reagan administration to combat youth drug use. The first time they met with President Ronald Reagan, they were seated in the Oval Office, when the president leaned back and propped his boots upon his desk.

"Well," Reagan said, "I wore my cowboy boots in honor of you boys."

The DARE program enabled Fortune to see many of the people he had admired, including one childhood hero, Gene Autry. When the Statlers were invited to Autry's home, Fortune noticed Autry's old Martin D45 guitar.

"You like that guitar?" Autry asked.

"Yes sir," Fortune told him. "That's the guitar I've seen you play on some of your movies and TV shows."

"Do you want to play it?" Autry asked.

Fortune said he could hardly answer, but he said yes and played the cowboy legend's guitar.

Autry treated the group to a Los Angeles Angels game, where Fortune met a favorite actor, Pat Buttram, Autry's sidekick and a star of TV's "Green Acres."

"I was sitting there between Gene Autry and Pat Buttram, and all I could think was that I wish I could call my dad," Fortune said. "Of course, we didn't have cell phones back then. I could not believe I was there."

Fortune remembers his time with the Statler Brothers as a "blessing" that gave him the chance to use the musical gifts God gave him.

Precious Memories; Remembering T. Tommy Cutrer

T. Tommy Cutrer was born in Kentwood, Louisiana on June 29, 1924 and was raised not far from there in Osyka, Mississippi. He was playing football for Osyka High School at age 14 when he was sidelined by osteomyelitis. After being bedridden for a year, he resumed school at St. Mary of the Pines in Chatawa, where the Sisters stressed elocution. Clear diction would stick with him; by his senior year he was working as emcee of a radio variety show in McComb.

He became successful as a country and gospel singer and instrumentalist and also as a businessman and politician, but his greatest fame came as a radio/television personality from the 1940s through the 1990s. As an announcer on the Grand Ole Opry and country music television shows, and as the host of nationally syndicated radio broadcasts, he became one of the best-known entertainers in country music.

Cutrer took on increasingly prominent disc jockey and emcee jobs at KARK, Little Rock (1943); WREC, Memphis (1944); WSLI, Jackson (1946); NUZ, Houston (1949); and KCIJ, Shreveport (1951-'54). Mostly he played country music, but also a bit of pop. It was the manager of the Houston station who, finding the pronunciation "cut-Trair" difficult, dubbed him simply "T. Tommy," and the on-air name stuck. In Shreveport, Cutrer was the first disc jockey to play Johnny Cash records, and the first outside of Memphis to play Elvis Presley records. During this time, he also worked on his secondary career as a singer of country and gospel music and a drum-playing band leader. Floyd Cramer and Jimmy Day would be Cutrer band members, and he'd record dozens of singles for such labels as Abbott,

Capitol, Mercury, Columbia and Dot, most of them in the 1950s. When T. Tommy lost his left leg in a car crash en route to Nashville, his ability to play music was severely limited, but the country music capital proved the site of his greatest country music success. Between 1954 and 1964 he achieved national fame as a disc jockey at WSM radio, the voice of the Grand Ole Opry, and, after a stint as owner-operator of WJQS radio in Jackson, as the emcee on the Flatt & Scrugg, Pet Milk Opry and Johnny Cash television shows. He was named the nation's top D.J. in 1957. As emcee of the broadcast Country Music Worldwide, he was heard across Europe, South America, and Africa.

Cutrer turned to politics in 1976, in an attempted run for Congress in Tennessee, and was successfully elected a state senator there in 1979; after four years in office he went on to be spokesman for the Teamsters union, as an operator of restaurants, and a return to radio. Music City USA, his nationally syndicated country music interview show, was heard on more than 130 stations in the 1970s. T. Tommy Cutrer was elected to the Disc Jockey Hall of Fame in 1980.

He was the father of three sons and two daughters; he married twice, first to Lucille Lang in the 1940s, then to Vicki Martin. He died on October 11, 1998.

World loses country ambassador, George Hamilton IV

"It's really nice to be important - but much more important to be nice." That was a saying George Hamilton IV lived by. The world lost the International Ambassador of Country Music on September 17 following a heart attack that previous Saturday.

During the memorial service at the Ryman Auditorium on September 24, Jett Williams told everyone of the love George had for her dad, Hank Williams, and how it was interesting that George had passed on her dad's birthday.

John D. Loudermilk spoke about George's first hit song and how it came to pass. Loudermilk had written the song "A Rose And A Baby Ruth" and hoped to record it. He left it with a record executive while he went off to summer Guard Camp. When he came back he found out that an unknown 19-year-old man from Winston-Salem, North Carolina, had recorded it and they had a hit song.

George Hamilton IV

1937 - 2014

George Hamilton IV grew up listening to the Grand Ole Opry. When he was young, he rode the bus several times from North Carolina to Nashville to see the Grand Ole Opry in person. He joined the Opry himself in 1960, joining many of the heroes he grew up listening to as a young boy.

Chet Atkins signed him to RCA Victor as a country artist. He got his first Top 10 country hit in 1960, with "Before This Day Ends," and then again with "Three Steps to the Phone (Millions of Miles)" and "If You Don't Know I Ain't Gonna Tell You." In 1963,

"Abilene," a tribute to a Kansas town, became his biggest hit and a four-week No. 1 country single.

He was never the rowdy, drinking, crying-in-my-beer kind of country singer that was in fashion at the time. George was a quiet, gentle man with a smooth voice who could calm you with a smile. One of the stories told by Ricky Skaggs was about being on a bus with George, his wife and some others when talk got a little rough. Ricky admits this was when he was young and brash and words came out of his mouth that should have. He said George just turned around and smiled at him with a look that reminded him of his mother. In tears Ricky told everyone how it made him realize that he shouldn't be using that language. George didn't scold him or even say a word. But it made a lasting impression on him.

In 1968, he and his wife Tink attended an event at Vanderbilt's Memorial Gym where Democratic presidential candidate Robert F. Kennedy was to give a speech. Kennedy was late and George was asked if he could entertain the crowd until Kennedy could get there. According to Frye Gaillard, at first George turned down the request saying he didn't feel he was good enough, but Gaillard convinced him by telling him George was all they had.

George told people he considered "opening" for Kennedy a highlight of his musical career and even returned a check that had been sent to him to pay for his time.

In 1973, George completed the "longest international concert tour in country music," performing 73 shows in three months. He became the first country artist to perform behind the Iron Curtain, playing in Czechoslovakia and in Russia in 1974. By 1976 he was known as country music's "International Ambassador."

He was a passionate advocate for country music and for his deeply held faith, frequently performing as part of Billy Graham's Christian crusades. George attended the Moravian church in North Carolina, but found a church home with the Baptists in his Franklin, Tennessee, home.

He also found a place he loved in the Opry. He greeted guests as they came to the Grand Ole Opry for backstage tours. He loved meeting people and the fans and tour guides loved him, as was shown at his memorial service when two pews of his fellow greeters were in attendance.

Others who performed at his service were Connie Smith, Marty Stuart, Ricky Skaggs and the Whites, Jimmy Capps, Jim "Moose" Brown, Gail Davies, Andrew Greer and Cindy Morgan, Barry and Holly Tashian, Joe and Carol Babcock and David Moody. Eddie Stubbs and Bill Anderson spoke along with his pastor and others who remembered him fondly.

At the end of the service a lone bagpiper came in playing and as he walked by the simple pine casket there wasn't a dry eye in the Ryman.

Stringbean Akeman's killer granted parole

The man convicted of murdering Grand Ole Opry star David "Stringbean" Akeman has been granted his request for parole by The Tennesse Board of Parole. On October 15, the board granted John Brown's request for parole.

The 64-year-old Brown had served 41 years of a 198 year sentence, and had been denied parole at least a half dozen times.

For the full story on Stringbean Akeman and his killer's parole, see our December issue.

The CFR News
is published monthly by
Gabriel Communications, Inc.
P.O. Box 210796, Nashville, TN 37221

615-673-2846
Larry Black, Publisher
Renae Johnson, General Manager
Paula Underwood Winters, Editor

Corey Frizzell holds benefit for singer/songwriter Whitey Shafer

Nashville's Artist to the Stars, Corey Frizzell, teamed up with Country Star, Jerrod Niemann to produce the star studded event, "That's The Way Love Goes - A Benefit for Legendary Singer Songwriter Whitey Shafer."

"Whitey has suffered from recent health issues with mounting bills." Said Corey, "He means a lot to me and to Country Music. When I was told what the Shafers have been dealing with, I decided I needed to do something for this Icon. So I called some friends and got to work."

The Benefit took place Tuesday, October 7th at Downtown Nashville's Honky Tonk Central (3rd Floor) with performers Jerrod Niemann, Lee Roy Parnell, Ken Mellons, Daryle Singetary, Billy Yates, Dallas Davidson, Rob Hatch, Lance Miller and special surprise guests..

If you'd like to contribute, please mail a check to P.O. Box 558, Ridgetop, TN 37152 or make a secure online donation through PayPal at trace-74@comcast.net.

Whitey Shafer began his musical career in the town where he was born, Whitney, Texas. He moved to Nashville in 1967, where he signed his first publishing contract with Blue Crest Music Publishing Company.

In the early 1970's, Whitey signed an exclusive contract with Acuff-Rose Music. In 1972, "That's The Way Love Goes," became a #1 hit for Johnny Rodriguez. Shafer wrote four songs for George Strait's 1985 album "Does Fort Worth Ever Cross Your Mind," which received the Album of the Year honors from the CMA and the ACM. In 1987, "All My Ex's Live In Texas," written with his wife at the time, Lyndia Shafer, also became a #1 hit song and was nominated for a Grammy and CMA Song of The Year.

Whitey has written with and for some of the greatest Artists and Songwriters known to Country Music. He befriended Lefty Frizzell, with whom he began co-writing. Their collaborations included "That's the Way Love Goes" and "I Never Go Around Mirrors," two of the most well known songs in Frizzell's catalog. "That's The Way Love Goes" was also recorded by Johnny Rodriguez and Merle Haggard. "Rainbow In Daddy's Eyes" is an all-out, pure country weeper recorded by Johnny Bush; "I Wonder Do You Think Of Me" was recorded by Keith Whitley. "All My Ex's Live In Texas," "Overnight Success," "Lefty's Gone," and "Does Fort Worth Ever Cross Your Mind" were just a few of the songs recorded by George Strait.

Whitey has written over 500 songs and continues his hit songwriting career with artists such as John Michael Montgomery, LeAnn Womack, and Kenny Chesney.

For more information, please visit the Benefit Facebook Event Page: https://www.facebook.com/events/722739027810428/

Nadine's Corner

Most folks have turkey for Thanksgiving, but here are a couple of side dish recipes to go with that turkey!

Mess of Greens

Ingredients
- 2 tablespoons butter
- 3 Tablespoons olive oil
- 1 small sweet onion, diced
- 3 garlic cloves, minced
- 1 smoked ham hock (about 12 oz.)
- 3 (1-lb.) packages fresh collard greens, washed, trimmed, and cut into thin strips
- Pepper sauce

Preparation
1. Melt butter with oil in a large Dutch oven over medium-high heat. Add onion, and sauté 5 minutes or until lightly browned. Add garlic; sauté 1 minute. Add ham hock, and gently stir.

2. Add half of collards and 2 cups water. Cover and cook over medium-high heat, stirring occasionally, 10 minutes. Add remaining collards and 8 cups water; bring to a boil. Cover, reduce heat to low, and simmer 2 hours. Add table salt and black pepper to taste, and serve with pepper sauce.

Spicy Option: Stir in 1/4 to 1/2 cup jarred jalapeño peppers, if desired.

KEEP CALM AND THANK GOD

Bill Anderson gets surprise during show in Branson

Bill Anderson had a big surprise at the Larry's Country Diner Show in Branson on Saturday night, September 27. As Bill closed his segment with the song "OLD ARMY HAT," some of the folks in the audience started yelling. When he stopped and asked them what they were yelling, one of the men said the man whom the song was written about was actually in the audience. Ed Hanley, who is 90 plus years old, was in the audience and made his way down to the stage.

It was very emotional for everyone. When he got on stage he thanked Bill and then said, "What I found out is…watch out what you tell Bill Anderson….he'll write a song about it."

The story behind "Old Army Hat" as told by Bill Anderson

It is a true story that happened to my friend and his father. The father is still living and he is from a little town in Tennessee. He just turned 90 years old. It was a few years ago when his son realized how bad he wanted to go see the World War II Memorial. His son took him up there, but it was a true story that the son told him to please not wear that old army hat up there. Of course the father made sure to tell the son he would wear the hat wherever he wanted to wear that hat! The part in the song where the little boy comes up to him….all that is true and really happened. The biggest challenge for this song was making it flow and fit, but still get the complete story told in less than 10 minutes. It was such a deep story, there were a few parts we just weren't able to write into the song. Walt Aldridge is my co-writer on the song and he saw the beauty and the value of the story and he really helped me organize my thoughts and get it all down on paper.

Kenny Rogers 2014 Christmas and Hits Through The Years Tour

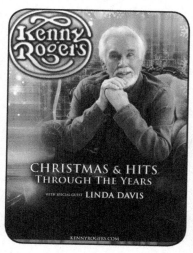

GRAMMY Award-winning Country Music Hall of Fame member Kenny Rogers will be performing holiday favorites and his classic hits across the U.S. and Canada when his 33rd Christmas tour – Christmas & Hits Through The Years with Special Guest Linda Davis - launches this November. The legendary Rogers will be joined by GRAMMY Award-winner Linda Davis on a festive 25-date run that begins November 12 in Niagara Falls, Ontario and wraps December 23 in Westbury, New York.

Just this month Rogers, along with his longtime friend Dolly Parton, received their fifth joint nomination as a duo for this year's CMA Awards. The title track duet from Rogers' new album, You Can't Make Old Friends, which is also featured on Parton's latest release, Blue Smoke, earned the collaborators a nomination in the Musical Event of the Year category. Rogers and Parton also received a GRAMMY Award nomination earlier this year.

Rogers generates a fun, family-friendly atmosphere annually with his Christmas & Hits shows, which have become a holiday tradition. His heartwarming performances of Christmas-time favorites like "White Christmas," "O Holy Night," "The Christmas Song (Chestnuts Roasting On An Open Fire)" and originals such as "Mary, Did You Know" are accented with the addition of a local choir and children in each tour city. Rogers also performs his big hits such as "Lady," "The Gambler," "Islands In The Stream," "Lucille," "Ruby, Don't Take Your Love To Town, "She Believes In Me," and "Daytime Friends," making this show a special treat.

Celebrating the holiday season, Kenny Rogers adds his legendary voice and incomparable style to Jim Brickman's original song "That Silent Night." This song, along with fourteen new recordings, will be available exclusively at Amazon on Brickman's album On A Winter's Night: The Songs and Spirit of Christmas. The album, set for release on October 7, can be pre-ordered at Amazon now. A portion of all album sales will benefit The Zach Sobiech Osteosarcoma Fund. The fund supports groundbreaking research for osteosarcoma, a rare and aggressive bone cancer.

Not one to rest on his laurels, Rogers is continuing to receive acclaim for his live performances and new studio recordings. The Milwaukee Journal Sentinel observes of Rogers and his latest release (and 22nd career Top 10 country album), You Can't Make Old Friends, "his voice is still an instrument to be reckoned with" and in a glowing review, Country Weekly notes "you have to give Kenny a ton of credit for being willing to spread his wings in new directions—and even more for pulling it off."

A trailblazing artist, Rogers has sold more than 120 million albums worldwide. Amazingly, he has charted a record within each of the last seven decades. He received the Willie Nelson Lifetime Achievement Award at the 47th Annual CMA Awards last fall. The first country artist to consistently sell out arenas, Rogers quickly became a pop superstar as well – his 28 Billboard Adult Contemporary Top 10s is fourth-best all time among men, trailing only Elton John, Neil Diamond and Elvis Presley. Rogers has recorded 12 No. 1 albums and 24 No. 1 hits and is the RIAA's 8th best-selling male artist of all time. He has received three GRAMMY Awards, 11 People's Choice Awards, 18 American Music Awards, eight Academy of Country Music awards and six Country Music Association awards. For more information go to: www.kennyrogers.com

Country Legends of the Past and Present

BY TOM WOODS

Lefty Frizzell

Lefty Frizzell topped the country charts six times, including the career-launching "If You've Got the Money I've Got The Time" in 1950, but his first smash hit might very well have been the one that earned him his nickname.

Born in Texas in 1928, William Orville Frizzell was known to friends and family as "Sonny" until one fateful day in 1942. At age 14, an argument or some other typical teen-age drama led to a life-changing schoolyard fight. That dust-up is when Sonny decked a classmate - with one wicked, left-handed punch.

It surely must have been an impressive shot, because from that day forward, Frizzell was known as Lefty.

But that's not why we remember Lefty Frizzell.

His musical legacy runs deeper. Much deeper.

He was already attracting attention for his singing ability, starting at age 12. His family had moved around from East Texas to Louisiana and Arkansas during his early years, where he was exposed to the sounds of Jimmie Rodgers. It wasn't long before he won a talent show in Dallas, and he was showcasing his amazing vocal range.

A natural, Lefty Frizzell had a voice that could twist lyrics like a pretzel or ride them like a roller coaster.

His debut hit, "If You've Got the Money I've Got The Time," rocketed to No. 1 and propelled his career to superstardom as the first of six No. 1 singles.

Other Lefty songs to reach the top of the charts were "I Love You a Thousand Times" (1950), "I Want to be With You Always" (1951), "Always Late (With Your Kisses)" (1951), "Give Me More, More, More (Of Your Kisses)" (1952) and "Saginaw, Michigan" (1964).

His music influenced Merle Haggard, Willie Nelson, Roy Orbison and many other performers who heaped praise on Lefty over the decades. It earned him many accolades, long after his time at the top of the charts.

Unfortunately, Lefty always had a penchant for trouble—from arrests to fights to heavy drinking—and it led to an early death in 1975 at age 47 from a massive stroke.

But death wasn't the end of Lefty's influence on country music.

Lefty was inducted into the Country Music Hall of Fame in 1982; he has a star on the Hollywood Walk of Fame; and "If You've Got the Money I've Got The Time" earned him a Grammy Hall of Fame Award.

George Strait recorded an homage "Lefty's Gone" in 1985 and Roy Orbison paid tribute in 1988 on the Traveling Wilburys album, (Roy's nom de plume was Lefty Wilbury).

Still, Lefty did a lot of things right.

If you've got to pick one star to define that pure honky-tonk sound of the 1950s, Lefty Frizzell deserves consideration for your vote.

Country Questions
By Dick Boise, CMH

Send questions to:
Dick Boise, , c/o CFR News,
P.O. Box 201796, Nashville,
TN 37221.

Q. Thank you for all the information on our good country sngers. I'm 88 years old, so you know I don't like the new "junk." I'd like to ask, where was David Ball from and how long has he been entertaining? I first heard him singing "Riding With Private Malone." I think he's great.

Dee Frisbie, Coffeeville, KS

A. Dee, thank you for your comments and there are many, many who do not like the new "junk" as you call it. You might notice, none of that "junk" finds its way on the Reunion shows. David Ball was born July 9, 1953, in Rock Hill, SC. He grew up around music most of his young life and played in his uncle's band. He moved to Nashville to begin his solo career in late 1980s. His first hit "Thinking Problem" was in 1994. In 2001, he found the hit "Riding With Private Malone." He did a fine job with that song on the Reunion show.

Q. I saw Martha Carson on a Family Reunion show and enjoyed her song very much. Could you tell me when and where she was born. I like the gospel songs the best.

Emma Kuhn, Carlisle, PA

A. Martha Carson was born in Neon, KY, March 19, 1921. Her real name was Irene Amburgey and she, along with two sisters, began on John Lair's Renfro Valley Barn Dance. Irene was nick-named "Marthie" by John Lair during that time of performing. She later met and married James Carson and continued to use the name Martha. They were very popular on the radio in Atlanta.

They later divorced and she went on to record for Capitol Records. I believe nobody sings "Satisfied" like Martha Carson.

Q. Years ago I remember watching the Glen Campbell TV show and I would see a young man who was very good on the five string banjo. I would appreciate it if you could find out his name for me. Thanks,

Pete Young, Stockton, CA

A. I know that originally John Hartford wrote Glen's hit "Gentle On My Mind" when he was appearing with him. Hartford died in 2001 of Non-Hodgkin lymphoma. But, I believe you remember Larry McNeely who was featured on the Goodtime Hour several times. He has recorded several LPs and I believe he is working in bluegrass bands now.

Q. My uncle has mentioned a name to me several times and I'd like to know more about this perosn. He said that Jerry Jeff Walker was from Texas and what else can you tell me about him.

Donna McCort, Dover, DE

A. Donna, your uncle was close about Jerry Jeff being from Texas. He was born in Oneonta, NY on March 16, 1924, as Ronald Crosby. He left the home area to travel and present his music soon after he graduated. You might remember a fine song that he wrote, "Mr. Bojangles." He is still active with his style of music in the Texas scene.

Road Stories

By Claudia Johnson

Gene Watson No Farewell Yet!

After more than 50 years as a country singer and songwriter, Gene Watson is not even close to saying farewell to the party that has been his life.

"I've been doing this a long time," said Watson, who was playing honkytonks and nightclubs by age 19 and admits that he has more road stories than he could ever recall. "Being on the road is my life."

A Texas native, Watson came from a musical family and cannot recall a time when he was not singing at church with his sister or performing at local functions with his brother. However, he clearly remembers how easily innocent young musicians could be duped.

"When I was 15 and my brother was about 12, there was a guy who came to town in Paris, Texas who was supposed to be a big producer and talent scout," Watson said. "He thought that Jessie and I had a lot of potential, so he put a show together at the coliseum. That was the big debut for The Watson Brothers. By the time the show was over with, he left town with the proceeds."

Watson is known today for a string of hits that includes "Fourteen Carat Mind," "Love in the Hot Afternoon," "Farewell Party," "Memories to Burn," "Got No Reason Now for Going Home," "Speak Softly," "Paper Rosie" and "Sometimes I Get Lucky and Forget." Long before the hits started coming,

Gene settled in Houston, Texas, where he developed a strong local following and staged his disc debut. In 1964, the Grand Ole Opry duo, The Wilburn Brothers, took Gene on the road briefly. Then it was back to the Texas honky-tonks and a string of local singles throughout the '60s.

"My cousin, Bill Watson, is a songwriter, so we decided to go to Nashville and check out what it takes to get a song recorded," he recalled. "That would have been in 1966 or '67. We thought with some of his songs and my singing, we might get someone to listen. Of course, it was to no avail."

Watson continued to work toward attracting the attention of radio disc jockeys and major record labels.

"We needed a record to get out there, so I did my first recording on an independent label called Sun Valley Records that started up just for this recording session," Watson said, referring to "If It Was That Easy," a song he wrote, admitting, "It wasn't very good, I thought that was something because I had my own record."

Finally, in 1974 while Watson was working as an auto body repairman, his recording of "Love in the Hot Afternoon" was noticed by Capitol Records, which picked it up for national distribution. It soon became the first of two dozen top-10 hits.

"I can safely say my entire career has been a learning experience," he laughed, as he recalled his naivety when he first became involved with music as an industry.

Like all other major-label artist, Watson was required to pay for his own recording sessions, yet the record label owned the recordings, meaning Watson's classics are owned by four different corporations. In recent years, Watson has completed a meticulous re-recording of 25 of his greatest hits for his own label, Fourteen Carat Music, giving him a kind of proprietorship over them he never had with the previous recording labels.

"I wanted these to sound as close to the originals as possible," Watson said of tracks on "The Best of the Best. "I had to work so hard to capture them the same way I did them originally. I just thank the good Lord above that He's let me keep my voice intact."

Watson admits he has a lot to be thankful for in addition to his clear and enduring voice. He quit drinking alcohol in 1980, and 10 years later gave up cigarettes. He's a colon cancer survivor since 2001 and was a 2002 inductee into the Texas Music Hall of Fame.

"I owe a debt of gratitude to Larry's Country Diner and Country Family Reunion," Watson said, adding that these programs are providing a venue for classic country music singers to connect with their fans and with one another. "So many of us never got to meet each other until we came on these shows because we were so busy. Being able to get together and talk is one of the reasons this is so much fun."

Watson's respect for country music is reflected in an ambitious 2014 project by his own Fourteen Carat Music label, "My Heroes have always been Country," that pays homage to his musical influence in which he covers classic songs by Buck Owens, Willie Nelson, George Jones, Johnny Cash and many others.

Watson said that no matter what songs he performs at his shows, his audience expects him to sing his own classic, "Farewell Party." Though the song is about unrequited romantic love, one line pinpoints how Watson feels about the dedicated fans who have enabled him to spend his life doing what he loves.

"At the end of my farewell party...I'll go away loving you."

Jim Ed announces Cancer in video on Facebook page

Jim Ed Brown announced via a Facebook post and video on September 30 that he was battling cancer with this statement:

"Some of you may have heard various rumors since I have had to cancel a few shows over the past few weekends. To clarify and put those rumors to bed, I wanted to just come out and explain what is going on. Two weeks ago, I was diagnosed with lung cancer. At that time, I was in shock and scared as I didn't know what that really meant. After testing, the doctors have asked me to take the next 4 months off from touring and to focus on chemotherapy and radiation treatments to shrink the cancer cells. I will keep you all updated on the progress. I am forever grateful for the love, support, and prayers during this time."

We sure do wish him a speedy and full recovery!

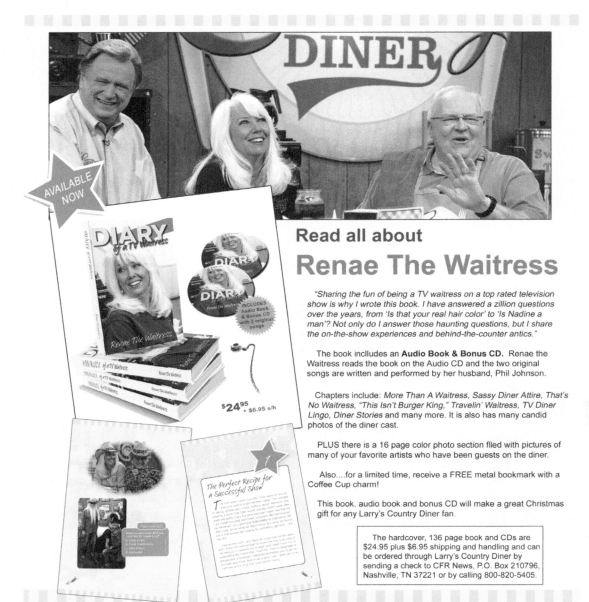

DINER

AVAILABLE NOW

DIARY of a TV Waitress

Renae The Waitress

INCLUDES Audio Book & Bonus CD with 2 original songs

$24.95 + $6.95 s/h

The Perfect Recipe for a Successful Show

Read all about
Renae The Waitress

"Sharing the fun of being a TV waitress on a top rated television show is why I wrote this book. I have answered a zillion questions over the years, from 'Is that your real hair color' to 'Is Nadine a man'? Not only do I answer those haunting questions, but I share the on-the-show experiences and behind-the-counter antics."

The book inclludes an **Audio Book & Bonus CD.** Renae the Waitress reads the book on the Audio CD and the two original songs are written and performed by her husband, Phil Johnson.

Chapters include: *More Than A Waitress, Sassy Diner Attire, That's No Waitress, "This Isn't Burger King," Travelin' Waitress, TV Diner Lingo, Diner Stories* and many more. It is also has many candid photos of the diner cast.

PLUS there is a 16 page color photo section filled with pictures of many of your favorite artists who have been guests on the diner.

Also....for a limited time, receive a FREE metal bookmark with a Coffee Cup charm!

This book, audio book and bonus CD will make a great Christmas gift for any Larry's Country Diner fan.

The hardcover, 136 page book and CDs are $24.95 plus $6.95 shipping and handling and can be ordered through Larry's Country Diner by sending a check to CFR News, P.O. Box 210796, Nashville, TN 37221 or by calling 800-820-5405.

Larry's Country Diner RFD Show Schedule Nov. 2014
(These shows have previously aired)

JOHNNY RODRIGUEZ
Saturday, Nov. 1
10:00 p.m. Central
Sunday, Nov. 2
6:00 p.m. Central

JAMIE O'NEAL
Saturday, Nov. 8
10:00 p.m. Central
Sunday, Nov. 9
6:00 p.m. Central

TIM MENZIES
Saturday, Nov. 15
10:00 p.m. Central
Sunday, Nov. 16
6:00 p.m. Central

HOT CLUB OF COWTOWN
Saturday, Nov. 22
10:00 p.m. Central
Sunday, Nov. 23
6:00 p.m. Central

GEORGE HAMILTON IV
Saturday, Nov. 29
10:00 p.m. Central
Sunday, Nov. 30
6:00 p.m. Central

Help military families for the holidays

Many supporters would prefer to connect with a needy military family on a local level. Here are some suggestions to find local military families in need:

If you are located near a military installation, that might be achieved by contacting a military chaplain (Battalion Chaplain in the Army) or a Family Readiness Group Leader. Some installations run a Santa's shop program where donations are received so military families in need can "shop" for items for their family.

Do you know of any military families personally? Ask them if they are aware of any needs. Perhaps if you ask around, you'll quickly find someone you know who knows of someone who would be encouraged by your support.

Try contacting your local churches or schools to see if they are aware of needs.

Stay in tune with your local news to learn of opportunities to support military families.

Contact your local VFW, American Legion, or AMVETs - LINK.

Operation We Are Here also has a listing of local opportunity locators - LINK.

Availability of Jean Shepard's book "Down Through the Years"

We've been getting lots of calls about Jean Shepard's book "Down Through the Years" and why we no longer have it available. The reason is that Gabrield fulfilled it's contractual comittment and now the sale of the book reverts back to Jean.

As of now, Jean's website: www.jeanshepardcountry.com states that her book will be available there starting October 31. She will most likely have it available through bookstores as well, so you should keep checking with your local bookstore to see if they can order it for you.

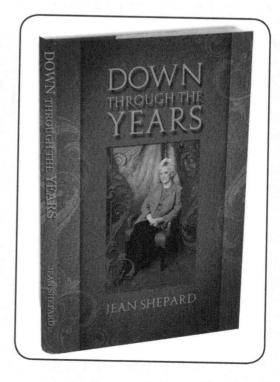

The Nashville BratPack — Kids of the Country Stars!

By Melissa Luman
Daughter of Bob Luman

Bobby Bare, Jr. and Melissa Luman

Jeannie Bare and my mom Barbara Luman were both pregnant at the same time - Jeannie with Bobby Jr. and my mom with me. Well, I came along 11 days before Bobby Jr. and both Bobs were on the road. Jeannie Bare was at the hospital with my mom when I was born. When Bobby Jr. and I were about a month old, the Lumans went to the Bares one evening for dinner and Bare told my dad to just put me in the crib with Bobby Jr. As he laid me down in the crib....Bare said, "Bob, let's breed em!"

Husker Du is a German memory game that we used to play all the time together when he was in off the road...I used to beat him every time... so, my mom took this picture to show the level of concentration my dad had while playing the game with me.…. even though he always lost! Through the years the game got lost, but I went on ebay and ordered the now vintage Husker Du game and I play it with my grandson.…. and yes.… he beats me every time!

We lived on the then famous Caudill Drive across from Orbison and Cash and you can imagine the tour buses that came to see our homes, not to mention the fans in cars. We had a BIG black mailbox and when my dad was on the road, on Saturdays I would get some albums and 8 tracks out of the drawers and take them to the mailbox and set 'em in there and sell 'em for about a dollar or two.

One day my dad came home from Nashville to find me selling his merchandise out of the mailbox. He really thought it was cool until I told him how much I had sold... and how much I sold them for. Needless to say, that was the last time our big black mailbox was used as a mini record store!

One day I was over at John Carter Cash's house playing, I was about 10 and JC was about 8. Johnny and June had gone out for the day, so it was just me and JC and, of course, the maids and the cooks who I adored dearly.

Ellen Reeves, Jeannie Bare and Barbara Luman.

JC had a trampoline out by the tennis courts and I said, "Let's go play on the trampoline," and John Carter said, "Oh we can't, the back/side door is locked and I can't reach the lock. Me, being 2 years older, was a bit taller, so I said, "I bet I can reach it." So we went to the door, I got up on the staircase that led to Johnny and June's bedroom, reached real high and unlocked that sucker. So out we went to the trampoline. Mind you, you could not really see the trampoline from the windows in the house, so we are out there jumpin' and playin' around and at some point the maids figured out that John Carter and I were missing. OH LORD!!! Well, all h#*l broke loose at 200 Caudill Drive.…(meanwhile we're still jumpin' and playin' on the trampoline!!!...)

Playing Husker Du

Back in those days only two people had phones in their cars.… the President of the United States.…. and Johnny Cash! The maids called Johnny and June and said the kids are gone… possible that they could have been kidnapped..." Cash kid and Luman kid.….."So Johnny and June immediately return home and about that time little Luman and Little Cash rolled in all sweaty from our trampoline jumpin' and boy oh boy did we get a TRUE CASH talkin' to.…. and I've never forgotten it!

Branson with Larry's Country Diner & Guests

Larry's Country Diner was performing LIVE in Branson at the Starlite Theatre September 23-28. A great time was had by all in attendance!

Rhonda Vincent and The Rage

Gene Watson

Gene and Larry having some fun!

Dailey and Vincent

Mandy Barnett

Jarett Daugherty cracks up Darrin Vincent!

Barbara Fairchild & Rudy Gatlin join Jimmy Fortune as Jimmy Capps plays

Mo Pitney

Michele Capps accompanies Bill Anderson.

Southern Raised were surprise guests as was Rory Feek and daughter Heidi.

The Starlite Theatre SOLD OUT!

Dave Rich – the singer with "a steel guitar pedal in his voice"

DAVE RICH   R C A   VICTOR RECORDING STAR

By Shirley Shaw

In the 1950s a handsome, talented teenager burst onto the Nashville music scene with a unique singing style that quickly propelled him on a fast track to stardom. Then something occurred that totally changed the course of his life. What happened to that young man, and where is he today?

Dave Rich grew up in a small west Kentucky town, in an area that produced such musical greats as Boots Randolph, the Everly Brothers and Merle Travis. His father bought Dave a $5 guitar when he was five years old and taught him basic chords. Growing up, he listened to country singers on the radio and sang along with Webb Pierce, Ray Price, Hank Thompson and other Grand Ole Opry stars.

When he was 14, his brother Spider began taking him along on gigs around the state with the western swing band for which he played guitar – Les Smithart and the Super X Cowboys. Dave honed his skills during this "on-the-job training" period with Spider coaching him on pitch and timing. He took Dave everywhere he went so his young brother could gain experience. The two recorded Dave's songs to play for anyone who would listen, and these efforts landed Dave a job as DJ at WRUS, a radio station in Russellville, Ky.

He admired the famous WSM DJ Eddie Hill, so he developed a similar on-air persona – The Old Starvation Boy. Dave says, "I talked about country things, portrayed myself as always being hungry, and mentioned all kinds of foods, like possum and grits, etc. It went over in a big way with the listeners. Everyone loved it; everywhere I went people recognized me as the Old Starvation Boy."

The DJ Dave replaced at WRUS had rented an armory on Saturday nights for dancing, so Dave got a band together and joined the group of entertainers. He says, "I still didn't have a car – had been hitchhiking back and forth to the station – so two or three of us decided we'd move to Russellville and room together. I was making $16 a week as a DJ and about $25 from the armory gig, and after I paid my band I'd run out of money by Friday, so I'd buy a Dr. Pepper and Hershey bar and live on that 'til I got paid. I didn't care; I was famous in the little town, all over Kentucky. WRUS was a 'super power' station that reached a 50-100 mile radius."

Then Les and his Super X Cowboys landed a TV show in Indiana and invited Dave to sing with them each week. After the performance he would drive 100mph to Russellville to wind up the armory show. By this time he had bought a Ford for $40, and with his job as DJ, singing gigs and appearing on the Saturday Night Jubilee, he was doing very well! But a recording contract still eluded him – they said he sounded too much like Webb or Faron or Hank.

He'd been reading in country music magazines about the process of writing songs, and he decided that he would develop his own singing style and write his own songs. After writing four or five, he sang them for Spider, who was so impressed he rushed Dave to their older brother's place of business.

The brother was Raymond Rich, who owned a successful automobile dealership in Central City, Ky. He was good friends with Mose Rager, a blues singer and guitar player credited with creating the thumb-picking style of guitar playing that he taught to Merle Travis. About that time another guitar player by the name of Chet Atkins (who was far ahead of musicians anyone had heard at the time) came on the music scene and was producing records for RCA in Nashville. Mose was so blown away by Chet he told Raymond, "Let's go to Nashville and find him."

The men learned where Chet lived, and when they knocked on his door, Chet (who had heard of Mose) invited them in and they stayed four hours, picking and becoming acquainted. Because of this contact Raymond knew Chet very well – even sold him his first new car.

So when Dave and Spider came rushing into his office and Spider told Raymond about the songs his little brother had written, Raymond didn't even listen to Dave sing. He had such faith in Spider and his assessment of Dave's talent, he told them to get with the engineer at the Central City station (where Dave now worked as DJ) and record one of the songs. Then Raymond drove to Nashville and left the tape of Dave's first song with Chet.

Dave didn't hear a word for two weeks, then Chet's secretary called to say he was to come to Nashville and sign a contract with RCA Records. "I was screaming riding down the highway. After all those years of trying they called me to come and record. I knew on my first session that Chet was sold on me."

The first release became famous overnight on the radio. Those were heady days for Dave. He said, "I would spend hours with Ralph Emery, who played my records 'til he went off the air, and I'd walk down to WLAC where Bob Jennings had a two-hour show, and he would play my records. I'd sometimes do the Friday night Grand old Opry on WSM. I remember when I finished recording 'Your Pretty Blue Eyes,' Chet came out into the studio and said, 'Dave if you'll keep singing like that, I'll record you as long as I live.'"

The inimitable singing style Dave had developed created quite a stir among singers at that time. His voice would slide effortlessly across a range of notes that many thought Chet was creating somehow with electronics. "DJs all over the country were playing my records because they listened to Ralph Emery, Bob Jennings and Eddie Hill. Eddie is the one who described me as 'the man with the steel guitar pedal in his voice.'"

During this time, while it seemed as if all Dave's dreams were being fulfilled, he was struggling with thoughts about God's plan for his life. Raised in church, he knew a spiritual relationship with God was more important than worldly fame, so after a life-changing experience one night in a revival service, he decided to quit the music business and enter the ministry.

At that time Dave was on the verge of breaking through with a smash hit, of perhaps becoming a millionaire, so everyone was aghast at his decision to quit singing and become a preacher. His brothers, also his business partners, spent hours telling him how he was letting everyone down, what people would think of him, what he was giving up on a 'whim' – he couldn't do that to them. His manager told him he could do more for God from a platform of stardom than he could ever do preaching to small crowds. Chet Atkins, his chin quivering, pleaded with Dave to go to school, learn all he could about the ministry, then make his decision.

Dave agreed to honor the remaining nine months of his contract, and it was during that time he recorded a song written by a newcomer to the Nashville scene: City Lights by Bill Anderson. In his autobiography Whisperin' Bill, Anderson relates this account of Dave's recording:

Chet listened to my record…and in a few days produced a great record of it by a young stylist named Dave Rich. Dave was a singer like Willie Nelson, in that for many years he was simply ahead of his time. He was a tremendous singer, but the general public never quite caught on to the acrobatics he could perform with his voice. He had the vocal ability to move from one note to another in much the same sliding way as a pedal steel guitar, and he sang the living fire out of "City Lights." He took the word array in the first line and turned it into five syllables. He was incredible.

Dave's last appearance was a two-week run at the Wisconsin State Fair where Jim Reeves was the headliner. Jim, who'd heard about Dave's decision to start preaching, told him he could preach better than Dave could – and proceeded to do so! Band members needled him about his religion, but then one of them came down with a blinding migraine headache, asked Dave to pray for him and the pain immediately left. Jim quizzed him about his knowledge of scriptures and finally called the band together, telling them to leave Dave alone, that he was sincere.

We'll never know what heights Dave might have reached in the country music industry, but 59 years later, he has no regrets about the decision he made all those years ago. His powerful ministry has impacted people all over this country and other parts of the world. He established many churches for the organization with which he was affiliated – and he never stopped singing. He estimates he has written about 100 gospel songs and recorded a dozen or so albums. He was thrilled to be inducted into the Rockabilly Hall of Fame, and was influential in seeing Jimmy C. Newman also added to that illustrious group.

Today Dave has returned to live in Central City where his son Enoch pastors a church. All of Dave's children – Enoch, Debbie and Necie – sing beautifully, as do his grandchildren. He enjoys communicating with multitudes of friends on Facebook and reminiscing about the many experiences of his amazing life. Like many of us old timers, he loves the Country Family Reunion series and Larry's Country Diner. Those gatherings truly are a reunion of many old friends from Dave's long-ago days in Nashville, but we who are blessed to know him through his ministry are happy he followed God's call.

Word Search Puzzle Answers on page after next

```
S I L L I G E I B O D E E R A N N O D
W A L T O N S P E Y T O N P L A C E T
A F N G I X A T V H O D D C O U P L E
L L E A R M E R E H W E S L E T S O Y
A I R A M E M U R P H Y B R O W N V D
J P M E R E E Y L M I A M I V I C E O
E E D V F N S F H L E C O O O P E O D
T R A I L I E R I O E R N D N J Y A Y
S E B T Y T M C L R R R C E S N A T D
O D O I I H I L L G R N A A G Q A K W
N I U G N G T A B A O I E D N R U C O
S H T U G I D S I E C M N T L E E A H
M W Y F N L O S L A N I E T E I E M D
P A O S U N O I L L O C D R I D K R E
O R U R N O G E I I E S A E P N U R G
E D I S N O R I E C H I P S M Y T A D
H Y N A P M O C S E E R H T E O L I M
O O R A G N A K N I A T P A C Y W E N
```

ALICE	GOOD TIMES	MIAMI VICE
BEN CASEY	GREEN ACRES	MOD SQUAD
BEVERLY HILLBILLIES	GREEN HORNET	MOONLIGHTING
CHIPS	HOWDY DOODY	MURPHY BROWN
CANNON	I SPY	ODD COUPLE
CAPTAIN KANGAROO	IRONSIDE	PEYTON PLACE
DOBIE GILLIS	JETSONS	RAWHIDE
DONNA REED	KOJAK	RIFLEMAN
DR. KILDARE	L.A. LAW	RIN TIN TIN
EMERGENCY	LASSIE	SOAP
FLIPPER	LOVE BOAT	ST. ELSEWHERE
FLYING NUN	MAD ABOUT YOU	TAXI
FUGITIVE	MAUDE	THREE'S COMPANY
GOMER PYLE	MEDICAL CENTER	WALTONS

COUNTRY'S FAMILY REUNION COLLECTION
Taped in 1997, 1998, and 1999. Includes FOUR different video series: Country's Family Reunion, Country's Family Reunion Two, Country's Famly Reunion Celebration, Country's Family Reunion Gospel, and Stories from the Golden Age of Country. $119.80

COUNTRY'S FAMILY REUNION NASHVILLE SERIES
Filmed in January of 2008 this is a 10 DVD collection that includes a "TRIBUTE" to the late Porter Wagoner, Hank Thompson and Billy Walker. Featuring 70 artists and songwriters. $119.80

COUNTRY'S FAMILY REUNION 2010
Country's Family Reunion 2010 was filmed in "2010 " right here in Nashville Tennessee with over 50 of your favorite artists sharing their laughter, their stories, and all your favorite songs on 12 DVDs! $119.80

BILL ANDERSON'S 50th ANNIVERSARY
No one in history has had more country songs recorded than Whisperin' Bill. Filmed in 2010, celebrate Bill's 50th Anniverssary with over 7 hours and 5 DVD's we've captured tons of great hits sung by the original artists. $79.80

A GRAND OLE TIME
Filmed in 2010, A Grand Ole Time includes 5 DVDs with over 7 hours of country music entertainment. Features Dallas Frazier, Jan Howard, Collin Raye, Jim Glaser, Rhonda Vincent, Ronny Robbins and many more. $79.80

SALUTE TO THE KORNFIELD

We gathered all the members of the TV show "Hee Haw" into one room and filmed it. What we got out of that taping is incredible, once-in-a-lifetime stuff that we're calling Country's Family Reunion: Salute to the Kornfield! This 5 DVD series was filmed in 2011. $79.80

GETTIN' TOGETHER
This wonderful 5 DVD set was filemd in 2011 and includes some brand new folk hanging with our CFR family (Dailey and Vincent, Don Edwards, Joey and Rory, and others), plus some of your favorites (Roy Clark, Johnny Lee, Neal McCoy, Bill Anderson, Jeannie Seely, Jean Shepard, and many more!) $79.80

COUNTRY'S FAMILY REUNION KINFOLK
On this special Country's Family Reunion gathering, filmed in 2012, we thought we'd ask all the family groups to sit a spell and sing some songs with us. Brothers, sisters, cousins, moms and Dads were all invited to join in the fun. The Gatlin's, the Whites, The Lennon Sisters, Rhonda Vincent and Darrin Vincent, and other family acts joined us. 5 DVDs with over 5 hours of content. $79.80

OLD TIME GOSPEL
The roots of a lot of the country music we love can be found in the Gospel songs of old. Filmed in 2012, this series is filled with songs celebrating the gospel music we grew up with so we called it Old Time Gospel. 5 DVDs featuring The Whites, Jean Shepard, Joey & Rory, George Hamilton IV and more. $79.80

SECOND GENERATIONS
A gathering of country music legends and the children of country music legends such as Marty Robbins, Conway Twitty, Faron Young, Tammy Wynette, George Jones, Roger Miller, Johnny Russell, Hank Williams, Dottie Westt. All on 5 DVDs with over 7 hours of content, including the 'Behind The Scenes' DVD filmed in 2012. $79.80

GRASSROOTS TO BLUEGRASS
Filmed in 1999, Jimmy Shumate, Melvin Goins, John Hartford, Jeanette Carter, Charlie Louvin, The Osbourne Brothers, and many more telling stories and singing songs about the history of Bluegrass music. This series is a must-have for any Bluegrass fan! $119.80

PRECIOUS MEMORIES - GOSPEL CLASSICS COMBO
Precious Memories includes 90 minutes of footage from the reunion members who've passed away, plus the detailed biography photo book. AND, Gospel Classics, a 3 DVD set with TONS of Gospel songs and stories, plus the Gospel Song Book. $119.80

SONGWRITERS COLLECTION
The Songwriters is a 6 hour, 5 DVD series featuring 22 of the best country music songwriters of all time... You'll hear how songs like "The Gambler," "Always," "All My Exes Live in Texas," "When You Say Nothing at All," "and more were written. Filmed in 2010. $79.80

GOD BLESS AMERICA AGAIN
God Bless America Again is devoted to songs that make us proud to be Americans and songs that allow us to enjoy our spiritual roots. ISongs you sang in church when you were growing up and songs that recall a time in America when we were free to openly express our faith without fear of ridicule-- A time that seems, on reflection, to have been filled with family, friends and faith. Filmed in 2013. $79.80

SIMPLY BLUEGRASS
In 2013 we asked Ricky Skaggs to pull together some of the best of the past, present and future of Bluegrass performers for Simply Bluegrass. Hosted by Ricky Skaggs and Bill Anderson, this is a reunion that all Bluegrass and Country fans will enjoy. This series has 5 DVDs with over 6 hours of great Bluegrass music! $79.80

Precious Memories; Remembering Buddy Killen

William Doyce "Buddy" Killen was born November 13, in Florence, Alabama. He started out playing music and ended up owning one of the best publishing companies in Nashville and around the world.

He began playing bass for a comedy group that appeared on the Grand Ole Opry. After the group broke up, he became a staff bassist with the Opry while playing on recording sessions and singing on music publishing demos. In 1953, Killen came to the attention of Tree Publishing founder Jack Stapp. Stapp gave Killen a job with the then up-and-coming Tree that paid 35 dollars a week.

During his early career he worked with artists such as Dolly Parton, Dottie West, Diana Trask, Exile, Roger Miller, Joe Tex, Ronnie McDowell and T. G. Sheppard.

Throughout the 1970s and '80s, Tree acquired a number of publishing companies, including those of Conway Twitty, Jim Ed Norman, and the Blue Book catalog owned by Buck Owens, which contained many of the songs from the Bakersfield group including Merle Haggard, Jim Reeves, Nat Stucky, and Jerry Chesnut, in all more than 50 catalogs.

When Stapp died in 1980, Killen became the sole owner of what would become Tree International. With his Killen Music Group, Killen published some songs on the soundtrack to the film Idlewild. He also co-published the popular "Me and My Gang" by Rascal Flatts and worked with artists such as Faith Hill, Trace Adkins, Kenny Chesney, Reba McEntire and Bill Anderson. He also worked at the W.O. Smith School of Music.

In 1989, a new chapter in the history of Tree began when Sony/CBS purchased the publishing company from Buddy Killen for 30 million dollars. After the sale of Tree to Sony/CBS, Buddy Killen remained head of the company but by the end of the year had stepped down to pursue other interests.

Killen died in Nashville, Tennessee on November 1, 2006, of pancreatic cancer.

(L-R) Buddy Killen, Burt Reynolds, Bobby Goldsboro, Charlie Fach

Country singers speak about Stringbean killer's parole

John A. Brown was convicted of killing killing David "Stringbean" Akeman and his wife, Estelle and was sentenced to 198 years in prison. He was released on parole in October of 2014 after serving 41 years of that sentence, much to the shock of many country music artists and fans.

Brown told the board in April that he had been "reformed" through his more than 40 years in prison. He said he knows he can never make up for the horrible crime he committed.

"I don't have any right to ask for forgiveness. It's unforgivable," Brown told the board.

Mac Wiseman called the board's decision a "great miscarriage of justice. It makes me question the legal system," he said.

Wiseman said did not discount Brown's contrition, but he did question how a man with two life sentences could be released.

"I fully believe that the good Lord forgives us for our mistakes," he said.

But, Wiseman added, members of the parole board "don't have the authority, spiritually or otherwise, to forgive that man, I don't think."

Brown's transformation from the 23-year-old drugging, drinking robber who ambushed Dave "Stringbean" Akeman and his wife, Estelle, in November 1973 at their Ridgetop home evidently convinced enough of the parole board to give him a pyschological emaminaiton to determine his propensity for violence. Once those reports came back and it was determined he had a job waiting for him, they decided to release him on parole.

Pastor Maury Davis of Cornerstone Church, located in Madison, reportedly offered Brown a position as a janitor. He is himself, a convicted murderer from Texas who served his sentence and went into the ministry.

Jan Howard and Mac Wiseman had shocked reactions to Brown's release.

Jan Howard, who was friends with the Akemans, attended the parole hearings and spoke to local news reporters after the news broke, saying, "He had ransacked their house and then shot them execution style in the back of the head while they were kneeling and praying for their lives," said Howard.

"This is a miscarriage of justice," said Howard. "He was tried, convicted and sentenced to 198 years in prison. Why bother if they're not going to carry it out?"

At 6'5", David "Stringbean" Akeman stood head and shoulders above everyone else on Hee Haw and was one of the show's most memorable characters. Akeman was a banjo player who played bluegrass and traditional country classics on Hee Haw and the Grand Ole Opry.

When he was young he entered a country music contest and awarded the top prize by Asa Martin, who had his own band. Akeman was introduced as 'stringbeans' during a performance in which Martin forgot his name and from that point on was known as Stringbean.

By creating a costume with a long tailed shirt and jeans given to him from fellow Opry performer Little Jimmy Dickens, who happened to be 4'11", Stringbean was able to accentuate his height. The extra long shirt combined with the tiny pants often caused people to begin laughing before he started his performance.

Stringbean and Estelle Stanfill were married in 1945. He made a good living playing at the Opry and performing on Hee Haw, but he lived a quiet life in his cabin on some land purchased with Grandpa Jones. Stringbean liked to walk to Grandpa Jones cabin, sit on his porch, and whittle during the morning. Then Grandpa Jones would walk to Stringbeans cabin and whittle on his porch during the afternoon. The only luxury item he purchased was a Cadillac Coupe Deville. Since Akeman grew up during the depression, he had a deep distrust for banks and he would stash large amounts of cash in different places around his cabin. He was also known to carry a wad of cash in his overalls, and on occasion, flash it around.

Rumors of Akemans fortune and where it may been hidden filtered through the criminal element in Nashville. Petty criminals (and cousins) John A. Brown and Marvin Douglas Brown heard the stories, and made a plan to find the money. On November 11, 1973, the two men drove to Akemans cabin and broke in. As the men searched the house, they listened to the Opry and even heard Stringbean.

They ended up spending too much time looking for the cash and were still in the house when Estelle and Stringbean drove up the driveway. Akeman heard noises and noticed commotion inside the cabin. He told Estelle to stay in the car, and he stepped out with a revolver and slowly entered the dark house. Stringbean struggled with the two men and he was shot dead. Estelle, hearing the gunshots inside the cabin, jumped out of the car screaming. John Brown chased her down the driveway where she fell pleading for her life. She was shot and killed, and left face down in the grassy pathway. The men left with a chainsaw, a pillowcase, and some guns. If they had searched Stringbean or Estelle, they would have found three thousand dollars in his overalls and two thousand dollars stuffed in her bra. The next morning Grandpa Jones walked over to Stringbeans cabin and discovered the bodies.

The police immediately focused on the Brown cousins. Informants, including Marvin Douglas Brown's fifteen year old girlfriend (he was in his mid twenties), confirmed the rumors being heard around town. The two men were heard bragging about committing the murders.

After being interrogated, the pair were charged with first-degree murder and sentenced to ninety-nine years each in prison. Doug Brown died in 2003 while serving his sentence.

Stringbean Akeman and his wife Estelle are buried together at Forest Lawn Memorial Gardens in Goodlettsville, Tennessee. A bluegrass festival is organized every year in Jackson County Kentucky in Stringbeans honor. During the Hee Haw intro, Akeman would play the scarecrow on the show, after his death the scarecrow was left in the cornfield as a memorial. A few years after the murders, a couple renting Akemans cabin claimed to have found rotting money in the chimney in excess of twenty thousand dollars. It was the treasure that everyone heard of, but the ravages of time and field mice destroyed it. However, the property owners have stated that this story was false. Even in death, the legend of Stringbean lives on to teach new generations of the history of bluegrass music. His music is still being sold, and archival footage of his performances can still be seen on you tube.

And there are some who feel that the pastor of Cornerstone Church is doing what people should do in giving him a helping hand. One person posted this on facebook: "Cornerstone, has done so much good for the Nashville area that that point alone is inarguable. Now, he, too, murdered someone in his youth. He was released, taken in as a janitor in a church in Texas, and has since done marvelous things with his life.

The disciple Paul was a murderer, and after Damascus road, he became the most effective arm for Jesus that ever existed in Biblical times.

Beyond the emotional upset that all of us in the music community share over this because of who the victim of this crime was, this man could very well do great things with what time he has left."

And while all that is true, people who knew Stringbean and Estelle may have a harder time of forgiving and no one will ever forget them.

Down Home
with Carol Bass

You have heard the saying, "You can tell the year a woman graduated from high school by the way she wears her hair and makeup!" Just like hair and make-up, a home can show its age too. Here are some dead give-a-ways known as age spots, see if you recognize any. But more importantly, here are some simple practical fixes.

LIGHTING

Lighting is like a hairdo, a dead giveaway of age. Perhaps it stands very tall and has an eagle attached? Talking about the lamp, not the hairdo. Is your ginger jar lamp with the pleated shade showing its age? It's a shame to throw that lamp away and purchase another one because it still works. So what else can we do? Let's think practically. I have a saying, when clients want to throw away perfectly good items, "If the patient is going to die anyway, let's _____." Meaning, if you are going to throw the lamp out and replace it anyway, why not try one wild thing first, like painting it. The finish, the shape, or the style of a lamp may be fine but it may be the color that is out-of-date. The lamp may be a classic but the shade is giving away its age. It could be a combination of things.

PRACTICAL SIMPLE FIX - SHADES, HARPS & SECERTS

There are paints out there today that will cover anything. I love a product called RUB N Buff. You can find it at most craft stores. Cost around $6.00 a tube, and comes in lots of colors. It is applied with your finger. I have changed old chandeliers, lamps, and accessories with the magic of rub n buff. A little paint or rub n buff, plus a new shade, and you have a new light fixture. Don't forget to remove the plastic on the new shade. A great way to change the height of a shade is simply to change the harp. Now, about that lamp with the eagle, it is time to send it to a thrift store. We can't make everything look younger.

Carol Bass, The Practical Decorator, Decorating for real people in real homes with real budgets and teaching other to do the same. 1-888-800-7507. www.ThePracticalDecorator.com

Linda Davis and Kenny Rogers together for Christmas Tour

Linda Davis will join Kenny Rogers performing holiday favorites and his classic hits across the U.S. and Canada when Kenny's 33rd Christmas tour – Christmas & Hits Through The Years. The 25-date run began November 12 in Niagara Falls, Ontario and wraps December 23 in Westbury, New York.

" There's no one I'd rather share Christmas cheer with than Kenny!" says Linda, "He is a great friend. He's asked me to open shows for over 20 years. We go that far back.. As far as Christmas goes, his fans adore him and turn out for our shows even when the weather is crazy. Whether they've seen the show already. His holiday concert is an event. I am so thrilled to be a part of it."

The 1st half of the show Kenny sings his most popular and biggest hits then he and Linda will sing 1 or 2 duets. Linda will also sing a song by herself from one if her CDs.

After the intermission and a set change the show will go with local children's choirs and fun audience interactive songs. A local high school or college choir is featured as the music moves into the sacred part of the show.

You can find out more about the tour at Kennyrogers.com or Lindadavis.com. There are Christmas CDs and all kinds of goodies in both their stores.

Nov. 12 -15	Niagara Falls, ON, Canada, Niagara Fallsview Casino Resort - Avalon Ballroom Theatre
Nov. 20	Moncton, NB, Canada, Casino New Brunswick
Nov. 21	Halifax, NS, Canada, Halifax Metro Centre
Nov. 22	Sydney, NS, Canada, Centre 200
Nov. 28	Fort Pierce, FL, Sunrise Theatre
Nov. 29	Sarasota, FL, Van Wezel Performing Arts Hall
Nov. 30	Saint Petersburg, FL, Mahaffey Theater
Dec. 2	Florence, SC, Francis Marion University Performing Arts Center
Dec. 5	New Buffalo, MI, Four Winds Casino Resort – Silver Creek Event Center
Dec. 6	Detroit, MI, Fox Theatre
Dec. 7	Evansville, IN, Ford Center
Dec. 11	Wheeling, WV, Capitol Theatre
Dec. 12	Van Wert, OH, Niswonger Performing Arts Center
Dec. 13	Wabash, IN, Honeywell Center
Dec. 14	Zanesville, OH, Secrest Auditorium
Dec. 16	Greenville, SC, Peace Center For The Performing Arts
Dec. 17	Richmond, VA, Altria Theater
Dec. 18	Verona, NY, Turning Stone Resort & Casino – Event Center
Dec. 19	Uncasville, CT, Mohegan Sun Arena
Dec. 20	Jim Thorpe, PA, Penn's Peak
Dec. 21	Norfolk, VA, Chrysler Hall
Dec. 23	Westbury, NY, NYCB Theatre at Westbury

Alan Jackson announces 2015 Keepin' It Country Tour

Georgia native Alan Jackson, recently announced his 25th Anniversary Keepin' It Country Tour, a 25-city trek that will kick off on January 8 in Estero, Fla., and end at Red Rocks Amphitheatre in Morrison, Colo., on May 17.

At his artist-in-residence performance at the Country Music Hall of Fame and Museum on October 8, Alan debuted a new song, "Angels and Alcohol," which he mentioned would be appearing on an upcoming album.

Keepin' It Country Tour Dates			
Date		Location	Venue
Jan.	8	Estero, Fla.	Germain Arena
	9	Tampa, Fla.	USF Sun Dome
Feb.	20	San Diego	Valley View Casino Center
	21	Laughlin, Nev.	Laughlin Events Center
	27	Los Angeles	Nokia Theatre LA Live
	28	Phoenix	Ak-Chin Pavilion
March	6	Grand Prairie, Texas	Verizon Theatre at Grand Prairie
	27	Augusta, Ga.	James Brown Arena
	28	Greenville, S.C.	Bon Secours Wellness Arena
April	9	Wilmington, N.C.	Cape Fear Community College
	17	Independence, Mo.	Independence Events Center
	18	Enid, Okla.	Enid Event Center
	24	Roanoke, Va.	Civic Center Auditorium
May	1	Sioux City, Iowa	Tyson Events Center
	2	Brookings, S.D.	Swiftel Center
	8	Green Bay, Wis.	Resch Center
	9	Bloomington, Ill.	US Cellular Coliseum
	16	West Valley City, Utah	USANA Amphitheatre
	17	Morrison, Colo.	Red Rocks Amphitheatre

Keith Bilbrey & family play in honor of Emy Jo's Mom

Keith Bilbrey, his wife Emy Jo and her family were on Family Feud recently. Emy Joe & Keith Bilbrey, Stephanie Warner (Emy Jo's daughter), Delacy and Sherry Bellenfant (Emy Jo's sisters) were filmed in July and the show aired October 29 and will reair on Christmas eve.

The Bellenfant family lost a dear member of their family when Emy Jo's mom passed away this year, so to honor her memory, each of the family members wore a button with her photo on it.

. The show was my Emy Jo's mom's favorite game show. They auditioned before she died and of course, passed the test to be on the show. At least her Mom knew they were going to be on. They taped the show a week to the day of burying their Mom.

They ended up getting 0 points but they were entertaining enough that they have asked them to come back in the spring!

Country Legends of the Past and Present

BY TOM WOODS - Marty Robbins

If you visit the college of musical knowledge and look up the phrase "crossover hit-maker," you just might find a picture of multitalented Marty Robbins alongside.

Versatility is the buzzword that best describes Marty.

Marty's first of 17 career No. 1 hits was "I'll Go on Alone" in 1952, a pure country ballad that established him in the genre and earned him a membership in the Grand Ole Opry.

But he also made a lasting mark in the 1950s rock 'n' roll era with "Singing the Blues" (1956) and "A White Sport Coat (And a Pink Carnation)" (1957).

Then came Marty's signature song "El Paso" (1959), which zoomed to No. 1 on all the charts, earned him a Grammy and opened a new door for a wave of gunfighter ballads and trail songs that would set a lasting tone for his music and harkened back to his Arizona roots.

Of course, Marty never strayed too far from his country music roots, either. "Don't Worry" (1961) was the next No. 1 for him and he produced seven more chart-toppers that decade before kicking off the 1970s with "My Woman, My Woman, My Wife" (1970), which went on to win another Grammy for Best Country Song.

He was named to the Nashville Songwriters Hall of Fame in 1975 and honored by the Academy of Country Music as the Artist of the Decade (1960-69). And during these two decades, he also cut rockabilly and gospel records, further showing his versatility.

But that flexibility was also followed his career outside the recording studio.

Besides being a singer, songwriter and musician, Marty earned fame as a talented actor and a competitive NASCAR stock-car driver.

He drove in 35 races, finishing in the Top 10 in six them (including the 1973 Firecracker 400). Marty mpeted at Talladega, Nashville, Atlanta and other ꞁcks and drove the pace car at the 1976 Indianapolis ᴜ0.

In the movies, he portrayed himself in several Nashville-related movies and as a race driver in Hell on Wheels in 1967. Marty starred with Chill Wills in 1972's Guns of a Stranger and portrayed a musician in 1982's Honkytonk Man with Clint Eastwood.

But Marty never saw that completed Eastwood film. He died a few weeks before its release from complications of heart surgery, following his third heart attack. Marty was 57.

Awards and more recognition continued to follow his death. Marty was inducted into the Country Music Hall of Fame in 1982 and "El Paso" earned him a spot in the Grammy Hall of Fame in 1998. He also has a star on the Hollywood Walk of Fame.

Country Questions
By Dick Boise, CMH

Send questions to:
Dick Boise, , c/o CFR News,
P.O. Box 201796, Nashville,
TN 37221.

Q. Dear Dick, we are country music fans and watch a lot of country programs and truly love them. Our question is about the Wilburn Brothers. How old are they and are they still living? We love the CFR News and The Diner on TV. Thanks.

Jan Biggs, Washington, MI

A. Thanks for your kind words and The Wilburn Brothers TVshow was very popular from 1963 to 1974. Both Doyle and Teddy were born in Hardy, Missouri, Doyle on July 7, 1930 and he passed away Oct. 16, 1982. Teddy was born Nov. 30, 1931 and he passed away Nov. 24, 2003. Two great country music talents that also helped many others in the business.

Q. I have always been a great fan of Jeanne Pruett and enjoyed her on the Reunion shows. Haven't seen much of her and wondered what is her status?

Mary Jane Scheucher, Elberfeld, IN

A. In her early years in Nashville, she worked in Marty Robbins Publishing Company and also wrote many good songs. She announced in 2006, that she was retiring from the Grand Ole Opry and from touring. According to her son, Jack Pruett, Jr., she will turn 80 the end of January. Her husband has not had good health and she takes care of him at home. She grows orchids and roses and watches HGTV and is a huge Braves fan. Also, a few of her cookbooks, Vol. 1 and 4, are still available for $15 + $3.00 s/h and can be bought by sending a check to Jack Pruett, 100 Countryside Dr., Hendersonville, TN 37075.

Q. I am an old school country music fan, however, why don't we ever hear or see some for he other s on the Reunion shows, like Travis Tritt, Lorrie Morgan, Don Williams? I do love to read aobut the "old singers" in the CFR News and really like Larry's Diner.

Sandy Whitehead, Seymour, IN

A. I guess, Sandy, that most of us old school country fans would enjoy some of the newer singers and many of them have been invited to come to the Reunion shows,. It is a task to be able to schedule talented, working, touring artists into a time period for the show tapings and it doesn't always work out for them. We thank you for the usggestions of who you would like to see and for your interest in the News and the Diner.

Q. Over the many years at this season of Christmas, I've always enjoyed the song Eddy Arnold sang that spells out Christmas. Could you find out for me who wrote that wonderful song? Thanks and have a Merry Christmas.

Sandy McCort, Hoosick Falls, NY

A. "Tis the Season" and thank you for that song question. I really don't know how many times I have enjoyed his version in my lifetime. Now for me, CHRISTMAS just would not be the same without it. That seasonal favorite was wirtten by Jenny Lou Carson and Eddy Arnold. He first recorded it for RCA Victor in 1949.

Road Stories

By Claudia Johnson

John Conlee: A Rose by Any Other Name

Would "Rose Colored Glasses" by any other name sound as sweet?

John Conlee will never know, but his 1978 hit actually began with another title.

"When I started writing it, I was using 'love colored glasses,'" he said. "During the process I thought of the old phrase 'rose colored glasses' and promptly changed it. I'm not sure of the genesis of the phrase, but the song certainly has kept it alive and spread it. The song may never have done a thing the other way. Like a lot of other things in life, some things are meant to be, and some things are not."

"Rose Colored Glasses" launched a successful career for the disc jockey-turned-performer. The song spent 20 weeks on the Hot Country Singles chart in 1978 and became Conlee's signature song. As the song became a country standard, Conlee's fans often asked about obtaining rose-colored glasses for themselves, so in the early 1980s his first road manager and the song's co-writer George Baber suggested offering them as a concession item. They remain his best-selling concert souvenir.

Conlee has released 29 singles throughout the years with 26 of them charting in the top 20 or better and eight reaching number one. He's toured extensively, but he has always made sure he was at home as much as possible.

"I was never on the road for months at a time, even when I was busiest in those early years," he said. "It's a balancing act. I could never have been happy being gone for three months at a time. There were times when we would go to the West Coast and stay a couple of weeks, but that was my limit. I'd think 'I got to see the farm before too much more time passes.'"

A native of rural Kentucky and a farm owner in Middle Tennessee, preservation of the family farm system is important to Conlee.

"The farm crisis reared its head in 1985," he recalled, explaining what compelled him to perform a concert in Omaha, Neb., that June to benefit the National Farmers Organization and other farming support entities. "Then, when Willie Nelson announced his plans for a September Farm Aid concert, I called and offered to help. I was part of the first 10 Farm Aid concerts, and Willie has kept on doing them."

The singer spoke passionately and knowledgeably about modern farming practices that have continued to destroy the farming infrastructure.

"The reason Farm Aid ended up being created was because this was not a front page story in the first place, even through it should have been," he observed.

Conlee admitted that he's never had a great memory for jokes or stories, but he did make a confession about the event he called "certainly a highlight of my career – of my life."

"For years I had in my mind and told people that Roy Acuff inducted me into the Grand Ole Opry," he said. "He did not. It was Porter Wagoner. I found that out by listening to an old tape of my induction! There is so much excitement at an event like that, it's easy to lose some of the details."

One event, however, he has not forgotten.

"Ray Charles and I both had hits with a song called 'Busted,'" Conlee said. "I heard his version as a teenager, never imagining that I would sing it or any other song on a record, let alone that it would become a hit for me too."

Conlee said that Charles tops his list of favorite artists, so he was thrilled to be slated for a Las Vegas performance in the early 1980s with the legendary soul singer, whom he had never met.

"It was around that time I had a song on the charts called 'I Don't Remember Loving You,'" Conlee said. "When Ray came out of his dressing room, he started singing the words 'I don't remember loving you.' It left me speechless."

Read all about
Renae The Waitress

"Sharing the fun of being a TV waitress on a top rated television show is why I wrote this book. I have answered a zillion questions over the years, from 'Is that your real hair color' to 'Is Nadine a man'? Not only do I answer those haunting questions, but I share the on-the-show experiences and behind-the-counter antics."

The book inclludes an **Audio Book & Bonus CD.** Renae the Waitress reads the book on the Audio CD and the two original songs are written and performed by her husband, Phil Johnson.

Chapters include: *More Than A Waitress, Sassy Diner Attire, That's No Waitress, "This Isn't Burger King," Travelin' Waitress, TV Diner Lingo, Diner Stories* and many more. It is also has many candid photos of the diner cast.

PLUS there is a 16 page color photo section filled with pictures of many of your favorite artists who have been guests on the diner.

Also....for a limited time, receive a FREE metal bookmark with a Coffee Cup charm!

This book, audio book and bonus CD will make a great Christmas gift for any Larry's Country Diner fan.

The hardcover, 136 page book and CDs are $24.95 plus $6.95 shipping and handling and can be ordered through Larry's Country Diner by sending a check to CFR News, P.O. Box 210796, Nashville, TN 37221 or by calling 800-820-5405.

AVAILABLE NOW

$24⁹⁵ + $6.95 s/h

Larry's Country Diner RFD Show Schedule Dec. 2014
(These shows have previously aired)

HOT CLUB OF COWTOWN
Saturday, December 6
10:00 p.m. Central
Sunday, December 7
6:00 p.m. Central

GEORGE HAMILTON IV
Saturday, December 13
10:00 p.m. Central
Sunday, December 14
6:00 p.m. Central

RAY STEVENS
Saturday, Decmeber 20
10:00 p.m. Central
Sunday, December 21
6:00 p.m. Central

MARGO SMITH
Saturday, December 27
10:00 p.m. Central
Sunday, December 28
6:00 p.m. Central

The Roys new CD:
Bluegrass Kinda Christmas

The Roys bring the holidays home with their newest CD, 'Bluegrass Kinda Christmas' (Rural Rhythm Records), available now to radio programmers via AirPlay Direct. The disc hit the stores November 18. The Roys' much-heralded sibling harmonies, spot-on lead vocals and agile musicianship shine a light on Christmas songs both new and old, creating a festive holiday ambiance that's apropos for any seasonal celebration.

Recorded during a hot Tennessee summer, 'Bluegrass Kinda Christmas' features Elaine Roy (Guitar), Lee Roy (Mandolin, Mandocello, Mandola), Clint White (Fiddle), Daniel Patrick (Banjo, Dobro), Erik Alvar (Bass), and Josh Swift (Dobro*), and was recorded at THE ROYS' own studio in Hendersonville.

"My memories of Christmas are so vivid," observes Elaine. "But most importantly, I think, was the complete sense of being loved that I felt at those family gatherings." For her brother Lee, the holidays were a time filled with music, family and fun - and this album presents those emotions as well. "The title track is actually the first Christmas song Elaine and I've written," he notes. "We wrote it with our buddy Steve Dean, and it's full of the energy and excitement I remember from being a kid."

The 10-song collection hums with a warm and companionable feel that sets the stage for lively fiddle runs and the bell-like sounds of the mandolin. Crisp, clear notes resonate throughout, sparkling like the sun on snow. Each track is compelling, but Elaine's angelic vocal on "O Holy Night" is a standout: soft as candlelight, she brings an instant sense of peace – and images of Holy places to mind. Lee's stirring interpretation of "There's A New Kid In Town" (Curly Putnam/Keith Whitley/Don Cook) is another highlight; filled with mature gravitas and nuance. The pair never shies away from fun and they excel on the upbeat classics "Santa Looked Like A Lot Like Daddy" (Buck Owens/Don Rich) and "Christmas Times A Comin'" (Tex Logan).

The busy Bluegrassers are already feeling the spirit of the season; on November 24, they'll make their first appearance at Country icon Charlie Daniels' annual Christmas 4 Kids benefit concert at the historic Ryman Auditorium. They'll wrap the 2014 touring season - appropriately - with a performance at the Christmas In The Smokies concert in Pigeon Forge, TN on December 13.

BLUEGRASS KINDA CHRISTMAS Track Listing:

1. Santa Looked A Lot Like Daddy
2. Santa Train
3. With Bells On
4. If We Make It Through December
5. Christmas Times A Comin'
6. Bluegrass Kinda Christmas
7. There's A New Kid In Town*
8. Winter Wonderland
9. O Holy Night
10. Santa And The Kids

The Nashville Brat Pack
Kids of the Country Stars!

I use to travel with my Dad on the road between 1978 - 1980. Dad's favorite color was baby blue. So I went out and got a baby blue stage suit so I would fit in with the suits that he & his band had. It was my first rhinestone suit. I still have both of the baby blue suits.

Dad even had a1970 baby blue Lincoln Mark III. He had to special order it in that color. He still had it when he died.

Back when I was about 19, Merle Kilgore and I both worked for George Jones at his Possum Holler Club in downtown Nashville. We went deep sea fishing down in Panama Beach Florida on a vacation together. We caught about 100 Spanish Mackerel that day. The problem was….. we were FLYING back home the next day. When we got back to the marina Merle asked some guys if they could clean all the fish and, pack them in coolers with dry ice so we could fly them back to Nashville. The guys said, "Yeah, it can be done. But, we would have to basically work all night to do it. It will cost you!" Merle replied, "Son, money is NO object. Just have then ready early in the morning." So we left. I was thinking maybe money is no object for you. But, I'm just a poor kid making a couple of hundred dollars a week. I was afraid of what my half was going to cost. Merle kept telling me. "Don't worry about it." So the next morning we are up and, about ready to head to the airport. I told Merle "Hey, we need to go get the fish." Merle looked me in the eye and, said, "To hell with those

By Robyn Young
(son of Faron Young)

The photo below was taken during a professional photo shoot that was done at our house when we lived on Brush Hill Rd. in Inglewood. They took all kinds of shots of Dad in different type settings. Star stuff and with the family stuff. I actually never remember any other time that Dad sat and played guitar with me. In all honesty, he was a pretty bad guitar player. His band used to hide his guitar or leave it off of the bus all the time, trying to get him to just go onstage without playing. It really made him mad. So he finally confronted them about it. They told him "Faron, you play the wrong chords all the time. "Dad said " Hell, nobody can hear me. It's just an acoustic guitar?" But, the band told him "WE can hear you! And, you are throwing us off!" So eventually he stopped playing a guitar onstage. All in all it was probably a brilliant move which led him to become an even greater entertainer than he already was. He connected with the audience more and, ultimately became a world class showman that few entertainers ever wanted to follow onstage.

fish! Do you have any idea what the airline would charge us to fly those things home!!!" Somewhere down in Florida, I suspect to this very day. There are two guys who would love to just kick the crud out of Me & Merle Kilgore.

the 21 Days of Christmas

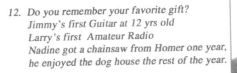

RFD ask the Diner cast to answer 21 holiday questions. We thought you would enjoy the answers.

with the cast of Larry's Country Diner

1. Egg nog or hot choclate?
   The Sheriff likes Egg nog

2. Colored lights or white lights on your tree/house?
   Larry has a HUGE tree with colored lights.

3. Do you hang Mistletoe?
   Nadine hangs mistletoe but Homer ignores it.

4. When do you hang your decorations?
   The whole cast decorates their trees the day after Thanksgiving.

5. What is your favorite holiday dish?
   Nadine's favorite holiday dish is pie (H E L L O)

6. What is your favorite holiday memory as a child?
   Renae was a child bride (17 yrs old) so her December 19th wedding is her favorite memory as a child….lol

7. What is on your Christmas wish list?
   Nadine's wish list has "Peace On Earth… like that's gonna happen!"

8. Do you open gifts on Christmas Eve?
   Keith opens his gifts on Christmas morning (the ones he hasn't already opened and rewrapped)

9. How do you decorate your Christmas tree?
   Renae has photo ornaments of her kids from their first Christmas and she adds to them every year

10. Snow….love it or dread it?
    The whole cast loves snow

11. Real tree or fake tree?
    The whole cast puts up fake trees after Thanksgiving so they can have decorations up longer. (Nadine says Homer wouldn't have the sense to keep a real tree alive)

12. Do you remember your favorite gift?
    Jimmy's first Guitar at 12 yrs old
    Larry's first Amateur Radio
    Nadine got a chainsaw from Homer one year, he enjoyed the dog house the rest of the year.

13. What's the most important thing about Christmas to you?
    The whole cast feels the most important thing about Christmas is to remember the birth of our Lord.

14. What is your favorite tradition?
    Nadine and Homer have all the grandkids over and Homer reads the Christmas story from the Bible.

15. What tops your tree?
    Larry's tree has a Star
    Jimmy and Keith have an Angel
    Nadine and Renae top their trees with Ribbons and flowers

16. Which do you prefer: giving or receiving?
    The whole cast prefers giving except Homer

17. What is your favorite Christmas song?
    Larry's favorite song is "Grandma Got Ran Over By a Reindeer"
    Nadine doesn't think that's funny !

18. Candy canes …yuck or yum?
    Nadine and Renae agree yuck…"give us chocolate".

19. Favorite Christmas movie?
    Everyone likes "It's A Wonderful Life"

20. What do you leave Santa?
    Nadine leaves cookies but Homer eats them before Santa arrives

21. Do you have a Christmas morning tradition?
    Keith and Jimmy's tradition is sleeping late.

Stage Clothes of the Stars

By Claudia Johnson

Rhonda Vincent - Royal Style

The Queen of Bluegrass, Rhonda Vincent, isn't just immensely talented, she's beautiful enough to be a cover girl, and in fact, she is. She's pictured on dozens of album covers not to mention numerous magazines, posters and billboards.

Having performed since she was only three years old, Vincent's stage style has undergone decades of transitions. Whether blond, brunette or raven-haired, her sparking blue eyes and stylish attire have remained unquestionably engaging.

"Starting out in a musical family, we always dressed alike or matching in color and style," she said of her family's band, The Sally Mountain Show, which included Vincent, her parents and her brothers. "Dressing for stage has been something I've been doing all my life. For as long as I can remember, there were always stage clothes, then there were regular clothes."

When the Missouri native first arrived in Nashville to record for Giant Records, she was provided with style professionals to help indentify her "look."

"I learned so much from that single experience," she recalled. "They tried 100 shades of blush on my cheek to find the exact color that works for me. They did my 'colors.' They told me I was wearing the wrong clothing size. The stylist went shopping and found all the perfect clothes for my body and in a style that enhanced my figure in the best way possible. I carry all of those lessons into what I do today."

Vincent acknowledged that throughout her career styles have changed to what she terms "the more disheveled look," with torn jeans and fitted t-shirts.

She sees traditional country and bluegrass music a "more of a classic music," so she dresses in gowns and the men wear suits for performances.

"At every show, there are compliments thanking us for dressing up," she said. "Most recently, I wore a conservative dress on the Opry Country Classics show at the Ryman. I thought it was a great dress, it just wasn't sequined or sparkly. My husband complimented me on the dress, but a lady came to me after the show and said that I should have dressed up and shown more respect to the Opry/Ryman stage, and dressed like Loretta Lynn. So in that instance, it was the actual dress I chose that was the issue. I've learned you can't please everyone all the time, but I always take great care in selecting what we wear."

For stage, Vincent said it's usually a sequined dress or gown, appropriate to the venue. If the performance is in a large performing arts center, she wears a long gown, creating a presence commensurate with the scale of the auditorium. For an outside festival, she wears a shorter gown, mostly for functionality, she explained.

"It's difficult to sign autographs wearing a gown at an outdoor festival," she said. "Also, when I find a pair of shoes I love, I buy two pairs – one that I can wear at festivals through the dust and dirt and not be afraid to ruin them. I just wear them, mud and all, and wipe them down later. I always keep a pair of rubber boots on board, in case it's raining. I rotate the shoes, dresses, and gowns from the bus, according to the season."

Vincent said that a major change accompanying a higher level of success is that she now owns dresses by such designers as Constance McCardle, Jackie Rogers and Vera Wang.

"It's fun to have something that is totally and uniquely my own," she said. "With maturity comes a confidence to maybe wear something a bit more sophisticated that I might not have worn a few years ago."

Like every woman, Vincent has one dress that stands out as a favorite. For her it is the green dress she wore on the cover of her "All American Bluegrass Girl" album. Stylist Jennifer Kemp, whom Vincent calls "the greatest," selected the green dress and some gold boots, and Vincent was seated on a green chair for the photo shoot. Vincent thought the shots would never be used and was stunned when the photographer sent her the photo.

"Still not convinced it should be the cover, I showed it to several people," she said. "They all said the All American Bluegrass Girl can wear whatever color she wants. I loved the idea of it being so different – something I pride myself on, to always do something different – so it became the cover."

Vincent said that the dress was discussed on radio shows and everywhere she went.

"I would have promoters wave my check before the show and say I wouldn't not get paid unless I wore the green dress," she said. "The years 2006 and

2007, I wore that dress almost every show at the demand of either the promoter or the fans. I still have it, and it was recently on display at the Tennessee Museum for the photographer's feature."

With the advent of social media and its instantaneous nature, Vincent has become increasingly conscious of when and where she wears her outfits.

"When I wore the same shirt two weeks in a row off stage, and photos were online when we were at a restaurant, someone asked if that was the only shirt I owned," she said. "With social media now, I need MORE new clothes! Will you tell my husband that I NEED them?"

Sounds like royalty – bluegrass royalty, that is.

Jimmy Capps inducted into NC Music Hall of Fame

Jimmy Capps dreamed of playing the Grand Ole Opry from the time he was a small child growing up in Benson, NC. He is now a regular on the Opry as part of the Opry Staff Band since 1967.

Jimmy started playing music professionally when he was only 12, working local dances. He began working with the Louvin Brothers which gave him his first shot on the Opry stage in 1958. Even though he had double pneumonia, he still managed to play that night.

He is one of the most respected session musicians in all genres having played on albums by rock and roll artists to traditional country artists. He plays on average of 500 sessions each year.

Jimmy was inducted into the North Carolina Music Hall of Fame on October 16, 2014 in Kannapolis, NC.

The N.C. Music Hall of Fame is open Monday through Friday from 10 a.m. to noon and then from 2-4 p.m. It is closed Saturday and Sunday. The museum is free, but does take donations. It is located at 109 West A Street, Kannapolis. North Carolina.

He was inducted into the Musicians Hall of Fame located in Nashville, TN in January.

Left: Jimmy playing and talking to the audience.

Above: Mark Capps (Jimmy's son), Jimmy, Michele, Michele's parents Dean & Jean Vonn.

Little Jimmy Dickens turning 94 this December 19

James Cecil Dickens, born December 19, 1920, better known as Little Jimmy Dickens, is a treasured country music singer famous for his humorous novelty songs, his small size, 4'11", and his rhinestone-studded outfits

Born in Bolt, West Virginia, he was the 13th child of a West Virginian farmer. During his childhood, he fell in love with music and had a dream of performing on the Grand Ole Opry. Dickens began his musical career in the late 1930s, performing on a local radio station while attending West Virginia University. He soon quit school to pursue a full-time music career, and travelled the country performing on various local radio stations under the name "Jimmy the Kid."

In 1949, now using the name Little Jimmy Dickens, he became a permanent member of the Grand Ole Opry. He also signed a record contract with Columbia Records, releasing his first single, "Take an Old Cold Tater and Wait," in the spring of 1949. The song became a Top Ten hit and launched a string of hit novelty, ballad, and honky tonk singles that lasted for a year, including "Country Boy," "A-Sleeping at the Foot of the Bed," "Hillbilly Fever," and "My Heart's Bouquet." Early in the '50s, he formed a band called the Country Boys, which featured a steel guitar, two lead guitars, and drums.

In 1965, he had his biggest hit, "May the Bird of Paradise Fly up Your Nose." The single topped the country charts and crossed over to number 15 on the pop charts. Although his next single, "When the Ship Hit the Sand," was moderately successful, Dickens wasn't able to replicate the success of "May the Bird of Paradise Fly up Your Nose." In 1968, he stopped recording for Columbia, signing with Decca Records, where he had three minor hits in the late '60s and early '70s. In 1971, he moved to United Artists and had two more small hits.

After receiving radiation treatments for a pre-cancerous condition on his vocal cords, he returned to the Opry stage in September 2014. He continues to perform at the Opry and is the oldest performing Opry member. He will turn 94 years old on December 19, 2014.

COUNTRY'S FAMILY REUNION

COUNTRY'S FAMILY REUNION COLLECTION
Taped in 1997, 1998, and 1999. Includes FOUR different video series: Country's Family Reunion, Country's Family Reunion Two, Country's Famly Reunion Celebration, Country's Family Reunion Gospel, and Stories from the Golden Age of Country. $119.80

COUNTRY'S FAMILY REUNION NASHVILLE SERIES
Filmed in January of 2008 this is a 10 DVD collection that includes a "TRIBUTE" to the late Porter Wagoner, Hank Thompson and Billy Walker. Featuring 70 artists and song-writers. $119.80

COUNTRY'S FAMILY REUNION 2010
Country's Family Reunion 2010 was filmed in "2010 " right here in Nashville Tennessee with over 50 of your favorite artists sharing their laughter, their stories, and all your favorite songs on 12 DVDs! $119.80

BILL ANDERSON'S 50th ANNIVERSARY
No one in history has had more country songs recorded than Whisperin' Bill. Filmed in 2010, celebrate Bill's 50th Anniverssary with over 7 hours and 5 DVD's we've cap-tured tons of great hits sung by the original artists. $79.80

A GRAND OLE TIME
Filmed in 2010, A Grand Ole Time includes 5 DVDs with over 7 hours of country music entertainment. Features Dallas Frazier, Jan Howard, Collin Raye, Jim Glaser, Rhonda Vincent, Ronny Robbins and many more. $79.80

SALUTE TO THE KORNFIELD

We gathered all the members of the TV show "Hee Haw" into one room and filmed it.What we got out of that taping is incredible, once-in-a-lifetime stuff that we're calling Country's Family Reunion: Salute to the Kornfield! This 5 DVD series was filmed in 2011. $79.80

GETTIN' TOGETHER
This wonderful 5 DVD set was filemd in 2011 and includes some brand new folk hanging with our CFR family (Dailey and Vincent, Don Edwards, Joey and Rory, and others), plus some of your favorites (Roy Clark, Johnny Lee, Neal McCoy, Bill Anderson, Jeannie Seely, Jean Shepard, and many more!) $79.80

COUNTRY'S FAMILY REUNION KINFOLK
On this special Country's Family Reunion gathering, filmed in 2012, we thought we'd ask all the family groups to sit a spell and sing some songs with us. Brothers, sisters, cousins, moms and Dads were all invited to join in the fun. The Gatlin's, the Whites, The Lennon Sisters, Rhonda Vincent and Darrin Vincent, and other family acts joined us. 5 DVDs with over 5 hours of content. $79.80

OLD TIME GOSPEL

The roots of a lot of the country music we love can be found in the Gospel songs of old. Filmed in 2012, this series is filled with songs celebrating the gospel music we grew up with so we called it Old Time Gospel. 5 DVDs featuring The Whites, Jean Shepard, Joey & Rory, George Hamilton IV and more. $79.80

SECOND GENERATIONS
A gathering of country music legends and the children of country music legends such as Marty Robbins, Conway Twitty, Faron Young, Tammy Wynette, George Jones, Roger Miller, Johnny Russell, Hank Williams, Dottie Westt. All on 5 DVDs with over 7 hours of content, including the 'Behind The Scenes' DVD filmed in 2012. $79.80

GRASSROOTS TO BLUEGRASS
Filmed in 1999, Jimmy Shumate, Melvin Goins, John Hartford, Jeanette Carter, Charlie Louvin, The Osbourne Brothers, and many more telling stories and singing songs about the history of Bluegrass music. This series is a must-have for any Bluegrass fan! $119.80

PRECIOUS MEMORIES - GOSPEL CLASSICS COMBO
Precious Memories includes 90 minutes of footage from the reunion members who've passed away, plus the detailed biography photo book. AND, Gospel Classics, a 3 DVD set with TONS of Gospel songs and stories, plus the Gospel Song Book. $119.80

GOD BLESS AMERICA AGAIN
God Bless America Again is devoted to songs that make us proud to be Americans and songs that allow us to enjoy our spiritual roots. ISongs you sang in church when you were growing up and songs that recall a time in America when we were free to openly express our faith without fear of ridicule-- A time that seems, on reflection, to have been filled with family, friends and faith. Filmed in 2013. $79.80

SIMPLY BLUEGRASS
In 2013 we asked Ricky Skaggs to pull together some of the best of the past, present and future of Bluegrass performers for Simply Bluegrass. Hosted by Ricky Skaggs and Bill Anderson, this is a reunion that all Bluegrass and Country fans will enjoy. This series has 5 DVDs with over 6 hours of great Bluegrass music! $79.80

SONGWRITERS COLLECTION
The Songwriters is a 6 hour, 5 DVD series featuring 22 of the best country music songwriters of all time... You'll hear how songs like "The Gambler," "Always," "All My Exes Live in Texas," "When You Say Nothing at All," "and more were written. Filmed in 2010. $79.80

Opry back at the Ryman through January 2015

The Grand Ole Opry is back at the Ryman for the winter months and will be there through January 2015 making this a great time to visit and be nostalgic.

The Grand Ole Opry started as the WSM Barn Dance in the new fifth-floor radio studio of the National Life & Accident Insurance Company in downtown Nashville on November 28, 1925. On October 18, 1925, management began a program featuring "Dr. Humphrey Bate and his string quartet of old-time musicians." On November 2, WSM hired long-time announcer and program director George D. "Judge" Hay, an enterprising pioneer from the National Barn Dance program at WLS in Chicago, who was also named the most popular radio announcer in America as a result of his radio work with both WLS and WMC in Memphis, Tennessee. Hay launched the WSM Barn Dance with 77-year-old fiddler Uncle Jimmy Thompson on November 28, 1925, which is celebrated as the birth date of the Grand Ole Opry.

As audiences for the live show increased, National Life & Accident Insurance's radio venue became too small to accommodate the hordes of fans. They built a larger studio, but it was still not large enough. After several months with no audiences, National Life decided to allow the show to move outside its home offices. In October 1934, the Opry moved into then-suburban Hillsboro Theatre (now the Belcourt); and then on June 13, 1936, to the Dixie Tabernacle in East Nashville. The Opry then moved to the War Memorial Auditorium, a downtown venue adjacent to the State Capitol. A 25-cent admission was charged to try to curb the large crowds, but to no avail. On June 5, 1943, the Opry moved to the Ryman Auditorium.

The auditorium first opened as the Union Gospel Tabernacle in 1892 and was home to the Opry until 1974. By the late-1960s, National Life & Accident desired a new, larger and more modern home for the long-running radio show. Ryman Auditorium was already 51 years old at the time the Opry

moved there, was beginning to suffer from disrepair as the downtown neighborhood around it was falling victim to increasing urban decay. Despite these shortcomings, the show's popularity was increasing and its weekly crowds were outgrowing the 3,000-seat venue. The Opry's operators were seeking to build a new air-conditioned theatre with a greater capacity and ample parking in a then-rural area of town, providing visitors a more controlled, safer, and more enjoyable experience.

In an effort to maintain continuity with the Opry's storied past, a large circle was cut from the floor of the Ryman stage and inlaid into the center of the new Opry stage. Even when the Opry moved from the Ryman Auditorium in 1974, fans still continued to visit, see the famous stage, take photographs and buy souvenirs, and major motion pictures continued to be filmed on location at the auditorium, including John Carpenter's Elvis (1978), the Loretta Lynn Oscar-winning biopic, Coal Miner's Daughter (1980), Sweet Dreams (1985) (the story of Patsy Cline), and Clint Eastwood's Honkytonk Man (1982). In 1992 Emmylou Harris and her band, the Nash Ramblers, performed a series of concerts there (the results of which appeared on her album At the Ryman). The Harris concerts renewed interest in restoring the Ryman, and it was reopened as an intimate performance venue and museum in 1994. Audiences at the Ryman find themselves sitting in pews, the 1994 renovation notwithstanding. The seating is a reminder of the auditorium's origins as a house of worship, hence giving it the nickname "The Mother Church of Country Music".

The Ryman Auditorium has been completely renovated and with the beautiful additions it makes a perfect showcase for artists to hold shows, tours, and exhibits.

Cheyenne: Gentleman Jim's Best Friend

By Claudia Johnson

East of Carthage, Texas, stands a life-size statue marking the grave of Jim Reeves, the velvet-voiced singer who died in a plane crash on July 31, 1964. Behind him is the grave of his dog, Cheyenne.

Reeves' nephew, John Rex Reeves, remembers when Cheyenne became part of his uncle's life. John Rex said that Jim was performing in Cheyenne, Wyo., when a couple that raised collies offered him one as a gift. Jim turned them down, explaining that his busy schedule did not afford him the time necessary to care for a pet.

"When he got back to Nashville, they shipped Jim a dog," John Rex said, adding that Jim softened to the beautiful animal. "It wasn't just how he looked. Collies are exceptionally intelligent, and they're easy to bond with people."

Jim decided to keep the dog and named him Cheyenne in honor of the collie's place of origin.

"When Jim would come off the road, he'd play with Cheyenne and became buddy-buddy with him," John Rex said. "It was really good for Jim. The collie was a soothing tool for Jim, and Jim adored him."

John Rex Reeves, 78, is the son of Jim Reeves' oldest brother, Buford, and only 13 years younger than his famous uncle. Jim's father died when he was eight months old, leaving Buford, at age 20, with a feeling of responsibility for his mother and eight younger siblings, who were living in the rural community of Galloway in Panola County, Texas.

"My dad had been working in the oil fields long enough to be able to buy a little house," John Rex said. "He moved them up to DeBerry, and that's were Jim lived until he was out of high school and had signed with the St. Louis Cardinals."

The Reeves children hunted for raccoon and squirrel and fished along the Sabine River, especially Jim and his older brother OD. John Rex, who lived three miles up the road, remembers tagging along and cherishes the memories of time spent at his grandmother's.

"There was always music around her house," John Rex said, noting that Jim, OD and other family and neighbors played and sang. "I not only remember listening to those jam sessions, we played baseball together. Jim taught me how to throw a curve ball. He was just like an older brother."

"We grew up around the oil and gas fields of East Texas, and there were all kinds of personalities that came in and out," John Rex said. "There was a lot of folklore, a lot of stories around campfires. We'd go down on the [Sabine] river and build a campfire. Jim was a wonderful storyteller, so he'd tell stories, and we'd play music. Actually, the first time I heard Jim play 'Am I Losing You?' was around the campfire."

When Jim joined the Louisiana Hayride, a popular radio show in nearby Shreveport, La., Jim took his young nephew backstage to meet the performers. This further instilled a love of music in John Rex, who first started singing at the Methodist Church where his family attended services.

He had even formed a trio before leaving for college to earn degrees in economics and accounting. John Rex later did two tours in the U.S. Army, where he was often called on to use his musical talents.

"During those years, I was busy and Jim was busy, but we got together when we could," John Rex said. "I actually played golf with him two weeks before his plane crash. He'd just returned from South Africa filming his movie, 'Kimberly Jim.'"

After all the years of protecting their mother, it fell to John Rex's father, Buford, to tell Beulah Reeves the worst news a mother could imagine – her son was dead. She had already buried an infant daughter in 1911 and a teenage son in 1935.

"That left Mama Reeves with six of her children," John Rex said.

Her youngest child's body was returned to Panola County for burial in a location where hundreds of thousands of fans from throughout the world have continued to visit in the half century since his death at 40.

True to his family roots, John Rex retired to pursue the passion for music he'd discovered as a child after a successful career with Nabisco. Since 1992, he's performed fulltime, appearing at venues across the U.S. and once each month on "Midwest Country" on RFD TV.

When the album "Jim Reeves and Friends–Radio Days, Vol. 2," was released in 2001, John Rex said he was pleased to see that the cover featured an old black and white photograph of Jim playing with Cheyenne, a fitting tribute to the relationship between a man and his dog.

Even more fitting was the small, temporary funeral home marker originally placed at the gravesite where Cheyenne was laid to rest near his best friend. It read simply, "1957- 1967 Jim's Collie Dog."

CPSIA information can be obtained at www.ICGtesting.com
Printed in the USA
LVOW02s1828260415

435601LV00003BC/3/P